From Foot Soldier

to Finance Minister

Takahashi Korekiyo

Japan's Keynes

Harvard East Asian Monographs 292

From Foot Soldier

to Finance Minister

Takahashi Korekiyo

Japan's Keynes

Richard J. Smethurst

Published by the Harvard University Asia Center
Distributed by Harvard University Press
Cambridge (Massachusetts) and London 2007

Printed in the United States of America

The Harvard University Asia Center publishes a monograph series and, in coordination with the Fairbank Center for East Asian Research, the Korea Institute, the Reischauer Institute of Japanese Studies, and other faculties and institutes, administers research projects designed to further scholarly understanding of China, Japan, Vietnam, Korea, and other Asian countries. The Center also sponsors projects addressing multidisciplinary and regional issues in Asia.

Library of Congress Cataloging-in-Publication Data

Smethurst, Richard J.
    From foot soldier to finance minister : Takahashi Korekiyo, Japan's Keynes / Richard J. Smethurst.
        p. cm. -- (Harvard East Asian monographs ; 292)
    Includes bibliographical references and index.
    ISBN 978-0-674-02601-8 (cloth : alk. paper)
    ISBN 978-0-674-03620-8 (pbk : alk. paper)
    1. Takahashi, Korekiyo, 1854–1936. 2. Statesmen--Japan--Biography. 3. Japan--Politics and government--1912-1945. 4. Finance, Public--Japan--History. I. Title. II. Title: Takahashi Korekiyo, Japan's Keynes.
    DS884.T3S64 2007
    336.52092--dc22
    [B]

                                                                                    2007011887

Index by Thomas Vecchio

♾ Printed on acid-free paper

Last figure below indicates year of this printing
17 16 15 14 13 12 11 10 09

Yasuba Yasukichi and Tamaki Norio

Acknowledgments

The research for my study of Takahashi Korekiyo began indirectly in the late 1980s, amid the debate that erupted over my book on Japanese agricultural development and tenancy disputes. Because some of my critics argued that I had underestimated the impact of the Shōwa depression on the countryside, I decided to study the Japanese economy of the early 1930s, and at the time gave several public talks on the effects of the depression and the massive crop failure of 1934 on rural northern Japan. As I investigated this period, the name Takahashi Korekiyo, often with the epithet "Japan's Keynes," appeared repeatedly. So I bought several biographies of him and began working backward, from the Shōwa depression to Takahashi's childhood. The more I read about him, the more fascinated I became by the man—until at last I decided to abandon the economic downturn for Takahashi.

Luckily for me, many Japanese scholars and journalists have written books and articles about Takahashi, and he also left a large paper trail of published and unpublished writings, in both Japanese and English. Thus, I have had the good fortune to be able to take research trips to archives in Tokyo, Iwate, and London, and to libraries in Tokyo, Kyoto, Ann Arbor, Princeton, New York, and both Cambridges. I wish to thank the staffs at the RBSG Archives, the ING Baring Archive, the HSBC Group Archives, and the Rothschild Archive in London, the Bank of Japan Archive and Constitutional History Room of the National Diet Library in Tokyo, and the Jewish American Archives in Cincinnati, and among these archivists I would like to single out for particular thanks Caroline Shaw at the Rothschild Archive and Ōmiya Hitoshi at the Bank of Japan Archive. I am also deeply indebted to successive Japanese bibliographers at the Asian Library of the University of Pittsburgh, Sachie Noguchi and Hiroyuki Good. A historian is only as good as his sources, and I am happy to report having been able to find them. Accordingly, I express my deep gratitude to the archivists and librarians who have helped me.

I have also had the opportunity while doing the research for this book to be affiliated with the historical section of the Institute for Monetary and Economic Studies at the Bank of Japan. A series of section chiefs—Shinpō Hiroshi, Ōkubo Takashi, Mutō Tetsu, and Shizume Masato—not only tolerated my presence, but also encouraged me greatly. Many of their staff members, particularly Ōnuki Mari, Hatase Mariko, and Fujii Noriko, aided me significantly in my research. Two old boys of the Institute, Ishida Sadao and Suzuki Kōichi, both superb economic historians, advised me from early on in my project. Another former staff member, Miyajima Shigeru, provided me with essential bibliographical guidance in the early years of my project. All of these people have spent hours consulting with me about my research, listening to my presentations both in Japanese and English, and acting as sounding boards for my ideas. And in the process, all of these people have become close friends—in fact, I originally intended to dedicate my book to them, but changed my plans for reasons that will become clear.

I also want to take this opportunity to thank the groups that have funded my research over the years: the Japan Foundation, the Fulbright Fellowship Commission, the Social Science Research Council, the University of Pittsburgh's Asian Studies Center and University Center for International Studies, and within those two centers, the Japan Iron and Steel Federation Endowment Fund and the Mitsubishi Endowment Fund.

I have also benefited from the advice, encouragement, and critiques of a number of Japanese and American scholars and students. At Keio University, my scholarly home in Tokyo in recent years, I am particularly indebted to Nishikawa Shunsaku, Maki Atsushi, and Tsuya Noriko. Gordon Berger, Keith Brown, the late Olive Checkland, Frederick Dickinson, Seymour Drescher, Steven Ericson, Sheldon Garon, Janet Hunter, Inaba Chiharu, Itō Yukio, Gregory Kasza, Ellis Krauss, Stephen

Large, Matsuda Koichirō, Mark Metzler, Thomas Rawski, Charles Schencking, Sugihara Kaoru, Suzuki Toshio, and Werner Troesken have all heard or read bits and pieces of the manuscript—and some have read it all. Their reactions and advice have played an important role in the development of the book's final version. I have given talks on Takahashi at the University of California, San Diego, Cambridge University, Chinese University of Hong Kong, Columbia University, Hong Kong University, Keio University, London School of Economics, University of Michigan, Osaka Gakuin University, Osaka University, the University of Pennsylvania, the University of Pittsburgh, and Portland State University, and have benefited from the reactions, often critical, of the various audiences. I want to thank the students in three successive undergraduate writing seminars for history majors at the University of Pittsburgh from 2004 through 2006, who read my manuscript as part of their course work and gave me amazingly frank critiques, considering the power I had over determining their grades.

Finally, I want to single out nine people to whom I am especially indebted: Nina Sadd, who not only edited my manuscript, but also reformatted it to meet the press's requirements. William Hammell, my editor at the Harvard Asia Center, and Julia Perkins, my copy editor, have both made important contributions to the final version of the book. Three civilians read all or part of the manuscript and commented on it: Albert Rosenberg, Joan Rosenberg, and William Smethurst—and their efforts rose far above the requirements of friendship and filial piety. Mae Smethurst not only read the manuscript and provided her usual editorial rigor, but also has had to live for twenty years with Takahashi in the house; of course, at the same time, I have had to live with Aristotle and Zeami. Finally, I want to thank two close friends, who died as this book neared completion: Yasuba Yasukichi, professor in the Faculty of Economics at Osaka University and then Osaka Gakuin University, and Tamaki Norio, professor in the Faculty of Commerce at Keio University. Both men helped to educate me in many, many ways. Yasukichi, whom I first met in Baltimore in 1957, has in his own inimitable way been an advisor, sounding board, and critic—we have spent hours over the years talking about Japanese economic history, and particularly the need for quantitative analysis of Japan's economic development. In his last article, published posthumously in 2005, he called on quantitative historians to test my assertions about rural standards of living in pre–World War II Japan. I now have in Pittsburgh Yasukichi's set of the Hitotsubashi group's *Long Term Economic Statistics of Japan*. Norio, a newer friend, was my host for almost a decade at Keio. We shared lunch and coffee two or three times a week during my visits to Tokyo, and talked at great length about the importance of qualitative as well as quantitative approaches to Japan's economy. He shared with me his knowledge of Meiji and Taishō financial history and bibliography; a large part of his personal library is now in my study. Norio also helped me in the onerous task of reading Takahashi's handwritten documents. I am deeply indebted to both men for their help and friendship, and have dedicated the book to their memories.

Contents

Reference Matter

Tables and Figures

Tables

Figures (following page 184)

From Foot Soldier

to Finance Minister

Takahashi Korekiyo

Japan's Keynes

Introduction

In the early morning of February 26, 1936, two young officers of Japan's Third Imperial Guards Regiment led 100 of their men, armed with rifles and machine guns, through the still-dark, snowy streets of Tokyo. When they arrived at the home of the 81-year-old finance minister, Takahashi Korekiyo, they smashed open his front gate, pushed into the house, and with their boots on hurried to the bedroom where the minister lay sleeping. One of the officers shouted "traitor" as he fired bullet after bullet into Takahashi's prostrate body; the other screamed "heavenly punishment" as he brutally hacked the octogenarian with his sword. Takahashi died in the attack, and his death gave new life and power to Japan's military and accelerated the country's movement toward World War II. Several Japanese scholars and journalists have written that Takahashi was Japan's last barrier to militarism.[1] After his death, the road to war began in earnest.

Why was Takahashi a target of military rage? Was he in fact the last barrier to militarism, and if so, how and why? How did this remarkable man, an illegitimate child born in 1854, who was adopted as an infant into an *ashigaru* (foot soldier) family, that is, into the lowest stratum of the samurai class, become one of Japan's most cosmopolitan government leaders, a man who combined a nationalistic love of his country with a realistic understanding of its insecure place as a second-level nation in a world of far more powerful European and North American states? How did he rise from penurious origins as a hereditary private in the feudal infantry to become a fluent speaker of English and a friend

of many British and American financiers and politicians? How did he
become "Japan's Keynes" and an advocate of economic development
that did not just make Japan richer, but that also improved standards of
living, a democratizing politician, a critic of militarism and of the view
that soldiers with proper "spirit" could defeat enemies with superior
weaponry? The primary goals of this book, a biography of Takahashi
from birth to assassination, are to trace his education as an autodidactic
financial and political statesman; to elucidate his efforts as an official
to make Japan and its people richer and to encourage the latter to play a
larger role in governing themselves; to assess the efficacy of his countercyclical monetary and fiscal policy during the Great Depression between
1931 and 1936; and to evaluate the role, if any, that his policies played
in the rise of militarism in the quinquennium before his death. Although
there are many biographies in Japanese of Takahashi, one of the two
most important financial statesmen in Japan between the Meiji Restoration and World War II, no one has published a comprehensive study
of him in English. No one has written about the connections between
his unusual education and his pathbreaking economic and political ideas,
even in Japanese.

Takahashi became finance minister for the first time in February 1913,
and from then until his murder 23 years later served in that post seven
times, as well as serving once as prime minister and once as minister of
agriculture and commerce. Between 1913 and 1927, as finance minister in
the Yamamoto, Hara, Takahashi, and Tanaka cabinets, and as agriculture
and commerce minister in the Katō government, Takahashi advocated
stringent limitations on military spending, civilian control of foreign policy and the military, support for Chinese efforts to build a unified nation
that could resist Western imperialism, and opposition to those Japanese
policymakers who used loans and military intervention or their threat to
gain footholds in various regions of China. In other areas of foreign policy, he promoted cooperation with the Anglo-Americans, including the
expansion of Japan's colonial empire only within the British and the
American imperialist framework. Domestically, he favored universal suffrage and greater control by elected political officials over the government's elitist bureaucracy. To promote economic development, he supported growing the economy while raising workers' wages to stimulate
further growth, improving productivity, and sharing the benefits of the

ensuing profits with the workers. Finally, he advocated using tax policy to encourage greater equalization of income between rich and poor; devolution of the land tax and of control over the content of primary school education to local communities; and limiting, to the extent politically possible, governmental authority to crack down on the supporters of so-called "dangerous" political ideologies.

But Takahashi is most famous for the policies he adopted after he became finance minister for the fifth time in December 1931, during the depths of the depression, policies that allowed Japan to return to full utilization of capacity and full employment by 1935–36, five years before the American recovery. Prices were falling sharply, unemployment was high and rising, farmers suffered from the collapse of agricultural commodity prices, the growth of industrial productivity stagnated, many factories were under- or unutilized, and industrial investment had virtually disappeared. To counter these problems, within a year of coming to office Takahashi engineered Japan's recovery by introducing a series of reflationary, countercyclical fiscal and monetary measures that dramatically reversed his predecessor's conservative, deflationary policies. In the monetary realm, Takahashi took Japan off the gold standard, ended the convertibility of paper money for gold, devalued the yen, lowered interest rates, and raised the limit on the Bank of Japan's issuance of bank notes. This led to a boom in Japanese exports even while the rest of the world's trade contracted.

In the summer of 1932, Takahashi also introduced a countercyclical fiscal policy. He increased government spending and made up the difference not by raising taxes, but by deficit financing—and deficit financing through selling low-interest government bonds directly to the Bank of Japan rather than on the open market. The government's spending increased the volume of money in circulation and stimulated demand. Growing domestic demand together with expanding exports encouraged production and re-employment—more people had more money to spend and Japan began to recover from the depression.

Takahashi recognized by 1935 that the economy had nearly recovered. He introduced a plan to bring the government's spending back into balance with revenues. This required him to reduce military spending, which he had been forced to increase during the public euphoria over the conquest of Manchuria in 1931–32 (a conquest that he himself decried). The army and navy, happy with more money, vigorously resisted his efforts to limit their growing budgets. Their ultimate resistance was Takahashi's assassination. And the army's and navy's efforts worked. Takahashi's successors as finance minister dramatically increased the military's budget and moved to a planned, command economy, not only speeding the road to war, but also to economic inefficiency and runaway inflation.

It is widely accepted by leading Japanese and Western historians of the depression that Takahashi was unusual in the world at the time. Japanese economic historians such as Gotō Shin'ichi have called him "Japan's Keynes," even going so far as to point out that Takahashi introduced his policies four years before the publication of Keynes's *General Theory*, at a time when most Western and Japanese financial statesmen advocated balanced budgets and higher taxes. Western scholars such as Charles Kindleberger, the author of the standard economic history of the depression, and Robert Skidelsky, Keynes's biographer, have also commented on Takahashi's uniqueness.[2]

This book elucidates four broad areas of Takahashi's life. The first has to do with his education. How did Takahashi, with his inauspicious beginnings and straitened childhood, come in maturity to hold a sophisticated set of political and economic ideas? Takahashi, because of the year of his birth and low rank, was essentially an autodidact; he had neither a classical samurai nor an elite modern education. His only usable skill was a fluent command of English, which he began to develop at the age of ten with foreign missionaries in Yokohama. In fact, Takahashi was one of a small group of low-ranking samurai born in the 1850s who learned to speak English well because they were either too young to study by rote memorization in late feudal schools, or too old to learn in the formally-structured classrooms of elite Meiji period schools such as Tokyo Imperial University. These men had the advantage of learning by speaking from childhood with native English speakers, not from textbooks. After studying with Clara Hepburn in Yokohama and working as a houseboy in Oakland, California, Takahashi, while still in his teens and early 20s, associated with some of the most important foreign employees of the Meiji government: the Scots banker A. A. Shand, the Dutch-American missionary Guido Verbeck, and the American educator David Murray. Takahashi even helped William

Elliot Griffis translate scatological Japanese into vernacular English. Many of the top Meiji leaders—for example, Itō Hirobumi, Yamagata Aritomo, Matsukata Masayoshi, Saigō Tsugumichi, and Inoue Kaoru—even though he often differed with them on policy issues, called on Takahashi, because of his language skills, to carry out crucial assignments. The two most important of these, writing Japan's first patent and copyright laws in the 1880s, and selling Japanese war bonds in London and New York in 1904–5, introduced Takahashi to the two men who had the greatest influence on his education, the French-educated industrial planner, Maeda Masana, and the German-Jewish-American financier, Jacob Schiff. What I have found is that Takahashi educated himself not by going to school (there is no evidence that he attended school at all as a child), but by reading and talking voraciously, and doing that reading and talking in both Japanese and English. Takahashi, although badly schooled as a youth, was, by the time he rose to the top levels of government in the last 25 years of his life, a well-educated man, and one who was not limited by the strictures of a formal education. While it is hard to "footnote" all of the influences on him, it is clear that he received his education through a lifetime of reading, talking, and serving in government.

The second area of study is Takahashi's service at the highest levels of government between 1904 and 1927. How many Japanese political leaders of his time shared *in toto* his forward-looking set of economic and political ideas: the primacy of economic growth and of sharing the benefits of that growth with the working class, the use of tax policy to ameliorate income differentials, civilian control of foreign policy and the military, opposition to excessive military spending and to the piecemeal exploitation of China, decentralization of government power, and democratization? The other "liberal" politicians, if we can use that term, in Japan in the 1920s, men such as Hamaguchi Osachi and Shidehara Kijūrō of the other major political party, for example, shared his views on foreign policy, militarism, China, and democratization, but not on the use of fiscal and monetary policy to stimulate economic growth.

My third subject is Takahashi's countercyclical policies during the world depression, and their efficacy. How was Takahashi able to introduce policies that most financial statesmen in Japan and the West in 1931–32 opposed as outrageously unorthodox? Even Marxist economists such as Ōuchi Hyōe joined leaders of the preceding Minseitō cabinet, and bureaucrats in the Bank of Japan and Finance Ministry, in attacking Takahashi as recklessly inflationary. When we look back from our contemporary vantage point, we may find it surprising that responsible economists and financial leaders advocated more deflation as the cure for deflation, but in the early 1930s this was orthodoxy—even Franklin Roosevelt campaigned in 1932 by accusing Herbert Hoover of inflationary fiscal policies. Moreover, Takahashi's monetary and fiscal stimuli worked. In his four years as finance minister, consumer prices did rise, by 20 percent, but nominal national wealth rose by much more, 60 percent—no other country in the world recovered from the depression so quickly. The economist Hugh Patrick was correct when he wrote that Takahashi carried out "one of the most brilliant and highly successful combinations of fiscal, monetary, and foreign exchange rate policies the world has ever seen."[3] But the largest share of Takahashi's increased government spending went to the nation's armed forces.

The fourth and final subject is the relationship between Takahashi's deficit financing and the rise of militarism. It is widely acknowledged that Takahashi was not a militarist. From the time of his association with Maeda in the 1880s and Schiff 20 years later, Takahashi developed a powerful critique of excessive military spending. But even if Takahashi opposed militarism, could one not argue that he helped the army and navy expand their power in the 1930s by increasing their budgets as he undertook his fiscal stimulus? The answer, I think, is for the most part, no. Takahashi, in an atmosphere of public clamor for more funds to support Japan's war in Manchuria, continually opposed the army and navy ministers' demands for more money. He even went so far at one cabinet meeting as to accuse the army minister, General Araki, of talking like an idiot. Although while Takahashi served as finance minister in the 1930s, the army's and navy's budgets grew sharply, he continually gave them far less money than they demanded, and he did this in a political context that encouraged compromise and mandated unanimous cabinet support (including that of the army and navy ministers) to approve the budget. In other words, the finance minister was not a free agent in budget-making during the depression years. In fact, Takahashi was one of the few leaders in the 1930s to stand up publicly, in the face of mortal danger, to the military.

Most of the research into primary documents for this book has been conducted in archives and libraries in Tokyo. Takahashi's papers are located in the Constitutional History Room of the National Diet Library and at Tokyo Metropolitan University. The papers of Matsuo Shigeyoshi, governor of the Bank of Japan when Takahashi was in London during and after the Russo-Japanese War in 1904–6, are found in the Archive of the Bank of Japan. I examined newspapers on microfilm at the Keio University Library and explored other primary sources at the Finance Ministry Archive. Outside of Japan I found useful materials at the ING Baring, HSBC, RBSG, and Rothschild archives in London, and at the American Jewish Archives in Cincinnati. I have also relied on various published primary sources: Takahashi's memoirs of the first 52 years of his life, published serially in the *Tōkyō asahi shinbun* and then issued as a book in 1936 after his death; three volumes of his writings; and materials published in multi-volume sets by the Bank of Japan and the Finance Ministry.[4] The most valuable documents (largely unused even by Japanese scholars) are the letters and cables Takahashi sent from London to Prime Minister Katsura Tarō, Finance Minister Sone Arasuke, Bank of Japan Governor Matsuo, and Elder Statesman Inoue Kaoru in 1904–5 (found in the Matsuo papers); the materials on the negotiations between Takahashi and Schiff, the Rothschilds, Sir Ernest Cassel, Baring Brothers, Parr's Bank, Kuhn, Loeb, and the Hongkong and Shanghai Bank during the Russo-Japanese War (found in the four London bank archives); and the Takahashi-Schiff correspondence between 1906 and 1920 (52 letters available in the Diet Library and the American Jewish Archives.) These two men, neither one a native speaker of English, exchanged letters in beautiful Edwardian English in which they not only provided each other with information on the events of the day, but also revealed a warm friendship. One of the subjects of their letters was Takahashi's daughter Wakiko, who lived with the Schiffs in New York in 1906–9, and who spent World War I trapped in London with her husband and children because of German submarine warfare.

Takahashi was not merely an important political leader: his life was also fascinating. While the primary goal of this book is to analyze Takahashi's education and involvement in government, there are many good tales to tell along the way. Among them are Takahashi's taunting of the prostitutes sent to service the foreign merchants in Yokohama in 1866; his run-in with a Chinese cook in Oakland, California in 1868; his recitation of English-language poetry to Lord Date of Sendai domain in 1869; his affair with a geisha in the early 1870s, while not yet 20; his year as an unscrupulous stockbroker in the mid-1870s; his study of social dancing in Washington, DC in 1886; his narrow escape from death when his horse fell into a crevasse in the Peruvian Andes in 1889; his shipboard meeting with the actress Lillie Langtry in 1904; his audience with her former lover, Edward VII, the next year; his efforts to find a Japanese spaniel (*chin*) for Queen Consort Alexandra in 1905; and many other adventures. One can trace Takahashi's success to his unorthodox early life—because of it he had a detachment and pragmatism, a gregarious and even insouciant conviviality that made it easy for him to chat up strangers, and a total lack of self-consciousness with foreigners, unusual for a Japanese of his lifetime.

ONE

A Remarkable Beginning,
1854–67

The Birth of a Foot Soldier

Takahashi Korekiyo was born in Edo on July 27, 1854, the illegitimate son of Kawamura Morifusa and Kitahara Kin, and named Kawamura Wakiji. His father Morifusa served the shogun in Edo Castle as a landscape painter of the Kanō School; Kin was a family maid. The Kawamura family's history as artists dated back to the mid-seventeenth century when Morifusa's ancestor Morihiro studied with the famous painter and connoisseur, Kanō (Morinobu) Tan'yū. From that time on, eight successive Kawamuras adopted the character Mori in their given name and Tan in their artist's name; Morifusa signed his paintings Tanshō.

Morifusa, who was 46 when fat little Wakiji was born, reportedly had an epicurean, magnanimous, and pietistic personality and a reputation for hard work. Morifusa lived well in a large, elegant home in the Hamamatsu-chō section of warrior-class Tokyo. He entered the day's happenings in his diary, in which he wrote every night, no matter how drunk; he ordered large amounts of sake every two or three days; and he held frequent drinking parties for his friends. When Kin left the Kawamura household after Wakiji's birth, Morifusa gave her a parting gift of clothing and 200 *ryō* in gold, an amount larger than the annual income of all but the highest-ranking members of the samurai class. He regularly took his children to worship at the nearby Buddhist temple, Zōjōji, the family temple and burial ground of the Tokugawa shoguns (his employers). In 1862, eight years after Wakiji's birth, the shogunal government (*bakufu*) raised Morifusa's annual stipend as a reward for his diligence. He wrote in his diary that he and his eldest son and artistic successor Mori-yoshi/Tan'eisai raced to the castle during two major fires in the following year to save the shogun's six-panel screens from destruction.

Unfortunately for Morifusa, his employment as the artist in charge of screens at Edo Castle depended on the continuation of the shogun's regime. When the Meiji government replaced the *bakufu* and began the creation of a modern centralized state after 1868, Morifusa lost his samurai status and its guaranteed income. He found himself unemployed in his early 60s and without job prospects; the reaction against the "feudal" arts in the 1870s meant that there was little demand for traditional-style paintings. In something of a comedown for a man who had led a secure and sometimes even luxurious life before 1868, he was forced to open a dumpling shop; when that business failed, Morifusa tried to support himself as an artist by selling his paintings. Like many under- or unemployed ex-samurai in the first decade of Meiji, Morifusa lived in straitened circumstances until his death in 1878.[1]

Morifusa married twice. His first wife gave birth to a daughter but died in 1838 when Morifusa was 30. He remarried a few years later and his second wife bore four sons and two daughters. When Morifusa's third son was born in the early 1850s, a beautiful young woman named Kitahara Kin, the daughter of a prosperous fishmonger to powerful samurai kitchens, came to the Kawamura household as a maid, and in 1854, at the age of sixteen gave birth to Morifusa's last child, Wakiji. Given the number of children in the Kawamura household, Morifusa and his wife decided that they could not support one more, and within four days of Wakiji's birth, negotiated his adoption by Takahashi Kore-tada, a samurai serving Sendai domain, one of the largest of the powerful, semi-autonomous "outside" (*tozama*) regimes of Tokugawa Japan.

Takahashi's adoption reveals much about the class structure of late feudal society. The Takahashi family was of *ashigaru* (light infantry) status, that is, members of the lowest rung of the samurai class (to some, they were not samurai at all). Men of this rank played an important role in the wars leading up to the establishment of the Tokugawa regime in the early seventeenth century because it was they who learned to use the newest military technology of the time, Portuguese-style fire-arms, and who were organized into rapid-fire units. While at the time most of these men were of peasant origin, they were given quasi-warrior status when Tokugawa Ieyasu came to power. *Ashigaru* were required to wear distinctive, shortened kimono; they also were often prohibited from studying in the regular domain schools for samurai.[2] One might call Wakiji's adoptive father a hereditary private in the army.

Takahashi tells us in his memoirs that Morifusa had the choice of sending him to the Takahashi family or to a richer household of candy-makers who lived in Mita, near the present-day campus of Keio University. Takahashi then goes on to write that "human fate is really strange. If I had been adopted into a candy-maker's family, I would probably have spent my whole life making candy. Needless to say, my life would have been very different than it is now. A person's whole life can be deter-mined in a moment."[3] In the modernizing Meiji era, young men from the lowest ranks of the warrior class had better opportunities for upward mobility than did those from even relatively prosperous commoner families.

When young Wakiji moved into the Takahashi household in the summer of 1854, his adoptive parents and grandparents lived together in a Sendai domain tenement just below and to the east of Atago Shrine (*Atago-shita*), within easy walking distance of the Kawamura house.[4] Although his new father served the Date family as a low-ranking samu-rai, his forebears had not always been *ashigaru*—in fact, his grandfather Shinji had started his life as a middle-level warrior serving the Okabe, lords of Kishiwada domain near Osaka. Around 1820, the domain offi-cials dispatched Shinji, while still in his 20s, to the Edo mansion to serve the lord during one of his periodic visits to the shogun's court. At about the same time, Kusama Kiyoko, the teenage daughter of a prosperous farmer from Sagami, entered the Okabe mansion (*yashiki*) in Edo both to serve the lord's family as a lady-in-waiting and to learn samurai etiquette. Takahashi's memoirs tell us that both Shinji and Kiyoko were renowned for their good looks, and that rumors soon began to spread that the couple was living together, a breach of domain rules. Kishiwada officials expelled the pair from the Edo *yashiki* and Shinji lost his samurai status and guaranteed income. To make ends meet while he looked for another warrior-class opening, Shinji took a job as a guard for another domain, and Kiyoko worked as a seamstress in a geisha house. Then, thinking that Shinji's chances of re-entering the samurai class were slim, the couple separated.

Kiyoko went to work in the home of a Tokugawa bannerman (*hatamoto*, relatively high-ranking and well-paid samurai who were direct vassals of the shogun) near the Yotsuya gate of Edo Castle. The Kōriki family had a long history of service to the *bakufu*—in fact, its status was so high that the wife of the current family head came from the Hosokawa, like the Date, one of the most important outside daimyo families. Shortly after Kiyoko entered the Kōriki household, her master fell ill and died, leaving his elegant widow, a young son, and his father, the former bannerman, behind. According to our source, the elder Kōriki lusted after his daughter-in-law to such an extent that she cut off her hair, became a Buddhist nun, and took vows of chastity. This apparently only increased his passion for her—so much so that she felt forced to leave her son in Edo and return to her natal home in Kumamoto. But before departing, the mistress took her young maid Kiyoko aside and told her, "I regret that I must leave this household. I fear that my son will fall prey to the schemes of others. Because I trust your loyalty to me, I entreat you to see that my child succeeds his father as the next Kōriki bannerman. Thus, I entrust to you the Kōriki genealogy and the family's treasure, Taira no Atsumori's flute" (*aoba*).[5]

Kiyoko, deeply moved by the words of her mistress, determined to carry out her injunction. Kiyoko went immediately to Shinji and told him that she planned to take her mistress's case before the magistrate—even though to do so, Shinji and she would have to separate permanently. Shinji, in urging his "wife" to take a different course of action, replied: "I have abandoned my wife and children back in Kishiwada and have deserted the domain that my family has served generation after generation. But we cannot relive the past. If we work hard, I can become a samurai once more and we can establish our own household and live together. I do not think going to the magistrate is the best way to handle the Kōriki case. You must persuade the elder Kōriki to have his grandson succeed as bannerman. And I shall strive even harder to become a warrior again." According to Takahashi's memoirs, the two parted in tears.[6]

Thanks to Kiyoko's efforts, the parties involved resolved the dispute amicably and the young son succeeded his father. The widow returned to Edo from Kumamoto full of thanks for Kiyoko's faithfulness, and as a reward allowed the young couple to use the Kōriki crest as their family coat of arms—it remains the Takahashi *kamon* to the present day. Kiyoko was still in her early 20s at the time. Shinji and Kiyoko were reunited and with a payment of 20 *ryō* in gold, Shinji was adopted by Takahashi Naoemon, an *ashigaru* samurai of Sendai domain, but one who was permanently assigned to the lord's mansion in Edo. Although the memoir does not explain how this upturn in Shinji's and Kiyoko's fortunes took place, or for that matter, where the 20 *ryō* came from, the widow Kōriki probably played some role in arranging for Shinji to re-enter the samurai class, albeit at a rank lower than he had held before his fall.

In 1824, soon after the adoption, Chokuemon died and Shinji, at age 34, succeeded as family head. Kiyoko subsequently gave birth to three children, two of whom were sons, but all died before reaching adulthood, the last in 1851. In order to insure the continuation of the Takahashi line, the couple then adopted a daughter from a prosperous family of jewelry-makers in Asakusa, and searched for a husband for her and thus an heir for themselves. One assumes that the money she brought with her allowed Shinji and Kiyoko then to adopt Horie Kakuji, the son of another Sendai domain samurai, as their son and Shinji's successor and to rename him Takahashi Koretada. Shinji died in 1854, only months before Koretada did what his predecessors in the Takahashi family had done for at least two generations before—adopt the young Wakiji and name him Korekiyo. Koretada, like the infant he adopted, had been born in the same area of Edo, between Shinbashi and Shiba, but 30 years earlier. He and his wife had six children, but only one lived to adulthood—thus, the adoption of the future finance minister. Takahashi's grandmother Kiyoko, who played the primary role in raising him, outlived not only her husband, but also her adopted son and daughter, and died in 1886 while Takahashi was abroad studying patent and trademark law.[7] This strong-minded, intelligent woman played an important role in Takahashi's development as a pragmatic, independent-minded official who did not bow to the fashions of the time.

Thanks to Kiyoko, Wakiji/Korekiyo, even after he entered the Taka-hashi household, continued to meet his father and his family—and on a few occasions, even his natal mother. The Takahashi, unlike many *ashi-garu*, were allowed to have a surname and to carry a sword (one, but not two); thus, family members could visit with high-ranking samurai fami-lies such as the Kawamura. After the Meiji Restoration, when Taka-hashi had returned from America and entered the government as an English-language specialist, he and his father often drank together. But although Takahashi knew that Kawamura was his father, and Kawa-mura knew that he knew, his father always addressed Korekiyo as Taka-hashi-san and gave no indication of their blood relationship. In the early 1870s Kawamura's wife came to Takahashi, who was not yet 20, but who was gainfully employed as an English teacher at the Daigaku Nankō, a school that was one of the forerunners of Tokyo Imperial University, and asked him for a loan to help out his family of birth.[8] It was certainly a sign of the changing times in early Meiji Japan that a man who had been a well-to-do samurai under the former *bakufu* had to call on his teenage, illegitimate, ex-*ashigaru* son, now an employee of the new government, to make ends meet.

Takahashi was fortunate to come into the world in a time of great change, and thus of opportunity. He was born in July 1854, the year after Commodore Matthew Perry and his "black ships" made their first visit to Japan. Takahashi grew up amidst the internal conflicts and Western pressures that led to the fall of the Tokugawa regime and the establish-ment of the modernizing Meiji government in 1868. While Kawamura must have been a competent artist, his talents were not essential to the new government as it modernized to defend itself from domestic and foreign enemies. Conversely, the skill that Takahashi had developed by the age of fourteen, a fluent command of the essential foreign lan-guage, English, put him in a good position to rise in the world. One man's talent, appealing as its results may be to devotees of Japanese art, was unneeded; the other man's ability was a passport to upward mobility. But why and how did Takahashi gain the opportunity to learn English? Part of the answer lies in Takahashi's personality. He was not a man to sit back and let fate come to him; throughout his life, he took positive steps to solve the problems he encountered. He was a man who was not discouraged by his mistakes and who learned from them.

The Late-Edo Education of a Foot Soldier-to-Be

Takahashi attributed to the lessons of his childhood the origins of his optimism and his concomitant pragmatic view that a problem could be solved if you studied the situation and acted. He told the following anecdotes to illustrate his point. The children of Sendai fief's *ashigaru* households played at a small shrine near the northeast gate of the domain's Edo mansion. One day in 1857, when Takahashi was three, a neighborhood girl took Takahashi and his friends there to play as usual. Soon word arrived that the wife of Lord Date was approaching the shrine to worship—thus, the girl in charge rounded up the children so that the daimyo's wife would not have to see dirty, lower samurai children as she prayed. But inadvertently, Takahashi was left behind. When the lord's wife, elegantly dressed as one might expect of someone of her rank, bowed before the shrine, baby Wakiji crawled out from behind the shrine, clutched her kimono, and said in baby talk (he was told later), "Auntie, that's a nice kimono you have on" (*obasan, ii bebe da*). The lord's wife said, "Whose child is this? He is really a cute child," and was told it was the child of someone called Takahashi. As this was said, Takahashi climbed into the lady's lap. Later that evening, after Takahashi returned home, a lady-in-waiting came to his home to tell his family that the lord's wife wanted to interview the child at her quarters the next day.

Takahashi's parents panicked. First of all, they feared they might be reprimanded for allowing their child to climb into the lady's lap—in the stratified society of the time, it was not good form for the children of privates to crawl onto the lap of the commanding general's wife. Second, no one had the kind of clothing necessary for an audience at the Date domain's primary "mansion." Thus, the Takahashis ran to the Kawamura house, the home of Takahashi's birth father. But the Kawamuras did not have the appropriate children's clothing either, so they pawned something at hand and bought young Korekiyo his first formal clothes. Much to everyone's surprise, the story had a happy ending and according to Takahashi helped to stimulate his optimistic view of the world. The lord's wife, overjoyed to see the cute young *ashigaru* child, instead of scolding him, showered him with presents. When he returned home, all the other *ashigaru* families in the neighborhood (Sendai domain *ashigaru*, who resided permanently in Edo and did not return home to the castletown with their lord, lived in tenements exclusively for families of their rank) said, "The Takahashi child is certainly fortunate" (*Takahashi no ko wa shiawase mono yo*). How often, after all, did the first lady of the domain entertain low-ranking children?[9]

A year or so later, probably sometime in 1858, word spread that a procession of samurai from one of the Tokugawa branch families (*kamon*), going to Kyoto to defend the Emperor's palace from potential threats, was about to pass through the neighborhood. Takahashi and other neighborhood children ran down to the main road in Shiba to watch the parade. As little Korekiyo reached the road, a woman he knew waved and called from the other side of the road, "Come here, come here." Without thinking, Takahashi bolted across the street. But he stumbled as he ran and fell, and as he did so, the horse of one of the outriders, speeding down the highway, stepped on him. Everyone panicked, thinking poor little Korekiyo was dead, but when they looked they found a horse's footprint on his coat. Again, as in the earlier case, people said that the Takahashi child was blessed. He concludes these anecdotes by writing, "I must have heard this talk. From childhood I believed myself to be lucky. No matter what misfortune I faced, no matter what failure I met, I believed that things would work out for the better—and I strove for this. Thinking back, this is why I became an optimist." And, I would add, a pragmatist.[10]

Takahashi grew up, looked after by his grandmother Kiyoko, in Sendai domain's lower estate below Atago Hill in Shiba—located near where two huge apartment buildings, about halfway between where Shinbashi and Hamamatsu-chō stations, stand today. The lower *yashiki* contained the homes of three *rusu-i-yaku*, important, high-ranking samurai in charge of their lord's dealings with the *bakufu* and other domains; three *mono-kaki-yaku*, officials in charge of keeping records and writing documents; and the row houses for 60 *ashigaru* households. The *rusu-i-yaku* changed from time to time, but they had high enough rank in the domain's pecking order to bring their wives and children with them from Sendai. Grandmother Kiyoko frequently helped these high-ranking families organize receptions and parties—her experience in the Kishiwada and Kōriki mansions prepared her to play a leading role in these families' "downstairs." Despite her *ashigaru* rank, Kiyoko went frequently to these upper-class samurai households—and this connection would have important consequences for her young grandson Korekiyo.

In 1859, when Takahashi was five, an energetic 28-year-old samurai named Ōwara Shindayū came from Sendai to serve as *rusu-i-yaku*. Ōwara realized, as not all samurai did in the years leading up to the demise of the Tokugawa regime, that the imperialist Western nations were not going to go away voluntarily. Japan, to protect itself from the West, needed to learn from the West; accordingly Ōwara encouraged young Sendai warriors to undertake foreign studies.[11] Although it may stretch credulity to argue that the child Korekiyo absorbed Ōwara's lesson at this time, Takahashi's view of Japan's place in the world, throughout his career as a mid- and high-level government official, was similar to Ōwara's in the 1860s. Takahashi believed that Japan benefited by learning from and cooperating with, rather than confronting, the superior wealth, technology, and power of the Anglo-American empires, even if it forced the newly industrializing Japan occasionally to eat diplomatic and economic crow.[12] About the time Ōwara arrived in Edo, his mother died and was buried in Jushōji, the official Sendai domain Buddhist temple, in Gotanda, about a two-mile walk from his and Takahashi's homes. Ōwara, a filial son, went every month to pray at her grave. Takahashi's grandmother Kiyoko also visited Jushōji regularly; one assumes that her connection with high-ranking families made it possible for the widow and mother of an *ashigaru* to visit the domain's official Buddhist temple.

One of the few roads to upward mobility for low-ranking samurai youths in late-Tokugawa Japan was through domain temples such as Jushōji. Boys would serve the temple as pages, learn to read and write, and gain "stock" toward promotion to higher warrior ranks. One day, when Kiyoko had taken young Takahashi to Jushōji, the chief priest asked her to help him find a child to serve as his page. Kiyoko immediately realized that this would be a great opportunity for Wakiji to rise above his hereditary duty as a private in the Sendai army and asked the priest if the young boy would do. The priest consented and the six-year-old Takahashi went to the temple to live.

When Ōwara visited his mother's grave, he stopped to have lunch and play a game of *go* with Jushōji-sama, as the chief priest was known. Takahashi was always at their side serving. He overheard Ōwara talk about the need for samurai to study Western military methods and foreign conditions, about which the Sendai domain warrior learned from his friend, the renowned modernizer Fukuzawa Yukichi. He also heard

Ōwara, a high-ranking samurai, say that in today's perilous conditions Japan needed to recruit men of ability, even if they came from the *ashigaru* class. (Apparently he did not mention the possibility of using commoners.) Ōwara, influenced by Satsuma domain's Ōkubo Toshimichi, later the primary modernizer in the early Meiji government, came to the conclusion that Sendai domain must send young people to the treaty port of Yokohama to undertake Dutch and English studies with native Dutch and English speakers. The problem was, whom to send? Here Takahashi's status as a member of the lowest class of samurai came to his aid. All but the highest-ranking Date retainers who came to Edo under the stipulations of the alternate residence system left their wives and children back home in Sendai. Only the 60 *ashigaru* in Takahashi's tenement, who lived in Edo permanently, had wives and children in the capital. Thus, Ōwara decided to expedite his plan by choosing two children from those readily available in Edo—Takahashi and his friend Suzuki Tomoo, later an official in the Bank of Japan—to study English in Yokohama.[13]

Takahashi Studies English

Yokohama was a dangerous town for a low-ranking samurai intent on learning a barbarian language in the summer of 1864. Satsuma samurai had murdered an Englishman named Charles Richardson near Yokohama in September 1862, and the British had bombarded the Satsuma castletown, Kagoshima, in retribution in August 1863. Chōshū domain had closed the Straits of Shimonoseki to foreign ships in June 1863, and in September 1864, soon after Takahashi's arrival in Yokohama, the British, French, Americans, and other foreign powers reopened the straits by military force. In the shadow of these actions and reactions, anti-Tokugawa, anti-foreign zealots actively sought out for assassination *bakufu* officials and Japanese who seemed too closely connected to the foreigners.

Takahashi's grandmother worried about sending her precious grandson to such a perilous place. Therefore she asked Ōwara for permission to go on her own to the newly opened treaty port to investigate the safest ways of living and studying there. She found that the foreign quarter, where Takahashi and Suzuki would study, and the Japanese city, where perforce they had to live, were connected by only one bridge. She worried that if anti-foreign activists destroyed the bridge, there would be no way out for young Korekiyo. So she asked Ōwara permission to go with the two ten-year-olds to look after them. Ōwara quickly assented—after all, how could two young boys keep house for themselves?[14]

Takahashi began his study of English by going daily to the foreign quarter to study with Clara Hepburn, wife of the medical missionary James Hepburn, famous for creating the Hepburn system of romanizing the Japanese language. As Takahashi wrote to William Elliot Griffis on June 3, 1905, "I began to learn the alphabet under Mrs. Hepburn in 1864–65. Mr. Momotaro Sato and a few young students of the clan of Kaga were with me in her class of English."[15] Takahashi went on to praise Dr. Hepburn's skills as a physician before recounting why he himself did not study medicine. "Dr. Hepburn had some medical students too. I remember that Mr. Sato and I were once asked by one of them to catch a cat for the purpose of dissection. So one day we killed and brought in the animal to the Doctor, and the next morning we were called into the operating room to look. But when I saw the procedure of dissection of the cat's eye, I was so horrified that I turned away for once and all from the medical profession."[16] Medicine's loss was government's gain. Takahashi's language studies continued for a year and a half with Mrs. Hepburn and later with the wife of James Ballagh, another American missionary, and ended only when, in the winter of 1866, fire destroyed much of the Japanese quarter of Yokohama and forced Takahashi, Suzuki, and Kiyoko to return to Edo.

The Japanese study of English was divided into two schools in the 1860s: older students in the tradition of Nagasaki Dutch studies, such as Fukuzawa Yukichi, who taught themselves to read by translating books and newspapers but who could barely speak, and younger ones such as Takahashi, Satō, and Hayashi Tadasu, later Ambassador to Great Britain and Foreign Minister, who studied with Mrs. Hepburn and other native English-language speakers, and who thereby developed oral fluency. When Takahashi returned to Sendai domain's lower mansion after the fire in 1866, Ōta Eijirō, one of the former (a translator who could not speak well) worried that Takahashi would lose his proficiency in spoken English if he did not continue to use it frequently. He proposed that Takahashi, now age eleven, take a job as a houseboy for one of the British banks in Yokohama. Takahashi, with his grandmother's approval, returned to Yokohama to work for Alexander Allan Shand, the 22-year-old acting manager of the Yokohama branch of the Chartered Mercantile Bank of London, China, and India, a bank known locally, because of the structure of its gate, as the "Iron Pillar Bank." The bank had three directors, of whom Shand, who would later become an important mentor and friend to both Japan and Takahashi, was one. Takahashi's primary tasks were to clean Shand's room and to serve him his meals.[17] There is an aspect of Takahashi's situation at the Iron Pillar Bank that tells us something about the similarities in British and Japanese class structure in the mid-nineteenth century. Each of the three directors had a houseboy: two of the houseboys were low-ranking Japanese samurai children and the third was the son of an enlisted man in the British garrison in Yokohama.

Although in his spare time Takahashi went to Ōta's place to study translation, he did not take instruction in English while at the bank. He improved his oral fluency, however, on the job by talking to his boss, Shand. He also fell in with the bank's grooms and cooks in all kinds of mischief; in fact, as we shall continue to see, Takahashi had a readiness to carouse in his early years. They drank, gambled, and made life difficult for the prostitutes sent to service the foreigners. The prostitutes came at night, led by older women who carried lanterns to light the way. Takahashi and his pals would knock out the lights, chase the escorts away in terror, and then steal the prostitutes' hairpins and other decorations before the young women could reach their patrons. Takahashi tells us that he soon earned a bad reputation among his peers and Sendai domain officials.[18]

One day, Suzuki Tomoo, the other child who had gone to Yokohama to study English in 1864, visited Takahashi and told him that he was being sent to America to study, but that Takahashi was being left home because of his bad behavior. Embarrassed by this, especially because news of his pranks had reached his grandmother, Takahashi decided that he must find some other way to go abroad. Through an acquaintance he found the master of a British whaling ship who was willing to hire him on as a cabin boy. When he went to see the captain, he was told that the ship was both a whaler and a sailing vessel; thus, it might take six months or more to reach London. On the other hand, everyone on the ship spoke English, so it was a great chance for the twelve-year-old to practice his conversational English. Takahashi replied that no matter how long it took or how rough the voyage, he wanted to go to England.

At this point an older and higher-ranking Sendai warrior named Hoshi Juntarō intervened on Takahashi's behalf. Hoshi had come to Yokohama to study British military methods and worked in the shop of an American named Eugene Van Reed, a merchant who sold guns to various domains and who also arranged for Japanese laborers to work in Hawai'i. Hoshi, impressed that Takahashi had taken the initiative to arrange his passage on a whaler, talked to Ōwara in Edo and arranged for young Takahashi to join the official group of five students going to America. Three of the students received scholarships for their study, but Suzuki and Takahashi, because they were still children, did not. So Hoshi talked to his employer, Van Reed, who came up with a solution. Suzuki and Takahashi would live with Van Reed's elderly parents in San Francisco and learn while they helped out around the house. Sendai domain would send their travel expenses and school money directly to the Van Reeds in California. Takahashi, his grandmother, and Ōwara all thought this an excellent solution and breathed easier.[19]

Takahashi Travels to America

How should a young Japanese dress in America? Ōwara, Kiyoko, and Takahashi agreed that it should be in the Western style. Korekiyo searched for Western clothes that would fit his twelve-year-old frame. He engaged a tailor to make him a cotton vest and pants and a silk frock coat. He also found a black cardboard hat with white cloth in the back to protect him from the sun. A bigger problem was shoes. The only Western men's shoes one could buy in Yokohama in 1867 were in large sizes for British soldiers. Finally, Kiyoko found used women's black satin shoes that would fit young Korekiyo. The night before he was to board ship in Yokohama his grandmother cut his hair short; Takahashi tells us he still had his hair when he was writing his memoirs in the 1930s. He must have cut quite a figure as he boarded ship for San Francisco!

But Kiyoko decided that Korekiyo needed more than his Western-style outfit to cross the ocean and enter a strange new world. He needed to take with him protection from the old as well. Thus, a few days before Takahashi's departure, the widow of a samurai handed her grandson a dagger and said, "I am not giving you this so that you can hurt someone else. A man must value his name. For righteousness and to clear away shame, there are times when we must die. I am giving the dagger to you for the rare chance you will need it." Then, according to Takahashi, Kiyoko taught him how to commit ritual suicide. On July 24, 1867, only three days before his thirteenth birthday, Kiyoko took her grandson to Yokohama to board the *Colorado*, a 3,750-ton paddle-wheel freighter, for America.[20]

The ship set sail for America the next day. While the three older samurai, led by a 32-year-old Sendai domain samurai, Tomita Tetsu-nosuke, lately a member of the Meirokusha, a diplomat, Governor of the Bank of Japan, and a founder of the school that became Hitotsu-bashi University, had staterooms, Takahashi, Suzuki, and the other younger students traveled down below on the orlop deck, not a pleasant experience as Takahashi describes it.[21] Large numbers of people slept in three-tiered hammocks in large rooms. The ship's crew fumigated them with red pepper each morning. Takahashi and his fellow travelers ate communal meals from large tin pails. Since most of their fellow shipmates were Chinese laborers emigrating to the United States, the standard fare was "Nanking pork mixed with fat." The travelers defecated and urinated into large 20-gallon tubs lined up at the rear of the ship over the paddlewheel, which, one assumes, washed the waste out of harm's way. The young Korekiyo found the odor of the Chinese food particularly unpleasant. But his trip was saved by three escapes. First, one of his fellow passengers, a 24-year-old Satsuma warrior named Itō Sukeyuki, who later became a fleet admiral (*gensui*) and chief of the navy's general staff, spent the entire voyage sitting down below drinking.[22] One day he asked Takahashi whether he drank. After the thirteen-year-old veteran of the "Iron Pillar" replied in the affirmative, the two spent the rest of the voyage happily in their cups. In fact, Takahashi drank up all of his $20 shipboard allowance, and that of his dry companion Suzuki as well. Second, Tomita and other older samurai on the higher decks smuggled food to their younger compatriots in steerage. And third, and maybe most important, Takahashi and Suzuki regularly sneaked up to the first-class toilet to relieve themselves. After 23 days at sea, on August 18, 1867, the *Colorado* arrived in San Francisco harbor.[23]

Takahashi wrote to his parents and grandmother about his shipboard experiences in a letter from San Francisco a few months later. The letter is far from a literary masterpiece; however, it is written in *sōrōbun*, the samurai epistolary style, and uses more than 100 *kanji*, revealing that Takahashi had learned to read and write his native language while he served as a page at Jushōji:

A few lines in the cold season to see how grandmother and mother and father are doing. We left at six in the morning on July 25th and spent 23 days at sea. We were on time and arrived in America at six in the morning. We left the ship and went to Van Reed's house safely. I wanted to send a letter by China clipper, but because of work I missed the deadline by three or four days. I finally had a letter to send by November 8th, but no ship was available. I apologize that my letter is late. Please show my letter to Jushōji-sama and after him to everyone else. The letters from father and grandmother arrived on November 19th by the Western calendar. I saw whales now and then while at sea. Tomita-san was a big help to me on the ship. The food was all right although I ate nothing but bread. The Nanking pork mixed with fat was inedible. Someone named Satō Momotarō, whom grandmother knows from Yokohama, traveled to America on the same ship.[24]

Takahashi Wakiji
December 3

TWO

Takahashi in San Francisco, 1867–68

A Dangerous Arrival in a Strange Land

Young Takahashi's eighteen months in San Francisco began inauspiciously, and his time there demonstrated how dangerous it was to be an energetic Asian child in a strange land in 1867. He, Tomita, and the others of the Sendai group were met at the ship by Ichijō Jūjirō, a fellow retainer of Lord Date, but one who had fled the domain a few years earlier to study in the United States. The group set off together to deliver Suzuki and Takahashi, the two youngsters who had come to America to study English, to Van Reed's house. But when they arrived there, they found no one home. So Takahashi and his shipboard drinking partner Itō decided to return to the ship. Takahashi describes their attire as they walked the streets of San Francisco. Itō was dressed in a woolen naval uniform with brass buttons, which Takahashi describes as "Kagoshima-style," that is, the uniform of the Western-style Satsuma-domain navy. Takahashi had on the same outfit: white cotton pants, black frock coat, cardboard hat, and women's satin shoes, which had looked strange enough when he boarded ship in Yokohama. But on the voyage across the Pacific, the frock coat had become threadbare and the cotton pants had shrunk up to his knees; he looked so odd that passersby occasionally hit the top of his hat to ridicule him. Trouble threatened Takahashi from the Japanese as well as the American side.

Tomita, who knew of Takahashi's bad behavior at the Iron Pillar Bank in Yokohama, scolded the thirteen-year-old for his excessive drinking on the *Colorado*. Tomita told Takahashi that he was not serious enough to study in America and should return to Japan on the next ship. It was only when he apologized and promised no further misbehavior that Tomita gave in—but it was clear that Takahashi was on probation.

Life in the Van Reed household, after the two youths finally settled there, seemed promising at first. They shared a pleasant room and for the first time since leaving home ate wholesome, if somewhat exotic, foreign food, and at the dinner table with their hosts. But the good life was short-lived. Gradually the quality of the food deteriorated. Instead of sending Takahashi and Suzuki to school, the Van Reeds ordered the two boys to cook, clean, and run errands. When the mistress went to market to shop, Suzuki and Takahashi trailed behind with large bamboo baskets to carry potatoes and other vegetables home. Not only did the two not go to school, but they were not allowed to study at night either because of the Van Reeds' fear that burning candles or kerosene lights to read by might cause fires. The final straw came at lunch one day when the mistress handed the two boys a few grapes, bread, and butter, and instructed them to eat outside with the dogs, not at the table as before. Clearly Eugene Van Reed in Yokohama had led his parents in California to have expectations about the purpose of the two boys' trip to America that were different from those of Ōwara, Wakiji, and his grandmother.

Takahashi reports in his memoirs that he became so outraged by this treatment that he stopped working. Suzuki, who had a more obedient and docile temperament, continued to work; soon Mrs. Van Reed gave orders only to Suzuki and ignored Takahashi altogether. This angered young Wakiji even more, so much so that when she gave orders to Suzuki to carry out some household chore or other, Takahashi heckled from the sidelines and told him not to do it. The Van Reeds soon wrote Takahashi off as a bad investment and looked around for some way to rid themselves of the burden of housing him. This led to one of the most amazing events in Takahashi's eventful life—one that virtually everyone who has written about Takahashi's life has mentioned—and one that had an important formative effect on the development of his character.[1]

One day Mrs. Van Reed came to the recalcitrant Takahashi and asked him to go with her to visit rich friends in Oakland. Takahashi, bored by his inactivity, immediately assented. In his memoirs, he paints an idyllic picture of the East Bay city in 1867.

Oakland at that time, as the name implies, was a forest of oak trees. The town was one block large, laid out on a cross system. Houses were scattered here and there, but there was a haberdashery, a millinery shop, a shoemaker, and a general store all in one cluster. The station where we got off the train was a station in name only—it had a large roof to keep the rain off, but no seats. The rich family (we visited) had a large house with a splendid view on the banks of a river. A young couple lived there, and they had many fields and garden plots and raised cattle and horses. They also had two servants, of whom one was Chinese and the other Irish.[2]

Takahashi Carelessly Signs a Document

When Takahashi returned home that evening, the Van Reeds asked him if he had liked the ranch in Oakland. After he answered that he found it a fine place, they asked him if he would like to live there. The Van Reeds went on to say that the young master, Mr. Browne, commuted every day to a bank in San Francisco, but that his wife, "who is very kind, can teach you." When Takahashi replied that he would like to go very much, Van Reed asked him to bring Ichijō as a witness and come with him. When Van Reed, Takahashi, and Ichijō arrived at their destination, which turned out to be a notary's office, they found Mr. Browne waiting for them. Van Reed then handed over a single type-written sheet of paper and asked Ichijō and Takahashi to sign it. The two Japanese had an incomplete command of English and the thirteen-year-old Takahashi was too trusting—he was overjoyed at what he had been told, that is, that he could go to Browne's house in Oakland to study. As he later wrote in his memoirs, "I was at an age when I trusted what people said, so I did not apply my learning to it. Moreover, since my teachers in Yokohama had been Mrs. Hepburn and Mrs. Barragh, I thought only women taught English." Ichijō, who was older and more worldly, read the document and said to Takahashi, "it says something about your going to Oakland and something else about three years." But Takahashi was not suspicious; in fact, when he told Suzuki about his new opportunity, Suzuki was jealous.[3]

Takahashi lived an idyllic life for a young boy in his first months in Oakland. Mrs. Browne taught him English calligraphy and reading, and made him clothes. She let him bring hot water and watch while she bathed her newborn baby. She debated Wakiji on methods of child-rearing. He thought her cruel for not immediately feeding and comforting her baby when it cried; she replied that what he suggested was the easiest way to spoil a child. But, Takahashi reports, she also came to see him as an honest, sympathetic young man. Takahashi learned to cook by assisting Mrs. Browne on the occasions she went to the kitchen. He agreed to look after the Brownes' cattle and horses if he were allowed to ride the horses. After Mr. Browne assented, Takahashi spent hours six days a week grooming and feeding the livestock, and Sundays riding around the countryside. Takahashi tells us he had only one weakness on the farm: hard as he tried, he could not milk the cows successfully.[4]

Takahashi also had his second sustained contact with Chinese (the first being in steerage on the *Colorado*) while in Oakland, and it was the outcome of this contact that began to teach him one of the most important precepts of his adult life: never accept at face value what you are told; always investigate below the surface. A rich neighbor of the Brownes employed a Japanese worker who could not speak English. Thus, they asked Takahashi to help out as an interpreter, and each Sunday he used his free time to ride one of Browne's horses to the Rogers's farm. But Takahashi, who liked to leave early on his day off, could not depart until he put the cows out to pasture, which he could not do until the Chinese cook had milked them. One weekend the cook for some reason did not milk the cows at his usual early time. Takahashi, in a rush to speed to the Rogers's farm (was their young daughter his attraction?), took the cows out to the fields before they were milked and hurried off to the neighbors. That evening, Mrs. Browne scolded Takahashi for his negligence.

The next morning, the situation worsened. When Takahashi went to chop wood for the cooking and laundry, which was one of his chores, he found the Chinese cook doing it instead. When he remonstrated with the cook, the cook countered by telling Takahashi that if he were not going to do his duties properly, then he could not be depended on. Therefore, the cook said he would do all the sawing and chopping of wood himself from now upon. Takahashi flew into a rage at what he interpreted as an insult, picked up an axe, and started after the cook.

Takahashi then writes, somewhat melodramatically (and inconsistently), the following paragraph in his memoirs:

When I left Japan my grandmother had told me to commit suicide rather than be shamed. She taught me the [samurai] method of disembowelment if I could not kill the person who shamed me. I put the dagger my grandmother had given me in my pocket. When the Chinese cook saw this, he put a small axe in his pocket. At that moment, the two of us seemed intent on killing each other. But I thought of the two *kanji* of my grandmother's admonishment: *kannin*, forbearance. When it was the time to be patient, be patient. But grandmother in counseling me to be patient had also told me to finish off my enemy first, and then myself. But if I killed him, what would happen to me? Doubts boiled up in my chest.[5]

When Mr. Browne returned from the city that evening, Takahashi burst into the living room and asked him what would happen if he killed the Chinese cook? Browne looked at Takahashi with a strange face and said, "If you kill a person, you get killed."[6] When Takahashi answered by saying that he could not let the cook's scorn go unavenged, Browne told the teenager that some of the fault was his and scolded him for putting the cows out too early and not sawing the wood. Takahashi went to his room in a huff.

Takahashi brooded all night and the next day, and came to realize that to give up his life to avenge a petty insult was idiotic. Thus, he went to Browne to ask permission to leave. "I can't work together with that Chinese guy (*yatsu*). I want permission to leave." Then came the bombshell. Browne replied, "You can't quit whenever you want to. I bought you for three years. Didn't your friend and you sign the document?"

Takahashi was stunned. He now understood what Ichijō had been trying to say when they signed the paper in Van Reed's presence. Takahashi had agreed to a contract for three years of indentured servitude. But there is comedy even in tragedy. Takahashi quickly realized that somehow he had to run away. Thus, he turned to Browne and said, "If this is so, please give me a day off. I want to go to San Francisco tomorrow and confer with my friends." Browne told Takahashi not to be impertinent and slapped him in the face. At the very moment that Takahashi was hit, he farted. "I was embarrassed," he wrote later, "so even though I was angry I could not refrain from smiling." Seeing this, Mrs. Browne came to Takahashi's defense and said to her husband, "Dear, you shouldn't act in such a violent way."[7]

Takahashi Escapes from Indentured Servitude

Takahashi went to San Francisco the next day to confer with Ichijō. The older samurai, according to Takahashi, was perplexed by the situation and could only say repeatedly, "What a fix. What a fix." Takahashi suggested running away, but Ichijō feared that, unaccustomed to the laws and practices of America, they might run into even greater difficulties if he did. So in the end, Takahashi returned to Oakland, but with a new resolve. "I decided, in my childlike way, to take matters into my own hands. Once I got back, I was disorderly about everything. If they were disgusted with me, they would fire me. So I stopped cleaning the lamps. I stopped doing the dishes. I randomly broke things. But it had no effect at all. Mr. and Mrs. Browne saw all this and never got mad. Not only that, but when Mrs. Browne admonished me for my bad behavior, she did it in a kindly way. I was puzzled by this."[8]

At this point, Takahashi tells us, President Andrew Johnson appointed Mr. Browne's father and the actual owner of the Oakland estate, John Ross Browne, Minister to China. He and his entourage, which included children a few years younger than Takahashi and several servants, came to Oakland to pick up their son and his family to depart for China. The maids did all of the cleaning duties and the family, in preparation for their journey, sold all of their livestock. Thus, Takahashi, even if he were to end his strike and want to perform his chores, had nothing to do. But being a gregarious fourteen-year-old, he soon befriended the Browne children and spent the next two months playing. As he wrote, "I played with the children every day and passed the days in pure pleasure."[9]

When the time finally came for all of the Brownes to depart for China, the elder Mr. Browne, that is, the newly appointed Minister to China, came to Takahashi, gave him 20 dollars in gold coins, and told him that he could arrange for Takahashi to work in the San Francisco customs office and live in the household of one of its officials. In the evenings after work, that man's daughter would tutor Takahashi in English composition. Young Takahashi, who had completely forgotten about the earlier unpleasantness during the two months of play, agreed to the arrangement. Moreover, each member of the Browne family gave Takahashi five or ten dollars as they left for China. When Takahashi went to the pier in San Francisco to see the Brownes off, he met the customs office official and liked him very much. Takahashi was told about his work and study regime, and that he would have his own private room for which the family had bought new blankets and sheets. To our naïve, young Takahashi, this all seemed too good to be true.

That evening Takahashi reported his auspicious news to Ichijō, who immediately told Takahashi not to go. Good as the new situation may seem, it would still be indentured servitude. Takahashi quotes Ichijō as saying, "He thinks he has bought you as a servant. The buying and selling of slaves ended with the Civil War. He is breaking the law. This is an opportune time to escape servitude, so do not go back."[10] Although Takahashi thought he was showing ingratitude, he did not go back to the customs official's house, and as one might expect, the family did not come after Takahashi. Although Takahashi had broken his "contract," clearly the customs official had no legal recourse.

Takahashi's immediate problem was how to live without the room and board provided by his "owners." The Brownes had given him 40 or 50 dollars, and Mrs. Browne had paid him four dollars a month during his time in Oakland. Takahashi had deposited all of this money in a bank and had a bankbook to prove it. So he could get by for the time being. At this juncture, fortune smiled again. Satō Momotarō, Takahashi's classmate from Mrs. Hepburn's school in Yokohama and a relative of a future colleague in London in 1904–5, Ambassador and later Foreign Minister, Hayashi Tadasu, offered him a job in a shop that sold goods imported from Japan. Takahashi moved into the shop and helped Satō make deliveries, which turned out to be profitable: the recipients of the goods tipped Takahashi and Satō 10 to 25 cents per delivery.[11]

Although Takahashi had escaped from his indentured service, he and his older colleagues, Ichijō and Tomita, thought it important for him to retrieve from the elder Van Reed the contract he had signed; this was particularly important because Takahashi's Yokohama classmate, Suzuki, still worked as a servant in the Van Reed household. Although the Japanese government did not have a consul in San Francisco, it did employ an honorary consul, an American named Brooks, whom the Tokugawa shogunate had appointed to look after Japan's interests in California. Brooks arranged for Tomita, Ichijō, and another samurai named Takagi Saburō to meet with Van Reed.[12] What ensued was a comedy of errors, which luckily, as with most comedies, had a happy ending. Takagi negotiated in his reasonably fluent, but heavily accented English. After he and Van Reed had reached what seemed an amicable settlement, Van Reed replied, "I agree." But Takagi heard "angry" instead and flew into a rage. In the end, Van Reed returned all of the money he had received from Browne when he sold Takahashi's contract to him, and returned the agreement that Ichijō and Takahashi had signed as well. All that remained now was to free Suzuki.[13]

This proved difficult both because Suzuki had turned out to be a better and more loyal servant than had Takahashi, and because he was reluctant to hurt Mrs. Van Reed's feelings by deserting her. Finally, unable to convince Suzuki to leave voluntarily, Takagi, Tomita, and Takahashi decided to abduct him. So a few days later, when Suzuki came out of the house with the Van Reeds, the three grabbed him and ran off. But they ran into a cul-de-sac and were trapped. When Van Reed blocked their escape and told Suzuki to return to the house, Tomita stepped up and shouted at Van Reed, "Me Tomita! Me Tomita! Japan!" Even Takahashi had to wonder what result Tomita expected from his outburst. Suzuki returned to the house, but left for good with the Van Reeds' approval a week or so later.[14] Ironically, the key American in these discussions in San Francisco in the summer of 1868 was an honorary consul appointed by the *bakufu*—but at the very time Brooks arranged for Takagi to negotiate with Van Reed, the government that had appointed him had been overthrown.

During the year and a half that Takahashi spent in America, momentous events took place back home in Japan. In November 1867, Tokugawa Yoshinobu resigned as Japan's last shogun with the expectation of becoming an important part of a new coalition government. In January 1868, samurai from Satsuma and Chōshū, domains that wanted predominant power for themselves and thus found the November compromise unacceptable, seized the imperial palace in Kyoto and declared a restoration of power to the emperor, one that had no role for the ex-shogun. In May, Yoshinobu surrendered Edo Castle, his seat of authority, to the imperial forces. In July, a group of Tokugawa loyalists were

defeated in a battle in the Ueno district of Edo, when they resisted the
new government militarily. The victors then ordered the shogun to surrender his landholdings and go into exile in Mito, and then in Suruga
province. In September, the imperial leaders brought the emperor to
Edo, declared it the national capital, and renamed it Tokyo, "eastern
capital." And in October a new reign name was announced: Meiji, that
is, "enlightened rule," in place of Keio. In other words, during the time
Takahashi was in America, the government came to power that he would
serve for almost his whole life, and the city of his childhood gained a
new name. But the transition was not to be easy for Takahashi: Sendai
domain, which he still served as a low-ranking samurai, remained loyal
to the shogun and resisted the Meiji government. It was in the late stages
of these events, while his domain still stood up to the new regime, that
Takahashi and his friends in San Francisco began to think about returning home.

Takahashi Returns Home

While, during the summer of 1868, the Sendai group worked to free
Takahashi and Suzuki from their servitude, news arrived from Japan of
the events taking place back home. A newspaper from Japan came to
the shop where Takahashi and Satō worked with a report of the July
4th battle in Ueno that had led to the defeat and destruction of the
shōgitai, the Tokugawa loyalists who had united to defend the shogun
against the new government. The San Francisco group, most of whom
came from domains that supported the Tokugawa, concluded that if it
took the imperial forces three days to defeat the rebels, the Tokugawa
might win an ensuing civil war. At this point, everyone began to think
of going home to see what was going on. It was decided that the older
samurai, Tomita and Takagi, would return home first, and let the
younger ones know when it was safe to follow. But months passed and
no word came from Tomita. So in December of 1868, Ichijō, Suzuki,
and Takahashi each bought a suit of ready-made Western clothes, purchased 50-dollar steerage tickets, and left for home.[15]

   Takahashi and his group returned to Yokohama in December 1868
with new dangers awaiting them. Takahashi and Suzuki carried passports issued by the former Tokugawa government that stated they were
peasants from Sendai. Since their domain opposed the new govern-

ment, Kiyama Seiichi, the non-Sendai man in their group, told them to throw their passports overboard to avoid complications when they passed through customs. But trying to enter Japan without any papers at all seemed even more dangerous. Here Takahashi's story, recounted in his memoirs, becomes a little improbable. Kiyama told the Sendai three to leave their luggage with him, go through customs pretending to be foreigners, and meet him later at an inn in Kanagawadai. So Ichijō, Takahashi, and Suzuki safely entered Japan singing foreign songs and speaking English. One wonders how the three Japanese, even in their new American suits, convinced the authorities they were not Japanese. And one finds it equally unlikely that foreigners could enter Japan in 1868 without passports or other papers. Whatever the potential stumbling blocks, the three safely made it to the inn—in fact, their only problem was that Kiyama did not follow soon after.

Kiyama finally arrived a few hours later and apologized for making them wait so long. He then explained why: "When I took Takahashi's baggage through customs, they found a pistol, and that caused an uproar. Why did you bring it with you?" Takahashi explained that in San Francisco he had traded his grandmother's dagger, the one he had almost used on the Chinese cook, for an American pistol. He then hid the pistol in the bottom of his trunk, never dreaming, he said naïvely, that it would cause a problem when he, a retainer in a domain of anti-government rebels, reentered Japan.[16]

The thinness of the cover of Takahashi's Western suit and skill in English became clear when the group arrived in Shiba, near the Sendai estate, in the city now called Tokyo. A young barber in Takahashi's neighborhood, who had been a childhood playmate, recognized him immediately, and using a shortened version of Korekiyo's childhood name, yelled, "Waki-san, Waki-san." The dangers they confronted also became clear quickly. Takahashi visited his natal family, the Kawamuras, who refused to take him in for fear of reprisals from the new government. The Sendai three, therefore, had no choice but to follow Kiyama to his home across town in Ushigome, where they stayed holed up for over a month while he tried to find a place for the three to live and work.

Deliverance came ironically from Mori Arinori, a 21-year-old Satsuma samurai, who himself had just returned from spending 1865–68 in Great Britain and the United States to become an official in the new government. Mori recognized the importance to Japan of young men who could speak and read English. Thus, in January 1869, he had the three Sendai samurai move into his home in Kanda under assumed names—for example, Takahashi Wakiji Korekiyo became Hashi Wakichirō, drawing one character each from his surname and childhood given name. Mori from Satsuma, two young samurai from Chōshū, the other principal government domain, and the Sendai three, that is, three men from the victorious domains, and three enemies, lived a communal life together while they worked to improve their foreign language skills. Mori instructed his young charges in English, Ichijō (under the name Gotō Tsune) taught them Chinese literature, and a third samurai took charge of calligraphy lessons. Because Mori served in the Meiji government, he was too busy to teach full time. Thus, to save time, Mori taught Takahashi, who in turn passed on what he learned to the other students. Shortly thereafter the government established Daigaku Nankō, a school devoted to foreign studies, and in March 1869, Takahashi, Suzuki, and Ichijō, because of their superior English-language skills, became "third-class instructors"; by February 1870, Takahashi had been promoted to the rank of "junior professor" (*shō kyōju*). Takahashi, at age fourteen, began a career in government that would last 67 years, until his assassination in 1936.[17]

About the same time, the daimyo of Sendai domain surrendered to the new government and was placed under house arrest in Zōjōji, the Tokugawa temple near Takahashi's childhood home in Shiba. Thus, Takahashi was no longer a fugitive from the government he served, but conversely became a target of a faction in his own domain that resisted surrender and continued to oppose the Meiji government. These anti-government, anti-foreign samurai began to arrest and even execute Sendai students of Western studies. In the name of protecting the imperial throne from contamination by things foreign (and presaging the young officer/terrorists of the 1930s by ignoring the fact that the emperor himself supported the new government), these dissidents set out to capture Takahashi and his two companions. One day Suzuki ran to Takahashi to say that two plainclothesmen from Sendai domain had captured Gotō—that is, Ichijō under his pseudonym—right in front of the school in Hitotsubashi, next to the Imperial Palace, the locale that had been the shogun's castle grounds until only a year earlier. The next day Mori took Takahashi and Suzuki to the Sendai domain office in nearby Hibiya and demanded Ichijō's release. He went on to say that he was adopting the three into his family; he subsequently wrote them into his family register, and for a short time, Takahashi was a dependent of Mori Arinori, and thus of a samurai from Satsuma.[18]

At about the same time, a messenger and then a letter came from Lord Rakuzan (Date Yoshikuni), the Sendai daimyo, saying that he would like to meet the two young students who had just returned from America. On the appointed day, Takahashi and Suzuki put on their American suits and walked to Zōjōji in Shiba to meet their domain's lord (eleven years after baby Takahashi had met his wife). When the daimyo greeted them, one of his advisors told them that it was not decorous to wear mufflers in the presence of the lord. Takahashi answered, "This is a necktie and wearing one is a sign of proper manners. Not wearing one is dressing like a laborer." So Japan began to segue into the "modern" world of Western clothes.

The lord asked, "How long did you stay in America? What is it like over there?" and a host of other questions. Takahashi and Suzuki answered them one by one until, finally, Date asked, "Can you make a foreign poem?" The two answered that they were utterly untrained in poetry. When the lord prompted them therefore to recite a poem, Takahashi replied, "I haven't studied poetry especially, but I have learned a couple of poems." Luckily he had memorized poems from Volume 4 of the Sargent Reader, and Takahashi recited two: "The Spacious permanent on high. With all the blue ethereal sky," and then, "The Spring is coming, the spring is coming. Hark, the little bird is singing."[19] I like to think that this interview marked the end of Takahashi's service to the old, feudal order, and the beginning of his long career as a bureaucrat and politician.

The Influences of Takahashi's Youth on His Later Life

What impact did the experiences of Takahashi's youth have on the development of his mature intellect and personality? Can we identify in our discussion of his first fourteen years and eight months any lifelong influences? The answer is obviously yes. By the time Takahashi began his long career in government by entering the Meiji government as an English-language teacher in March 1869, many of the skills, central intellectual convictions, and character traits of the grown-up Takahashi had already begun to appear.

Most importantly, the key to Takahashi's upward mobility from illegitimate child and adopted *ashigaru* to seven-time finance minister and prime minister was his command of English. This was not only because Takahashi spoke and wrote English skillfully, as his long friendships and elegant letters to foreigners such as Shand, Schiff, and Schuyler Duryee of the United States patent office attest. Also and more significantly, the Meiji oligarchs, the primary leaders in Japan's effort to catch up with the West in the late nineteenth and early twentieth century, entrusted important tasks to Takahashi: interpreting for David Murray, a highly-paid American advisor on education in the 1870s; writing Japan's first patent and trademark laws in the 1880s; and negotiating Japan's foreign loans to pay for the Russo-Japanese War in 1904–7, for example, because they recognized that he had the requisite language skills to perform these assignments. In the process of using his command of English to carry out these and other duties, he proved to Itō Hirobumi, Yamagata Aritomo, Saigō Tsugumichi, Inoue Kaoru, and Matsukata Masayoshi that he could carry out complex jobs successfully. In this way, the linguistic foundation Takahashi began to build in Yokohama and San Francisco provided the underpinning to his later career.

Second, Takahashi associated from childhood with men who committed their lives to making Japan rich and strong by learning from the West. Beginning in 1859, when at age five he met Ōwara Shindayū at Jushōji, Takahashi studied, worked, and played with men in Edo, Yokohama, San Francisco, and Tokyo whose names read like a "Who's Who" of Meiji/Taishō government and business leadership: the Bank of Japan official Suzuki Tomoo, the silk merchant Satō Momotarō, the central banker and entrepreneur Tomita Tetsunosuke, the fleet admiral Itō Sukeyuki, the diplomat and exporter Takagi Saburō, and finally and most important for Takahashi's early career, the liberal Westernizer and future conservative education minister, Mori Arinori. Takahashi's lifetime opposition to a Japanese quest for diplomatic autonomy and economic autarky, and his costly resistance in his final years to the chauvinistic and unmodern (or even anti-modern) blather of men like General Araki Sadao, starts with his fraternization from early childhood with men who understood realistically Japan's weakness, and thus its need to make itself rich and strong by learning from and cooperating with the West.

Third, Takahashi spoke almost daily for over four years, from age ten to age fourteen plus, with foreigners—certainly a rare experience among Japanese youths or among Japanese in general in the closing years of Tokugawa rule. Frequent conversations with teachers and employers such as Clara Hepburn, Alexander Allan Shand, the Van Reeds, and the Brownes, with ships' officers, neighbors, and fellow-servants on the voyage to and from and in California, with foreign teachers at Daigaku Nankō, and many others helped him build his command of the English language; they also allowed Takahashi to overcome any feelings of inferiority he might have felt in dealing with Americans and Europeans. What strikes one, as we shall see as the book progresses, was Takahashi's ease and self-confidence in his frequent dealings with foreigners during his long life.

Fourth, Takahashi did not have a mainstream education, even by late-Tokugawa standards. Unlike the best-educated samurai of his time, who studied either Chinese classical literature and Confucianism, or Dutch studies, or both, Takahashi seems to have had little in the way of a formal education. Takahashi does not mention in his memoirs going to school at all as a child. We know from the letter he wrote to his parents from San Francisco in 1867 that he had learned the *sōrōbun* epistolary style, probably at Jushōji or from his grandmother, before beginning his study of English. We know he studied English for over a year with Mrs. Hepburn and Mrs. Barragh, in classes together with other young men, some of whom, like Satō, were not even samurai. But, as we have seen, his educational opportunities in his last year in Yokohama and in California were limited; he may have learned more from speaking English to his masters and fellow employees than in more traditional teaching settings. Thus, I will argue that Takahashi did most of his learning, both in childhood and later, on the job as a kind of "intern" or policy apprentice. He learned from people with whom he worked and corresponded and in the process he gained many mentors, but few if any masters. And here his command of English helped out. Takahashi read foreign books and newspapers all his life—in fact, a photograph taken of him in 1935, only a few months before his murder, shows him reading Beatrice and Sidney Webb's book on Soviet Russia.

He also learned from corresponding with many people in both Japanese and English. Takahashi's later correspondence with the Jewish-American financier Jacob Schiff is a good example; as one reads through it, one realizes that the two men were not only warm friends, but were also continually teaching each other about international politics and economics. The gregarious Takahashi learned by living, not by attending Tokyo Imperial University.

Fifth, Takahashi was born, raised, and lived almost his entire life in the city of Edo/Tokyo. The language he spoke from childhood until his death was the language of the capital, one that developed to allow samurai from all over Japan to communicate with one another when on duty in Edo. Most Tokugawa-era members of the warrior class grew up in their domains far from Edo. The languages they learned in childhood were their local dialects, often unintelligible to samurai from other parts of Japan; thus, the need for a common language. Takahashi, although he served the lord of Sendai, a region of the country with one of the most distinctive dialects, never actually went to Sendai as a youth. He served the northeastern domain, but lived only in Edo, and communicated with his fellow Sendai warriors, and for that matter, with the lord's wife when she entertained him as a child, and the lord when Takahashi had his audience in 1869, in the samurai Edo language (as distinct from the very different, working-class Edo dialect), an ancestor of the standard Japanese later taught in the modern school system. In other words, by the end of the Tokugawa period, Takahashi was a young man whose local language was also his "national" one. By Japanese standards of the 1860s, he had an urbane beginning.

Sixth, Takahashi's unusual childhood, his mastery of English, and his foreign experience made him an unusually internationalist and cosmopolitan man for his times. Although Takahashi called himself a nationalist, and the evidence demonstrates that in some senses he was one, he was never a chauvinist. Throughout his mature career, Takahashi committed himself to the nationalistic goal of enriching Japan and its people—that is, he was committed to the *fukoku* half of the Meiji slogan, *fukoku kyōhei*, "rich country, strong army." But Takahashi's rich country was one in which the people's standards of living were more important than the government's wealth, and thus what that money could buy, its military power. He staunchly opposed using Japan's growing wealth for excessive military spending and militaristic adventures. He supported Japan's empire-building only as long as it was carried out within the framework of Anglo-American imperialism. Takahashi believed that enriching Japan, his nationalistic goal, benefited from participation in the world economic order; he opposed autonomous enterprises that threatened Japan's place in that order. He moved comfortably in the Anglo-American world, and encouraged his followers in the Bank of Japan and the Finance Ministry to do so as well. While I would certainly not say Takahashi was a full-grown cosmopolitan internationalist at age fourteen, his youthful experiences helped create the foundations for the development of this part of his intellectual framework.

Seventh, Takahashi had an unusual detachment and rationality, and these traits began to develop even in his youth. As we have seen, Takahashi led an unconventional life as a child. He associated regularly with foreigners. He was a free spirit who got drawn into low-level rascality from time to time. He had the ability, even as a teenager in San Francisco, to find pragmatic solutions to problems he faced—for example, his escape from indentured servitude. While Takahashi clearly had a hot temper and a strong, almost solipsistic sense of self as a child, traits that he never entirely overcame, he was perforce not limited by the conventions of his day. He could look at problems almost as an outsider, apply his reason to their solution, and solve them pragmatically. As Ozaki Yukio, a frequent political opponent, wrote in his autobiography, Takahashi, because of his unusual early life, "was free from prejudice too, and in that respect he probably had no equal in the country. . . . For the Japanese, who are normally bound by convention and formality, Takahashi was a rarity. Such a man would not be thrown into raptures by public praise or cast into despair by criticism. Later, this trait helped him to earn acclaim as a 'national treasure' for managing the vital issue of the nation's finances."[20]

Eighth, and finally, Takahashi was a brave man. Throughout his mature life, he involved himself in projects that required him to take physical and intellectual risks: for example, his trip to manage a silver mine high in the Peruvian Andes in 1889, and his outspoken opposition to militarism, in the face of repeated death threats, in the 1930s, when pusillanimity in publicly confronting the army's aggressive and chauvinistic leaders was the order of the day. One can see the origins of this courage in the thirteen-year-old going off to San Francisco in his cardboard hat and satin shoes, and in the fourteen-year-old escaping from indentured servitude and then avoiding successively the police of the new government and of the recalcitrant faction of Sendai domain's warriors. Takahashi's unusual childhood provided the foundations for his unusual life.

THREE

Many Mentors, Few Teachers: Takahashi's Career in and out of Government, 1869–81

The two major Japanese financial statesmen of the first third of the twentieth century were Inoue Junnosuke and Takahashi. Each reacted differently to the world's economic crisis in the early 1930s. One reason for this dissimilarity is that the economically orthodox Inoue had an elite education at the top schools and university of mid-Meiji Japan, and on graduation entered the Bank of Japan, where he spent his entire career (except for a few years in its sister bank, the Yokohama Specie Bank) until he became Finance Minister for the first time in 1923. The low-ranking Takahashi, on the other hand, had little formal education, many different jobs, and learned primarily in the workplace from his various mentors. From the time he began to teach English at Daigaku Nankō in 1869 until he joined the Bank of Japan in 1892, Takahashi served in eight different governmental ministries, offices, or schools, and in eight non-governmental jobs. As a bureaucrat, he taught at Daigaku Nankō and Tokyo English Language School, worked in the Education, Finance, Interior, and Agriculture and Commerce ministries, headed the Agricultural College, and established the Copyright and Patent Office, where he became Japan's first Patent Commissioner in 1889. In the private sector, he worked as an errand boy and *shamisen* carrier for a geisha, ran an English-language school in Karatsu in western Ja-

pan, translated for the *Nichinichi shinbun*, taught English in a private
school in Tokyo, did freelance translation, sold securities for a brokerage firm, managed a ranch, and in 1889, led a group of Japanese miners
to dig for silver in the high Andes. Because Takahashi experienced
many ups and downs in this period of his career—for example, the
silver mine enterprise in Peru ended in complete failure, and Takahashi
had to return to Japan to tell the shareholders that they had lost their
investments—he gained from these experiences a degree of pragmatism
and flexibility and a sense of detachment and irreverence that Inoue did
not receive at the Imperial University in Tokyo.

Guido Verbeck, an Important Influence on the Young Takahashi

Almost as soon as the adolescent Takahashi began teaching English at
Daigaku Nankō, the government sent his mentor and protector, Mori
Arinori, to the United States as its diplomatic representative.[1] Mori, fearing that the young Takahashi might wander astray without proper guidance, asked Guido Verbeck to look after him. Thus, in mid-1869, Takahashi moved into Verbeck's house as a student-apprentice (*shosei*) on the
school grounds in Surugadai just north of the Imperial Palace. Verbeck
(1830–98) was one of the most influential foreign teachers and advisors
to Japan's Meiji leaders in the 1860s and 1870s. The Dutch Reformed
Church had sent him to Nagasaki in 1859—even before more strategi-
cally located treaty ports such as Yokohama and Kobe were opened to
foreign intercourse. In Nagasaki, not only did Verbeck proselytize for his
church, but also and more importantly for Japan's entry into the modern
world, he taught English, social sciences, and Western technology to
students who later ranked among the giants of Japan's Meiji period
leadership: for example, Ōkubo Toshimichi, Itō Hirobumi, and Ōkuma
Shigenobu. After the Meiji Restoration these men served in the group
that took over the reins of government, and in 1869 Ōkuma had Verbeck
called to Tokyo to become assistant head (primary foreign teacher and
administrator) of the Daigaku Nankō. One of the first of several thousand foreign employees of the Meiji government (*oyatoi gaikokujin*), Verbeck became a trusted advisor to the new government and played a
significant role in the abolition of feudal domains, their replacement by
prefectures under central control, and the institution of universal edu-

cation and military conscription—among the most important reforms of the first Meiji decade.[2]

Takahashi studied history with Verbeck and heard lectures on the Bible, which he tells us he read every day. Because the youth had had very little spiritual training, even during his three years at Jushōji, and had faced a number of daunting experiences in his short life, Verbeck's teachings had a powerful impact on Takahashi. In a sense, because he had spent so much of his childhood in an adult world, and a strange adult world at that, Takahashi was a man-boy: experienced in the ways of the world beyond his years, but spiritually underdeveloped. The tolerant Verbeck was not the kind of missionary who proselytized directly, but one who spread his religious beliefs by living them as he taught English and the sciences. Nor did he pressure Takahashi to become a Christian. Takahashi did not convert to Christianity, but in spite of his various peccadilloes during the 1870s, he remained one of his mentor's most loyal and trusted disciples. When Verbeck decided to sell his home and return to California in 1878, he turned to young Takahashi, not to his far more highly placed former students, for help in selling his home. Takahashi's lifelong magnanimity and his tolerance toward what he saw as the foibles of others (and himself) may well have developed from his ten years of close association with Verbeck. In 1935, shortly before his murder, the finance minister told the journalist Imamura Takeo, who in 1952 published the anecdote in his seminal biography of Takahashi,

There is no good other than in God's truth. Men have God's heart in them. When that heart shines in humans, people become God, and earth becomes a kind of heaven. But our various desires and passions cloud God's soul. Even so God's soul does not disappear from us, and we do not fall completely into depravity. When we are controlled by our passions and desires, we not only wound others, but also ourselves. Finally we recognize that we have erred, realize that "this is not good," and return to the correct path. Even if no one teaches us, we naturally follow this path.[3]

Takahashi also learned under Verbeck's tutelage that man had a divine calling for hard work. While one may not necessarily accept Imamura's view that Takahashi, like Benjamin Franklin, was an exemplar of Max Weber's "Protestant ethic," that is, the view that one serves God by working hard and accumulating wealth, nevertheless there is a striking similarity between the two self-made men. Both Takahashi and Franklin were autodidactic, hardworking, and flexible pragmatists who had a propensity to fall down, pick themselves up, and start all over again. Both had university-educated rivals—John Adams in Franklin's case—who thought their practicality lacked in principle. Moreover, if one reads Franklin's autobiography and Takahashi's memoirs, one finds they both had an immodest ability to package themselves, to create and recreate a self-image, for public consumption. But there is a difference as well: Takahashi lived an intemperate youth, drinking to the extent of poisoning himself; Franklin seems to have avoided such youthful excesses.[4]

The Road to Perdition and Back to Tokyo

In spite of Verbeck's influence on Takahashi, he was not able to cure his young, headstrong protégé of his propensity to get into trouble, that is, to "cloud" God's soul. While still fifteen, Takahashi once more succumbed to the "demon sake," fell into a dissipated life, and finally left the government temporarily to live with and work for a Tokyo geisha. At work here were not only his corporeal temptations, but also his excessive pride as a hereditary foot soldier in competition with upper-class samurai "betters." One day Takahashi returned to his room at Verbeck's to find three splendidly dressed young samurai waiting for him. All three were lower-level students at Daigaku Nankō, but were the sons of the chief advisors (*karō*) to the lord of Echizen domain in Fukui. The three told him that their domain had sent them to Tokyo to study, but that their fathers had learned that they were neglecting their studies and ordered them home. Their dilemma was that they owed a great deal of money— 250 *ryō*, more than 50 times Takahashi's adoptive father's annual income—and they could not return home until they had paid off their debt. The situation here is almost comical: the major generals' sons, who are students, come to the private's son, who is a teacher, to ask him to raise more money than he has ever seen in his life.

Takahashi, undoubtedly proudly, but one must also think naïvely, agreed to help and went to the home of a distant commoner relative in Asakusa to find the money. His cousin in turn borrowed the money from a number of sources, lent it to Takahashi (he was required to place his seal on the promissory note, making him the borrower of record), who passed it on to his three new "friends." The three in turn paid off their debt, told their fathers they would straighten up and work hard, had their orders to return home rescinded, and then invited Takahashi to dinner to thank him for finding the money for them. Dinner turned out to be at a splendid restaurant named Kashiwaya in Ryōgoku, one of the finest Edo/Tokyo geisha districts of the 1860s and 1870s. Takahashi tells us that this was the first time (but far from the last) that he had seen geisha in a real *tatami*-style room.

The host for the evening was an Echizen merchant named Fukuiya (Fukui Kazuemon), who clearly profited from his close relationship with the people who ran the domain, that is, the young men's fathers. He and the three upper-class samurai were dressed in splendid silk clothing, had gold decorations on the handles of their swords, wore their hair in the old Edo topknot style, and appeared to be on close terms with the geisha—they obviously came to the restaurant often. Takahashi, on the other hand, wore a cotton kimono and *haori*, carried cheap swords bought only because all government officials including Daigaku Nankō teachers had been ordered to carry swords, and wore his hair in a makeshift topknot as it had not grown back from his time in America—one pictures the plump Takahashi looking something like a fledgling *sumō* wrestler. Takahashi reports that although he was the guest of honor, his hosts and the geisha ridiculed him for his inferior attire. At this point, Takahashi's *ashigaru* pride (perhaps his feelings of inferiority vis-à-vis upper samurai) took over. Already deeply in debt, he nevertheless asked Fukui to obtain swords and kimono like the other three wore and to make arrangements for him to take them to dinner to reciprocate. He invited the three to his room at Verbeck's, or went out with them nightly to learn to sing and dance in the newest mode. Verbeck clearly could hear the racket, but even if he did not, Takahashi had to have the guard open the gate for him every night when he returned home drunk. Takahashi felt ashamed, but rather than abandon his newly dissolute life, he decided instead to move out of Verbeck's room and move in with Fukui. Takahashi went to tell Verbeck about his decision. The mentor replied that Mori had feared something such as this and had asked him to take care of Takahashi. Verbeck then added, in an important lesson to Takahashi about one's need to make decisions for oneself, "If you want to leave to live elsewhere, you are free to do so. And feel free to move back in again if you want." As Takahashi stood to leave, Verbeck, in another unexpected gesture, presented his large, leather-bound, annotated family Bible to his young protégé—the one he had used when he lectured the youth on Christianity—and asked Takahashi to read it at least once a day, no matter what happened.[5]

After Takahashi left Verbeck's home, he fell entirely into dissipation. He spent most of his time with geisha and frequently missed work at Daigaku Nankō. One day, he went with some young women entertainers to see a play in Asakusa. A foreign colleague saw Takahashi wearing a geisha's long undergarment and drinking as he sat in the stalls of the theater. Embarrassed, but unable to give up his dissolute way of life, in March 1871 the sixteen-year-old Takahashi resigned from Daigaku Nankō, thus losing his only source of funds to pay the interest on his 250 *ryō* loan (in their insouciant upper-class way, the youths from Fukui apparently made no effort to repay Takahashi) and to cover room and board at Fukui's (rich merchants do not give young teachers free rides). Takahashi then began to pawn his new clothing and his books, except for Verbeck's Bible, which he dutifully read every day. When that money was gone, Fukui evicted Takahashi, forcing him to move in with Okimi, one of his geisha friends. Okimi already supported her parents and a variety of other dependents, but she liked young Wakiji; thus, he became her *hakomochi*, carrying her musical instrument to and from her evening engagements, to pay for his keep.[6]

Takahashi confesses in his memoirs that he was disgusted with himself and believed that this was not the way for a man to live. He also writes that at this point good fortune intervened. He accidentally met an acquaintance from his Yokohama days, who told him that Karatsu domain in Kyushu had just established an English language school and was looking for someone to teach English there. The former colleague had recommended Hayashi Tadasu, another Yokohama classmate and a future Minister to the Court of St. James and Foreign Minister, but he had turned down the job to go abroad as secretary in the Japanese Legation in Washington. Takahashi jumped at the opportunity not only because it gave him a chance to redeem himself, but also because it paid 100 yen per month plus board—he could therefore use the salary to buy Western clothes suitable for the job and to pay off his debts. In June 1871, the adolescent Takahashi set off for Kyushu to become a schoolmaster.[7]

The decade between the Meiji Restoration in 1868 and the suppression of the Satsuma Rebellion in 1877 was a fascinating time of transition. At the beginning, the new central government based its power on a coalition of some of the most powerful late-Tokugawa feudal domains, an army drawn from these realms, and the pre-existing land-tax systems, run by each of these domains in their own territories, not by a central authority. The new government, whose leaders were drawn from the domains that overthrew the Tokugawa in 1868, ironically depended for its revenues on taxes, collected in grain from the territories of the defeated shogun and some of his closest supporters. The domains whence they came were quasi-independent. By the late 1870s, the Meiji leaders had abolished feudal domains, prohibited the carrying of swords, and had created a centrally-directed prefectural system, an army based on the conscription of non-samurai, and a new, nationally directed land-tax system, paid in money. As this process unfolded, domains all over Japan enthusiastically established schools of Western studies as a first step toward creating their own modern, European-style armies. As Takahashi was told in 1871, "In Karatsu domain they have not yet set up a school of Western studies. The domain officials thought they would establish an English-language school first and then create French-style infantry units and look for drill and bugle instructors. They already have the latter two, but no English teacher."[8]

To travel to the domain on the western shore of Kyushu, Takahashi took a ship from Tokyo to Kobe, another from Kobe to Nagasaki, and then a small boat from Nagasaki to the border of Karatsu. He traveled with the French-style drill and bugle instructors, both former samurai of the *bakufu*. The domain officials sent palanquins and a horse to the port to pick up the three new instructors from the east. It turned out that neither of the military instructors could ride a horse, so Takahashi, who had learned to ride in Oakland, took the horse and arrived well ahead of the other two, who were carried by palanquin bearers.

The samurai of Karatsu, like those of most domains in the late-Tokugawa–early-Meiji era, were divided over the issue of how to deal with the West. Whereas by the early 1870s the majority recognized, as did the lord of Karatsu, that Japan needed to learn from the militarily powerful West before it could rid itself of the unwanted imperialists, a minority opposed any connection with foreigners or Westernizing

Japanese such as Takahashi. One evening while Takahashi was out drinking with some of his employers, arsonists from the anti-foreign faction burned down the school. Takahashi petitioned the lord to demonstrate his support for opening the country to the outside world by re-establishing the school within the domain's castle. The lord consented—in fact, he moved out of the castle and Takahashi ran English classes in the daimyo's former living quarters.

When Takahashi opened the school, 50 students enrolled, and by the time he departed, he had trained 250. Among them were a number of men who rose to eminence later in their lives, particularly Amano Tameyuki, an economist who studied at Tokyo Imperial University, taught at Waseda University, and wrote for Ishibashi Tanzan's *Tōyō keizai shinpō*, and Tatsuno Kingo, an architect who studied with the British builder Josiah Conder and later designed the Bank of Japan building and Tokyo Station. Takahashi emphasized English conversation in his school and taught almost entirely in the language of instruction—a far cry from the rote memorization and copybook method used by earlier students such as Fukuzawa Yukichi at Tekijuku in Osaka and Katsu Kaishū in Nagasaki. Takahashi even sought out the captain of a foreign ship that entered the port of Karatsu so that his students could practice English conversation with the crew.

By the end of 1871, Takahashi had established the school on such a firm footing that he made two new proposals: first, he memorialized the domain authorities to allow him to admit female students. They approved, and the first girls, the daughters of the domain's reformist officials, entered the school in early 1872. Second, he proposed the hiring of a foreign teacher. Takahashi left for Tokyo to confer with Verbeck about finding someone like Griffis in Fukui, and at the same time to order English-language books from abroad for the school's library.

While Takahashi was in Tokyo, an event occurred in Karatsu that tells us much about the difficulties of Japan's transition from a self-contained, inward-looking polity to the forward-looking, international world of men such as young Takahashi. Messengers arrived in Tokyo to inform him that the neighboring Imari Prefecture had seized power in Karatsu, imprisoned those in the domain's leadership committed to learning from the West, placed all of the domain's other samurai under house arrest, confiscated the books of the domain's paper business that provided the funds for teaching English and military drill, closed the school, ordered the execution of all Christians, and were investigating whether or not Takahashi himself was a Christian who should be killed. Earlier in 1871, the central government had abolished feudal domains and established prefectures, but given its inability to assert complete control over all of Japan, Tokyo appointed the reigning feudal lords and their warriors as regional governors and officials. The Imari Prefecture officials who seized power in Karatsu were in fact the leaders of the anti-foreign faction of the former Imari domain. Although Takahashi was clearly identified as one of the enemy—an advocate of opening the country to foreigners—he nonetheless took the risk and returned to Karatsu. Takahashi boarded a ship from Tokyo to Nagasaki, and then took an "express palanquin" from Nagasaki to Karatsu. He petitioned the new authorities and they allowed him to reopen his school. But the Imari government did not pardon the incarcerated Karatsu officials, and one of Takahashi's staunchest supporters even tried to hang himself in prison. It was not until the Home Ministry in Tokyo intervened and ordered the prisoners released that they were able to return home.[9]

Takahashi Returns to Tokyo

Takahashi returned to Tokyo in October 1872. Maejima Hisoka was in the process of establishing a postal system in Japan and needed someone to translate British and American regulations. Thus Takahashi entered the Postal Division of the Finance Ministry. Takahashi, although only eighteen, had already become something of a rationalist (and at the same time, perhaps not unrelated, a contrarian) who preferred to do what made sense to him rather than obey rules for their own sake. He soon proposed to his immediate superior that he be allowed to work at home—he had moved back in with Verbeck and not only could go to him or his fellow students for help with translation, but also would have access to better English-language dictionaries—and was given permission to do so. Maejima, however, was more orthodox. When he got word of this arrangement, he ordered Takahashi to come every day to the office, and the young bureaucrat began to be given assignments other than those for which he had been hired. Takahashi got into a shouting match with his boss and resigned—probably only moments before he would have been fired—from the Finance Ministry after only a few months on the job.[10] The independence to resign from an office rather than to obey orders with which he did not agree would be important for Takahashi throughout his career.

Takahashi's colleagues likely saw his abrupt decision to resign from government not as a virtue, but as another example of his weakness of character. One finds in the Takahashi papers at the National Diet Library a remarkable English-language letter, written by the eighteen-year-old to someone named Nobu, a friend from his California days, on December 15, 1872, in which Takahashi attempts to explain his seemingly unorthodox behavior.

Having transgressed, repented of and rectified my faults, and finding myself now in the state of perfect reformation, I feel little backward to write you this letter. Last summer I received a letter from Messers Gataby and Naitow, in which they evidently expressed my faults, and my unworthiness to be their friend, which has been the cause of their breaking off the friendship that existed between them and me. . . . From this time I have understood that every of my friends in America, among whom you are, must have forsaken me. The more I think about this subject the more it has distressed me. . . . At this time my mind was confused in darkness and as I had no friends to consult with, I have consulted with the Bible which is still and forever the guide of my soul. It is needless for me to tell you the importance of the Bible; for by your letters and compositions to your father and brothers, I know you [are] already intimately acquainted with it, and I may add, if you pardon me, that I think you are the seed that fell on the good ground and not that which fell on the road or among the rocks. Yours very affectionately, K. Hashi[11]

After his departure from the postal service, the "reformed" Takahashi decided to return to school and took the entrance examination, passed, and in March 1873, still only eighteen, entered the Kaisei Gakkō, a reorganized and expanded successor to the Daigaku Nankō. The former teacher became a student, for a short time at least, in the same school. Takahashi decided to matriculate at the school because it had expanded its curriculum and now taught Western law, science, engineering, and mining, of which he knew nothing, and many of his former students had become students there. Takahashi continued to live with Verbeck, whose home became a meeting place for many foreign employees of the Meiji government. Among them were a missionary and economist named McCurdy, who taught at the Kaisei Gakkō, and one of the most famous *oyatoi gaikokujin*, William Eliot Griffis, who had taught for some years in Fukui, and had come to Tokyo to teach science.

Both employed Takahashi as a helper in the translation of Japanese-language materials. Takahashi translated orally while Griffis wrote down what he said. Takahashi tells us that Griffis's younger sister, who later taught at the Hitotsubashi School, sat in on the sessions, and that one of the books he read was *Shank's Mare*, the comic travels of two Edo men, Yajirobē and Kitahachi, through the 53 stations of the Tōkaidō Road. The book contains obscene language and the young Takahashi could not bring himself to repeat it in front of a woman (although interestingly Takahashi had learned obscene English), so when he translated these sections, Miss Griffis left the room. Takahashi received 20 yen per month for his translation work. During this period in 1872–73, Takahashi also made an arrangement with a classmate named Suematsu Kenchō to trade English for Chinese classics lessons. Suematsu, who would become a journalist, study at Cambridge University, and in 1882 publish the first (partial) English translation of the *Tale of Genji*, had a good classical education. Takahashi, meanwhile, had superior English-language skills, but lacked a foundation in Chinese. So they tutored each other in their spare time, and Suematsu became proficient in English so quickly that they began to translate English-language newspaper articles for the *Nichinichi shinbun*, for which they were paid 50 yen per month.[12]

Takahashi went to see Mori shortly after the latter's return from the United States in July 1873, and was persuaded that he had studied long enough and that it was now time for Takahashi to put his language skills to better use. Mori told him that the Education Ministry had recently hired David Murray, whom both he and Itō Hirobumi had met in the United States, to advise on educational reform, and that Takahashi should apply to be his interpreter. Takahashi did so and was selected, and in October 1873, after only a few months in school and while still just nineteen years of age, he rejoined the bureaucracy, this time as an official in the Education Ministry. For the next two years, he served with Hatakeyama Yoshinari as one of Murray's interpreters.

The Education Minister at this time was Saigō Tsugumichi, an important early-Meiji leader from Satsuma, and the Deputy Minister was Tanaka Fujimaro. The two occasionally held parties for Murray and his wife, accompanied by their wives. Takahashi frequently found himself

interpreting for Mrs. Murray, Mrs. Saigō, and Mrs. Tanaka. In his memoirs, Takahashi relates stories of Mrs. Saigō breastfeeding her baby in
front of foreign guests, Itō Hirobumi's wife getting drunk at dinner with
the Murrays, and a visit to the home of Katsu Kaishū, one of the heroes
of the Meiji Restoration, whose son had studied with Murray at Rutgers
University. When Murray and Katsu moved beyond talk of Katsu's
son and began to discuss mathematical problems, Takahashi could not
interpret because he did not know the necessary vocabulary. The two
older men therefore communicated by writing out their questions and
answers. Mrs. Tanaka, the wife of the Deputy Minister, even moved in
with the Murrays for four months in the former Kaga domain estate in
Hongō (now the site of Tokyo University) and Takahashi found himself
frequently called to interpret. In October 1875, the government assigned
Murray to organize its exhibit at the upcoming World's Fair, and he left
Japan to go abroad. The Education Ministry thereupon reassigned Takahashi as Principal of the Osaka English Language School.[13]

The experience of serving as interpreter for Murray and his wife had
an important impact on Takahashi's development. For two years he was
in continual contact with foreigners on both an official and a personal
level. The young Takahashi moved in and out of the Murray household
almost daily. Takahashi's experience in dealing with foreigners on such
an intimate level was clearly atypical for a Meiji Japanese. It is no wonder
that later in life, both in Tokyo and when he traveled abroad on official
business, Takahashi could socialize among foreigners with complete
ease. Men such as Fukuzawa Yukichi, who was fifteen years older than
Takahashi, and Inoue Junnosuke, who was fifteen years younger, learned
English through reading in school and used it only in formal situations.
As a result they did not develop Takahashi's or Hayashi Tadasu's level
of oral fluency—and certainly not their command of colloquial and even
vulgar English. During those two years, Takahashi also socialized with
some of nineteenth-century Japan's most prominent modernizers, including Mori Arinori, Saigō Tsugumichi, Itō Hirobumi, Katō Hiroyuki,
and Katsu Kaishū. He interpreted for these men and their wives not
only in formal settings, but often in relaxed situations over dinner and
drinks as well. Takahashi was clearly influenced by what I would call the
"conservative progressiveness" of their thought. Mori and Katō, leaders
of the Meirokusha, a group of intellectuals committed to modernization

within the context of pre-existing (some would say, re-invented) Japanese social structures, preached a doctrine of change within continuity. Murray emphasized something similar, that Japan should develop new institutions, in his view educational ones, based on Western science, law, economics, etc., but should do so in a Japanese context. Takahashi's belief during the second half of his career that the government's primary duty was to encourage (but not direct) Japan's economic development from the bottom up, and that this could best be done within a framework of international cooperation, began to develop here. But Takahashi also began to see something else that he would continually emphasize in his later career: Japan came first, and cooperation second. One worked within an international framework because it helped Japan grow, not because of a belief in some higher economic law. Yet while Takahashi wanted to adapt, not adopt, Western ideas and institutions, he had already developed a willingness to tolerate dissent and heterodox points of view early in life. Takahashi concluded a letter to his "dear friend Naiki," written on August 10, 1874, with:

It is said that the foreign church in Tsukiji is filled with the Japanese on every Sunday. First one seat is filled with our girls who sing hymns beautifully. You may imagine how the unalloyed labors have begun to be useful to the harvest. Japanese translations of the bible are publicly sold at Tsukiji. Our government seems to have understood that how foolish and vain it is to try to extend its authority over the faith of its people. I hope the government will grant religious toleration in a [few crossed out] couple of years.[14]

Finally, men such as Mori, Itō, and Saigō began to discern that Takahashi, in spite of his occasional falls from grace, was a useful young man: few Japanese in the 1870s had his fluency in English, the essential foreign language of the day.

But October 1875 brought another detour in Takahashi's career. Ichijō Jūjirō, his former colleague in San Francisco and at Mori's, Verbeck's, and Daigaku Nankō, returned from assignment as a junior diplomat in France, resigned from the foreign ministry, and cut himself off from the world to study Buddhism. People tried to persuade Ichijō that his talents and his skills in Chinese studies, English, and French were needed in the foreign office, but he would not return to public life. Finally young Takahashi went around to convince him, and the two became involved in a lengthy debate over religion.

Ichijō promised that if he lost the debate he would return to the government, while Takahashi vowed that he would resign from the Education Ministry and join Ichijō in the study of Buddhism. Ichijō, who had studied Taoism and Confucianism before the Restoration, Christianity with Verbeck, and now Buddhism, had the clear advantage and accordingly won the debate. Takahashi once more resigned from government, returned the salary advance he had received to prepare for going to Osaka, and moved in with Ichijō. For the next six months, the two spent their days and nights studying and debating Buddhism, but, Takahashi reports, they could not see eye-to-eye on its meaning. So in May 1876, Takahashi left Ichijō's place, moved back to Verbeck's house, and went to work as an English teacher in the Tokyo English Language School.[15]

The mid-1870s were a volatile time in Japanese politics. One segment of public opinion, including some of the government's own leaders, advocated the "opening" of Korea, in other words, aggressive Japanese military intervention on the nearby peninsula. Samurai from Saga, Hagi, Kagoshima, and other places challenged, sometimes militarily, the policies of the Tokyo government. Political leaders such as Gotō Shōjirō and Itagaki Taisuke called for some form of democratic government; grassroots political movements all over Japan began to demand a larger role in governance; and debate sprang up everywhere over politics, foreign policy, and the economy. In this milieu, Takahashi helped to set up an English-language debating society in his school. In one debate under these auspices, Takahashi argued against free trade. This brought Takahashi to the attention of the organizers of a Japanese-language debating society in downtown Tokyo, and he was enlisted to debate Baba Tatsui, an enthusiastic supporter of the people's rights movement, on the issue of free trade versus protectionism.

Takahashi's anti–*laissez faire* speech shows that in 1877, at age 22, he had already developed some of the main principles of his adult political and economic philosophy—in fact, he gave the speech again half a century later at Keio University (with a new introduction). Takahashi argued that the European powers, when they advocated free trade, did so not out of principle, but for their own self-interest. Free trade gave them an economic advantage because they could produce industrial goods much less expensively than Japan could. Under the tariff restrictions imposed by the unequal treaties signed with the Europeans and

Americans, Japanese imports exceeded exports, and 8,000,000 yen of gold specie left Japan every year. For this reason, at such an early stage in Japan's economic development, free trade was not to its advantage. Military theory taught that one should only fight battles one can win. Because Japan could not defeat the Western powers, either economically or militarily, it should focus on defense and eschew aggressive action elsewhere—including military intervention in Korea, which brought with it the danger of retaliation by the powers. If an industrially "backward country" such as Japan wanted to develop its industry, encourage exports, and maintain an autonomous economic situation, it needed to stimulate export industries and through protectionism shield itself from unnecessary imports. Necessary imports would be foreign technology and raw materials, but not luxury items or goods Japan could produce domestically. This is vintage Takahashi in its embryonic form: a firm national defense, but not a military powerful enough to involve itself in foreign adventures; development of the Japanese economy domestically and for export within an international context, but in that context only because it benefits Japan's growth, not because of some "global" principle like free trade.[16]

Typically for this topsy-turvy period in Takahashi's career, he soon left the English school, in spite of his success as a teacher there. A Tokyo newspaper reported that the school's headmaster had spent an evening in a local red light district and was forced to resign. Takahashi and another colleague resigned in sympathy, and Takahashi returned to the private world once more. Yet his past intruded once again. Fukui Kazuemon, the merchant who had turned Takahashi out in 1871 when he could not pay his debts, came to him with a business proposition. Fukui said he had begun a milk business and was raising capital. Would Takahashi and Suzuki Tomoo, his fellow servant from San Francisco days, like to invest? They gave Fukui a few hundred yen, and each month afterward received a small return on their investment. In the spring of 1877, Fukui came again and said he was expanding the business to establish a cattle, pig, and horse farm in Nagano, and convinced Takahashi and some of his friends to invest in it—one actually invested 2,000 yen. Fukui then went on to suggest that Takahashi, who had experience in America with farm animals, would be the right person to go to Nagano to help set up a market for selling them. Takahashi accepted and in March 1877 went to Nagano to negotiate with the prefectural government. As one can imagine, local officials questioned the ability of this brash, young Tokyoite to reform markets that had worked well locally for years. In fact, one wag remarked that, "When Takahashi says stock farming [*bokuchiku*], he means to plant trees and bamboo [also *bokuchiku*, but written with different Chinese characters] in Nagano Prefecture."[17] Finally Takahashi got his way and new markets were organized, but much to his chagrin Fukui sent him no cattle to sell in them. Takahashi contacted Suzuki to investigate why, and the latter reported that he searched and searched, but could not find Fukui. Takahashi returned to Tokyo—his account of his trip home sounds like his own version of *Shank's Mare*—and set out himself to locate Fukui. But Fukui was not to be located; Takahashi had been deceived again, and in late 1877 found himself in a familiar situation, unemployed and deeply in debt since Suzuki and he felt obligated to repay their friends' losses. And at this very time, Verbeck, apparently miffed over Murray's moving into what he saw as his territory in the Education Ministry, left Japan for home. Takahashi sold Verbeck's home for him, and accordingly had to find a new place to live.[18]

Japan in the autumn of 1877 was at yet another crucial turning point in its development as a modern state. The conscript army had just put down what turned out to be the last samurai rebellion of the Meiji era, and the government was in dire financial straits. In addition to lacking capital, it faced other significant problems, not the least of which were those related to public health. Cholera, for example, was prevalent. The Interior Ministry set up a commission of Japanese and foreign experts under the leadership of its Hygiene Bureau director, Nagayo Sensai, to draw up regulations for cholera prevention. Needed were people who could read English-language documents. Takahashi's language skills saved him once again, and he joined the Interior Ministry to take charge of translation of cholera-related documents for the commission. The work was urgently important because of Nagayo's fear of an epidemic, so Takahashi worked literally day and night to complete the job. But the work, which included translating a book on the use of microscopes and documents on a cholera epidemic in Russia, was so time-consuming that Takahashi enlisted more and more people to help. In the end, he created a system much like the one he had used with Griffis. Takahashi read the documents and translated orally; others, usually more adept at formal Japanese, wrote down what he said and rewrote it in the appropriate style. A sign of the importance of English-language skills in the new Japan is that one of Takahashi's helpers was Ōwara Shindayū, the high-ranking Sendai domain official who had befriended Takahashi at Jushōji in the 1860s and sent him to study English in Yokohama.

After Takahashi finished his translation work for Nagayo, he worked as a freelance translator for Nishimura Shigeki, the head of the Education Ministry's translation bureau. Takahashi wrote that he translated books on the history and economics of the United States, but he must have done others as well, since he and two young university students translated the Cambridge economist Alfred Marshall's *The Pure Theory of Modern Trade*. Later Marshall sent Takahashi a letter of thanks, which Takahashi still had in his possession in the 1930s. The translation work paid well—one yen per page of English into Japanese, and two or two-and-a-half yen for Japanese into English. Takahashi had more translation work than he could handle, farmed some of it out, and still made a good deal of money.[19]

In 1878, Takahashi's landlord, a merchant from Kanazawa, and several of his rich friends approached Takahashi about opening an English language school. He agreed and in September he, Suzuki, and several others established an English language school to prepare young men for university study. Takahashi continued to translate even as he taught English, but he also delved into another, more dangerous field: speculation in silver futures. In the inflationary period of the late 1870s, when the government ran chronic deficits because of the cost of suppressing rebellions, creating a modern infrastructure, establishing expensive model factories for modern, transplant industries, and paying the salaries of foreign advisors, the value of paper money vis-à-vis silver fell steadily. The finance ministry, worried about this trend and not yet fully understanding its root causes, sold silver in Yokohama in an attempt to reverse the drop in the value of the yen. Takahashi's landlord approached Takahashi and told him that selling silver futures was a sure way to make money. If the government continued to sell silver, the downward trend would be reversed and those who sold silver future certificates cheap would make a big profit when the price rose. Takahashi tells us that he agreed to invest in this scheme because he wanted to make money for scholarships for his poorer students. He made a big profit in the first few weeks—1,000 yen on a 5,000-yen investment. But Takahashi and his co-investors, who were neophytes in finance, did not realize that the cause of the fall in the value of the yen—excessive government spending—was too fundamental to stop through government intervention. The finance ministry soon abandoned its efforts to sell silver in order to stabilize its value, but the people to whom Takahashi had entrusted money continued to speculate. In the end, everyone in the group, including Takahashi, lost their investment—the 5,000 yen Takahashi had made through translation was gone. The value of paper money did not recover until Ōkuma Shigenobu, Sano Tsunetami, and Matsukata Masayoshi introduced their deflationary fiscal and monetary policies several years later.

As the value of Japan's currency continued to fall, Takahashi decided to undertake the study of market prices. Thus, he met occasionally with a man named Yokota Hirotarō from Tosa domain in Shikoku to learn about stocks. After a while, Yokota proposed to Takahashi that now that he had become knowledgeable in the stock market, they should open a brokerage firm of their own, and in 1880, they did so. In his description of his short career as a stockbroker, Takahashi tells us that he and his fellow brokers had different sets of rules for their rich clients and what he calls their "country" (*inaka*) clients. Takahashi bought and sold according to his good customers' wishes, on the market, did not demand immediate payment for losses, and even made up part of these losses on occasion. As for country clients, when they asked Takahashi to sell to secure a profit, he recommended they wait longer in order to make even bigger profits. But if these stocks eventually lost money, he demanded immediate payment to make up the difference. He sold their stocks at prices that were less favorable than the ones used for rich clients. And he plied them with "fancy food so they came to trust us." Takahashi concludes this section of his memoirs by telling us,

I soon came to realize that what we did was no more than gambling. I learned all I needed to know about commodity and stock markets, and after four months, we liquidated our business. We lost 1,500 yen in addition to our original investment of 6,000 yen. Yokota and I each paid half of the losses and we went out of business.

Imamura sees this interlude in buying silver futures certificates and working as a stockbroker as an important part of Takahashi's education.

"As finance minister, Takahashi criticized speculators as gamblers. He himself well understood the contrivances and spirit of speculation from his own youthful experience."[20] In my view, it also shows a slightly unsavory and manipulative side to Takahashi's character, one that reappeared in 1889–90 when he went to Peru to manage a silver mine, and in 1904–5 when he went to London and New York to sell Japanese bonds during the Russo-Japanese War.

In April 1881, several of his friends approached the 26-year-old Takahashi about joining the Education Ministry to help oversee the management of education, and he agreed. But Hamao Arata (1849–1925), Assistant Minister of Education and later two-time president of Tokyo Imperial University, disapproved of Takahashi because of his checkered background. Hamao did not think a drunken, womanizing speculator was an appropriate person to play a role in guiding Japan's educational system. Takahashi in his familiar brazen style visited Hamao in his office to explain why his bad behavior should not be held against him. Takahashi, in a somewhat self-serving statement, went so far as to say:

I am annoyed that you think I continue to do this sort of thing. [Although he had been doing so up until a month or two earlier.] I have come to give a full account of my actions and clear up any misunderstandings. . . . I want you to understand that the Takahashi you see today is a different Takahashi. I want to join the Education Ministry because I want to take part in educational policy, rather than teach, as I have done up until now.

Hamao relented and Takahashi joined the ministry—but as it turned out, he was hired to research and write trademark and patent laws, not help run Japan's educational system. Takahashi's career as a pedagogue ended in 1881.[21]

During this period, an important event took place in Takahashi's life. His grandmother arranged for him to marry a woman named Saigō Oryū, and the bride and groom moved into the Japanese-style part of Verbeck's house. Takahashi's first son, Korekata, who went to London with him in 1904, was born in this house in March 1877. The couple had a second son, Koreyoshi, in 1881, but Oryū died young, in 1884. In 1887, after Takahashi returned from studying patent laws in the United States and Europe, he remarried. His second wife, Shina, bore him several more children, including Wakiko and Koreaki.[22]

FOUR

Japan's First Trademark
and Patent Laws, 1881–89

A month after Takahashi entered the Education Ministry in 1881 to oversee regional education, the government transferred him to the newly
established Agriculture and Commerce Ministry in order for him to carry
out what became his first major achievement as a bureaucrat: the writing
of Japan's first and second sets of trademark and patent laws.[1] Takahashi
wrote in his memoirs that he came to this task because of conversations
he had had with David Murray seven years earlier. James Hepburn,
Takahashi's former mentor in Yokohama, wanted to republish his Japanese-English dictionary, first issued in the 1860s, and spoke to Murray
about the danger of its being pirated. Murray and Takahashi talked about
this, the issue of patents and copyrights in general, and the difficulties
of protecting foreigners' intellectual property under the treaty port system in which non-Japanese were not subject to Japanese law. Takahashi
went to the Maruzen Bookstore to look for works on the subject and
found nothing, read a short article in the *Encyclopedia Britannica*, and then
proceeded to the Education Ministry to persuade the deputy minister of
the necessity of protecting the intellectual property of someone as important to Japan as Dr. Hepburn. Nothing came of his effort, but Takahashi saw it as the genesis of his interest in the subject.

At the same time, he clearly understood that something more was at
work here. Europeans and Americans, upset over Japan's infringement
of their patents and copyrights in its rush to industrialize, pressured the

Japanese government to create a legal framework for the importation of foreign technology. The Japanese, seeing discussions over the establishment of such laws as a lever to negotiate an end to the humiliating unequal treaties, wanted laws (or at least negotiations over laws) as well. What the government needed was an official with adequate English-language skills to read British and American statutes and to use them as a basis for writing Japan's laws. Takahashi was chosen for the job and joined the research section of the Industrial Bureau of the new ministry.[2]

Takahashi, on the advice of the chief of the Industrial Bureau, decided to write trademark laws first. He immediately faced two problems: first, explaining to Tokyo merchants, most of whom came from the late-feudal, Edo-period milieu, the difference between trademarks and *noren*, literally, shop curtains, which bore the logo of particular shops and served as the traditional "trademarks" of those enterprises; and second, distinguishing between names for products that were unique to specific companies and those that were generic. The businessmen feared in the first case that a loyal chief clerk (*bantō*) could not, under new trademark laws, establish a branch business by borrowing, as was the custom, his former employer's logo, and in the second that some entrepreneurs could register terms such as *masamune*, meaning high-grade, pure sake, so that other brewers could not use the term in their advertising. Takahashi and his two or three assistants spent two-and-a-half years translating foreign laws, adapting them to conform to the particularities of Japanese institutions, and writing and rewriting them to present to the *sanji-in*, the primary legislative body of the early-Meiji Japanese government. As he did this, Takahashi also lectured widely on trademarks:

I used *masamune* as an example. It is a word that is widely known to the public to mean high-grade sake, and is in the public domain. Thus, no one could monopolize it with a trademark. But the name Marukan for vinegar or Kikkō-man for soy sauce, even though widely known to the public, could be trademarks because these names and their symbols brought to mind specific producers. Thus, these producers could have monopolies on their names and logos and have them protected by law. . . . I earned a big reputation for brandishing drawings of *masamune* and Marukan, and making my explanations in a loud voice.

The *sanji-in* voted Takahashi's proposal into law in January 1884. Then a year later, with the Emperor in attendance, it passed an amended law rewritten to iron out some of the glitches in the earlier version. The *genrō-*

in, or cabinet, also passed the law handily. Takahashi reports having spent a great deal of time after the government promulgated the law explaining its meaning to the business community.[3]

Takahashi and his staff next wrote a proposal for a patent law to protect Japanese inventions and presented it to the *sanji-in* in early 1885. Again there was resistance, this time on the grounds that the regulations would be difficult and expensive to enforce. Mori Arinori, who was a member of the council, argued vigorously on Takahashi's behalf, and the bill finally passed and went forward to the *genrō-in*. Takahashi was appointed a temporary member of the *genrō-in* so that he could present his proposal to its members. He did so successfully, and the new patent law went into effect on July 1, 1885. The government appointed Takahashi Japan's first Copyright and Patent Commissioner. Takahashi, in spite of his earlier indiscretions, had begun to use his English-language and other skills to make a name for himself.[4]

About this time, Itō Hirobumi, the ranking government official in charge of investigating new (that is, Western) institutions, wrote to Saigō Tsugumichi, the Minister of Agriculture and Commerce, that someone should be sent abroad without delay to study patent and copyright laws. Although Japan now had its first set of laws, Itō believed that they needed to be revised on the basis of a thorough investigation of American and European models. Neither Itō's letter nor Saigō's response indicated that Takahashi was the one to be sent— Takahashi's involvement with an official named Maeda Masana in a rejected development proposal might have discredited him with the government's top leaders—but they asked Takahashi to make a detailed proposal of what needed to be studied. Finally, in the midst of a power struggle, Maeda, Takahashi, and their supporters were swept from the ministry—but while Maeda and the others left government at least semi-permanently, on November 16 the government ordered Takahashi to go abroad to make the study.[5]

Takahashi Travels to America for a Second Time

Takahashi recorded that he was so busy between November 16 and his departure on the November 24 that his "eyes spun." Naturally he had to reserve ship accommodations for his entourage and himself. A variety of friends and acquaintances asked Takahashi, now a recognized specialist in English and America, to take their sons with him—at least until the young men could find places to study. Takahashi felt a duty to bring Japan into the modern world by encouraging young men to study abroad. Thus, he left Yokohama with several others in tow; one of them, Kushida Manzō, later became president of Mitsubishi Bank. First-class cabins for trans-Pacific voyages were hard to find at the last minute, and in the end Takahashi sailed on a freighter with one of his group down below in steerage, the same place he had been 20 years before on his earlier trip to America. Prior to his departure, he went to the imperial palace to be received by the emperor, and also to the Agriculture and Commerce Ministry, where he was promoted to secretary, the highest position he had yet held in government. He also attended a round of farewell parties, standard practice for officials about to go abroad on long journeys. Virtually all the people who attended these parties, with the exception of Takahashi's relatives, were Japanese with extensive experience in Europe and America: his fellow travelers such as Tomita Tetsunosuke from his days in California; teachers and students from Takahashi's various English-language schools; and men such as Makino Nobuaki, who had studied in America, and Maeda Masana, who had lived in France for nearly a decade. A number of these men had also been associated with Ōkubo Toshimichi, the driving force behind Japan's industrialization before his assassination in 1878. Some, like Maeda and Makino (Ōkubo's son), were Ōkubo's protégés, and others were prefectural officials involved in regional economic development, a subject of importance to Takahashi throughout his career.[6]

A storm raged for the first three nights of Takahashi's voyage, and virtually no one came on deck or to the dining room until the 27th. One of his younger traveling mates appeared that morning, and with a laugh told Takahashi the following story, which he recorded in his memoirs:

I did something really awful. I got over my seasickness and the weather turned bright, so I came above deck to wash my face and searched for a place to do so. I saw a cabin that looked like a washroom. It had something attached to the wall with water trickling down. We have been taught to respect Western inventiveness, but this looked inconvenient. As soon as I scooped up water to wash out my mouth, a foreigner entered. I decided to watch him to see how he used the device. He stood in front of it and urinated, and I realized that I had washed my face in urine.[7]

Another of the youngsters ate breakfast by himself one morning, and never having eaten Western food before, simply ordered the first three items on the menu. The steward served him three different kinds of bread.

Takahashi, who could distinguish a urinal from a wash basin, learned lessons more fundamental to his economic education on his travels from Yokohama to San Francisco, Chicago, and New York. In his usual gregarious way, he quickly made friends with several of his American traveling companions. One was a businessman named Horace Fletcher who owned shops in Yokohama, San Francisco, and Chicago that sold Japanese ceramics, textiles, and lacquerware. Another was a missionary named Cole who, unafraid to mix God and Mammon, told Takahashi to be sure to visit the commodities market when he stopped over in Chicago. Cole then related an anecdote of a trip to the market by President Chester Arthur. The market was closed for ten minutes for the president's visit, and when his speech threatened to go too long, several traders yelled, "Make it a short speech." According to the missionary, it did not matter to the traders whether Arthur was "president or a country policeman." In America, nothing stood in the way of commerce.[8]

The night after his ship docked in San Francisco, Takahashi boarded a ferry to Oakland to indulge his nostalgia for the time when "the cows and horses were [my] friends." He writes:

It was a moonlit night and I walked here and there looking for the Browne family or people I had known from the old days. I finally came to the place where the Brownes' house and the station had been. When I looked up, I saw a huge oak tree. This was the towering tree where I kept my cows and horses every day. My hundred chickens roosted there at night. Meeting this familiar tree in the bright moonlight, I could not keep deep emotions from stirring in my heart.

The same evening, Takahashi visited Mrs. Verbeck, who lived in a nearby community, and talked with her and her second son until late into the night. Two days later Takahashi left Oakland for Chicago.[9]

Takahashi relates several experiences he had on the way to New York, his ultimate destination, that deserve to be included in that they formed part of his economic education. From the train window he observed the agricultural development of the American plains states:

In many areas, the land along the railroad right-of-way was divided into 600-acre plots, and the government and the railway company owned every other one. If a person lived on the government land for six months, he could buy up to 160 acres for twenty-five cents per acre. . . . Many people seemed to own 500 or 600 acres.

One of Fletcher's assistants explained to Takahashi and his entourage the workings of the American businessman's Chicago shop. Because of the pressing demand for traditional Japanese goods such as kimono and furniture, Fletcher not only sold imported goods, but also had brought Japanese craftsmen to Chicago to finish the goods according to the individual customer's requirements. Before Takahashi left Chicago for New York two days later, he visited a stockyard and the commodities exchange. He had a long talk with Takahashi Shinkichi, the Japanese consul in New York, about business conditions and opportunities for selling Japanese goods in America. Such experiences reinforced an important element in Takahashi's mid-career economic thought: the growth of Japan's export trade depended on the modernization and development of the manufacture of traditional goods such as raw silk, tea, lacquer, and ceramics, not on the products of heavy, transplant industry.[10]

Consul Takahashi told the younger Takahashi that his clothes were "Japanese-made and shameful to look at." In fact, the only acceptable part of Takahashi's outfit was the silk high hat that Verbeck had given him ten years earlier—although even there the color was wrong. The two therefore went out to order a morning coat, a frock coat, and an overcoat. While Takahashi awaited the completion of his new clothes, he used his time to explore New York. He crossed and was impressed by the mile-and-a-half long Brooklyn Bridge with its 240-foot towers (only two years old at the time), drove through Central Park, and visited the stock market. He also attended a performance of Gilbert and Sullivan's *Mikado*, and a show called the "Japanese Village," brought to New York to show Japanese customs to Americans. Alas, Takahashi did not record his thoughts on the operetta, but he did make a speech to resident Japanese about the shame of the latter display. He told them that it was "indecent and shamed us in front of foreigners." The proud, nationalistic Takahashi recognized that Japan must learn from the West, but even so, he did not want his country embarrassed in front of Americans. Even while Takahashi realistically recognized the power of Anglo-American money and technology, he nonetheless held a nationalistic resentment toward British and American condescension.

While in New York, Takahashi visited several prominent attorneys in order to begin his study of patent law. One famous New York patent lawyer told him that a primary reason for the advanced state of British technology was the protection provided inventors from patent infringement, which gave inventors a financial incentive to invest time and money in developing new technology without the fear that others would reap the benefits of their efforts. He reinforced Takahashi's view that if Japan wanted to develop industrially, it needed to protect industrial designs through patent and copyright laws. Takahashi met prominent New Yorkers and even became a temporary member of the Union League Club. He associated with a number of young Japanese who would become important business leaders in the future, particularly Ōkubo Toshikazu, son of the late advocate of industrial development, and Matsukata Kōjirō, son of the current Finance Minister. And he heard from Tokyo that in preparation for putting a new constitutional system into effect, the government had reformed the bureaucratic system. The government established a cabinet with a prime minister and subordinate ministries and ministers, in the European fashion, and in the process appointed General Tani Kanjō the new Minister of Agriculture and Commerce, who, as one of his first duties, furloughed Takahashi's patron and mentor, Maeda Masana.[11]

On New Year's Day 1886, Takahashi went to the Japanese club in New York and bowed to the imperial portrait. The next day he departed for Washington to study American patent laws. Kuki Ryūichi, the Japanese Minister to the United States, took Takahashi to meet the Deputy Secretary of the Interior, and the same day, he met the secretary of the patent office, Schuyler Duryee, who opened the doors of the United States Patent Office to Takahashi, and who would become his mentor and lifelong friend. Takahashi received permission to go daily to the patent office, and Duryee explained its organization to him. He then took Takahashi on a tour of the accounting, application, investigatory, drawing, and decision-making divisions, the library, and the model-making room. In each section, Duryee introduced Takahashi to the primary people. They in turn explained their methods of keeping account books, making blueprints, using lithographs, and various other technical aspects of their work. Takahashi was particularly impressed by the speed at which the secretaries typed up letters after taking dictation.

He spent several weeks learning in this way about the American process of investigating and issuing patents, and then sent a questionnaire to Duryee and to the New York lawyer he had met in December. He also approached Duryee about collecting a five-year set of the weekly patent office gazette and other documents, which contained detailed information about the patent-approval decision-making process. Duryee told Takahashi that a complete set would cost him $3,000, but that if he agreed to trade Japanese publications for American ones, he could give Takahashi the materials he wanted free. Takahashi replied that there were as yet no Japanese documents, but that he planned to begin issuing them when he got home, and would send those. Duryee agreed to this arrangement, and Takahashi sent the materials to the Patent Bureau in Tokyo, where they were kept until their destruction during the Great Kantō Earthquake of 1923.[12]

Takahashi in his memoirs depicts the difficulties (and perhaps pleasures) of research: "I had to question people in each division about detailed matters. There were many women among the employees. I had no trouble associating with men, but I had more difficulty with women. So I thought about what to do." Takahashi's answer was to take dancing lessons. He found a dancing school run by a family named Sheridan. He asked Mr. Sheridan whether someone like himself, who had never danced, could actually learn to do so. Sheridan replied, "Can you walk?" When Takahashi answered in the affirmative, Sheridan said, "Then of course you can dance." Takahashi, not one to do anything halfway, be it work or play, every morning practiced dancing at Sheridan's before going to the patent office. At the school, he met many women, some of whom worked in the patent office. One day, a Miss Perry told Takahashi that he was in for a big surprise in the near future. When he asked what it was, she replied that she shouldn't really say, but since he was a foreigner and lived in a single room, she would tell him. "We are going to have a surprise party at your place soon!" Takahashi, as one can imagine, was mystified. "I had no idea what a surprise party was." His landlady explained that it was an event where couples come to your home suddenly with baskets of food. You too are expected to provide a basket. Then everyone gathers around the piano and sings and dances—and eats. One day, Takahashi learned that tonight was the night. He hurried home and together with his landlady prepared food for the evening's event. Takahashi reported that, "We passed a very enjoyable evening."[13]

Shortly afterward, Sheridan came to say that he had been asked to organize a performance by his young students in which they would wear Japanese clothing and dance the Russian boatmen's dance. He asked Takahashi for help in finding the proper costumes for the children. So Takahashi took Sheridan's daughter to a museum in Washington where they had kimono, and using them as models she and two dozen mothers made new ones for their children to wear on stage. When they were completed, Takahashi organized a session so that the girls could practice putting on their kimono. As one might have predicted, the girls, given the American woman's custom of wearing the right side of her jacket over the left, put their kimono on backward. Takahashi took it upon himself to teach them how to wear a kimono. Takahashi's experience of assisting Okimi seems to have born fruit in America fifteen years later. Moreover, he showed his usual tolerance: in spite of his pride in being Japanese, he did not report objecting to the use of Japanese costumes in a performance of a Russian dance. His only regret was that he had to leave Washington for London before the performance took place.[14]

Takahashi, undoubtedly unusual for a mid-Meiji-period Japanese, saw the *Mikado* a second time before leaving the United States. The Takahashi papers contain the following report from a Washington newspaper of his visit to the theater:

On Monday night last two pleasant-looking Japanese gentlemen connected with the legation in this city presented themselves at the box office of the National Theater, where the Mikado is being played. They said that Minister Kuki was unable to accept the invitation of the manager to be present that night to witness the performance, but had sent them as his representatives. The attachés were given prominent seats, for the manager had expected to make quite a card of the Japanese minister's presence. The two pleasant-faced Japanese gentlemen seemed to enjoy the performance greatly, but at times they laughed at the attempts of the Americans in imitating the Japanese. When the Mikado himself came in they spoke some unintelligible words in their own language, and laughed. Nevertheless, they heartily enjoyed the opera, and applauded more than once. After the performance they repaired to a café, where they in turn tried to get even with the Americans playing Japanese by playing Americans themselves, and ordered each a whiskey cocktail and drank it, but they did not seem to like it, for they ordered a bottle of claret to finish off with.[15]

It might perhaps seem natural, then, that even convivial, English-speaking Japanese like Takahashi, meeting this kind of condescension abroad, would develop strong nationalistic feelings.

Takahashi, in his usual gregarious way, developed a personal as well as a professional relationship with Duryee, and went several times to Duryee's home in Virginia for dinner. Shortly before Takahashi left Washington for his trip to London, he was invited one last time, just after Duryee's youngest son had been born. Over dinner, Mrs. Duryee said, "We are about to part with Takahashi-san, with whom we have become close. We shall have difficulty remembering Takahashi-san's name. We have not yet named our new son, so would it be all right to give him your name?"

Takahashi replied, "That would be fine, but which will you use, Takahashi or Korekiyo? Takahashi is my surname, like Brown or Smith. Korekiyo is my equivalent of a Christian name."

She replied, "Then why don't we use both, Korekiyo Takahashi," and they gave their son his full name. Takahashi wrote he heard later that when their son grew up and went to school, Korekiyo Takahashi was too long, and he was called "Kore."[16]

Takahashi and Schuyler Duryee immediately began a long-lasting correspondence. Although some of the letters found among the Takahashi papers are merely cover letters for technical documents from Takahashi or Duryee, others are personal and often quite moving, and reveal Takahashi's ease in dealing with foreigners—and the depth of his warm personal feelings toward foreign friends like Duryee. On December 20, 1886, Takahashi wrote to Duryee to say that he had arrived home and had told his children about the Duryee family in America. "My boys were very glad . . . and they asked me many questions regarding my acquaintance with you and your family." Duryee wrote on December 28 to say, "It is very pleasing to know that the Good Shepherd so carefully guided your little flock during your long absence, and I venture to remark that the moistened eyes with which your dear boys welcomed you met with a hearty and feeling response from their father. I can imagine that the first few moments of a meeting of parent and child after so long a separation must be a silent communication."[17]

Before departing from the United States, Takahashi made a number of professional and non-professional stops in Baltimore, Philadelphia,

New Haven, and New York. In Baltimore, he dined with President Daniel Coit Gilman of Johns Hopkins University and his wife. In Philadelphia, he went to see Edwin Booth perform the title role in Sir Edward Bulwer-Lytton's play, "Cardinal Richelieu," and wrote that Booth's skills reminded him of the great kabuki actor, Danjurō IX: "I felt strongly that a master is a master whether in the east or west." While in the City of Brotherly Love, an attorney named John Welsh lectured him on the importance of protective tariffs. In New Haven, Takahashi spoke at length with a patent attorney named Ahl, who also took him to visit several factories including that of the Winchester Repeating Arms Company. Takahashi records in his diary that his work in the United States progressed so rapidly that he was able to complete it within three months. On March 30, 1886, he sailed for Liverpool.[18]

Takahashi summed up his experience in America in a remarkable letter he wrote on April 16, just after reaching Britain, to a man named Takamine in the Agriculture and Commerce Ministry in Tokyo. Although Takahashi is communicating with a Japanese official in his own ministry, he wrote in English, and I might add, in impeccable English. One wonders if he is trying to advance his career by impressing his superiors with his foreign-language skills. Further, Takahashi wrote at some length about the American patent system, "its vast importance, its intimate connection with and direct influence upon the prosperity of a country." He then praised his government for recognizing the importance of protecting its inventors' and industrialists' properties. "We are fortunate in this matter for we can profit by the long experience of other nations in this important factor of civilization." Finally, he asked Takamine to urge the minister to make "a liberal appropriation" for the patent bureau, a precursor to Takahashi's request, after his return, for an independent bureau.[19]

Takahashi's First Trip to Europe

Takahashi's arrival in London was a comedy of errors, but revealed his resilience and fearlessness in speaking English to native speakers, even to those who did not have an American or elite-British accent. Only on entrance into the harbor did he learn from an Englishman he met on the ship that Liverpool was not London, that he needed to take a train to the capital, and that the men who came to the ship to take people to hotels were from local, not metropolitan, establishments. Takahashi investigated London hotels in travel books in the ship's library, found they all cost more than he could afford, and opted for a rooming house. He found an advertisement in one of the books for such a place, wrote down the address, and forwarded his luggage there without contacting the landlord ahead of time. When Takahashi arrived at Charing Cross Station, he hired a carriage and went straight to 7 Barchester Gardens, the location of the rooming house. He rang the doorbell and a young woman came to the door.

Takahashi said to her, "I am Japanese and I am looking for a room." She replied, "Currently we do not have a vacant room."

A woman who looked like her mother then appeared and said, "Why did you come directly here? You should have asked at American Express."

Takahashi agreed that she was right, but added, "Even so, don't you have a room? I am in a fix since my luggage is on its way."

Takahashi reports that "at this point, the girl's father appeared. He was interested in Japan and as I answered his questions, everyone seemed to relax. Finally the mother said, 'We have one big room we haven't used for a long time. It is not prepared for rental, but why don't you take a look at it.'"

The room turned out to be too large and to be badly appointed, but it was late at night and Takahashi had nowhere to go—so he took it. When Takahashi went around the next day to the Japanese Consulate to meet Sonoda Kōkichi, a former samurai from Satsuma and future president of the Yokohama Specie Bank, who was the consul in London, several of his compatriots there tried to persuade Takahashi to move, but he refused. Takahashi, in contrast to so many of his Japanese compatriots of the time, was fearless in his willingness to communicate with foreigners. (One can only wonder what the novelist Natsume Sōseki, famous for his reluctance to speak English during his four years in London, would have done in Takahashi's situation.)

Similarly, one night when Takahashi and his friends gathered for "a Japanese dinner (well, at least a sukiyaki dinner)," the landlady said, "Since all of you are Japanese, why don't you gather around the piano and sing a Japanese song?" Takahashi reports that they were all without talent. But finally Takahashi agreed to sing "Umegae no chōzubachi," that is, "Umegae's Washbasin," if one of his compatriots played the piano. The problem was that Takahashi knew only the first verse and it was short. But since the landlady did not know Japanese, he decided to sing the first verse repeatedly, and in the end sang it 25 times. She was satisfied and the party went on until the wee hours of the morning. One wonders if Takahashi was being ironic when he recounted this story in his memoirs, as Umegae of the song was a servant in a samurai household who was secretly sold to a house of prostitution. When she, in distress, struck the washbasin of the title, gold coins fell from the sky, allowing her to buy her freedom.

Takahashi decided to leave for Paris almost immediately after arriving in London. One of his English advisors told him that the British patent office, unlike its American counterpart, would not freely give him information, did not do good research, and certainly would not allow him to look at all of the relevant documents. The man advised Takahashi to make his study by working with patent attorneys, but then went on to say that since these men traveled abroad in the summer, there was no point in his staying in London. Takahashi does not comment on the inconsistency here: why leave London in April when the patent attorneys will leave town in July? Nevertheless, on April 23, he, along with Consul Sonoda and his wife, departed for Paris.

The primary reason for Takahashi's visit to Paris seems to have been to meet the new Minister of Agriculture and Commerce, Tani Kanjō, the man who had furloughed Maeda Masana. In fact, over dinner in Paris, a finance ministry official who was in Europe at the time attacked Takahashi vehemently over his role the year before in supporting Maeda in the *Opinions on Promoting Industry* (*Kōgyō iken*) debate over industrial policy. But Tani seemed to have forgiven Takahashi and invited him to join the group that would meet the President of France. While Takahashi waited for the day of the appointment to meet the president, he visited the Patent Section of the French Commerce Ministry to continue his investigations. Takahashi gave them a list of questions in English and was told to come back the following Saturday with an interpreter. The French-speaking Japanese assigned to him was Hara Takashi, a young secretary in the legation, and Takahashi met for the first time the man who would be his primary political mentor later in his career: a future president of the Seiyūkai political party, which Takahashi would join in 1913, and a future prime minister, under whom Takahashi would serve as finance minister from 1918 until 1921. When Takahashi returned, he was given a detailed explanation of the French system, and how it differed from the American one. Then, with his customary cheek he asked for all of the specifications of French inventions since 1876, and received them.[20]

On May 5, two days after his meeting with the French President, Takahashi returned to London and moved into the Sonodas' home. Takahashi was introduced to the appropriate people at the British Patent Bureau and went there frequently to carry out his investigations. He reports that as he studied the British system, he found it backward compared with the American one—so backward, he wrote, "that I wanted to teach the British myself." He, as he had been told before he went to Paris, found that he had little to learn in London, so he decided to collect materials as he had in Washington and Paris, send them home, and move on to his next destination. Takahashi approached the Director of the Patent Bureau, and was told that if he applied through diplomatic channels, "We shall have no trouble giving you the documents." But Kawase Masataka, the Japanese Minister to Great Britain, decided Takahashi's request was not important enough to bother the British government and refused to help him. Fortunately, his friend Sonoda had no such qualms and agreed to make the request as Japanese consul in London. The British Patent Office staff sent all the requested materials to the consulate, which Takahashi then sent back to Japan.

Although Takahashi was now ready to move on to Berlin, he had one more goal before leaving Britain—a tour of the English factory district. As many Japanese since the visit of the Iwakura Mission fifteen years earlier had done, in early July Takahashi had the experience of seeing modern British industrial might firsthand. Over nine days, he visited knitted goods, weaving, spinning, flannel, textile machinery, steel, and engine factories in Nottingham, Sheffield, Leeds, Manchester, Oldham, Bolton, Liverpool, and Birmingham, as well as the Manchester stock exchange. Takahashi remarks that the division of labor he observed in Leeds impressed him: men worked in the textile machinery factory and women in the spinning and textile mills. He also comments that because of an election, the pubs in Manchester were closed and one could not get a drink, he was told, without a doctor's prescription. One assumes that he missed his evening pints.[21]

A week after his return to London, Takahashi traveled by train, boat, and train again to Berlin. The morning after his arrival, July 18, Takahashi went to the legation to greet Shinagawa Yajirō, the new Minister to Germany, who had been deputy minister of the Agriculture and Commerce Ministry in 1884–85 during the debate over Maeda's industrial development proposal. Shinagawa had encouraged Maeda and his subordinates such as Takahashi, but was an important enough member of the early-Meiji leadership group that he could not be cashiered as easily as Maeda had been. Thus, he had been "exiled" to Berlin after Maeda's fall from grace in November 1885. Takahashi spent the rest of July writing his report on his investigations in the United States and France (he does not mention Britain in this regard) and listening with some German-speaking friends to lectures by a statist German professor named Müller. The titles of the lectures are instructive: "Bismarck's Political Life from 1861 until the End of the Franco-Prussian War," "The Supreme Power of the Monarch," and "The State and Organization of the National Territory."

Takahashi hired an English-speaking German as his interpreter, and in early August visited the Patent Commissioner for the first time. Takahashi immediately asked for the relevant materials, as he had in the United States, France, and Britain, and was shown an English-language document the staff had prepared for the Melbourne Exhibition. He was told that unfortunately, there were no duplicates, but that Takahashi could copy it by hand, and he did so. As for his request for materials, he was told, as in London, that, "This request should be made from the Japanese legation to the Foreign Ministry, and then from the Foreign to the Home Ministry." Minister Shinagawa made the appropriate request and Takahashi successfully received his fourth set of detailed explanations and blueprints.

In Berlin, Takahashi met a man named Kawashima who was a member of a well-known Kyoto family of silk-textile makers. Kawashima carried samples of his firm's brocades around continental Europe taking orders and found that occasionally French and German makers would steal both his designs and his color distributions. Naturally his business would have benefited from copyright protection. But he told

Takahashi that protecting his designs would not be adequate; the color distributions had to be protected as well. To prove his point, Kawashima showed Takahashi samples of both his company's and its imitators' textiles. Takahashi learned that patent and copyright protection was more complicated than he had thought, and this exchange served to reinforce his and Maeda's view that the protection and development of traditional industries were essential to Japan's export trade, and thus to its economic growth.

While in Berlin, Takahashi met with a German patent attorney named Hugo Pataki who lectured him at some length about the flaws of the German system. One problem was that the courts, which played the greatest role in protecting patents, did not have jurors and other officials with sufficient scientific knowledge to make difficult technical decisions. Thus, they often handed down flawed judgments. The British and American legal systems were based on common law, that is, on the precedent of earlier decisions. Because modern technology was new, there was not an adequate accumulation of cases to enable judges to reach decisions. But in both countries, the government entrusted final authority over the protection of inventions to the patent office. Takahashi returned home with this in mind. He needed to create in Japan a strong, independent patent and copyright commission staffed by knowledgeable scientists, technicians, and legal experts.

Takahashi left Berlin on September 3, more than eight months after he had arrived in New York, and stopped for a few days in Hamburg, where he was greatly impressed by a large-scale farm and ranch on the outskirts of the city. Takahashi was particularly struck because the proprietor of the farm was doing what Maeda Masana had advocated in Japan, but on a much larger scale. The German farmer imported foreign seedlings particularly suited to the local climate and soil, searched for and used the best cultivating techniques of other regions and countries, improved irrigation and drainage systems, introduced appropriate modern technology into what was a traditional industry, and did market research to insure that he grew crops that would sell locally. In the evening, he served his guests a sumptuous dinner, the ingredients of which, except for ocean salmon and port wine, came entirely from his own estate.[22]

Takahashi Returns Home to Controversy

Takahashi left London for home on October 7, 1886, sailed quickly to Colombo and Hong Kong, and arrived in Yokohama on November 26. He immediately found himself involved in heated debates over both the establishment of an independent patent and copyright bureau and the character of Japan's patent system. One of his colleagues met him at Shinbashi Station, the Tokyo terminus of the railroad from the port of Yokohama, and told him to go immediately to the Agriculture and Commerce Ministry even before going home to see his family. When Takahashi asked why, Sugiyama replied that the Agriculture and Forestry Division of the Ministry had recently sold land and earned 80,000 yen, which they planned to divide among the ministry's divisions. But since the top officials knew that Takahashi would soon be home, they decided to postpone the final decision until they had conferred with him. Takahashi went to Deputy Minister Yoshida Kiyonari and brazenly requested that all of the money be used to create an independent patent and copyright bureau in its own new building. Yoshida replied that he could not give a definitive answer right away, and would postpone his decision on how to use the money until Takahashi had submitted a report on his findings in the United States and Europe. Takahashi, with the aid of two assistants, immediately set to work. A few days later, Sugiyama came to see him and said, "Deputy Minister Yoshida told me that he was not at all amused by your demeanor the other day. He thinks you are a crude type who acts too much like an American. 'To stand in front of someone and speak rudely—Takahashi is a frank man who shows no restraint.' What did you say to him?"

"I talked about my research abroad and that we needed to revise our patent and copyright laws completely to protect Japanese inventions and designs. . . . To make these laws work well, we need to have a completely independent bureau in a new building. I asked for all of the 80,000 yen for this purpose. He said he couldn't answer right away—that I had to finish my report first."[23]

Takahashi worked hard on his report, completed it in a month, and submitted it to his superiors in January 1887. He then set to work writing drafts of new patent, trademark, and design regulations. About the time Takahashi submitted his report the government shuffled the ministry's top personnel and Kuroda Kiyotaka, a key Meiji leader from

Satsuma, and Hanabusa Yoshitada, whom Takahashi had met in London, replaced Tani and Yoshida. Minister Kuroda, who had to approve the regulations before they could be presented to the full cabinet, resisted endorsing Takahashi's draft. Finally, after conferring with Hanabusa and other superiors, Takahashi went directly to Kuroda and asked him for his signature and seal. Kuroda replied, "I don't understand these laws at all. They may be necessary, but if we promulgate them, it will cost money. Only Finance Minister Matsukata approves expenditures. So go explain this to him. If he endorses it, I'll stamp my approval." Takahashi went quickly to visit Matsukata, explained the drafts in detail, and gained his approval. Thus, Kuroda signed off on the draft law and submitted it to the cabinet for its consideration.

When debate over the proposal began in the executive body, Takahashi faced strong opposition to his proposal from Inoue Kowashi, a governmental leader deeply involved in creating Japan's new legal system. Takahashi argued that the patent commissioner should have the power to decide about the strength of evidence in patent applications and must have the final authority in approving or disapproving patents. Inoue countered by arguing that this proposal undermined the authority of the legal system; final authority must reside with the Supreme Court and the judiciary, not with the patent commissioner, who was a subordinate of the Minister of Agriculture and Commerce. Takahashi rebutted by explaining what he had learned in Germany: judges did not yet have the scientific education to make nuanced technical distinctions. Thus, it was necessary to have the patent bureau do the investigations and make the required decisions. Inoue recognized the validity of Takahashi's argument and approved the proposal as a temporary expedient, that is, until judicial officials could acquire the needed technical knowledge. On December 18, 1887, the government replaced Takahashi's old patent and copyright laws with his new ones, and they went into effect on February 1, 1889. Japan now had laws to protect Japanese inventions. The law also established an independent Patent and Copyright Bureau in its own building, and two days later Takahashi was appointed its director.[24]

Takahashi's laws were meant to protect Japanese inventors and artisans such as Kyoto's Kawashima, and not foreign patents; the new law did not prevent Japanese from copying foreign machines when they were imported into Japan. In the spring of 1888, while the debate over

Takahashi's proposals was underway, Kuroda became Prime Minister, and was replaced as Minister of Agriculture and Commerce by Inoue Kaoru, who, when he was foreign minister in 1887, had been vilified for negotiating a treaty draft that some thought compromised too much with the foreign powers. Inoue sent his secretary to tell Takahashi to draft legislation to protect foreign machines from imitation by Japanese entrepreneurs. Inoue wanted such laws because of his fear that without them, foreigners would not sell new-model machines to the Japanese, and that this would slow Japan's industrial development. Takahashi met with the new minister, and related a conversation he had had in London with the secretary of the British patent office. The Englishman had explained to Takahashi that while Japan had many demands in the debate over revision of the unequal treaties, it had very little leverage because the foreign powers had little to gain by compromise; patent protection was its best bargaining chip. If Japan passed laws to protect foreign inventions before the treaties were revised, it would lose that leverage. At first, Takahashi reports, Inoue angrily resisted this line of argument, but in the end he came around to Takahashi's point of view and agreed to postpone the introduction of such legislation. Takahashi tells us that his discouragement over Inoue's appointment as minister turned to admiration. He had met few people who changed positions "without fear, when they realized their earlier concept was wrong."[25] From this point, Inoue, one of Japan's late-Meiji-period "elder statesmen," became another of Takahashi's mentors.

FIVE

Maeda Masana and the Debate over Industrial Policy, 1882–85

One of Takahashi's key mentors in his education as a policy apprentice was a young bureaucrat named Maeda Masana, who in the mid-1880s advanced a proposal for Japan's economic development that challenged the top-down, heavy-industrial approach of men such as General Yamagata Aritomo and Finance Minister Matsukata Masayoshi, Japan's two most powerful military and financial leaders at the time. Although Maeda was an intense Japanese nationalist who opposed the fledgling political parties that advocated democratization, his *Opinions on Promoting Industry* (*Kōgyō iken*), in its first, unrevised version from 1884, advocated a grassroots, bottom-up industrialization based on traditional industries, and accordingly had a strong market-based flavor. Some have called Maeda an advocate of dirigisme, that is, of direct government control over the economy, but this misses the point of *Kōgyō iken*, and of its influence on Takahashi.[1] Although Maeda opposed giving the people their choice of political leaders, he did advocate allowing them a large role in economic decision-making—the government's job was merely to assist, not to direct. If Maeda and his followers such as Takahashi had not lost the 1884–85 debate over industrial policy, Japan's economic, and possibly even its political, development might have had a far less authoritarian, top-down flavor.

Maeda affected Takahashi's development in a number of ways. Maeda's intense nationalism impressed Takahashi. As Takahashi wrote years later, in an oft-quoted statement, "After two days of talking with Maeda, I realized that my concept of the state was shallow. The state was not something separate from the self. The state and the self were the same thing."[2] Both men, although nationalistic, feared army and navy influence in government and opposed excessive military spending. Maeda in his policy proposal gave highest priority to agriculture, sericulture, and other traditional industries, secondary importance to river transport, shipbuilding, and harbors, and lowest priority to military spending. As Shinobu Seizaburō, the dean of Marxist historians of Taishō democracy wrote, Takahashi was committed to the "bourgeois" principle of civilian political control over the military. Both men were empiricists who emphasized "fundamentals," that is, the need to formulate policy initiatives on the basis of research into existing conditions, rather than on abstract theory. Maeda wrote:

We must establish a national industrial policy by questioning things . . . We must understand in detail the present state of our agriculture, industry, and commerce, and only after that can we plan for its development in the future. . . . In discussing the industry of our country, [the theorists] run after theory and ignore our country's reality. They say "protection," they say, "*laissez faire.*" There are a hundred ideas and each meets the standards of developmental theory. All are exceedingly wrong. They must learn that there are special national conditions of industry, and that theory does not cross national boundaries.[3]

When adapting foreign models to existing domestic conditions, Maeda explained, "We must study the real economic institutions of the Western countries and their efficacy." Takahashi relentlessly harped on the need to get down to basics:

I constantly say "fundamentals, fundamentals," (*konpon, konpon*) and during the Hara cabinet years, I was told, "You always say fundamentals and nation." This began after I met Maeda in the Ministry of Agriculture and Commerce. Today, when a problem arises, I do not look for temporary solutions. We must investigate what caused the problem. I learned this years ago when we created Maeda's *Kōgyō ikensho*.[4]

Both men wanted the populace to share in the benefits of economic growth. Maeda, as we shall see, sharply criticized Finance Minister Matsukata because his deflationary policies in the early 1880s impoverished the countryside; during the depression in the 1930s, Takahashi would write, "Production in the broadest sense means all the people are working. It is good when everybody is working and making an income without wasteful government spending. There is no other way than full employment."[5] Both men believed the key to industrial development was inexpensive capital. Maeda wrote repeatedly in *Kōgyō iken* that Japan had not progressed industrially because the high interest rates caused by Matsukata's policies prevented investment, and Takahashi throughout his career emphasized the government's need to pursue the kinds of monetary and fiscal policies that provided businessmen with inexpensive capital. Finally, although both men believed in development driven by central government programs, they also believed that local officials and producers had better information to allocate resources than did bureaucrats in Tokyo. In other words, although they might not have phrased it this way in 1885, Maeda and Takahashi understood the efficacy of market information.[6]

Maeda Masana

Maeda was born Maeda Kōan in March 1850 in Satsuma domain, the son of a doctor of Chinese medicine. In 1858, in response to the changing times, his father sent Kōan to study Western medicine and Chinese literature with Yagi Yahei, a student of Ogata Kōan, the renowned scholar of Dutch studies. Yagi knew Dutch and was involved in Satsuma's trade with China through the Kingdom of the Ryūkyūs. Maeda, not yet ten, became involved in this commerce and learned before most Japanese did the economic importance of foreign trade. Maeda writes that in his childhood, he "had not played war like his friends, but lived a happy life of nurturing because of his love of raising plants." Ōshima and his co-authors suggest that Maeda's childhood interests in plants and foreign trade are connected with his later view that Japan could best develop economically by emphasizing the modernization of traditional, agriculture-related industries, such as sericulture and tea, whose products could be exported.[7]

In 1865, the Satsuma leaders decided to send fifteen samurai abroad to study. Maeda applied for one of the openings, but was not selected. Mori Arinori, a higher-ranking and older Kagoshima/Nagasaki compatriot, joined the fifteen, and began his career as a "conservative modernizer"; it was he who became Takahashi's protector and mentor in

1869, and who introduced Maeda and Takahashi to each other in 1883. Although Maeda did not have the opportunity to travel to Europe or the United States at this time, the domain officials seem to have recognized his talents as a student of things foreign because they sent him to Nagasaki to assist the domain's official there in charge of international dealings. At the same time, he entered a school of foreign studies run by a second-generation Chinese scholar named Ga Reishi. Ga, along with key Meiji leaders such as Ōkubo, Ōkuma, and Itō, had studied English and Western studies with Guido Verbeck, and in turn Ga's students included men such as Mutsu Munemitsu, Japan's foreign minister during the war with China in 1894–95. In 1866, Satsuma domain sent Godai Tomoatsu, a leading advocate of learning from the West, to Nagasaki to export the domain's products and to begin to buy the British weapons that Satsuma would use in the overthrow of the Tokugawa *bakufu* a few years later. Maeda assisted him, and in this position not only learned about the Western world, but also associated with some of the central leaders of the Meiji Restoration and later Meiji government: Sakamoto Ryōma and Takasugi Shinsaku, important organizers of the cabal that overthrew the Tokugawa; Ōkuma, Itō, and Katsura Tarō, all prime ministers-to-be; Gotō Shōjirō, a pioneering advocate for a democratic polity; and Inoue Kaoru, a future finance and foreign minister and one of Takahashi's mentors.

Nagasaki, although ostensibly under shogunal control, had in the mid-1860s the atmosphere of a free port in which anti-Tokugawa dissidents, *bakufu* modernizers, and foreign merchants mixed freely. In this milieu, Maeda was drawn into the ferment leading up to the overthrow of the shogunate. He was in Nagasaki when Chōshū and Satsuma, the two domains that led the anti-Tokugawa (*sonnō*, literally, "revere the emperor") movement, formed their alliance to overthrow the shogunate; he joined the group even though Chōshū samurai had killed an elder brother in 1863. Maeda was only a teenager, so his role in the Meiji Restoration was small; nevertheless, Sakamoto, the man who engineered the partnership between the two powerful Western domains, sent the sixteen-year-old Satsuma samurai on a secret mission to Chōshū. He and his fellow travelers had to slip through the Tokugawa blockade, and he wrote of the passage: "My goal was to travel abroad, and I thought only of foreign travel. I thought if I die now my chances of foreign travel will be lost." While Maeda committed himself to "revering the emperor," in other words, to half of the famous "revere the emperor, expel the barbarians" mantra, he learned early in life of the importance of learning from, not expelling, the barbarians—or learning from the barbarians in order to expel them later.[8]

When Maeda returned from Chōshū to Nagasaki, Verbeck encouraged him to edit and sell a Japanese-English dictionary, and together with an elder brother, Kenkichi, and the future Japanese consul in New York, Takahashi Shinkichi, he set to work to revise and enlarge a dictionary entitled, "The Translator's Pocket English-Japanese Dictionary." They completed their task in January 1868, but could not find a publisher in Japan prepared to print English letters. So in March 1868, Maeda and Takahashi went to Shanghai to find a printer, and Maeda did not return to Japan until the job was completed in February 1869.[9] Both the fourteen-year-old Takahashi (Korekiyo) in San Francisco and the eighteen-year-old Maeda in Shanghai were outside Japan in 1868 and missed out on the Meiji Restoration. Although Maeda and Takahashi did not meet until 1883, fifteen years after the Meiji Restoration, and although they came from opposing domains in the civil war of 1867–69, they associated with many of the same people from early in their lives. Maeda knew Mori, Itō, and Verbeck and his circle in Nagasaki, where the Dutch-American teacher taught before moving to Tokyo; Takahashi associated with the same men, but a few years later, in the capital.

There is a good reason that Takahashi and Maeda did not meet in the first ten years of the Meiji period. In 1869, Ōkubo and Ōkuma, the two key leaders in Japan's early-Meiji efforts at industrialization, sent Maeda to France to study, and he stayed there for almost eight years, returning to Japan only in March 1877. Maeda, who arrived in France discouraged over what he perceived as the insurmountable gap between Western enlightenment and Japanese backwardness, soon had powerful lessons in reality: the Franco-Prussian War, the Paris Commune, and its failure. Between July 1870 and May 1871, Maeda watched the French army, in spite of its modern equipment, collapse before the Prussians; he saw Napoleon the Third—to Maeda the symbol of French prosperity—chased from the city; he saw destitution, hoarding, black marketeering, and usury during the long siege of Paris. Maeda concluded that France looked superior to Japan only because it had a head start in developing modern technology; at a "spiritual" level it was inferior. Japan, to catch up with the West, need not change its fundamental principles such as its emperor-centered polity, but only to borrow technology. In other words, over the course of 1870–71, Maeda became a nationalistic, conservative modernizer.[10]

Between 1871 and 1873, many of the Meiji government's key leaders, including the most powerful, Ōkubo, traveled to the United States and Europe to attempt to renegotiate the unequal treaties and to learn first-hand about Western "civilization." In April 1873, Ōkubo arrived in Paris, where he met his young protégé Maeda and encouraged him to study methods of stimulating Japanese industrial production. Maeda, given his childhood interest in both trade and plants, decided to study agricultural economics and policy, and came under the tutelage of Eugene Tisserand, Deputy Minister of the French Agriculture and Commerce Ministry. Tisserand emphasized to Maeda the importance of agriculture and agriculture-related industries in the early stages of industrialization, both to produce goods for export and to obviate the need to import foodstuffs, and of the centrality of modern science and technology in increasing agricultural productivity. Maeda also learned of the usefulness of trade fairs, which were in vogue worldwide in the late nineteenth century, as a venue for promoting a nation's goods while learning about developments elsewhere. The French government decided to sponsor a Paris World Exhibition in 1878, and Maeda, who saw it as an opportunity to stimulate Japanese exports and improve Japanese technology, went to work in the office of the exhibition, and at the same time set about persuading his government to enter exhibits. He lectured on the subject to Inoue Kaoru, while the future *genrō* was still in bed during a September 1876 visit to Paris. Inoue, according to Maeda, "jumped out of bed with enthusiasm" and then returned home to report to Ōkubo. In December, Maeda received an order to return home to join the industrial development branch of the Interior Ministry and to prepare for the exhibition.[11]

By the end of 1877, under Tisserand's tutelage, Maeda's views about Japan's industrial growth had expanded well beyond using the Paris World Exhibition to sell traditional Japanese goods. He also began, with like-minded men such as Fujimura Shirō, Governor of Yamanashi Prefecture, to conceptualize a method of agricultural development that came to be called "The Meiji Agricultural Method" (Meiji *nōhō*.) Meiji *nōhō* entailed sending successful farmers from more highly developed agricultural areas of Japan to disseminate new farming techniques to less advanced cultivators; experimenting with and exchanging plants from one part of the country to another; importing foreign seeds, plants, and farming methods; carrying out domestic exhibitions and competitions of agricultural products; raising private capital to carry out irrigation, drainage, and land-reclamation projects; and establishing agricultural research centers to test and disseminate improved seeds and plants. Maeda returned home from France in 1877 with seeds and seedlings he had gathered there; collected animals, plants, and seeds from all over Japan; and established the Mita Agricultural Testing Center on grounds of a former Satsuma domain estate to experiment with his new acquisitions. The "successful farmers" involved in Meiji *nōhō* then tested the products of these centers on their own farms, often at substantial financial risk.[12]

The Japanese government decided to enter the Paris Exhibition in 1878, and appointed Ōkubo as director, Matsukata as vice director, and Maeda as the head of the advance party and the day-to-day organizer of Japan's exhibit. Maeda gathered more than 40,000 Japanese items— goods as diverse as furniture, silk textiles, raw silk, cocoons, pottery, tea, and kimono—to display in France, and even shipped trees to Paris to create a Japanese garden. As part of his gradually emerging developmental plan, he took with him two men from Yamanashi Prefecture, a grape-producing region, to study winemaking in France. Maeda even went so far as to write a French version of *Chūshingura*, the story of the 47 loyal samurai who avenged the unfair death of their lord, a story that holds an important place in Japanese theater and cinema even now, 400 years after the actual event and more than a century after Maeda's effort. He produced the play with French actors in order to "show how the Japanese respected the gods and Buddhas, the principles of loyalty and filial piety, their duty to their lords, propriety, love, and trust." Thanks to Maeda's efforts, the Japanese exhibit was a great success, and played an important role in the boom of "things Japanese" (*Japonisme*) sweeping France at the time. While in Paris, Maeda heard that Ōkubo, his patron and the government's most powerful modernizer, had been assassinated.[13]

Maeda remained in Paris for a short time after the exhibition ended to clean up afterward and to help the Mitsui Trading Company establish a Paris branch. In May 1879, he returned home to join the commercial branch of the Finance Ministry, and then after its establishment, the Agriculture and Commerce Ministry, to promote industrial development. On his return, Maeda wrote a report entitled, "An Opinion for Direct Trade" (*Chokusetsu bōeki ippan*), in which he advocated that Japan take control of its own trade rather than import and export through foreign merchants in treaty ports such as Yokohama and Kobe. To do this, Maeda recommended the creation of an export-import bank, with branches abroad, to deal with foreign currency, and also encouraged the establishment of trading companies to buy and sell Japanese goods directly; his role in setting up the Mitsui branch in Paris was part of this plan.[14]

After Ōkubo's death in 1878, two different approaches to Japan's economic development began to appear. One approach, favored by Ōkuma Shigenobu, a former Hizen (Kyushu) samurai who was finance minister in 1879–81 and whom Maeda served, by Kuroda Kiyotaka, another Satsuma man, and by Maeda himself, advocated modernizing and subsidizing traditional industries to produce export goods. The other, favored by Matsukata Masayoshi of Satsuma and by Inoue Kaoru of Chōshū, urged fiscal retrenchment to stop inflation, and emphasis on heavy, transplant industries that produced the kinds of goods needed by the military. While Ōkubo still lived, he had been able to avoid conflict between the advocates of these two positions—in fact, when Maeda married Ōkubo's niece, Matsukata served as the go-between at the wedding. But in 1881, Matsukata forced Ōkuma from office, and Maeda was sent back to Europe to study economic and industrial conditions there, likely "exiled" because of his differences with the more powerful Matsukata. In January 1883, Maeda returned home, submitted his report, "A Survey Report on European Productive and Economic Affairs," to Agriculture and Commerce Minister Saigō Tsugumichi, a confidante of Matsukata, and then took a leave of absence due to illness. Ōshima thinks that given the predominance of Matsukata in financial affairs in 1883, Maeda's illness may have been "more convenient than real." Maeda returned to the ministry later in the year, after Shinagawa Yajirō, who was sympathetic to the Ōkuma/Maeda approach, became Deputy Minister, because, Ōshima writes, "he must have thought the situation was shifting more in his favor." It was at this time, in late 1883, that Maeda began to work on his developmental proposal, *Kōgyō iken*.[15]

Opinions on Promoting Industry

Japan was in the depths of a recession, caused by Matsukata's efforts to staunch inflation, when Maeda returned to the ministry in 1883. Between 1881 and 1884, when Maeda made his policy proposal, the price of a *koku* (4.96 bushels) of rice halved, from 10.59 yen to 5.29 yen, and each farmer's real tax burden doubled. As an advocate of the primacy of agriculture to industrial development, Maeda could not stay silent in the face of the rural suffering caused by Matsukata's deflationary policies. He therefore set about writing a proposal to study current economic conditions as a basis for a developmental plan, and presented it to Saigō in February 1884. Shinagawa, who also wanted to encourage industrial development, supported Maeda's proposal, and in February, Saigō approved it and advised him to carry out the proposed survey. Maeda's innocuous-sounding proposal was welcomed by most of the government's leaders, including Matsukata, because they wanted to know the current state of the economy and of public opinion in order to establish an industrial policy before a parliamentary system was established. Matsukata at this stage did not know that Maeda's interim study, when it was submitted six months later, would be sharply critical of his policies. The impending Maeda–Matsukata confrontation is replete with ironies: Matsukata and Maeda both came from Satsuma and were Ōkubo protégés, and Matsukata, who knew no foreign languages, employed Maeda as his interpreter when French Finance Minister Leon Say lectured the future Japanese finance minister on the dangers of inflation when Matsukata was staying in Paris during the World Exhibition in 1878. Maeda's language skills helped dig his own policy grave.[16]

Maeda began his nationwide survey that became the basis of *Kōgyō iken* in March, and amazingly, completed a seventeen-volume interim report in five months, by August. A primary source for understanding the process is Takahashi's autobiography, in which he writes: "There was a secretary in the Agriculture and Commerce Ministry named Maeda Masana. He was an extreme idealist who earnestly devoted himself to researching methods of economic development." Takahashi then explains that he met Maeda through an introduction by Mori, their mutual former "conservative-modernizing" colleague.[17]

Matsukata, as part of his deflationary policy, encouraged ministries to retrench by reducing the size of their staffs. Maeda did not like the idea of superiors dismissing subordinates. Thus, Maeda brought those slated for dismissal, some 40 or 50 men, to his *Kōgyō iken* team, which became the Fourth Section (*shika*) of the ministry. To save the same amount of money, Maeda then had the ministry eliminate horse carriages as a means of transportation for its members. The joke at the Agriculture and Commerce Ministry at the time was, "*Nōshōmushō uma o haishite, shika o oki*," ("the ministry eliminated horses and set up deer"), using a homonym for "fourth section." Maeda and his castoffs worked diligently to research and write *Kōgyō iken*. He himself moved into a small house on the grounds of the ministry and worked night and day without returning home. Takahashi reports, "his subordinates, carrying lanterns, left home in the dark, entered the ministry before the front gate opened, and returned home well after nightfall. These men worked with extraordinary efficiency," and one even died from overwork. Takahashi, who worked all day on his patent and copyright laws, joined Maeda's team at night.[18]

Maeda sent out a request to prefectural governors to make local surveys in May, gathered materials as fast as he could, and developed policy recommendations. By summer, he forwarded his seventeen-volume interim report to the printers, and on September 1, with only the Saitama Prefecture regional study complete, sent copies marked "secret" to prefectural governors and to a select number of government officials. Maeda apparently circulated the incomplete report because he wanted to get his policy concept on the table quickly. The following excerpt from Maeda's proposal reflects not only his remarkable view of Japan's economic needs, but also the origins of many of Takahashi's developmental ideas:

> Our people's clothing, food, and housing are inadequate. Many people cannot even be called people. They have debts, but no savings. They have no ability to cope with crop failures. We cannot raise taxes because there is nothing more to collect. We cannot improve military preparation, education, health and hygiene, flood-control, and other public works. We call ourselves a nation, but we are not advanced enough to be a nation. Thus, we have established a plan for what the government must do. We must concern ourselves with the livelihood of our citizens.[19]

Maeda proceeded to discuss French and Belgian policies, which he had studied abroad, and wrote about the need to develop regional, traditional enterprise before heavy transplant industry by providing local producers with low-interest, unsecured capital. This would raise rural standards of living and create wealth as a foundation for the later development of transplant industry. In the process, he criticized the efforts of Finance Minister Matsukata to stop inflation: "We cannot ignore our domestic conditions. What we (meaning Matsukata) are doing now is like running a child off a cliff."[20]

He then gathered the governors in Tokyo in order to answer their questions about the proposal, made revisions, and in January 1885, distributed the complete proposal, now in 30 volumes. But there were many fewer policy proposals in the completed *Kōgyō iken* and what remained advocated a more centrally-directed developmental plan that allowed Matsukata to cut the central government's expenditures by transferring its public-works spending, much of which primarily benefited the military, to the regions. Because of this final version of *Kōgyō iken*, historians long saw Maeda as a card-carrying member of the top-down, militaristic school of economic development. As one source states: "[*Kōgyō iken*] was the overall plan for Meiji absolutist industrial development, and accordingly holds crucial importance as the blueprint for semi-feudal and militaristic Japanese capitalist development."[21]

In 1969, Ariizumi Sadao, a historian working at the Constitutional History Room of the National Diet Library, published an article that dramatically revised this view of Maeda. While editing the Maeda papers there, Ariizumi came across a copy of the original interim report and found that its policy recommendations differed dramatically from those in the final version of *Kōgyō iken*. The interim report recommended industrial development based on traditional, agriculture-related industries and local initiative, the final report on public works for the military and central control. Why were there two versions of *Kōgyō iken*, and why was this not discovered until 1969? Maeda's interim report, as we have seen, sharply criticized the deflationary policies of Finance Minister Matsukata, which hurt the entrepreneurial, owner farmers who served as the core of Maeda's concept. Maeda went so far as to write, "Matsukata's ideas are fundamentally upside down." The government could not allow a middle-level bureaucrat in the Agriculture and Commerce Ministry to publish a document that disparaged the Finance Minister, especially when he was one of the government's most powerful officials, and Saigō Tsugumichi, the Agriculture and Commerce Minister and

Maeda's chief, was Matsukata's close associate. Matsukata ordered the recall of all copies of the interim report, and did such a good job of suppressing it that it did not reappear for almost a century. Moreover, in spite of the revisions, Matsukata refused to sign off on even the final, eviscerated *Kōgyō iken* document.[22]

The Industrial Bank Debate

One part of Maeda's interim plan called for the establishment of an industrial bank. Although this proposal did not survive Matsukata's revisions of November 1884, Maeda did not give up. He rewrote his industrial bank plan and resubmitted it in early 1885. Matsukata, who also wanted an industrial bank, although one of a very different stripe, decided to meet the challenge and sent in a counterproposal. As Takahashi, Maeda's spokesman before the *sanji-in* during the industrial bank debate of 1885, wrote,

The Finance Ministry's proposal called for establishing a central bank first and then local branches. It wanted to relieve the government of the cost of contributing 800,000 yen per year for public works by shifting the burden to the industrial bank. But our ministry's proposal was for setting up local branches first and the central bank later. Prefectural banks would be set up only after prefectures had made various preparations such as establishing agricultural testing stations, agricultural cooperative associations, circuit teachers, and other organs of agricultural improvement. When the prefectural bank had raised 1,000,000 yen locally (from private sources), the government would contribute a matching amount. Only when a number of prefectural banks were in operation would a central financial organ be set up.

The two ministries also differed on the purpose, nature, and conditions of the loans the bank would make. The Finance Ministry, which wanted to lend money to powerful and well-connected entrepreneurs such as Iwasaki, Mitsui, and Sumitomo for large-scale public-works projects, proposed to make lending decisions centrally, to require land as security, and to have the Agriculture and Commerce Ministry oversee the loans and collect the payments. The latter's plan was to lend small amounts of capital to local farmers and small and medium-scale entrepreneurs for regional economic development, to have lending decisions made locally, and to require no hypothecation.[23]

The Maeda papers include memorials from Kyoto and Ishikawa prefectures on which industries they would support and how they would raise local capital. Kyoto officials wanted to develop Nishijin silk textiles, dyed goods, and pottery, copper, and lacquerware. They would raise money for loans from wealthy local farmers and wanted matching funds from the government to provide the producers with low interest loans. They also stated that they feared the establishment of a centralized industrial bank because it would not make loans to local producers. The Kyoto government wanted the capital controlled regionally because a prefectural-level bank would lend to local businessmen and would have a better idea of local conditions and risks. Ishikawa urged development of the sericulture and raw silk industries. It requested governmental matching funds to establish a development bank in Kanazawa, the prefectural capital, for 30 years to make low interest loans. The Ishikawa memorial contained a detailed proposal about qualifications and security for loans. Both memorials reinforced Maeda's proposal to the *sanji-in*.[24]

One fascinating aspect of the 1885 *sanji-in* debate over the creation of an industrial bank is that while Matsukata's finance ministry proposal had the strong support of Yamagata Aritomo—the driving force behind the army and the Home Ministry in the mid-1880s—and Inoue Kaoru, and the less ardent, but still significant support of Itō Hirobumi—who at the time was beginning the process of writing Japan's forthcoming constitution—that is, of three future *genrō*, Matsukata could not push it through the legislative body. Maeda had the backing of men such as Yasuba Yasukazu, a Meiji leader who served as governor in Fukushima, Fukuoka, Aichi, and Hokkaidō prefectures, and of other men with regional experience. The *sanji-in* divided more or less evenly over the issue.[25] Takahashi presented Maeda's position. Tajiri Inajirō, Kanmuchi Tomotsune, and Katō Wataru from the Finance Ministry opposed him. The debate dragged on without conclusion, so a decision was made to have a meeting of the *sanji-in* with the two ministers present. Maeda's and Takahashi's problem was that while Matsukata was a hands-on finance minister, Saigō was a minister in name only; in fact, he had returned from a government mission to China just before the proposed meeting and missed much of the ongoing debate. Takahashi and several others undertook to brief Saigō on the matter, and explained the issues at stake and the impasse. Saigō

listened to the report and then stated that Takahashi had been presenting his own, not the ministry's, position to the *sanji-in*. "Everything
Takahashi has said up until now is his own personal opinion, and not
the ministry's view; he should be fired." Takahashi, as one can imagine,
was nonplussed.[26] The next day Saigō met with various members of the
Agriculture and Finance Ministry staff in a long meeting. Takahashi
presented the consensus view, Saigō then asked each person for their
opinion, and all agreed with the Maeda/Takahashi position. Deputy
Minister Shinagawa, who had run the ministry in Saigō's absence and
was a supporter of Maeda's proposal, then stood and said to the minister, "Since everyone here agrees with Takahashi's opinion, please use
his views." Saigō replied, "Thanks to everyone I have learned a great
deal today. I shall now go to see the finance minister." When he returned late in the afternoon to the ministry he reported that Finance
Minister Matsukata had withdrawn the Finance Ministry proposal for
an industrial bank.[27]

The Demise of Kōgyō iken

Although the outcome of the debate over an industrial bank would
seem to have been a draw, it was in fact a victory for Matsukata. On
December 22, 1885, in preparation for the forthcoming opening of a
parliament in 1890, the government established a European-style cabinet system. Tani Kanjō, a general with no interest in industrial development, became Minister of Agriculture and Commerce, and immediately cleaned house. Tani quickly sacked most of Maeda's staff, and
on December 31, he furloughed Maeda—that is, Maeda received a
salary, but had no duties. Maeda returned briefly to the ministry in
1889–90 for one final try at bottom-up economic development, but his
budding governmental career as a developmental planner did not out-
live the decade. Although the government later adopted some of his
ideas about agricultural improvement, Maeda spent most of his life
until his death in 1921 involved in a variety of privately funded schemes
to improve agricultural productivity, and deeply embittered. Only two
members of Maeda's circle survived the Agriculture and Commerce
Ministry purge, and both of them were sent abroad—Takahashi to
Washington, London, Paris, and Berlin to study patent laws, and Deputy Minister Shinagawa to Berlin to head Japan's legation there.[28]

Several Japanese scholars have written about why Maeda's industrial bank proposal failed in 1885. Foremost, as we have seen, Maeda's plan to privilege the bottom-up development of traditional, agriculture-based industries over centrally-directed heavy, transplant industries ran counter to the needs of men such as General Yamagata, who favored those industries that would most benefit the military. They also ran counter to the interests of well-connected entrepreneurs—*zaibatsu* business conglomerates in the making—such as Iwasaki, Mitsui, Sumitomo, and Yasuda, a connection that Maeda saw and criticized. But there were other reasons as well. According to his biographer Soda, Maeda was a heavy-handed administrator, "outspoken to the point of abnormality," whose plans to restructure the Agriculture and Commerce Ministry aggravated most of his colleagues. Even before the final denouement of the debate, four section chiefs in the ministry wrote to Saigō to denounce Maeda. They delivered the same letter to Tani when he took office in December. Maeda did not have the strong support of the key members of his own ministry.[29] Other groups besides the Finance Ministry and the Agriculture and Commerce Ministry also had an interest in the outcome of the debate. Both Maeda's and Matsukata's plans challenged the authority of the Home Ministry, and particularly its interest in controlling regional public works projects. In other words, intricate, inter-ministry power struggles played a role in the downfall of *Kōgyō iken*. Finally, the ongoing power struggle between officials from Chōshū and Satsuma, the two pre-Restoration domains that provided most of the Meiji government's top leaders, seem to have played a part. Although Matsukata and Maeda both came from Satsuma, Matsukata's primary support came from Chōshū men such as Yamagata, Inoue, and Itō; Maeda drew his support from Satsuma men such as Kuroda Kiyotaka. In the end, it was probably the complicated, conflicting views about how Japan should best industrialize and modernize, and about which ministries should play the leading roles, that brought Maeda down. Compared to the Home, Army, and Finance Ministries, the Agriculture and Commerce Ministry was an upstart—and as we have seen from Matsukata's proposal for an industrial bank, the Finance Ministry saw Maeda's ministry as a subordinate organization to do its dirty work.[30]

Although Takahashi and Maeda worked together closely for less than two years, Maeda's views had a powerful influence on the development of Takahashi's mature political and economic philosophy. They reinforced Takahashi's nationalism and empiricism. They formed the foundations for his views that economic growth should come first, national defense second—in fact, a national defense that exceeded the government's ability to pay for it, that posed a threat to the people's livelihoods, was not national defense at all. That "rich country" meant rich people, not just rich government. That entrepreneurs who had detailed knowledge about production and markets, rather than central planners who lacked such knowledge, should lead the economy; the government's role was to assist through research, subsidies, low-interest loans, and as he learned later, fiscal and monetary policy, not direct control. And that government power should be decentralized wherever possible. As Takahashi wrote in December 1916: "We must change the system of concentrating power in the central government and expand the power of local officials. To bring about the recovery of farm villages, we must abolish our uniform educational system and establish schools that are appropriate to local needs. We must decentralize financial organizations to revive the farm economy."[31]

It is safe to say that Takahashi never escaped the impact on his thinking of Maeda's developmental concepts. In the 1930s, when Takahashi served as finance minister many years after the *Kōgyō iken* debate, he wrote, "I have increasingly come to realize that if Maeda's plan had been carried out as originally conceived, all kinds of promising new enterprises would have arisen to support various regions. What bright prospects there were! What things would have grown up here and there! Even today, I think it regrettable that his plan was not put into effect. Occasionally, when I think back, I realize that this failure hurt Japan very much."[32]

Of all the members of Maeda's 1884–85 team, only Takahashi survived to have an important bureaucratic career. Even Shinagawa, who had been one of the leading members of the group that overthrew the *bakufu* and established the Meiji government in 1868, never afterward matched his colleagues Itō, Matsukata, Yamagata, and Inoue in power and position. Why did Takahashi alone survive? One reason seems to have been that in 1885, the government needed to send someone abroad to study patent and copyright laws, and in the end, Takahashi, in spite of his involvement with Maeda, was the best man available.

He had already spent several years working on the subject, and his English was excellent. Another is that his defeated friends, Maeda and Shinagawa, seem somehow to have worked behind the scenes to save his career. Shinagawa wrote to Takahashi on January 27 (1886?) to inform him that he had heard from Maeda, who had said, "Korekiyo's case differs from mine. Korekiyo should continue to serve our country, that is, its industrialization, by remaining in the civil service. I pray he will stay in the ministry."[33] And Takahashi, throughout his life, had a survivor's instinct to pick himself up and move on after he had fallen down.

SIX

Managing a Silver Mine in Peru,
1889–90

In spite of his involvement in the Maeda Masana debacle four years earlier, as 1889 opened, Takahashi at age 34 seemed firmly situated on the ladder to career success. At the very time that Maeda's own career as a public official stumbled to its end, Takahashi became commissioner of an independent patent and copyright office free from subordination to any government minister except the prime minister. He had achieved a goal that was important to him: he served as his own immediate superior. To reinforce the upward arc of his career, in the spring of 1889, the government also appointed him Principal of the Agricultural and Forestry College in the Komaba district of Tokyo, replacing Maeda's older brother Kenkichi.

Takahashi as Principal of the Agricultural and Forestry College

Although Takahashi served only half a year as head of the agricultural college, his experience there demonstrates not only his continuing commitment to Maeda's developmental ideas, but also his pragmatism as a problem solver. Takahashi thought that the function of the college was to train technicians to apply scientific methods, including quantitative analysis, to agricultural development. Takahashi wanted only the brightest students for his college, so they were recruited through a rigorous selection process. After graduation, the technicians, predominantly the sons of the very middle farmers—including the small land-lords, owner farmers, and upper tenant farmers (*gōnō*)—whom Maeda saw as the key to agricultural and industrial development, would return to the countryside to teach science and new farming techniques to poorer, landless tenant farmers. The government would reinforce their efforts by providing low-interest capital for rationalizing land use, creating and improving irrigation and drainage systems, and investment in the development of new, market-oriented crops. Imamura has criticized Takahashi for promoting a method of rural improvement that left the "feudal" landlord system in place; however, given the low level of literacy and education among poor farmers in the mid-Meiji period, sending well-trained technicians to the countryside to provide developmental leadership made a great deal of sense.[1]

Takahashi immediately faced two problems at the school. First, the students found the food unpalatable and asked Takahashi to do something about it. They told him that the contractor who provided the food was a friend of one of the school's administrators and that the leadership therefore made no effort to solve the problem. Takahashi offered the students two alternatives, both of which he saw as potentially useful to their education. The school would provide the students with money for them to do their own shopping, preparing, and serving. Takahashi particularly liked this solution because he thought students at an agricultural college should have direct knowledge of the market prices of the goods that farmers produced. The other alternative was that the students would select the food procurers and preparers, but not do the shopping and cooking themselves. Under both potential solutions, the school would turn complete responsibility for overseeing the kitchen and dining room over to the students. Takahashi reports that the students selected the latter course.[2]

Second, the school's curriculum called for students to perform a six-month, on-the-job internship before graduation, but the Agriculture and Commerce Ministry did not provide the necessary financing. The students petitioned Takahashi shortly after he became principal for help in finding the money. He agreed to do so and immediately went to the agriculture and forestry bureaus in the ministry to request funds. Each provided six or seven hundred yen per year for the internships, and the problem was solved. The students, as Takahashi records, gave him a gold tablet to thank him for finding solutions to these problems. Both Takahashi's arrangement for devolving control over the dining room to the students and his emphasis on the need for internships reflect his evolving views about the decentralization of power, the need for grassroots economic development, and the importance of hands-on, as opposed to theoretical, solutions to problems.[3]

On October 31, 1889, the college held a farewell party for Takahashi on the occasion of his resignation from the presidency. The students thanked Takahashi warmly for his efforts on their behalf, and he in turn exhorted them to work for the good of Japan so that it could some day "surpass the civilized powers . . . in strength and wealth," not an unusual sentiment for government officials and business leaders in the mid-Meiji period. But while calling on the students to work for Japan, he added that they should also "*promote . . . the well-being of the people*" (italics added).[4] This is a sentiment Takahashi reiterated throughout his career: economic development should raise standards of living, not just make the state rich and powerful.

Takahashi's Decision to Go to Peru

Takahashi wrote in his memoirs that when he visited America and Europe to investigate patents and trademarks in 1886, he realized how few Japanese went abroad for business, and that those who did operated largely in big cities such as New York, London, Paris, and Berlin. These merchants usually did not know the local languages and customs well and were ridiculed as a result. Takahashi, upon returning to Japan, reported this to Maeda and concluded that perhaps Japanese business-men "should try to sell goods in places where people are less arrogant, for example, South and Central America, where people speak Spanish and Portuguese." Several years later, Maeda visited Takahashi, reminded him of this earlier conversation, and then reported that six or seven men, headed by Fujimura Shirō, former governor of Yamanashi, had made a secret agreement with a German named Oscar Heeren to manage a silver mine at a place named Carahuacra, more than three miles high in the Peruvian Andes.[5] The plan had developed to the point that a Japa-nese mining engineer had been sent to Peru to evaluate the situation.

Heeren was a well-to-do German who had come to Japan briefly in the late 1860s, "lived like a daimyo in Tsukiji,"[6] the foreign settlement in Tokyo, and then returned to Germany. Later, while serving as a diplomat in Lima, he married the niece of the president of Peru, and became governor of the central bank. He and the president invested in a plantation, but lost money. Heeren surmised that it was because "native Peruvians do not make good farmers."[7] He proposed, therefore, to bring Japanese farm workers to Peru, whose work habits he admired from his time in Japan 20 years earlier. In 1888, Heeren sent a Japanese employee named Inoue Kenkichi to Japan to recruit investors and workers. Inoue brought with him a piece of Carahuacra silver ore to stir up interest in the enterprise, and this ploy was highly successful. Inoue spoke to his friend Shiroyama Seiichi, who in turn introduced him to Fujimura. Fujimura sent the silver ore to an expert named Iwaya Tachitarō, who assayed it and found it to be so-called ruby ore, silver of the highest quality. About the same time, a German mining magazine published an article praising the quality of Carahuacra silver ore. Fujimura, overjoyed by this, all but forgot Heeren's original plan to establish a farm, and organized a consortium of seven men including himself, with a capitalization of 50,000 yen to invest in the mine. Fujimura then sent the mining engineer, Iwaya's assistant Tajima Haruo, to Peru to investigate the mine and negotiate with Heeren. Tajima left Japan on November 28, 1888, arrived in Lima two months later, and in March cabled that he had signed a contract with Heeren to mine silver at Carahuacra and to organize a farm. The joint company would have 1,000,000 yen in capital, half from Heeren and half from the Japanese. Tajima reported that the company had already bought four mining sections for 250,000 yen and that the Japanese group owed half of this amount, which had to be paid by November 1889. The Japanese side also had to find 400 farmers to dispatch to Peru by March 1890. The seven Japanese investors were shocked to find that they owed more than double their present investment, but buoyed by news of rich silver ore deposits, decided to raise the remaining capital publicly.

It was at this time, in the spring of 1889, that Maeda, enthusiastically swept along by the possibility of organizing a Japanese-capitalized enterprise in a precious metal and in a non-North American or European country, approached Takahashi about joining the investors. Takahashi, convinced by Iwaya's assay of the metal and by Tajima's report, agreed to invest 10,000 yen, all of his savings at the time. Maeda then searched for investors and added prominent bureaucrats such as Ōkubo Toshi-kazu, Makino Nobuaki, Kuki Ryūichi, Iwaya—20 all together. The group raised 500,000 yen and founded the Japan Peru Mining Corporation. After securing investors, a manager was then required to oversee the mine. Although Maeda pressured Takahashi to take the job, he resisted. He felt that he could not desert the patent office just as it was beginning to function in its new structure. Maeda then went over Takahashi's head to Inoue Kaoru, Minister of Agriculture and Commerce at the time, who agreed that Takahashi should go. In October 1889, just as his rejuvenated career in government was beginning to take off, Takahashi resigned as patent commissioner to manage the Carahuacra mine of the Japan Peru Mining Company.[8] At the time, Takahashi wrote a memorandum about his decision, which not only explains his motives for going to Peru, but also presents his prescription for Japanese economic development, namely that the government should guide but not direct the economy, and that the key to success in industrialization is inexpensive capital.

Takahashi opens the memorandum by stating that when he traveled abroad as a young man, he learned lessons that became the foundation for his later life. Yet as a callow youth, he made many mistakes. Following his work in patent law and industrial development, in 1889 he felt that it was time to seek other ways to serve his country. He continued:

I see few enterprises in agriculture, forestry, or industry in Japan for which there is adequate money to pay labor costs and make profits. . . . We do not have spare capital. The funds that are available must be used for commercial businesses, thus slowing and limiting the growth of agricultural and industrial enterprise. Available capital does not match our abundant labor supply. Some-how we need to find surplus capital to make long-range plans. If we cannot do this, we cannot increase our national wealth. Our urgent duty today is to find ways to increase our capital. How can we do this? Our country is poor in capital, but it has excess labor. Together with my colleagues, I want to use this surplus to open up foreign resources and bring them back to Japan. We have therefore decided to go into the [silver] mining business in Peru.[9]

Takahashi then proceeded to extol Peru as a country with fertile soil and a climate appropriate to agriculture. But more to the point, he stated that Peru was rich in mines from which precious metals could be extracted, a fact that was well known, as Peru's gold and silver had allowed Spain to become the richest country in Europe. When he and his fellow investors decided to create a mining enterprise in Peru, they needed someone to manage the mine, and Takahashi reports that he "reluctantly" agreed to it. Takahashi writes that following the seclusion of the Tokugawa era, during which time Japanese nationals were prohibited from traveling abroad, this was a great opportunity for a first Japanese industrial enterprise overseas. To compete with Western powers economically, Japanese needed to expand business activities abroad in order to gain control of their own markets. (Takahashi uses the phrase "to chase deer (*shika o ou*) in the central plain," a Chinese expression that advises conquering the central plain in order to rule China.) Takahashi concludes his memorandum with the following: "I do not take the government duties to which I was appointed lightly, but I think that which I am resigning to do is more important for Japan. These are the reasons for my current action. I do not know what the outcome will be."[10]

Takahashi Goes to Peru

On November 16, 1889, Takahashi left Yokohama for his third trans-Pacific voyage, and arrived in Callao, the port of Lima, 53 days later, on January 7, 1890. All but seven of those days, two in San Francisco and five in Panama, were spent at sea, and as before, the trip across the Pacific was rough. Takahashi left Tokyo in the late fall chill, met similar weather in San Francisco, and then sweated through torrid temperatures as he visited fourteen ports and crossed the Equator between the Golden Gate and Callao. Takahashi met with Kawakita, the Japanese consul in San Francisco, who advised him about the dangers involved in such an overseas enterprise as Takahashi was undertaking. He told Takahashi that a British company had recently signed a contract with the Peruvian government to extend its railroad system, and that customs duties and mining rights had been offered as hypothecation. The consul warned Takahashi to find out whether his mine had been included in the agreement. Takahashi replied that it could not possibly be involved since he and his fellow investors had done a thorough job of investigating the mine before signing their contract. In fact, Takahashi countered, "we sent Tajima, who is traveling with me now, to Peru to make an independent survey of the mine. We would not have signed an agreement if Tajima had not corroborated Heeren's original information." Takahashi added that the extension of the railroad system based on such loans was good news for those wishing to develop enterprises in Peru.[11]

In his memoirs, Takahashi relates another experience from his voyage down the west coast of Mexico, Central, and South America that reinforced his lifelong view that to be a "rich country" meant raising people's standards of living, not just making the country rich:

I had the habit of visiting steerage passengers when I called on foreign ships. This was because at age thirteen, I went to San Francisco and back in steerage, and I understood its discomforts. I have never seen such wretched conditions as those on the Santa Rosa. . . . The steerage passengers had neither cabins nor blankets. Many slept on deck with their baggage, cows, and pigs. They slept on a thin straw cover on the deck. When the ship rolled, the animals' urine and excrement ran across the deck onto the mats. Because the people had no training in hygiene, they used eating utensils to collect their children's urine and feces . . . . These passengers occasionally bought food from the cooks, but since they were very poor, it wasn't enough. Their neighbors feasted, and the children saw it and cried. Families fought over what was in the common pot. I don't have words to express how sad it was.[12]

Running a Mining Enterprise in Peru

Takahashi spent a little over a month in Lima before leading his team to Carahuacra, and during that time he had a number of problems to iron out. His first was to establish a working relationship with his partner Heeren, whom he had not met before. Heeren had built splendid living quarters and an office for Takahashi and his associates to live and work in, but Takahashi at first resisted using them because he did not want Heeren to dominate the enterprise. Takahashi viewed the silver mine as the first in a series of Japanese enterprises abroad; Heeren saw the mine as a profit-making business venture. This potential source of conflict was compounded as Heeren's original reason for looking to Japan for aid in a Peruvian project was to develop a farm; more than Japanese capital, he wanted Japanese farm workers. But Takahashi and his fellow investors had little interest in the agricultural part of the venture. Given their view that what Japan lacked for its economic development was adequate capital, the investors viewed the Carahuacra silver mine, for which they had great hopes given Tajima's report and the German mining article, as an important step in Japan's industrial growth. In a sense, Takahashi and his colleagues were industrial planners, not businessmen.

Takahashi spent ten days convincing Heeren that the Japanese investors' money was to be used for the mine, not farms; that Japanese miners, not farm workers, would be coming to Peru (unbeknownst to Heeren, one assumes, they were already on their way); and establishing the extent of the Japanese investors' liability. On January 18, Takahashi and Heeren reached an agreement, and over the next week or so, Heeren introduced Takahashi to Peru's principal leaders: the president, prime minister, and finance minister, as well as the German and Spanish ambassadors and the local representative of the Bank of England. Takahashi also had to adjust to the new climate and food and to make arrangements with a local doctor to help the advance team of carpenters and miners, which would arrive from Japan in late January, to do the same.[13]

On January 27, 1890, Yamaguchi Shin, an engineer who became Takahashi's most trusted lieutenant in the Andes, arrived, leading the advance party of seventeen miners and carpenters. These men were ill-educated in book learning, but highly skilled in their trades. They were young, vigorous and in their prime, and provincial in their outlook; none of them had left Japan before. As one can imagine, this combination of traits was potentially explosive.

Yamaguchi told the following story of their trip across the Pacific, which aroused Takahashi's fears. Two or three days before they arrived in San Francisco, late at night, Yamaguchi heard raucous noise arise from the steerage deck below. When he investigated, he found his Japanese workers entangled in a free-for-all with Chinese laborers on their way to America. After the ship's first mate had quieted things down, Yamaguchi talked to his charges to find out what had caused the melee. He learned that the Japanese "seethed with indignation" toward the Chinese for two reasons: the Chinese had negotiated with the cook for control of the common pot, leaving the Japanese with unappetizing scraps, and the Chinese combed out their pigtails every day and left their "filthy hair" everywhere. One evening, the Japanese decided on a prank for revenge. The Japanese tied the pigtails of two Chinese men together and then to a nearby post. When the Chinese awoke, they stood up, almost pulled their hair out, screamed in pain, and attacked the two nearby Japanese culprits. In due course, the other Chinese and Japanese joined in the melee, and a violent fight "boiled up like a tea kettle." At this point, one of the Japanese drew a sword and waded in, but luckily, some of his cohorts grabbed him before he could slash anyone. Yamaguchi told Takahashi that the tension disappeared only when the ship passed through the Golden Gate into beautiful San Francisco Bay. Having heard Yamaguchi's report, Takahashi had the workers sign an agreement that they would work according to rules that he laid out, which included a "no fighting" provision.[14]

Takahashi, Tajima, Yamaguchi, a technician named Koike, and the miners and carpenters spent the next two weeks in Lima preparing for their ascent to Carahuacra. Everyone was outfitted with cold-weather clothing, which particularly disconcerted one of the Tokyo carpenters who preferred to work in the nude and in warm weather. Takahashi also arranged for a doctor to examine all the members of his group to make sure everyone was physically fit enough to work three miles high in the Andes. When on February 8 the preparations neared completion, Takahashi invited the whole party for a final dinner—complete, given Takahashi's own predilection, with sake for all. After dinner, a noise arose from the workers' barracks. Tajima went to investigate and calmed things down. But fifteen minutes later the uproar broke out again. The workers attacked Tajima himself, and Yamaguchi had to level three drunken miners in order to bring the situation under control. In the end, however, the blame for the continuation of the scuffle fell on Tajima. Koike, who also was knocked down, gave the following post-mortem:

After this, we better not have the technicians and engineers try to stop the miners' and carpenters' fights. If Tajima had not come, the workers would have settled things among themselves. The other men attacked Tajima only after he tied one drunken worker up by the hands. In such situations, he will struggle to get free, taking the skin off his wrists, and not be able to work. The worst thing to do to a drunken craftsman is to tie him by the hands. Tajima's behavior tonight was not suitable for a mining engineer.

The next day Takahashi read the men the riot act and they promised once again to abide by the rules.[15]

On February 12, Takahashi departed from Lima to take his group by train to Chikura, 13,000 feet high in the Andes, and then on foot, horse, and mule to Carahuacra, 5,000 feet higher. Because of the drastic change in altitude, for which the Japanese had neither preparation nor prior experience, it was decided to turn a one-day train trip into a three-day journey, so the group did not reach Chikura until February 14. Chikura, as Takahashi describes it, was a desolate place. It had one hotel for foreigners and people from the metropolis run by a Frenchman, and another for natives. Native dwellings were scattered here and there, and range after range of mountains ringed the town. The town was on the tree-line, below which forests flourished, and above which one saw nothing but rocks and sharp cliffs. The mountaintops were in sun in the morning and rain in the evening and it was cold. No matter how many layers of clothing one wore, one could not escape it. The Japanese, unused to high altitudes, were nauseated. They did not have enough blankets to protect themselves from the cold and had to buy more from local people. The miners complained that if it stayed so cold they would freeze to death. Takahashi replied, "I came here to serve the state, so I am prepared to die in this enterprise. If you are cold, take my clothes." They miners responded that they could not take the boss's clothes and no longer complained. After two days in Chikura, the men gradually adjusted to the thin air and on the morning of February 16, Takahashi, his men, and their mules left Chikura to climb higher into the Andes.[16]

By noon, the group reached the village of Casa Barca, where Takahashi met and conferred with an American mining engineer named Henry Guyer, the Peruvian representative of Fraser and Chalmers, a Chicago-based mining machinery firm. The two discussed what kinds of smelting machinery to use at the mines at Carahuacra and nearby Santa Barbara. As several of the miners were ill from the cold and altitude sickness, the group waited until the 17th to continue on to Yauli, the closest settlement to the mine. The group split into two parties, with the miners and their guides going first, and Takahashi, Yamaguchi, and a Heeren employee named Cardenes coming later.

Takahashi writes in his memoirs that the trail was precipitous, the weather bleak and cold, and snow fell. They passed skeletons of horses along the trail. To the right was a 1,000-foot drop, to the left a gentler, but still steep slope. Cardenes led the way, Yamaguchi came next, and Takahashi rode last, on a mule. At one particularly dangerous spot, Cardenes stopped his horse to look back toward the other two. Yamaguchi, who was close behind, stopped his horse too, but the abrupt halt drove its saddle back to its hindquarters. Yamaguchi was startled and accidentally applied his spurs. The saddle slipped off the horse altogether and Yamaguchi was thrown onto the rocks below. His horse reared, and fell into the deep valley to the right. In turn, Takahashi and his mule fell into the valley to the left; luckily it was not deep and they fell onto soft snow in a level place.

Takahashi describes the scene:

When Yamaguchi fell, I thought, "that's it." I climbed out of the snow and yelled, "Is Yamaguchi dead?" A voice cried, "I didn't die. I didn't die." I replied, "Don't give up," and flew to his side. Yamaguchi looked at me and smiled. Then, enduring his pain, he stood up. Yamaguchi's horse had fallen one hundred feet farther and had landed in the snow upside down, with its head in the snow and its feet sticking up. Cardenes jumped from his horse, ran into the valley, and presently reappeared leading Yamaguchi's mount. It was a sad sight—blood came from its mouth, legs, and side. Since Yamaguchi was also hurt, he could not ride his own horse, so he rode my mule, I rode Cardenes's horse, and Cardenes took Yamaguchi's injured mount.

The snowfall did not let up, and the air grew colder. But the three men forged ahead and climbed to the 18,000-foot level, within half a mile of Carahuacra. But even though they were so close to their destination, their challenges were not over: the trail ahead fell precipitously, was buried in snow, and was only five feet wide. Cardenes, an expert horseman, slid his horse down the slope on its front legs. Takahashi and Yamaguchi followed by sending their horses ahead and sliding down the hill safely on their rumps. At the bottom of the slope they met the miners' group, and everyone went on to Carahuacra together.

After reaching the mine site, Takahashi wrote two poems:

If you look at the Andes upside down, they are not so tall.

When you roll over in the Andes, Mt. Fuji is mist in the foothills.

Yamaguchi added:

The horse that fell with me; is that its voice whinnying in the valley?

And after he had heard their story, Koike added:

The height of a fallen horse—twenty thousand feet.[17]

Having led his team to Yauli and Carahuacra and inspected the mine sites, Takahashi had many problems to solve. Although the group currently at the mine was only an advance one, there to study how best to organize and exploit it, the main party would be coming to Peru before the end of the year. Takahashi had to buy and set up mining, transporting, and smelting equipment, establish regular food supplies, and work on a host of other details essential to the success of the enterprise. After the mine's opening ceremony on February 27, at which offerings of sake, chicken, and test ore were made to three gods: Ōyamatsumi no mikoto, the legendary god of mountains; Inari Daimyōjin, an important Shintō deity; and the god of the Carahuacra mountain, Takahashi returned to Lima to run the business from its company headquarters. Even before departing for the capital, Takahashi began to make plans to obtain rice, corn, and potatoes locally, set up a ranch to raise sheep and cattle, and find mules to transport enough food to feed 100 people. Along the way back, he met with Guyer and other purveyors of mine equipment and visited other mines to study their organization and equipment. The Takahashi papers at Tokyo Metropolitan University include a letter from Guyer to Heeren and Takahashi, dated March 13, 1890, in which he describes the kinds of equipment that he thinks would be most suitable for Carahuacra. The letter includes a discussion of a tramway to transport ore, and of the generation and transmission of electricity to run the railway and other mine equipment, advanced technology for Japanese in the mid-Meiji period. Another letter, from Castle Brothers, a food wholesaler in San Francisco, dated May 27, provides a list of foods that could be sent to Peru, and their prices. And on the journey down the mountain, as on the way up, Takahashi had his requisite share of adventures. At one point, for example, he barely survived being buried alive when his mule sank halfway into a bog.[18]

Once back in Lima, Takahashi conferred at length with Guyer about mining and refining equipment. Since Guyer's company had put machinery in place for two other mining companies in Peru, and both had succeeded, Takahashi and Heeren decided to rely on Fraser and Chalmers, and signed and sent a letter of intent to Guyer. Takahashi needed money to pay for this, and most of the Japan Peru Mining Company's capital in Peru was already gone. He therefore cabled Tokyo for an additional 20,000 pounds, only to receive a reply that the Japanese economy was in a recession, and such a sum of money was not immediately available. But the Tokyo investors added that they would raise and send the money as soon as they could.[19]

Everything Passes Like a Dream

On March 26, less than a month after Takahashi returned to Lima, Koike suddenly appeared at the company office. His visit was unexpected, so Takahashi surmised that something critical had happened, perhaps a fight between the Japanese and Peruvian workers. But it was more critical than that. When Takahashi asked Koike why he had come unannounced from the mine, he replied that what had happened was so consequential that he had been sent secretly by Yamaguchi to report. Five days earlier, when Koike had been exploring the company's mines, he discovered that they had been dug to the very bottom and were virtually depleted of ore. He immediately notified Yamaguchi. The next day, he secretly assayed the little ore that was coming from the mines and found that the best had 1.5 or 2 parts silver in 1,000, paltry when compared to the ruby ore brought to Japan by Tajima, which had been 20–28 parts in 1,000. Yamaguchi and Koike knew that Takahashi was renegotiating contracts, and that they needed to report to him before he signed anything binding. Koike told the workers that he had to go to Lima for medical reasons and came as fast as he could.[20]

Takahashi immediately went to speak with Tajima, the mining engineer who had appraised the mine, had reported to Tokyo about its high quality, and had signed the first contract with Heeren. When pressed on whether he had in fact investigated the mine site prior to signing the contract, Tajima admitted that he had not gone to the site at all. In his defense, he explained that he "never thought someone like [Takahashi] would be connected with this company." He confessed to having read a report in English in a Peruvian school magazine, then translated it into Japanese and sent it back to Tokyo. Tajima then vowed to go to the mine immediately to verify his report.

Takahashi at first did not know how to react. On the one hand, he had his and his co-investors' hopes and plans for self-reliant Japanese industrial development, and thus he wanted to believe Tajima; on the other, he had heard from Koike and Yamaguchi, whom he trusted, that the mine was barren. Since Takahashi was a realist, he leaned toward believing Koike and Yamaguchi. They had actually investigated the mining site, while Tajima had not. Moreover, Takahashi had every reason to be cautious. He was considering the purchase of mining equipment. He had decided to rent a ranch for fifteen years, and had chosen someone to purchase mules. He had signed a letter of intent with Guyer for refining machinery and was within one telegram of closing the deal. Estimates had come from the shipping company about the cost of bringing workers to Peru. In other words, he was in the process of committing a great deal of money, and his colleagues back in Tokyo were raising the necessary capital. Takahashi thought and thought about what to do, and then decided he needed to talk to someone who knew more about mining than he and who could evaluate the conflicting reports; he chose Henry Guyer as his man.

Guyer, who was ill when Takahashi arrived, got out of bed and while still in his pajamas talked with Takahashi at some length. Takahashi explained the genesis of the Carahuacra project, the investors' trust in Tajima's report, and their commitment of 125,000 yen to buy the mine. He then told Guyer of Koike's story, and Takahashi's realization that Tajima's report was a fabrication. What Guyer then related to Takahashi both confirmed his suspicions about the mine and also gave him what must have been an important lesson in the *realpolitik* of business. Guyer said that he himself had almost bought the Carahuacra mine. Miners often discovered pockets of rich ore in worked-out mines, and it was this kind of ore that was reported in the German mining magazine and taken to Japan. Because of these reports, Guyer had investigated the mine twice, but found the same low-quality ore as Yamaguchi and Koike, 1.5/1,000 per unit. Guyer had reported all of this to the New York office of his company, which was associated with Takada Shinzō's company in Japan. The Japanese investors therefore should have known of the poor quality of the ore before they invested 125,000 yen in a mine that was probably not worth 2,000. Guyer then went on to say that the year before he had heard a rumor that Tajima had bought the mine. "If Tajima had come to see me, I would have spoken to him frankly about the mine. But I don't like to interfere in other people's business unless I am asked. Now that I have heard what you have said, it is indeed regrettable." One can conclude it must indeed have been regrettable since Guyer was about to sign a several-thousand yen deal with a Japanese company to develop a mine he knew was barren.[21]

Takahashi left Guyer's place convinced that Koike was correct: the mine was barren. What to do next? Clearly he had to talk to his partner Heeren, who had invested half the company's capital. When Takahashi told him what Koike had reported, Heeren reacted angrily, and demanded to know why Takahashi had allowed Koike to leave the mine. Fearing that word of the situation would get out, and realizing that he would certainly be bankrupted if the mine was indeed non-productive, Heeren initially could not believe the report of a "Japanese technician." Eventually, however, he came around to accept the inevitable, that what little ore remained in the mine was of a very low quality.

The question then was what to do? Should Takahashi and Heeren abandon the project altogether, go bankrupt, and absorb their losses, or should they find some way to continue? One of Heeren's subordinates proposed buying equipment to crush and refine large amounts of low-grade ore so that at least something would be salvaged from the mine. The problem with this solution was where to find money to buy the machinery for such a large-scale operation. The company had spent most of its capital, and the prospect of raising more in Tokyo during a recession seemed slim. Finally Takahashi came up with a solution worthy of his lesson from Guyer. After a week of continual negotiations, he and Heeren signed an agreement by which Tajima's original contract was rendered null and void, and the Japanese investors agreed to buy out Heeren's half of the company for 60,000 pounds (an amount as large as its original capitalization) and form a new company to refine low-grade ore. However, the company would have six months to make up its mind: if the Japanese investors could not find the money to fulfill their obligations in such a time, they promised to give up all their rights to the mine and its equipment. In the meantime, Heeren would take responsibility for paying, feeding, and housing Tajima, Yamaguchi, Koike, and the miners and carpenters. Takahashi would return to Tokyo to explain the situation to the other shareholders, and consult with them to determine whether to invest heavily in trying to make something of a barren mine worth less than one-twentieth of what they originally paid, or to liquidate the company and cut their losses. Takahashi, although he did not tell Heeren, had already made up his mind. He planned to recommend that the investors declare bankruptcy. This would avoid further losses by the Tokyo investors, which Takahashi thought inevitable if they pursued the mining project. It would also mean that Heeren, who had really wanted to farm, not mine, would get no compensation from the Japanese investors and would go completely bankrupt.[22]

On April 10, 1890, only three months after he had arrived full of hope for Japan's future, Takahashi sailed from Callao for home. In his memoirs, he describes the sadness of the occasion. "Ah, life is ephemeral and everything passes like a dream. Ah, the Andes. Ah, the people of Peru." Yamaguchi, who had to remain at Carahuacra to oversee the mine and miners until Takahashi cabled them to return home months later, wrote a Chinese poem for the occasion.

> Seeing Takahashi off at Callao Harbor
>
> Parting with deep feelings at the ocean's mouth.
> What will people say of us,
> Parting to return home,
> We rely on the benevolence of heaven. [23]

Takahashi had much to worry about on his way home. While he was in Lima, he could not send candid cables to Tokyo, because Heeren, who was far better connected in Peru than Takahashi was, read every cable and letter he sent. Takahashi had to stop the Tokyo investors from raising and sending to Peru the very capital he had been asking for only weeks earlier, but if he did so from Lima, Heeren would recognize Takahashi's double game. The danger was compounded by the fact that every report from Lima to Tokyo had been glowingly positive; the Tokyo investors had no reason to think anything was amiss at Carahuacra. So it is not surprising that they misread his last, intentionally vague, cable from Lima: "If we do not increase our capital, the mine has no prospects. I am coming home shortly." Takahashi tried to convey to his fellow investors that they should do nothing until he arrived home; his investors understood it to mean everything was going well, and they should raise additional capital as quickly as possible. Takahashi returned home on June 5 with a real crisis on his hands: how to keep the investors from sending good money after bad.[24]

Takahashi first went to see Maeda and then met with all the shareholders. He explained in detail the situation in Peru, including Yamaguchi's and Koike's discoveries, his realization that Tajima's report was false, and his revocation of Tajima's contract with Heeren. The investors were stunned. In their euphoria over the prospects of a successful Japanese enterprise abroad, they had completely misread Takahashi's cable, thought things were going well, set out to raise more capital, and sent an engineer named Yamada Naoya to Lima to take charge in Takahashi's absence. Takahashi convinced them that the mine had no prospects, praised them for sending no further capital to Peru, remonstrated with them for sending Yamada, who might resurrect the earlier contract, and quickly contacted San Francisco for him to come home.

On June 21, Takahashi cabled Heeren that despite his best efforts he could not get the shareholders to agree to an investment of 2,000,000 more yen. Thus, the contract between the Japanese investors and Heeren was off. They had lost all of the money they invested, all of their rights to the mine, and their dream of a Japanese mine abroad. Yamaguchi heard on July 2 that there would be no new company, started down the mountain from Carahuacra with the miners on July 4, left Lima on July 17, and reached Yokohama on September 10. During the three months that Yamaguchi spent alone with the miners high in the Andes he had to struggle to keep them under control. One time they attacked the mining office in Yauli, and on another occasion they had a knife fight with locals in which some were wounded.

Although the Japan Peru Mining Company was essentially bankrupt after the summer of 1890, there were still a few items of business to conclude. Takahashi had no money to reimburse the miners for their back wages and could only grant them a token payment from his own pocket. Tajima absconded with thousands of yen, came home to Tokyo, and set out to build himself a mansion. But Takahashi and Fujimura had him arrested and charged with fraud; on October 20, 1890, he was found guilty and sentenced to three and a half years in jail. Koike sued the company for back wages and went to court. He calculated that the investors, who were prominent people, would settle out of court, and he was partly correct; several paid him small amounts of money rather than face the embarrassment of a trial. But Takahashi himself and others did not succumb, and a year later, after the case finally went to trial, Koike lost his case.[25]

Years later, Takahashi summed up his experience as follows:

The Peru silver mine incident was not only Japan's first enterprise in Peru, but also a pioneering effort in Japanese enterprise abroad in the Meiji era. Japan and Peru had no treaty to establish diplomatic relations. We did not exchange diplomats. We Japanese did not have a clear understanding of Peru. No wonder people were surprised when they learned we planned to operate a silver mine high in the Andes. But the incident became well known because many prominent Japanese were involved.

The enterprise failed because the report by Tajima, the engineer dispatched to investigate the mine, turned out to be false. We became the laughing stock of Japan, and people who did not know the truth thought of it as a case of corruption. Slanderous abuse centered on me.

Time heals all. I don't write now to rebut old charges. Over half the participants are dead, and there is no one left that I need to persuade about our faded dreams. I have documents and my remembrances close at hand and want to lay out the truth for future generations.[26]

What did Takahashi learn from his failure in Peru? First, the venture must have reinforced Takahashi's view that it was necessary to do basic research before plunging into a project and that one should be more circumspect when evaluating such basic research. Second, the gregarious Takahashi, who had a tendency to trust people with whom he dealt, clearly learned to be more cautious and even to be more devious. His method of negotiating with Heeren, as Takahashi liquidated the mining company, presaged some of the techniques he used in raising money in London during and after the Russo-Japanese War in 1904–7. Third and most important, the experience reinforced Takahashi's view, which he would emphasize throughout his career, that Japanese industrialists and businessmen needed access to inexpensive capital in order to succeed and stimulate Japanese economic growth. But given the paucity of domestic sources of capital, to whom could Japan turn for such capital? People have wondered why Takahashi, who is generally viewed as an advocate of an inflationary monetary and fiscal policy, supported Matsukata Masayoshi's efforts to go on the gold standard, which was clearly deflationary, in 1896–97. The reason is that Takahashi realized after the failure of the Peru venture that the best potential source of industrial capital for a developing country such as Japan was abroad, especially in major money markets such as London, Paris, Berlin, and New York. Without conforming to the international gold standard system, Japan would not have easy access to those markets.

Coda

After the Japan Peru Mining Corporation failed in 1890–91, Takahashi found himself deeply in debt. He owed 16,000 yen, but had only 10,000 yen in assets. He was therefore forced to sell his home to make up the difference, and had to find another place to live. He finally found a small rental property, for which he paid seven yen per month, a few blocks from his former 5,000-square meter residence, complete with Western and Japanese-style buildings. Takahashi was also unemployed. Friends tried to help him, and offers of a position in Hokkaido, or as a prefectural governor, came in, but Takahashi turned them all down. As he explained, "When I had served in government before, if I disagreed with a superior I argued with him. But if I had to rely on my position to provide food and clothing for my family, I could not serve the nation selflessly. I might be forced to obey an order I did not agree with. I could not rejoin the government under these conditions."[27]

Takahashi found that he could receive a small monthly pension from the government, one-third of his salary for three years, but this was not enough for a family of four, including his wife, two sons, and himself, to live on. Takahashi therefore concluded that he must "bury himself in the country," and the family must somehow support itself there, maybe even by farming. He called his family together, explained his failure in Peru, and told them that they must all work together to make ends meet. "Korekata who was 14 was silent after I said this, but Koreyoshi who was 10 said, 'Then I shall sell clams to help out.' Everyone swallowed their tears when they heard this."[28]

SEVEN

Entering the Bank of Japan,
1892–1904

Before Takahashi joined the Bank of Japan in 1892, his career prospects seemed bleak: he remained under a cloud of suspicion because of the failed Peru project and other misadventures, and he was mired in debt, ready to do almost anything to make ends meet. Yet within seven years Takahashi rose through the bank's ranks, from serving as a marginally important official overseeing the construction of the bank's new building to becoming its second in command—all without any banking experience whatsoever. His meteoric rise came through his personal connections and talents, even through he advocated and implemented policies for Japan's economic development that were mistrusted as unorthodox by many of the nation's most powerful leaders. During his period of service ending in 1904, Takahashi developed a philosophy for Japan's development that was more Keynesian than Keynes—that is, Takahashi's concern was not merely recovery from a severe downturn, à la Keynes in the world depression of the 1930s, but also long-term economic growth.

Takahashi argued that the government had a duty to stimulate economic growth through investment in infrastructural facilities such as railroads, harbors, banking systems, and modern educational institutions, and that it should provide inexpensive foreign exchange for export industries, especially crucial ones such as the raw silk industry. In the area of monetary policy, Takahashi advocated the stimulation of exports through low interest and exchange rates, and promoted governmental provision of inexpensive, short-term capital to manufacturers, especially those who produced for the export market, but recommended that the investment of such capital should be controlled by manufacturers themselves. Further, he argued that Japan should join the gold-standard nations, seemingly a deflationary step that ran counter to his other policies, but one that was necessary as it would allow Japan to borrow money for industrial ventures in the City of London, the center of the financial universe, as well as its subsidiary markets in New York, Paris, Hamburg, and Berlin.

Expanded and improved infrastructure and inexpensive foreign exchange and investment capital meant more production and exports, higher company profits, greater investment in new factories, more jobs, greater domestic demand for goods, and ultimately, more economic expansion. The perspective on economic development and the government's fiscal health that Takahashi developed in this period was that Japan benefited triply from growth: growth raised the citizens' standards of living, made the state itself richer, and, accordingly, led to increased tax revenues and a balanced budget without cutting expenditures. As did his opponents in the policy debate, Takahashi advocated a balanced budget, but in his view it was achieved through growth, not through savings, frugality, and economic contraction, which his opponents espoused.

Takahashi Enters the Bank of Japan

Takahashi's colleagues and friends, including many who did not share Maeda's and his own approach to economic development, sympathized with Takahashi after the Peru debacle. Although public opinion and a segment of officialdom saw the venture as the failure of a bubble company, that is, of one that had some kind of speculative stigma attached to it, powerful government officials agreed with Takahashi that he had accepted the task of running the mine for selfless, patriotic reasons, and thus they searched for a job for him. Shinagawa Yajirō, Takahashi's former superior at the Agriculture and Commerce Ministry, wrote Takahashi to praise him for his skill and upright behavior in liquidating the mining company. Saigō Tsugumichi and Matsukata Masayoshi, who had both been opponents during the *Kōgyō iken* debate in 1885, expressed concern about him, and Maeda, who felt responsible for Takahashi's participation in the Peru scheme, asked Kawada Koichirō, Governor of the Bank of Japan, for help.[1]

In April 1892, Maeda called on Takahashi to inform him that Kawada had asked to meet him. Over the next few weeks, Takahashi visited the governor several times at his home in Ōmagari, near the old Kanze *nō* theater in central Tokyo, to explain the causes of the Peru venture's failure, and to talk about what work Takahashi might do in the future. Kawada immediately dissuaded him from "burying himself in the country," and suggested that Takahashi take over the presidency of the Sanyō Railroad from Nakamigawa Hikojirō, Fukuzawa Yukichi's nephew and a Keio Gijuku graduate, who had left the railroad to become head of the Mitsui Corporation. Takahashi turned down the offer on the grounds that he knew nothing at all about running a railroad (although a lack of knowledge of silver mining had not kept him from going to Peru). Kawada then asked Takahashi to join the Bank of Japan, adding that he could not join the bank as a regular officer because misunderstandings about the Peru failure had not yet disappeared, and banks, after all, depended on people's trust.[2]

Constructing the New Bank of Japan Building in Tokyo

Kawada hired the 37-year-old Takahashi in June 1892 to coordinate the construction of the new Bank of Japan building, one of Japan's first large-scale Western-style structures, which was running behind schedule, over budget, and had design flaws. His superior on the job was the architect Tatsuno Kingo, who had been one of Takahashi's students in 1871 at the English-language school in Karatsu.[3] Takahashi began his work, he wrote in his memoirs, "With the state of mind of an apprentice. I went to work early every day, listened to my subordinates explain things to me, and learned."[4] But Takahashi's apprenticeship ended quickly when he found that Tatsuno was a better architect than project manager. Takahashi soon had the opportunity to utilize his ability to solve problems pragmatically when he rationalized the construction office's procurement process. One day, Tatsuno's construction office ordered Takahashi's subordinate business office to requisition steel rods. It in turn contacted the manufacturer, who replied that he could not produce the number of rods the construction office wanted as quickly as it wanted them, but in the end, agreed to produce and deliver them as a costly rush-order. The following day, with Tatsuno's permission, Takahashi went to the warehouse, which was overseen by the construction section and therefore was outside his bailiwick, and found a large number of the same kind of steel rods piled in a corner. The construction section had no inventory of what was actually in the warehouse. Takahashi, again with Tatsuno's approval, created an inventory and began the process of keeping records of everything that went in and out of the warehouse.

Takahashi next discovered a flaw in the process by which the bank procured building materials from abroad. The Ōkura Trading Company was the sole purchaser of imported goods for the construction job. One day, while inspecting the company's invoices to his business office, Takahashi found that they were invariably dated on the day of the month when the exchange rate was the lowest. He contacted Ōkura and was told that all materials came from England, and that the British shippers sent their invoices to the Hongkong and Shanghai Bank, which in turn sent them to the trading company. Ōkura then paid HSBC on the basis of that day's exchange rate. "I told [Ōkura] to send us HSBC's invoice together with theirs so we would not be defrauded in the future," Takahashi wrote.[5]

Ōkura, under contract from the construction office, also had the responsibility to find stonemasons to face the building. The company had subcontracted the job to four master masons (*oyakata*, or straw bosses) from the Osaka area, and each hired one-quarter of the workers. The workers frequently went on strike for higher wages and refused to return to the job until their demands were satisfied. Ōkura had no way of preventing these delays short of raising the masons' wages; thus the job was over budget and behind schedule. Takahashi's solution was to end the contract with Ōkura and complete the building under the direct supervision of the construction office. He negotiated a contract directly with each of the four *oyakata*, assigned each one a side of the building, and arranged that they would receive a bonus of 500 yen for each day ahead of schedule the work was completed and pay a similar fine for each day it was behind schedule. Takahashi reported that "afterward the four bosses competed with each other rather than work as a group." This application of market principles expedited the construction process considerably.

Takahashi also encountered difficulty in procuring the stone used for the building's façade. The Hattori Company had a contract to cut and transport the stone from a quarry on the Izu Peninsula, but the construction office had no control over the timing or quality of stone that arrived in Tokyo. The quarry workers cut stone according to their own convenience, not the construction office's, and as a result stone often arrived weeks late, or stone needed later was shipped before stone needed earlier. Takahashi's solution was to send a representative from the construction office to the quarry and at the same time to appoint someone in the business office in Tokyo to communicate with him directly. This solution required the construction office to surrender some of its authority to the business office, but Tatsuno agreed to the proposal and the process of procuring stone improved considerably.

Finally, there was the issue of deciding how best to affix the building's façade. Tatsuno's original blueprint for the building, designed in the European Beaux-Arts tradition, called for stone walls on all three stories of the building. But Tatsuno learned from reports of an earthquake in Gifu the previous year that it was dangerous to use heavy materials on the higher floors. Thus, without telling Governor Kawada, Tatsuno revised his design to use brick on the second and third stories. Accordingly, workers had to remove large sections of stone from the higher areas in order to replace them with brick, causing the project to fall even further behind schedule. When the governor asked Takahashi why construction was progressing slowly, he replied that one reason was the shift from stone to brick.

On hearing this, the governor turned red in the face and declared, "What? Brick above the first floor! Who approved that? I entrusted construction to specialists, but I told the directors it would be all stone, and that is what they approved. The construction people can't just change things when they feel like it." Again, Takahashi devised a solution. He reported to Tatsuno, "the governor has no objection so long as the exterior is stone. I am an amateur, but could we apply a thin veneer of stone to brick walls on the second and third stories?"

Tatsuno replied that it was theoretically possible: one could tie three-inch thick pieces of stone together with iron rods and cement them to the brick. So, when the building was completed in 1893, the walls of the first floor were constructed entirely of stone, the second-floor walls were brick faced with stone, and the third-floor walls were brick filled with hardened mud and also faced with stone.[6] Takahashi's adeptness at hands-on problem-solving allowed Tatsuno and his workers to complete the new building expeditiously and closer to budget. As a reward for this, on September 1, 1893, Kawada appointed Takahashi a regular member of the bank and simultaneously the chief of the newly established Western Branch of the Bank of Japan.

Takahashi Opens the Western Branch of the Bank of Japan

The appointment to commence his career as a banker in Shimonoseki, at the southwestern tip of the main island of Honshu, was beneficial to Takahashi for three reasons. It allowed him to begin his work in the financial arena far removed from critics who had tried from the beginning to derail him. For example, the well-connected Tajiri Inajirō, who had a solid education in economics at Tokyo Imperial and Yale universities, and who in 1893 was Deputy Minister of Finance and thus far above Takahashi in rank, criticized his appointment as allowing a speculator into the Bank of Japan. The appointment also allowed Takahashi, a neophyte banker who did not have a university education and who had learned all he knew on the subject from an intensive reading of London and New York newspapers and foreign and Japanese banking laws in the summer of 1893, to learn on the job as he strove to integrate the Kyushu economy more closely into the national one. By coincidence, it placed Takahashi in Shimonoseki when many of Japan's primary leaders came to negotiate a treaty to end the Sino-Japanese War in 1895.[7]

When considering from today's perspective Japan's steady economic growth from the Meiji Restoration to the present, it is easy to overlook how long the process of creating a unified Japanese state and economy took. One element of this slow progression toward integration was the difficulty in establishing uniform interest rates nationwide. When Takahashi arrived in Shimonoseki to head the first Bank of Japan branch west of Osaka, businessmen in western Honshu and Kyushu paid considerably more to borrow money than did their counterparts in Osaka (according to Takahashi, as much as 7 to 10 percentage points per year more). Takahashi immediately committed himself to bringing interests rates down to Osaka/Tokyo levels. One economic historian who has studied the connection between the establishment of branch offices of the Bank of Japan and interest rates has found that the cost of borrowing fell dramatically in Kyushu after the establishment of the Western Branch: from 1881 until the establishment of the Western Branch in 1893, interest rates were an average of 3.09 percent higher than the national average, but from 1894 to 1909 only 0.85 percent higher.[8]

Takahashi took another step in 1893 that prefigured his actions as finance minister in the 1920s: he used Bank of Japan funds to save the 110th National Bank from bankruptcy. The 110th Bank, which like many mid-Meiji-period banks was based on the investment by former samurai of the stipend bonds given them when they were bought out of their warrior status in the mid-1870s, invested heavily in land-reclamation projects in Yamaguchi Prefecture. Because of repeated storms in the early 1890s, many of the reclamation dikes washed away, and "600,000 yen went up in foam." But when Takahashi investigated, he found that the government's stipend bonds that provided the bank's capitalization had risen sharply in value, and as a result even if the bank wrote off the reclamation losses it was still solvent. Unfortunately its former and potential customers did not know this. Takahashi decided to commit Bank of Japan funds to keep the 110th Bank from going under so that companies and other banks would deal with it again. Takahashi viewed saving this samurai bank as a good investment for the Bank of Japan. But here, as in his later efforts to save banks and companies, he made a commitment only after thorough investigation.[9]

As indicated by the differential in interest rates, Kyushu in the 1890s was not yet fully integrated into the national economy. Kyushu companies sold large amounts of coal, rice, and other products to central and eastern Japan, but bought very little in exchange. Every year the Bank of Japan had to ship about four or five million yen in convertible notes from the Osaka branch to western Honshu and Kyushu. Moreover, local entrepreneurs tended to invest in traditional industries, and Tokyo and Osaka investors showed little interest in Kyushu. Thus, Takahashi set as one of his priorities building a reputation for western Japan's financial and business world. He brought the Sumitomo and other eastern industrialists to the region to investigate local opportunities, particularly the modernization of coal mining, and he convinced Tokunaga Gen'ei, the richest man in the Shimonoseki area, to establish a cotton textile company. Takahashi's posting to the Western Branch gave him the opportunity to practice and expand upon some of the ideas about local development that he had learned from Maeda Masana. His work in Shimonoseki played an important role in the formation of his ideas about how best to promote economic growth.[10]

The Sino-Japanese War

The Sino-Japanese War advanced Takahashi's career and education in several ways: it brought him once again to the attention of major governmental leaders such as Finance Minister Matsukata; it helped mold his view that empire was desirable, but only if created and managed carefully within the framework of what was acceptable to the British and Americans; and it led him to realize that joining the gold-standard nations was important both to Japan's national prestige and to its ability to borrow abroad for industrial development.

The war, Japan's first major imperialist war, broke out in August 1894, while Takahashi headed the Western Branch of the Bank of Japan in Shimonoseki. Because the government established its wartime head-quarters in nearby Hiroshima and its major ports for sending troops and goods to fight the war were located in the Shimonoseki/northern Kyushu area, most of the country's major civil and military officials, including the Meiji emperor, came to the region. In fact, the Seventh Session of the Imperial Diet took place not in Tokyo, but in Hiroshima.

Takahashi had two major tasks during the war. First, the war with China over the "independence of Korea," that is, to pry Korea out of the Chinese "tribute system," was financed entirely by domestic funds. Takahashi was charged with selling war bonds in the region. He describes the process as similar to that used by the Tokugawa sho-gunate in raising funds during the feudal period. The bank set up a quota of 700,000 yen for Yamaguchi Prefecture and of that, 100,000 yen for the city of Shimonoseki. The prefectural governor, mayor, and other prominent figures visited company and bank officials to pressure them to contribute. The fundraisers' technique was to tell x that y had agreed to contribute a certain amount, and that he, x, should pledge as much or more. The same was done in rural areas. Takahashi reports that a combination of coercion and patriotic war fever allowed the government to raise locally more than double its original quota, and that some well-to-do farmers even mortgaged land to buy war bonds.

The government had a voracious demand for funds during the war and pressured the Bank of Japan to find even more money. When Takahashi visited the convalescing Kawada in Osaka, the governor told him that Prime Minister Itō had demanded 300,000,000 yen "to lend to the Korean government so it can reform itself." He wanted Kawada to lean on Mitsui and Iwasaki, much as the Tokugawa *bakufu* had pressured merchant houses such as the Kōnoike, to "lend" them money, and if that did not work, to use Bank of Japan funds. Takahashi incurred the governor's wrath by adamantly opposing Itō's proposal, because, Takahashi said, "the Western powers are likely to be very concerned if the Japanese government lends money directly to the Korean government at this time." Takahashi also feared that excessive borrowing to fund the war would crowd out investment capital for productive enterprises.

The second major task was dealing with the economic hardship the war caused locally. The region had a bumper rice harvest in 1894, usually a reason for rejoicing, but the military had seized all available ships in the area and none were available to transport the rice. When farmers sought places to store their crop, they found that the military had also taken over all local warehouses. As soon as a well-to-do farmer built a storage facility for his grain, the army requisitioned it. Because banks invested heavily in war bonds, capital was tight in the Shimonoseki region in 1894–95, and banks therefore did not have capital to lend to farmers and businessmen. Small and middle-scale farmers, who borrowed at high interest rates in the best of times, had no access whatsoever to bank funds during the war. Unfortunately for the region, Takahashi and the Bank of Japan could do nothing for them until the war was over. This experience must have had an influence on the view Takahashi propounded only a few years later that the government should limit defense spending to the greatest extent possible because of its detrimental effect on the nation's economy.[11]

Takahashi served in Shimonoseki when Chinese and Japanese officials held treaty negotiations there to end the Sino-Japanese War. During March and April of 1895 he had an opportunity to meet and consult with Prime Minister Itō, Foreign Minister Mutsu Munemitsu, and a number of their subordinates, and to serve as an important conduit for providing information to his superiors in Tokyo. Takahashi not only wrote about these conversations in his memoirs, but he also sent three letters, of which two were addressed to Governor Kawada, that are still in existence. In them he indirectly criticized the prime minister, praised Finance Minister Matsukata, supported the latter's effort to go on the gold standard by receiving the Chinese indemnity in London in pounds, and encouraged Governor Kawada to support Matsukata.[12]

In mid-March, Itō, Mutsu, and the Chinese negotiator Li Hongzhang arrived in Shimonoseki to begin negotiations. Takahashi reports that the government commandeered all inns and restaurants in the Amida-dera section of the city. On March 20, Itō and Li met for the first time and Li asked for a cessation of military operations and preparations during the negotiations. Itō replied the next day that his government would agree to a ceasefire if the Chinese allowed the imperial army to occupy three of its cities, the Chinese troops in those cities surrendered their weapons, and the Japanese were granted control over local railroads in north China. Moreover, Itō added the demand that the Chinese government pay the costs of the Japanese soldiers in China during the ceasefire/occupation period. According to Takahashi, Li silently looked over the Japanese memorandum, and uttered, "harsh, harsh." When the negotiators came together again on the 24th for a third meeting, the Chinese withdrew their request for a ceasefire and called for immediate peace negotiations. The Japanese stated that they would present their government's peace terms the next day, and the meeting ended. As Li was returning to his inn after the meeting, a young man broke out of the crowd and shot and wounded him.

In the end, in spite of the attack on Li and the understandable outrage of his entourage and public opinion back home, the Chinese granted the Japanese more or less what they demanded: the cession of the island of Taiwan and the Liaodong Peninsula (the southern entrance to Manchuria), the opening of additional treaty ports, tariff limitations on Japanese goods imported into China, the right to establish Japanese-owned factories in Chinese treaty ports, and an immense indemnity of 300,000,000 taels (500,000,000 yen.) Then on April 23, Russia, with the backing of France and Germany, sent the government of Japan a memorandum formally requesting it to return the Liaodong leasehold to China:

The possession of the peninsula of Liaotung [Liaodong], claimed by Japan, would be a constant menace to the capital of China, would at the same time render illusory the independence of Korea, and would henceforth be a perpetual obstacle to the peace of the Far East. Consequently, the government of His Majesty the Tsar would give a new proof of its sincere friendship for the government of His Majesty the Emperor of Japan by advising it to renounce the definitive possession of the peninsula of Liaotung.[13]

Takahashi reports that he was stunned by this triple intervention: "We were punished for our overwhelming victory," but he well understood that the Japanese government could not resist the power of three European countries and had no choice but to give in.

In March, when negotiations had just begun, Matsukata became finance minister once again, an appointment that Takahashi welcomed, even though he recognized that Prime Minister Itō and Matsukata were not on the best of terms.[14] In this context, three letters written by Takahashi, two to Governor Kawada in March, and another to Takahashi Kenzō, reveal not only his reading of the current political situation and desire to go on the gold standard, but also his views, frequently reiterated in the future, of the dangers of arousing Chinese anti-Japanese nationalistic feeling and of carrying out an overly aggressive foreign policy that would antagonize the Western powers.

On March 19, before the attack on Li, Takahashi wrote to Kawada about events in Shimonoseki and of his support for going on the gold standard:

From what people say, Matsukata wants to receive an indemnity [from China] in British pounds to follow Germany in becoming a gold-standard nation. I would like your Excellency to use his influence with Count Matsukata on behalf of my theory [support for going on the gold standard]. . . . When it looks as if peace negotiations will be completed and Count Matsukata comes to Shimonoseki would be a good time.

In Takahashi's view, however, Matsukata's appointment created short-term political waves:

Count Itō was in good form last night and over drinks on shipboard he laid out his foreign policy strategy. During his chat, he ridiculed the stupidity of various other officials, and especially that of Count Matsukata. Those present worry about the future of the current cabinet. Count Matsukata is waiting in the wings, and people have confidence in his moral stature. It would be popular if Matsukata returned to the premiership after the war.[15]

On March 31, four days after the attack on Li, Takahashi wrote a second letter to Kawada, in which he expressed his fear of Chinese anti-Japanese sentiment and of foreign intervention:

Yesterday our minister in charge of negotiations and Li met and agreed to a ceasefire. Over the next three weeks until April 20, an armistice will be in effect in three provinces including Shandong. Both sides will stop troop movements and re-supply. This is to prevent further war preparations under the cover of a ceasefire. The emperor, out of sympathy with Li, has ordered our negotiator [Itō] to sign the agreement. I [Takahashi] worry that Li will return home and ask the powers to support him in blocking a settlement. Li may want them to open hostilities against us. . . . His return will arouse the anger of the Chinese people. To quiet the wrath of the Chinese people we should wire the government in Beijing that the attack was the action of one crazed individual, and that the Japanese people as a whole feel sympathy for Li.

We must avoid earning ourselves a bad reputation during the war and arousing the anger of the powers toward us. As with the impact of the Ōtsu Incident [an assassination attempt on the Russian crown prince, later Tsar Nicholas II, during a visit to Japan in 1891], they might think that we have only a gold-leaf veneer of civilization. Russia has two ships, 2,500 troops, and three torpedo boats at Vladivostok.

There are no cases to my knowledge in which peace negotiations failed after an unconditional ceasefire was signed, but I fear we may have weakened our position by doing so. . . .[16]

On May 23, after Japan had agreed not to take possession of the Liaodong Peninsula, Takahashi wrote to Takahashi Kenzō about cautious empire-building: "We must govern Taiwan with the long-term future in mind. . . . To secure the peace in the Far East, we must allow Korea to stand between China and Japan as an independent nation. If we are patient, wait for ten or fifteen years, and devise a well thought-out strategy, Korea will inevitably become our territory."[17]

One can detect elements of Takahashi's later foreign policy and political philosophies in these letters. He was a nationalist who supported the development of Japan's nascent imperialist ambitions. He believed that Japan should build its empire within the framework of European and American imperialism because the powers were richer and stronger than Japan. Careful planning and patience, not precipitous military action, were crucial. He supported joining the gold-standard nations not only because it would give Japan access to foreign capital for economic development, but also because membership was de rigueur for major (imperial?) powers. He also, I suspect, supported the gold standard for careerist reasons. Although Takahashi had had and would again have conflicts over policy with Matsukata Masayoshi, the latter stood astride the Japanese financial world at the end of the nineteenth century. As a 40-year-old fledgling financial statesman trying to restart his career after a major setback, Takahashi found it useful to throw his support regarding the gold standard to Count Matsukata.

Takahashi Joins the Yokohama Specie Bank

In August 1895, Governor Kawada asked Takahashi to join the Yokohama Specie Bank (*shōgin*) as manager of the main office in Yokohama. Kawada wanted Takahashi to reform the bank to use Bank of Japan funds to provide low-interest loans to Japanese importer-exporters, both to increase foreign trade and to ensure that such trade be conducted through Japanese—not foreign—companies, an idea that, Kawada knew, Takahashi fully supported. Kawada had previously appointed Koizumi Nobukichi, a Keio University–trained protégé of Fukuzawa Yukichi, for this purpose, but he had failed because of his own ambivalence and the resistance of the bank's president, Sonoda Kōkichi, whom Takahashi had befriended in London in 1886.

From its inception in 1880 the bank had had two roles, and they sometimes clashed. The driving force behind the planning and creation of *shōgin* was Ōkuma Shigenobu, finance minister until his ouster in 1880. Ōkuma thought that the Japanese government, in the midst of rampant inflation, needed to fill its "coffers with gold and silver coins." According to Ōkuma's confidante Fukuzawa (and *shōgin*'s fourth-largest founding shareholder), this would allow Japan to issue secure paper money, which Fukuzawa saw as part and parcel of a modern economy.

A government faction led by Itō ousted Ōkuma from power on February 28, 1880, the very day that the bank opened its doors. However, his successor, Sano Tsunetami, and *his* successor, the more famous Matsukata, who became finance minister in 1881, believed even more strongly in the necessity of stockpiling gold and silver. Matsukata, under the influence of Leon Say, wanted to stabilize Japan's currency by establishing a central bank as the sole issuer of paper money. A minority view, advocated by Maeda Masana, held that the *shōgin*'s primary role should be to serve as Japan's import-export bank, which would lend low-interest foreign exchange to Japanese exporters and importers. Kawada appointed Takahashi manager of the main office of *shōgin* to impose Maeda's view on the bank's recalcitrant chief executives. Takahashi, from the time of the *Kōgyō iken* debate ten years earlier, had believed in the necessity of providing low-interest capital to exporters and manufacturers, and his appointment to the Yokohama Specie Bank allowed him to put his views into practice.[18]

As soon as Takahashi arrived in Yokohama, he committed himself to what he had done before in Tokyo and Shimonoseki: learning and problem-solving. Since he knew very little about exchange rates, Takahashi conferred every day with his subordinates who specialized in such matters, especially Yamakawa Yūki. Takahashi, ever the pragmatic nationalist, soon found a flaw in the Yokohama Specie Bank's method of operation: the Hongkong and Shanghai Bank (HSBC), not the *shōgin*, set Japan's official yen exchange rate each day. HSBC, having received the price of silver ingots, that is, the basis for the exchange rate, from London overnight, set the day's price, then announced it when the bank opened. Since the *shōgin* opened at nine, but HSBC and other foreign banks in Yokohama did not open until ten, the Specie Bank, although it received the ingot price at the same time as HSBC, could not carry out exchange transactions until an hour after it had begun operations. Takahashi proposed abolishing this colonial practice and instead having the Yokohama Specie Bank, which after all was Japan's official foreign-exchange bank, determine Japan's official exchange rate. Takahashi also found that foreign companies, and even large Japanese enterprises, used foreign banks such as HSBC, not the Specie Bank, to buy their foreign exchange. Takahashi proposed to attract these potential customers to the *shōgin* by giving them a discount of one-sixteenth of the exchange rate offered by the foreign banks. The governor also gave Takahashi permission to use Bank of Japan funds to establish a lending fund of 4,000,000 yen of 2 percent bonds. Having received permission from the Ministry of Finance to do so, Takahashi made the rounds of major companies such as Nippon Yūsen Shipping Company, Mitsubishi, and Standard Oil, and succeeded in attracting them to the *shōgin*.[19]

Takahashi recounts in his memoirs an anecdote from this first tour of duty in Yokohama that reveals both his penchant for learning on the job and the development of his thinking about the government's role in financial affairs. A French exporter of raw silk from Japan, who was a customer of the *shōgin*, went bankrupt and the bank lost some tens of thousands of yen. Three French banks had also lent him money and had taken even heavier losses. A few weeks later a report came from the Specie Bank branch in Lyons that the French banks, recognizing that the importer-exporter had been an excellent customer for many years, and that he had long experience in the field, decided to write off his debts, and moreover, to extend him additional credit. They concluded that he had gone bankrupt through no fault of his own, but because of an economic downturn in France; the weavers who regularly bought raw silk from him did not have the money to continue to do so. The letter concluded by asking what the *shōgin* intended to do in this case. Takahashi reported, "I was deeply moved by the kindness, wisdom, and morality of the three banks. I replied that the Yokohama Specie Bank must act in accordance with the French banks." With the French example in mind, Takahashi and the bank soon afterward forgave the debt of a Japanese entrepreneur, Asabuki Eiji, after his cotton textile company went bankrupt.[20]

The most critical event during Takahashi's service as manager of the home office of the Yokohama Specie Bank was Japan's enrollment among the gold-standard nations. In October 1893, just as Takahashi went to Shimonoseki as a fledgling banker, Finance Minister Matsukata had set up the Currency Investigation Commission to decide whether Japan should have a silver- or a gold-based currency. The committee deliberated for three years and was split on the issue; in the end fewer than half the members recommended adopting the gold standard. The businessmen, led by the leading Meiji-era entrepreneur Shibusawa Eiichi, opted for silver, because under it the exchange rate continually depreciated and provided an advantage to exporters. The bureaucrats, led by Matsukata, lieutenants from the finance ministry such as Tajiri Inajirō (who had opposed Takahashi's entry into the Bank of Japan) and Soeda Juichi (another Takahashi rival), and navy officials favored gold. Since the price of gold remained steady, unlike that of silver, the adoption of the gold standard made the importation of warships and other munitions from Great Britain less expensive. The absence of a mandate from the committee notwithstanding, Matsukata had already made up his mind. Once Japan obtained the Chinese indemnity in London in 1896–97, it had the specie reserves in the Bank of England necessary to act. The New Coinage Law that put Japan on the London-centered gold standard went into effect in October 1897. Takahashi played an important, if secondary, role in this process. From his time in Shimonoseki on, he had backed Matsukata's efforts, and one reason Governor Kawada transferred Takahashi to the Specie Bank in Yokohama was to help repatriate part of the Chinese indemnity.[21] By supporting Matsukata's proposal, Takahashi gained the patronage of the great man, even though they did not agree on how best to stimulate investment and demand. In March 1897, as the government made its final plans to go on the gold standard, Takahashi was elected Vice President of the Yokohama Specie Bank. At the end of the year, the Bank of Japan's leadership decided to send Takahashi abroad to inspect the Asian and European branches of the Yokohama Specie Bank.

Takahashi's Fourth Foreign Journey, January–October 1898

By going on the gold standard, Japan entered the "Pax Britannica," that is, the British world order. This allowed Japan to borrow from abroad for economic, colonial, and military development, something it had largely avoided for the first quarter-century of its modern development. Before Takahashi's scheduled departure for Europe in early 1898, Itō Hirobumi replaced Matsukata as prime minister, and Inoue Kaoru became finance minister for the only time in his long career as a bureaucrat and elder statesman, despite the fact that he considered himself one of Japan's foremost experts in financial matters. Inoue, who took office on January 12, asked Takahashi to postpone his departure until the two had a chance to talk. When they met, Inoue told Takahashi, "The Ministry of Finance wants to float a foreign loan of two hundred million yen. I would like you to investigate what terms we can get." Takahashi's inspection trip therefore took on a new dimension.

Takahashi left Kobe for London by ship on February 11. When the ship made its first call at Shimonoseki, friends and geisha from his days there boarded the ship and partied with him to the next port, Nagasaki. Takahashi was entertained at Nagasaki by the leaders of the Mitsubishi shipyards, and was seen off on his departure by Thomas Glover, the man who 30 years earlier had sold the Satsuma and Chōshū domains the weapons they used to overthrow the shogunate, and who in 1898 was serving as an advisor to the Mitsubishi Corporation. After Nagasaki, Takahashi visited Shanghai, Hong Kong, Singapore, Colombo, Bombay, Aden, Suez, and Marseilles, before arriving in London on April 28. Over these two and a half months, Takahashi discovered problems and suggested solutions at several of the branches he visited. This, Takahashi's fourth long trip abroad, was his first to Asia, and to two increasingly important Japanese export markets, China and India. In Shanghai and Hong Kong, leading Chinese merchants entertained Takahashi, and this experience reinforced his view that Japan's future on the mainland of Asia would depend more on expanding trade relations in cooperation with Chinese entrepreneurs than on military intervention and conquest. In Bombay, rich businessmen entertained him with music and classical dance, and he was taken to see Parsi and Hindu burial rites: the former featuring corpses being devoured by vultures, the latter involving cremation of dead bodies on large, outdoor funeral pyres. In his memoirs, Takahashi concluded his description of these rituals with the following statement, which reveals much about his evolving views of Japanese empire:

I thought that because India was an English colony, it would have switched to European civilization, but wherever I looked, I could find no evidence of this. I concluded that the British had an enlightened colonial policy. They made no effort to change local customs and religious beliefs, and left such things alone. I thought this was how colonies should be run. I approved heartily.

As always on his trips abroad, he befriended shipmates, in this case German and French businessmen, and demonstrated his ease in dealing with foreigners in English.[22]

Within a few days of his arrival in London, Takahashi had met two people who would play important roles in the next few decades of his life. The first was the 29-year-old Inoue Junnosuke, who had entered the Bank of Japan upon graduation from Tokyo Imperial University in 1896, and had subsequently been sent abroad to study at Parr's Bank in London. Later, as Governor of the Bank of Japan during the Hara and Tanaka governments, Inoue would cooperate with Takahashi in the use of Bank of Japan funds to rescue endangered companies during the financial crises in the decade after World War I. But when Inoue was made finance minister in the Hamaguchi/Wakatsuki government in 1929–32, the two became bitter rivals when Inoue did a volte-face to fiscal and monetary rigor and took Japan back on the gold standard at the pre-World War I price of gold.[23]

The second man was Alexander Allan Shand, a Scots banker "the Japanese could trust." Shand was born and had his earliest banking training in Aberdeen. In 1863, he joined the Chartered Mercantile Bank of India, London, and China in Hong Kong, and in 1864, at the age of 20, he became the acting manager of the bank's branch in Yokohama, where the eleven-year-old Takahashi served (and caroused) as a houseboy. From 1872 until 1877, Shand, as an advisor to the Ministry of Finance, persuaded the Japanese to abandon the American national bank system for the British model, based on a central bank, as a method of controlling the issuance of paper money and therefore inflation, which was a major problem for Japan in the 1870s. Shand returned to Britain in the late 1870s after the tragic death of his son on a holiday in Hakone. Back in London, he joined the Alliance Bank, which merged in 1892 with Parr's Bank, and for the rest of his life served as an important ally in the City for Japanese financial officials. Shand helped the Yokohama Specie Bank open a private account at the Alliance Bank in 1881, which Parr's Bank took over after the merger. It was Shand, assistant manager of the head office of Parr's Bank, to whom Takahashi turned in the spring of 1898 to investigate the possibility of selling Japanese government bonds in London.[24]

Shand introduced Takahashi to his superiors at Parr's, especially William Dun, a director and later general manager, and A. J. Fraser, another director. The three of them talked with Takahashi at length of the difficulties a small country such as Japan with no credit record would face in trying to issue bonds in the international market. The problem, Fraser told him, was that London investors knew little about Japan. If Japan attempted to float a 16,000,000 pound (200,000,000 yen) loan in 1898, it therefore would simply not sell. The most the London market could absorb would be 5,000,000 pounds—4 percent bonds with a selling price of 90 (Japan would receive 90 but pay back 100), which Fraser thought would do well. But if the Japanese tried to float too large an issue, they would undoubtedly have to provide security, such as land-tax revenues. Shand introduced Takahashi to other members of the London financial community as well: he specifically mentions the head of the Chamber of Commerce, a financial journalist, and a member of Shand's and Takahashi's former Yokohama employer, the Chartered Bank. Takahashi spoke to each of them about Japan's prospects of floating a loan in London, and then, having "gathered all of their opinions, formulated my own, and reported to Count Inoue."[25]

Shand also lectured Takahashi on what he considered to be the indispensable qualities of a banker: Pay attention to detail. See the big picture as well as the small. Be polite and kind to all clients and be willing to warn those who want to invest in risky enterprises of the hazards involved, but always politely; people will thank you later if you keep them from borrowing for some dangerous business scheme. Do not put the bank's money into chancy investments, not only because the money will be lost, but also because the bank's reputation will be tarnished. Do not disclose your clients' dirty laundry. Shand certainly remembered Takahashi's unseemly behavior in Yokohama 30 years earlier, but whenever Takahashi began to talk of working for Shand in Yokohama before the Restoration, Shand changed the subject. To Shand, reserve and reticence were essential qualities for a banker. Shand became Takahashi's close friend and associate in 1898, which would benefit him and Japan in 1904–5 during the Russo-Japanese War.[26]

Takahashi traveled to Belgium, France, and Germany in June 1898, mostly, he reported, for tourism: art museums, theater performances, churches, and parks. But he also took the opportunity to meet bankers and the younger Japanese businessmen and students in Europe at the time. He made inquiries about the chance of success for Japanese bonds on the continent, and learned two things: first, that Inoue Kaoru had not entrusted this investigation to Takahashi alone, but had asked Japanese diplomats in Europe to make similar inquiries; second, that the French and German securities specialists to whom he talked did not think Japanese bonds would sell well at the time, unless the return on the bonds was better than for other competing issues. One such specialist commented: "If the return on Japanese bonds was good enough, we might be able to recommend them to people who had inherited their fathers' estates, or to widows, or to aristocrats." Europeans in 1898 knew little about Japan, and serious investors would not buy Japanese bonds. Takahashi left the continent for London on July 10, and left Liverpool for New York two weeks later. Katō Takaaki, the Japanese Minister to Great Britain, whose Twenty-one Demands to China Takahashi would oppose in 1915, and in whose cabinet he would serve in 1924–25, saw him off at Euston Station in London. Katō said that the finance minister had also contacted him about the possibility of floating a loan in London; Katō cabled back to Inoue that he had seen and agreed with Takahashi's report.[27]

Takahashi spent ten days in New York conferring with the branch chiefs of the *shōgin* and Mitsui Trading Company. Schuyler Duryee, Takahashi's friend from his days in Washington studying patent laws, visited him, and the two along with others went to Coney Island to eat and "enjoy themselves until midnight." On August 10, Takahashi left for Niagara Falls, and then took a transcontinental train via Denver and the Rocky Mountains to San Francisco. He arrived there on August 16, and the next day began his inspection of the Yokohama Specie Bank branch in San Francisco. Takahashi discovered the branch was running a chronic deficit caused by exchange remittances to Hong Kong. Reminding the local branch chief that the primary duty of the *shōgin* was to promote Japanese, not global, trade, Takahashi warned,

If the losses came in remittances to Japan I would not worry. But the government set up the Yokohama Specie Bank to facilitate trade between Japan and the world. In contrast to that mission, you have emphasized American trade so that business with China and Hong Kong has grown. You must focus your work on Japan and make China and Hong Kong a secondary business.

Takahashi also visited Mrs. Verbeck, who was too ill to see him, had a long talk with her daughter, and concluded, "they looked poor and I found it very sad"—sad, because the family of one of the most important modernizing foreign teachers in Japan during the 1860s and 1870s, and one of Takahashi's first mentors, had fallen on hard times.[28]

The Yokohama Specie Bank Becomes a "City Bank"

During Takahashi's first three years at the *shōgin*, the bank transformed itself from one that amassed gold and silver for the Bank of Japan to underwrite Japan's currency into one that also provided inexpensive foreign exchange for Japanese and foreign importer-exporters to stimulate economic growth. But Takahashi had even greater plans for the bank. His first task on returning home was to report to Matsuda Masahisa, the new finance minister in the Ōkuma cabinet, about the possibility of floating Japanese bonds on the London market: "it will not be difficult if the loan is not larger than one hundred million yen," half of what Inoue had requested. Then Takahashi turned to his next goal, to make the Yokohama Specie Bank into a bank that provided inexpensive capital to entrepreneurs for all kinds of trade-related business activities, not solely the purchase of foreign exchange. He explained to his superiors at the bank that the San Francisco branch sent all of the profits it garnered in foreign-exchange transactions to the New York office, which in turn passed them, along with its own profits, on to the primary branch in London. London amassed a large amount of money, but since the managers there allocated it only for foreign exchange and trade with East Asia, they had more money available than opportunities to spend it. Takahashi recommended that the government take 2,000,000 pounds from the China indemnity, combine it with the monies forwarded from San Francisco and New York, and deposit it in the Bank of England as capital for business other than exchange transactions—specifically, for business that would stimulate Japanese imports and exports.

In November 1898, Field Marshal Yamagata replaced Ōkuma as prime minister after he had served less than five months, and established a cabinet of Meiji current or future political heavyweights: Admiral Saigō Tsugumichi, as home minister; future three-time prime minister General Katsura Tarō as army minister; future two-time prime minister Admiral Yamamoto Gonnohyōe as navy minister; future prime minister Kiyoura Keigo as justice minister; Admiral Kabayama Sukenori as education minister; and Matsukata as finance minister. On January 26, the finance minister called Bank of Japan governor Yamamoto Tatsuo, Takahashi, and a finance ministry bureau chief and future Bank of Japan governor, Matsuo Shigeyoshi, to his office to discuss how to facilitate trade with China. Should Japan, Matsukata asked, have a special financial organ, such as a branch of the Industrial Bank of Japan, in China to provide capital to facilitate trade? The influence of Takahashi's recent trip to China and South and Southeast Asia is apparent in his reply:

If we set up a new bank or use the Industrial Bank in China, we must employ people who understand Chinese business practices. At present, the only Japanese with such knowledge work in the Yokohama Specie Bank. . . . Therefore, the government should give that bank ten million yen in silver [China had a silver-based currency] and allow it to provide businesses with inexpensive capital in addition to its foreign exchange transactions. When Japanese merchants and industrialists in China look for money to expand their trade and business, they should choose the Yokohama Specie Bank. The government should permit the bank to lend silver-based loans to those companies found to be financially sound. We can transfer this business to the Industrial Bank in the future, when that bank has trained qualified people.

Takahashi reports that Finance Minister Matsukata agreed with his view and transferred 600,000 pounds (10,000,000 yen at the time) to the Specie Bank. By the end of the nineteenth century, the *shōgin* had clearly become a financial organ to provide industrial and merchant capital as well as foreign exchange. A month later, on February 28, 1899, the government called Takahashi back to Tokyo and appointed him Vice Governor of the Bank of Japan.[29]

Vice Governor Takahashi

Takahashi's first few years as Vice Governor were marked by a host of nagging difficulties. He mediated a dispute between Governor Yamamoto Tatsuo, later finance minister and a Takahashi rival in the Seiyūkai political party, and his subordinates, who found Yamamoto domineering and unwilling to listen to their views. He had to deal with personnel problems both during and after the row, when many of the subordinates tendered their resignations; interestingly, given his later conflicts with Yamamoto, Takahashi persuaded Finance Minister Matsukata to retain the governor even if the subordinates carried out their threats to quit. He supported the central bank's policy of helping troubled local banks and companies, but strove to establish orderly rules for doing so, believing that decisions in the past had been made out of personal favoritism, not rigorous investigation. He also set up a system of reorganizing the banks after their recovery. Under the new guidelines, he arranged for the Bank of Japan to rescue several endangered Kyushu banks. He dealt with the problem of how best to store and ship silver coins minted in Osaka for the Chinese government and arranged for the Yokohama Specie Bank, not the Japanese postal service, to set the official exchange rate for silver-based trade with

China. Under the old system, the same exchange rate stayed in place for three or four days at a time, which allowed foreign bankers to profit from the differences between it and the gold-based exchange rate, set daily by the Specie Bank. Takahashi became involved in a dispute over Yamamoto's efforts to abolish the payment of year-end bonuses to bank members. Although Takahashi opposed the proposal, the bank employees believed he was behind it—in fact, Takahashi was so unpopular with his subordinates at the time that he offered to resign. Takahashi recalled his first few years as Vice Governor as follows:

When I worked at the Yokohama Specie Bank I felt like a chrysanthemum blooming in the fields. I wasn't a gaudy person widely known to the public, but I worked in a comfortable atmosphere. The Bank of Japan, on the other hand, seemed like a beautiful fragrant rose. The work was flashy, and I had a big public reputation. But one could not escape the thorns in the shadows of the flowers.[30]

The year 1902 brought Takahashi new pleasures and new trials. On January 1, he and his family greeted the opening of the year in their new home in Omote-machi, next to the Canadian Embassy and across from the crown prince's residence in the upscale Aoyama district of Tokyo. It would be here and in his newly acquired second home in the seashore city of Hayama, close to the imperial villa, that Takahashi lived for the rest of his life. On a trip from the bank to Hayama during a heavy rainstorm, Takahashi, thinking of his wife and young family, including his fifth child Koreaki, born the previous year, composed the following poem:

Crying faces, swollen faces, frowning faces—
the rain in Hayama I cannot see.

Within less than a decade of entering the Bank of Japan, Takahashi's career was back on track and flourishing.[31]

The Bank of Japan as a "City Bank": Government Capital and Economic Development

Takahashi, possibly from the time of his service as an interpreter for David Murray in the early 1870s, and certainly from the time of his association with Maeda Masana in the industrial policy debate of the mid-1880s, came to believe that the most important function of the government was the encouragement of economic growth for the Japanese state and rising standards of living for its citizens. But one should not assume from this that Takahashi was a *dirigiste* who believed in a government-led command economy; rather, Takahashi felt that businessmen, not bureaucrats, should make decisions about which goods to produce and what markets to develop. To Takahashi, the government's role was to stimulate growth through monetary and fiscal policy, the creation of infrastructure, and the provision of inexpensive, low-interest, short-term capital and foreign exchange. During his two decades in the Bank of Japan and its subsidiary Yokohama Specie Bank, Takahashi strove to direct bank policy to achieve such goals.

One of the themes that runs through Japanese financial history from Matsukata in the 1880s, through Yamamoto Tatsuo between 1898 and 1904, and Katsura Tarō after the Russo-Japanese War, to Hamaguchi Osachi and Inoue Junnosuke in the 1920s and early 1930s, is that Japan's perceived economic stagnation (which overlooked the fact that Japan's economy was growing by an average of more than 3 percent annually) was caused by over-consumption. These men, in language reminiscent of Tokugawa-period Confucian sumptuary regulations, railed against excessive spending, especially for luxury goods and imports: luxury was morally bad and deflation morally good. To these men, luxury and radical political activity, which they also feared, went hand-in-hand. The way to curtail such problems was to reduce government spending, raise interest rates, and encourage frugality and saving. Yamamoto became governor of the Bank of Japan in October 1898, and raised interest rates six times over 1899 and 1900, in the face of vigorous opposition from his vice governor, Takahashi.

Takahashi represented a different breed of financial leader, one whose views were best represented by the editorial policy of the *Tōyō keizai shinpō* (East Asian Economic Review), a renowned journal that was known even in the increasingly militaristic 1930s for its support of democracy and economic growth that raised standards of living, and for its opposition to militaristic imperialism. Founded in 1895 by Machida Chūji, later a leader of the Minseitō political party, the journal criticized Yamamoto for his high interest rates. The editors of the journal argued that this policy reduced the amount of money in circulation; lowered consumer prices, share prices on the stock market, and demand; and contracted exports and increased imports, thus damaging domestic producers and increasing unemployment.[32] Takahashi was clearly on the side of the *Tōyō keizai shinpō*.

Despite opposition from his own boss, Yamamoto, whom Takahashi publicly criticized, he introduced policies to stimulate the economy. The best way to rectify Japan's trade imbalance, Takahashi wrote, was to stimulate exports, not reduce imports. This could best be done through the provision of inexpensive capital to manufacturers. Takahashi carried out a policy of turning long-term into short-term lending. He wrote, "Continuing, continuing again. To the Bank of Japan, continuing is the norm, receiving repayment for lending unusual. The bank should require repayment of all or almost all of its lending when the loan's term ends. We must reduce lending that stretches beyond the repayment period." He added, "Private banks should follow the same road. Avoid extending loans beyond the repayment date and increase the volume of capital available for short-term lending." Short-term lending not only would increase the money's efficacy, but also would make their capital more liquid so that banks could more quickly move money from unprofitable to profitable enterprises. During the decade or so that Takahashi served as vice governor, the Bank of Japan's turnover rate for lending increased from 7.9 times in 1898 to 15.7 times in 1910 and 15.4 times in 1911, almost a doubling. He also fought to contain, with moderate success, Yamamoto's high-interest-rate policy because it made the capital he wanted to provide businessmen more expensive. When Yamamoto's term ended in 1904, the government appointed Matsuo Shigeyoshi, a Finance Ministry bureau chief who agreed with Takahashi's views, to succeed him. In other words, over a decade in the Bank of Japan, Takahashi, much as he had done with the Yokohama Specie Bank, transformed it from one that carried out transactions to increase specie reserves, to one that provided inexpensive industrial capital, especially to export industries such as the producers of raw silk.

Conclusion

When Takahashi became a regular member in the Bank of Japan in 1893, he came to his position with a conviction, formed by his work in developing Japan's first patent and copyright laws, his involvement with

Maeda Masana's proposal to build Japan's economy on the basis of an alliance between the government and rural entrepreneurs, and his effort to import raw materials through a Japanese-controlled silver mine abroad, that his nation's primary goal was to make itself and its citizens richer. He also brought along a belief that while national defense was necessary, it should receive lower priority than economic growth; in fact, Takahashi felt that excessive military spending endangered, rather than enhanced, development. The decade before the Russo-Japanese War gave him the opportunity to practice what he believed, and from 1893 to 1904, he developed his economic thinking further. He went from wartime branch manager who watched as local businesses and farmers became endangered by the war effort, to using Bank of Japan capital to save banks, to having the Yokohama Specie Bank provide exporters with inexpensive foreign exchange, and then business capital, then to having the Bank of Japan do the same thing, but on a larger scale. Takahashi came out of his first decade as a banker with the key economic principles of the rest of his career as a financial statesman in place. The way to build a healthy economy was to keep interest rates low, invest government money, and encourage the investment of private money to expand production, exports, demand, and jobs—this would even allow the government, as the economy grew, to increase its tax revenues without raising tax rates. Growth, not frugality and contraction, as his rivals advocated, was the way to grow the economy and balance the budget.

EIGHT

Fundraising During
the Russo-Japanese War: 1904

A central event of Takahashi's life was his service as Japan's Financial Commissioner in London, New York, and continental Europe in 1904–7. Takahashi's subsequent career as a financial and political leader would have been much different had he not undertaken this assignment and not spent the better part of three years in Europe and North America negotiating for Japan with some of the richest and most powerful men in the world, including Lord Revelstoke (John Baring), Lord Nathaniel Rothschild and his younger brother Alfred, the Paris Rothschilds, Jacob Schiff, and Ernest Cassel.

Although Takahashi was already a rising star in the Bank of Japan and had won the attention of Japan's elder statesmen, his success in raising the money that Japan needed to defeat Russia speeded Takahashi's rise to the top of Japan's political hierarchy. Men such as Matsukata, who likely distrusted Takahashi because of his support in 1885 for Maeda Masana and his proposals for decentralized economic growth, learned that this fearless, English-speaking, middle-level bureaucrat was a man who could get things done. Within a few years of his final return to Japan in May 1907, Takahashi, with the support of Matsukata and the others, became Governor of the Bank of Japan in 1911 and Finance Minister in 1913. Takahashi's Russo-Japanese War service in the West also influenced his career in another, equally important way. It reinforced many of the lessons he was already learning about Japan's priorities. The government should focus on creating the environment for the private sector to carry out Japan's economic development. The fruits of that development should be shared by all Japanese, not just by a few government-sponsored entrepreneurs. National defense was important, but its costs should be kept within the limits of that which the economy could bear, and therefore, Japan should conduct its foreign policy within an international, especially Anglo-American, context. Without British and American capital, technology, raw materials, and moral support, Japan could not have defeated Russia in 1905.

Takahashi Goes to London

The Japanese navy attacked the trapped Russian fleet at Port Arthur in Manchuria on February 8, 1904, and declared war two days later, thus beginning the Russo-Japanese War. Even before the surprise opening sortie, the two Meiji oligarchs most concerned with financial matters, Matsukata and Inoue, and Governor of the Bank of Japan Matsuo Shigeyoshi, at the request of Hayashi Tadasu, the Japanese Minister to Great Britain, decided to dispatch a financial agent to London in order to sell Japanese treasury bonds to cover the costs of purchasing warships and other weapons from the West. The three men in Tokyo knew that Japan could not fund the war entirely from tax revenues and domestic borrowing; the Japanese government's general and special accounts budget for 1903 amounted to 360,000,000 yen, a sum that was smaller even than the first, unrealistically low estimates of total war costs.[1]

On February 12, Count Inoue appealed to Takahashi to accept the "onerous task" of traveling to London to raise funds, explaining that from the first Matsukata had thought him the best person for the job.[2] Takahashi was instructed that the war would cost about the same as the Sino-Japanese War, 450,000,000 yen, and that he would need to raise 100,000,000 yen of that amount abroad. Inoue also told Takahashi that imperial permission had been given, although it was still a government secret, to use customs duty revenues as security for the foreign loans. Little did the Tokyo leaders imagine as the war began that they would have to raise eight times that amount abroad and also dip into tobacco and liquor monopoly revenues as hypothecation before the final peace, or that the terms of the foreign borrowing would have serious political repercussions at home. Takahashi demanded one assurance from the government before accepting the overseas assignment: that he be given sole authority for all borrowing from foreign sources during the war. The next day, Inoue handed him a document that guaranteed full cooperation from Minister Hayashi and his staff in London, and promised that Takahashi would have complete power for all borrowing abroad. The document assured him that neither the government in Tokyo nor its agents, such as the Yokohama Specie Bank and the Industrial Bank of Japan, would seek or respond to loan proposals from foreign banks without his approval. On February 17, Finance Minister Sone Arasuke submitted to the cabinet a resolution to appoint Bank of Japan Vice Governor Takahashi Korekiyo as Japan's financial commissioner for fundraising on the London market. On February 22, Sone presented Takahashi with an official letter of appointment and detailed instructions about how to proceed when he reached London. Entitled "Orders concerning Selling Treasury Bonds," the directive ordered Takahashi to operate under the direction of Hayashi Tadasu, Japan's plenipotentiary to the British government.[3]

Two days later, Takahashi and his amanuensis Fukai Eigo departed for Honolulu and San Francisco, crossed the United States by train, and spent five unfruitful days in New York meeting with bankers. Takahashi later wrote that the New York bankers he met at this time saw the Japanese as "plucky children challenging a powerful giant. While they sympathized with us, they did not have capital to spare because it was wrapped up in their own industrialization. Americans had little experience in issuing foreign bonds and I saw we had few prospects in New York." When Takahashi challenged one banker to back up his pro-Japanese feelings with money, the American replied, "Sympathy and pockets are different." In early March Takahashi sailed empty-handed for England.[4]

As one can imagine, Takahashi faced formidable odds in selling Japanese war bonds in London in the spring of 1904. Were British financiers likely to be any more sanguine about Japan's prospects for victory over the behemoth to the east, Russia, than the New Yorkers were? After all, at the outbreak of the war Russia's national budget was ten times, her foreign trade three times, and her specie holdings eight times larger than Japan's.[5] Yamakawa Yūki, manager of the London branch of the Yokohama Specie Bank and Takahashi's friend from his days at that bank, had cabled Takahashi while he was still in New York, "There is no prospect whatsoever of selling government bonds here now. The Specie Bank has not a penny's worth of credit." He went on to advise Takahashi to raise the money in New York, because if he came to London he would find only "shame." By shame, Yamakawa probably meant the terms demanded by those London banking houses willing to talk about a loan to Japan, terms that the Japanese government would not consider unless absolutely necessary. For example, Baring Brothers and the Hongkong and Shanghai Bank (HSBC) had floated the possibility of a Japanese loan in February, even before Takahashi left Tokyo, but the terms were the same as those demanded in loans to the government of late-imperial China: high interest rates, low paying price, customs duty revenues as security, and a twelve-month monopoly on all Japanese government foreign loans. And Baring Brothers and HSBC soon balked even at this much. On March 7, the London office of HSBC notified the Yokohama branch that the bank would not act on the loans now because of a "continental feeling." They also wanted American participation before going forward on the loans, and New York's cooperation seemed unlikely. On March 4, Hugo Baring wrote from New York to his elder brother Lord Revelstoke that James Stillman, chairman of the National City Bank, was pro-Russian and thought Japan could not possibly win the war. On March 8, Revelstoke replied to Hugo that the bank would not take part in the Japanese loans at all for the present. According to him, "the highest people prefer neutrality just now." On March 14, in another letter to Hugo, Revelstoke wrote, "Neither you nor I are enthusiastic about the [Japanese] loan." An American presence in the loan syndicate seemed crucial, and the odds of it happening did not seem to improve with time; on April 6, Hugo cabled that Stillman, a key player in New York, was "positive in declining Japan during the war." The London market in April 1904 reflected Anglo-American investors' dim view of Japan's prospects for victory; Japan's prewar bonds fell in value by 25 percent in the first two months of the war.[6]

Takahashi had several allies, one known and the others as yet unknown to him. The known supporter was Alexander Allan Shand, Takahashi's employer in Yokohama in 1866–67 and his primary advisor when he visited London in the spring of 1898. In April 1904, Shand was serving as manager of the Lombard Street branch of Parr's Bank, and was the first non-Japanese with whom Takahashi met after his arrival in London.[7] Despite the seemingly insurmountable odds, over the next eighteen months the persistent Takahashi, by force of his own intelligence, bravado, and cunning, in combination with luck and political, social, and religious tensions of which he as yet understood nothing, and with the crucial help of Shand and the other allies, sold 800,566,000 yen (82,000,000 pounds) worth of Japanese bonds, 47 percent of the war's total cost of 1,700,000,000 yen, in London, New York, and later in French and German markets.[8]

A brief anecdote from Takahashi's journey across the Atlantic illustrates two aspects of his success in dealing with foreigners. Takahashi wrote and spoke English fearlessly. He had an open, friendly disposition, abundant (perhaps even excessive) self-confidence, and concomitantly, an un-Japanese way of engaging in conversations with strangers. On the Atlantic voyage Takahashi met and conversed with the actress Lillie Langtry about the techniques Japanese actors used when they died on stage. Takahashi recounts the conversation in his memoirs:

Although Miss Langtry and her maids kept to themselves, one day she spoke to me on deck. "When Japanese actors die on stage," she stated, "the color of their faces changes naturally. Do you know their secret? I would like to know if they use some kind of make-up to do this." I replied, "I don't really know, but now that you mention it, the Japanese actors' faces do change color gradually when they die. I don't think they use make-up, but do it by psychological control." She seemed not to believe me, and answered, "I think you are wrong. Maybe you know, but won't tell me." We then talked of other things.

Even though other passengers told him that she was in such bad financial straits that she was selling her jewels to make ends meet, Takahashi dutifully recorded her name and address in the address book he used for the next two years in London; one assumes he did not mention the Jersey Lily when he had an audience with Edward VII the next year.[9]

Takahashi's unpolished diary, written in English almost daily while he was in London and New York in 1904, reveals a man meeting ever more important bankers, financiers, and journalists, then in mid-May, finally forming a consortium to issue the first set of war bonds for his government, which by then desperately needed money to continue the war—all with Shand's crucial advice.[10] The diary reads:

April 7: "Shand called on me and had talk." *April 12:* "Called on Mr. Dun, Whalley, Shand [Dun and Whalley were Shand's superiors at Parr's Bank] as previously arranged and talked over the 'Treasury Bills' . . . Met Mr. Koch [W. M. Koch of Panmure Gordon] at the Specie Office and talked freely." *April 13:* "Mr. W. Foot Mitchell [former representative of Samuel, Samuel and Company, a major British trading firm in Yokohama, a confidant of Matsukata, and in 1905, a director of the Chartered Bank in London] called on me at the Hotel . . . Loan with hypothecation of railroads could only be advisable—to take Americans in conjunction with London market. . . . The Bankers doubted as to the [Japanese] government holding up the gold standard. . . . The people in heart think the Russians will be the final victor in the war. This scares people for Jap. bonds. Met Sir [Ewen] Cameron [Head of the London office of HSBC]. He thinks the best thing to be done to get money is to sell 4% bonds [from 1902] as suggested by Mr. Koch. Arranged to meet Lord Rothschild and his brother Alfred Rothschild with Sir Cameron and presented the letter of introduction from Sir Macdonald [British minister to Japan]. Mr. Shand came to see me afternoon on my request and we talked about the form of the treasury bill and of the means of making good feelings of Cameron and Rothschild." *April 15:* "This night stayed in the B'k go-down little after 12 and caught cold. Myself, Fukai, Kikuchi, Korekata [Takahashi's son] and servants remained." *April 18:* "Mr. Shand called on me 9½ AM as he telegraphed me last evening. Handed me their proposition as basis for consultation. All directors [of Parr's Bank] should be consulted. . . . But he thinks for business there will be no objection. Mr. Parr, Mr. Dun and the Chief Manager Whalley will be all-right and Mr. Frasier too. About H. S. Bk. [HSBC] Mr. Fraser is co-director with Sir Jackson and Mr. Shand is one of very old friend, he will be very careful to bring about all things in a satisfactory way. But proceed with utmost care not to speak of subject to anybody, but to proper and necessary persons only."

The diary continues:

April 19: "Called on Mr. Koch with my son on way to shopping. Introduced to his partners. Sir Ewen Cameron [HSBC] sent two letters, answered. Mr. Shand came to see me as previously settled." *April 20:* "Parr's Bank wanted to see me. Mr. Dun and Whalley told me they felt sure about the legal points in regard to the [British] neutrality. They will proceed and want to confer manager of the Specie Bank [Yamakawa] in regard to the question whether they will invite H. S. Bk. or not. Told Yamakawa to go to see Mr. Whalley and Shand 3 o'clock this afternoon, and spoke him to take Tatsumi with, and for the first time gave an idea of the conference. Yamakawa and Tatsumi came to see me at 4½ and they agreed to speak to Cameron and invite H.S Bk. on same footing. Called Cameron to come to see me. He came 5½, and told him that I did lay before my government his views as well as other proposals made by others. Accepted the one offered by others—the Specie Bk and Parr's. I desired them strongly to invite you [HSBC] to associate on the same footing, which they were willing and as they are going to ask you about it tomorrow, I am telling you to prepare for it. I hope this will be made a fixed channel for the Jap. Government and H.S. Bk. He took it in good feeling. I told him the point was for the Treasury bills of small amount just for trial. Yamakawa will convey those to Shand tomorrow at 10. Mr. Shand will perhaps come to see me with Mr. Bright the Solicitor on points of the legal technicalities about the Treasury Bills at 11 AM."

By mid-April, an arrangement to issue Japanese bonds was beginning to take shape, but the terms suggested were even harsher than those floated by HSBC and Baring Brothers in February, and the bonds would meet only a third of Japan's immediate financial needs: at most 3,000,000 pounds at 6 percent interest, repayment in five years, selling price of 92 pounds (that is, the Japanese government paid principal and interest as if they had received 100 pounds, buyers paid 92, and the Japanese government received 89 or 90.) The arrangement also stipulated that customs duty revenues would be held as security, and that a British tariff commissioner such as Sir Robert Hart in China would be appointed to oversee the Japanese government's collection of its own customs duties, by far the greatest insult to the proud Japanese, who were only then regaining from the Western powers the treaty right to set their own customs duties.[11]

Given his government's pressing need to pay for imported weapons, the outflow of Japan's gold reserves, which fell below 7,000,000 pounds in May 1904, and the widespread view in London that Japan would have to abandon the gold standard, Takahashi was not in a position to quibble over the terms, but he "would not hear" of the appointment of a tariff commissioner. Takahashi declared, "It is a mistake for you to think of Japan and China as similar. The Japanese government has never fallen even one cent behind in repaying interest or principal. This is true for domestic as well as foreign bonds. It upsets me greatly that you equate Japan with China." Takahashi wrote that "the bankers agreed with me and backed down, saying the pledge of security is enough."[12] He then cabled the terms to his government in Tokyo, which replied that it could not do with less than 5,000,000 pounds, which was still only half of what it urgently needed, that the principal should be repaid in seven, not five years, and at a price of 93, not 92 pounds. The London bankers agreed to these changes, and the loan negotiations moved forward. Nonetheless, as one of Takahashi's early biographers, Imamura Takeo, wrote, these were "colonial" terms: the kind imposed by Western powers on Asians. A typical loan by London bankers to North American and other European countries would bear only 4 or 5 percent interest, with repayment in 25 years, and often with no security required at all.[13]

Over the next three weeks, Takahashi conducted daily negotiations to determine the participants and to complete the details of the first set of Russo-Japanese War loans. In his diary, Shand's name appears almost daily, and names such as Parr's Bank, Hongkong and Shanghai Bank, and their officials appear regularly. So too do those of the Rothschilds, Revelstoke of Baring Brothers, and various other prominent financiers. At ten in the morning on April 22, a London banker named Henry R. Beeton visited Takahashi and suggested that he try to enlist the services of one of London's first-rate financiers as Japan's primary advisor during the war. Takahashi wrote in his diary, "In his opinion . . . if Sir Earnest Cassel (old Broad St.) is the man he would recommend, though he is not sure whether he will take into his hand or not. He says the Jews are the first-rate financier[s], and Cassel is most influential in London. He can invite Rothschild as well as Morgan and so on. Bring out big loans so as to make Anglo-American concern." In the margin of the passage above, Takahashi added, "He says if Japan is to beat her foe on land as she did on sea, better wait till then, but in the meantime must prepare for occasion by seeing Cassell." Thus, the name of Ernest Cassel, one of Takahashi's two unknown angels, enters our story for the first time. His name appears in Takahashi's diary many times over the next eight months, but Takahashi does not make an entry to report actually meeting the shadowy Cassel until eight months later, when in New York on December 16, he wrote, "Met Sir Earnest Castle at the dinner at Mrs. Schiff."[14]

At 11:30 on April 22, just after Beeton's departure, Sir Marcus Samuel, one of London's most powerful businessmen, called on Takahashi. Samuel told Takahashi that he was aggrieved because, although he had a long-standing relationship with the Japanese government, he had not been included in the current negotiations. He thought that his company and HSBC were best positioned to help Japan, and he wanted to make the two enterprises Japan's permanent foreign lending houses. Takahashi deduced that Cameron of HSBC had told Samuel of the current loan negotiations, and replied evasively, "Nothing can be decided in haste, and though I have an idea something must be decided as to the proper channel for the Government, I have not yet given full considera-tion on the matter, nor have I sufficient time to consider over the matter in full." Although Samuel was not included in any of the consortia that underwrote Japanese bonds, he became the largest single purchaser of them. But in the end, in spite of the possibility of a return greater than that from almost any other security available to these London investors, the high risk of the Japanese bonds narrowed to three the number of banks and financiers that issued Japanese bonds: Parr's Bank (Shand's bank), Hongkong and Shanghai Bank (which had had a major presence in Japan since before the Meiji Restoration), and the London branch of the Yokohama Specie Bank (a quasi-official Japanese bank). Although Lord Revelstoke, head of Baring Brothers, played a key role in the nego-tiations, his bank did not participate in the syndicate.[15]

Jacob Schiff Enters the Picture

On May 3, as Takahashi and the three banks concluded their negotia-tions to issue bonds that not only would cost the Japanese government dearly, but also would satisfy only half its financial needs, Takahashi met the last of his angels, Jacob Schiff. On that day, Takahashi made the following entry in his diary: "At dinner at Hills, many distinguished guests, among whom Mr. Shipley of New York, Green of Rothschild, Junior Levita and his father who is a director of the Chartered Bk. Cur-zon of Panmure Gordon and Co. Spyers, etc." Shipley is crossed out and Schiff inked in below. At Arthur Hill's dinner party, Takahashi met Jacob Schiff, senior partner of Kuhn, Loeb of New York, one of the richest and most powerful financiers in America; Hill introduced Schiff to Takahashi as an "unexpected guest." Schiff not only turned out to be the key to Japan's fundraising success in 1904–6, but also would become Takahashi's lifelong friend and mentor.[16]

Born into a middle-class Jewish family in Frankfurt in 1847, Schiff emigrated to New York as a teenager in 1865, and by 1904 had become one of the richest men in the world. Through hard work, his marriage in 1875 to Therese Loeb, daughter of his employer, and a discerning eye for good investments, by the turn of the century Schiff had made Kuhn, Loeb one of New York's two great investment banks. As did the other of the two, J. P. Morgan's company, Schiff and his investors helped finance the building of the American railroad system and reaped the benefits as America expanded westward. Like many other rich men at the turn of the century, Schiff became a generous philanthropist who invested millions in various causes. Although Schiff contributed extensively to Christian and secular charities, the primary focus of his largesse was Jewish organizations, especially those that assisted the new Jewish immigrants driven to America from eastern Europe by its pogroms. Schiff was committed to the idea that Jews should assimilate into American society, but without giving up their own religious beliefs and practices, and that he personally had a duty to help newer and poorer immigrants go through this process. He was also committed to using his financial leverage to reform, or if necessary to overthrow, the anti-Semitic Russian monarchy.[17]

References to Schiff in Takahashi's diary continue on May 4: "American firm is Kwun-Rose and Company. 1st rate financier in America." Then on May 6: "American business almost settled. Agreement between the American House and the issuing Bk. here have been settled on at 5 PM. Prospectus was approved by the Americans." May 7: "Cameron when he came said Sir Ernest Casttle said if only English he will not take a penny but as Americans came in he will take 50,000. . . . Schiff [written in Japanese syllabary] after audience to the King yesterday going to spent the Saturday End at Casttle's with family." May 9: "Mr. Shand came with Mr. Schiff. He was the person with whom I dined with Mr. Hills. He said last Monday 2nd was Bk Holiday and not in the City. On Tuesday, he met Lord Revelstoke and told him that he sent telegram to his American houses that now is the time to open business with Japan. Customs security and 8 per cent treasury bond will go very well. What do you [Revelstoke] think. Revelstoke looking at him, told him the loan on something same basis has just been concluded. Want you [Schiff] take half of 10,000,000. Cameron (HSBC) was called in talked over. . . . On Thursday everything was settled. When Schiff saw the King in Audience, he was told the King was satisfied to the American participation. That show Anglo-American combination in the Far East. The King was glad that his country alone was not to supply money to Japan. These were all confidential. Schiff asked me to call on him [in New York] on way to Japan."

And finally on May 10: "Mr. Schiff came with Mr. Otto H. Kahn and Shand. They brought telegrams of full prospectus. . . . Agreement was duly drawn and signed and exchanged at the date of the 7th inst. Applications for allotment etc coming from everywhere. Mr. Kahn says the King was very much pleased to see the Americans coming in."[18] Amazingly, within a week of meeting Takahashi at Arthur Hill's dinner party, Schiff had agreed to help the Japanese raise their needed 10,000,000 pounds by underwriting 5,000,000 pounds of Japanese bonds, an amount equal to that of all three issuers in London, through Kuhn, Loeb in New York; he had arranged for a contract to be drawn up and signed and a prospectus to be written in New York and cabled to London. And Edward VII gave his approval. How and why did this happen so quickly?

Takahashi produced two other accounts of his meeting with Schiff, both more coherent in their exposition since they were written after the fact. One appears in Takahashi's memoirs; the other, ghostwritten by Fukai Eigo, and then revised by Takahashi, appears in volume 1 of the official biography of Schiff, drafted by his close associate Cyrus Adler and published in 1929. Takahashi attended a dinner party at Hill's, where, as Takahashi reports, he:

happened to sit by the side of Mr. Schiff. Over dinner, he asked me detailed questions about the Japanese economy, the conditions of our production, and the people's morale during the war. I answered as well as I could. Near the end, I told him about my satisfaction over the agreement with the London bankers to issue five million pounds of bonds, but that the Japanese government wanted to issue ten million. The London bankers at this time thought that more than five million was out of the question, and I had reluctantly agreed. We talked of other things and parted.[19]

The next day Shand came to see Takahashi and told him that "Schiff of Kuhn, Loeb, which was the Parr's Bank agent in New York, wants to issue five million pounds of Japan's bonds in New York." Takahashi was "dumbfounded" because he had never heard of Schiff or Kuhn, Loeb before Hill's party. Takahashi had no idea to what he should attribute his fortuitous meeting; he concluded after his talk with Schiff at Hill's dinner that Japan's "good fortune occurred because of an accidental meeting."[20] But the meeting was far less accidental than Takahashi imagined.

It is widely accepted that Schiff supported Japan in 1904–6 because of his hatred of the Romanov dynasty and its anti-Semitism.[21] The skeptic, who may think that people act out of personal self-interest and not for idealistic reasons, may question such a "truism," but the evidence I have found supports the view that Schiff lent money to the Japanese primarily out of his desire to help his co-religionists in Russia; although he took a considerable financial risk in 1904, he ended up making money. From the 1890s until the Russian Revolution in 1917, Schiff was a leader in the movement to end the persecution and suffering of Jews in the Russian empire. He compared the plight of Russian Jews to that of their ancestors in Egypt, and according to Naomi Cohen, his most recent biographer, "doubtless saw himself as another Moses." Cohen quotes Schiff as writing in 1907, "I am so grateful to God that He so placed me to be able to be of some help to our co-religionists" in Russia. She then adds that his "struggle for Jewish liberation in Russia took on the emotional overtones of a personal crusade, almost as if the czar were hounding him, Jacob Schiff."[22] For more than 20 years, Schiff poured millions of dollars and hours of his time into lobbying officials such as Presidents Roosevelt and Taft and their successive secretaries of state into battling the public views of successive pro-Romanov journalists and American ministers to St. Petersburg, and into using his power in the world of money to prevent investment in Russia by New York and London banks and financiers.

In the first week of February 1904, just before embarking on one of his frequent trips to Europe, Schiff held a meeting of important New York Jewish leaders at his home. He told them, "Within 72 hours war will break out between Japan and Russia. The question has been presented to me of undertaking a loan for Japan. I would like to get your views as to what effect my undertaking of this would have upon the Jewish people in Russia."[23] In other words, a month before Takahashi arrived in Great Britain, and three months before Schiff and Takahashi met at Hill's, Schiff was already considering a loan to Japan, and considering it although almost every other financier in New York thought the inevitability of Japan's defeat made the risks of such a loan too great.

Waiting for Schiff in Europe was his close friend and frequent traveling companion, the elusive Ernest Cassel. While Cassel did not actually underwrite Japanese war bonds and although he never came out of the shadows into the forefront of our story, he appears to have played an important role in bringing the key players together to form a loan syndicate. Cassel, like Schiff, was born in Germany, in Cologne in 1852, and also emigrated as a teenager, in his case to London. He met Schiff in 1879 as a result of their mutual interest in investing in North American railroads. Over the next 40 years the men made many investments together (including in Pittsburgh's Westinghouse Electric Company); Kuhn, Loeb handled Cassel's financial affairs in America; and the two men exchanged more than 1,500 letters (in German) on finance, family, and politics. Cassel especially endeared himself to Schiff by saving his daughter Frieda from a mountain-climbing accident in Switzerland in 1890. In addition to being one of the richest financiers in London and, along with Lord Rothschild and Lord Revelstoke, one of three key advisors to the Treasury and the Bank of England, Cassel served as primary financial advisor to Queen Victoria's son, both when he served as Prince of Wales and when he reigned as King Edward VII—thus his sobriquet, "Windsor Cassel."[24]

Schiff arrived in London in 1904 in the aftermath of the 1903 pogrom at Kishinev, outraged over both the complicity of the Russian government and its repeated denials that there had been any atrocities. He arrived, however, not directly from New York, but from Germany, where he had gone after the February meeting with Jewish leaders. On his way back to New York via London, he met his friend Cassel in Frankfurt. Although there is no evidence that the two spoke of loans to Japan at the time, given Schiff's prior interest in the possibility of a loan and Cassel's intimacy with Schiff and his own anger over the Russian pogroms, it seems likely they did. Moreover, before meeting Schiff in Germany, Cassel had been in contact with an important mutual business associate, Lord Revelstoke. Revelstoke and Baring Brothers wanted to help the Japanese government—they had floated a loan proposal even before Takahashi left Tokyo—but had stepped back and refrained from active participation for two reasons: they had extensive investments in Russia that they did not want to endanger, and they and their government did not want Britain to side with Japan unless New York money came in. Given Stillman's and National City Bank's opposition to loans to Japan, and the silence of the Morgans and other Protestant New York financial houses, Schiff's interest seemed god-sent.

Thus, Cassel and Revelstoke became the go-betweens in bringing British and American capital together to support Japan.[25]

While much of the background to this story is shadowy, there are fascinating bits of evidence that seem to indicate that Schiff's meeting with Takahashi was not accidental, but was arranged, probably by Cassel and Revelstoke, and these conjunctions explain why the loan arrangements progressed so rapidly. The Baring journals indicate that on Tuesday, May 3, the very day on which Schiff and Takahashi met at Hill's in the evening, Revelstoke wrote a letter to one of his associates in which he stated that a loan to Japan of 10,000,000 pounds had been arranged, half to be handled by Parr's Bank and the Hongkong and Shanghai Bank in London, the other half through Kuhn, Loeb in New York. In other words, Schiff and the banks had completed an agreement to issue the bonds *before* Schiff and Takahashi met that evening. The next day, May 4, Schiff wrote from Claridge's Hotel to tell Revelstoke that "things were falling into place in New York." He also said that he had met Takahashi the night before at Hill's, and that Sir Ewen Cameron, manager of the London office of HSBC, was also there. And again on May 4, a note to Revelstoke was received from the foreign secretary, Marquess Lansdowne, to say that he had informed the prime minister of the "admirable arrangements," and that the latter wanted Revelstoke to brief him. Then on May 5, a meeting took place among Cameron, Schiff, and Revelstoke to secure the final terms of the loan. And finally on May 8, Whalley of Parr's Bank wrote that Schiff, Revelstoke, Cameron, and "the Japanese gentleman" were coming to see him.[26] This was Takahashi's first meeting with Schiff since the dinner party five days earlier. The details of the loan had been completed without the two key players meeting again, and with one entirely outside the loop.

This evidence seems to indicate the following: Schiff wanted to lend money to the Japanese because of his hatred of Russian anti-Semitism. Through Cassel and Revelstoke he learned of the London plans to issue Japanese bonds, which failed to provide the Japanese with all the funds they needed. Schiff agreed to provide the other half of the money, and did so even before he met Takahashi. Cassel and Revelstoke arranged for Schiff and Takahashi to meet at Hill's dinner party to bring the Japanese government into the picture. In fact, given that Hill called Schiff an "unexpected guest," it is likely he agreed to attend only after he heard Takahashi would be at dinner. While Cassel's role is nebulous, the Japanese government recognized its importance. The government presented imperial decorations for services to Japan to Revelstoke, Schiff, Sir Thomas Jackson, chairman of HSBC, Cecil Parr of Parr's Bank, A. M. Townsend of HSBC, and Cassel. Shand, who did the leg-work in bringing everyone together, received nothing.[27]

Revelstoke and Cassel had an additional motive for supporting Japan: the desire to bring about closer cooperation between London and New York finance. Cassel, who as we have seen would not buy Japanese bonds in May 1904 unless the Americans came in, explained it as fol-lows in a letter to Takahashi in the summer of 1905:

I was not in London at the time of the first issuance of Japanese bonds. I tele-graphed Baring Brothers and bought 50,000 pounds worth. There was a rea-son for this. I wanted to bring the British and American people closer together. I saw that the Americans [Schiff?] burned with true sympathy for Japan early in the war. I helped bring about the issuance of Japanese bonds in the two countries to unify their sympathy for Japan and to create intimacy between the United States and Great Britain, which had been previously estranged.[28]

It was the efforts to achieve this goal that impelled both Edward VII, who after all was related to the Russian dynasty, and Lord Lansdowne to praise Cassel, Schiff, and the others for their "admirable arrangement."

The first Russo-Japanese War loans were issued on May 11, 1904, one-half of the sum by Parr's Bank, HSBC, and the Yokohama Specie Bank in London, and the other half by Kuhn, Loeb in New York. The Japanese government, desperately in need of money to meet wartime expenses, agreed to terms it would have refused three months earlier: throughout April and early May, Bank of Japan Governor Matsuo re-peatedly cabled Takahashi from Tokyo instructing him to conclude the loan negotiations as quickly as possible in order to replenish Japan's rapidly diminishing specie holdings. Because the lenders considered the loans to be risky, they issued 10,000,000 pounds of bonds at 6 percent, a selling price of 93½ pounds, and issuing fees of 3½ percent, so that the Japanese government received 9,000,000 pounds but paid back 10,000,000, for seven years, with customs duty revenues as hypotheca-tion. Because the Japanese government feared being forced to abandon the gold standard and thereby lose all access to foreign funds, it had no choice but to accept these terms.[29]

Schiff's investment turned out to be a sound one. Several days before the bonds went on the market, the Japanese army defeated the Russians at the Battle of the Yalu River and advanced from Korea into Manchuria. When the bonds went on the market in London and New York on May 11, investors stood in queues two or three blocks long to place their orders, and the issuing banks closed by mid-afternoon. Demand reached 26 times the supply of bonds in London, 5 times in New York.[30] One should not presume that this reflected sympathy over pockets; rather, the chance to buy reasonably low-risk, 6 percent bonds at 93½ came to market rarely. As the *Wall Street Journal* reported on May 9, 1904, two days before the bonds went on sale, "The Japanese bond issue is likely to be surprisingly popular here. . . . A number of institutions in New York regard it as an excellent investment."[31] In other words, Schiff ended with the best of both worlds. On the one hand, as he confided to Takahashi, he underwrote and bought Japanese bonds for reasons other than making money:

I am not buying Japanese war bonds simply for profit. I do so because Japan is at war with Russia. Thus, my loans are indispensable money [for Japan]. We are Jews. We have many Jewish brethren in Russia. But the Russians torment our brethren. The Russian czars have a history of persecuting Jews. Saying "stop torturing Jews," we sometimes lend money to the Russians. But after they have taken our money, they start the persecution again. Jews are disgusted with the czars. We pray for the fall of the Russian monarchy. Now Japan has gone to war with Russia. If Japan wins the war, a revolution will surely break out in Russia. Thus, the monarchy will be buried. Because I pray for this, I am lending money to Japan.[32]

And Schiff and his clients, of course, also made money.[33]

The events in London in the spring of 1904 played an important part in Takahashi's education. To begin with, Takahashi grasped more quickly than most in Japan that New York, because of America's rising industrial power, would in the future surpass London as the world's financial capital. From 1904, the Japanese began to look to New York as an important source of foreign funds.[34] Takahashi also became increasingly aware from this time that Japan would be wise to ally itself with Great Britain and America, the two richest nations (in Britain's case, empire) in the world in the early twentieth century. Takahashi's Russo-Japanese War experience proved to him that the Anglo-Americans had a greater capacity to provide Japan with markets, raw materials, technology, and capital than any other set of nations in the world. It became a leitmotif of Takahashi's letters, speeches, and articles from 1904 until the end of his life that Japan's foreign, defense, imperial, and fiscal policies should fit into the Anglo-American framework.

One anecdote from 1904 especially illustrates this idea. Takahashi wrote in his memoirs that Schiff left for New York before the bonds were issued, but was in daily communication with Revelstoke in London. On one occasion, Schiff cabled Revelstoke to ask him what the lenders would do if they had to collect their security, that is, the Japanese customs revenues, and had no tariff commissioner in Yokohama to oversee the process. Revelstoke answered in one word, "Warships!" and Schiff immediately agreed that no commissioner was necessary. The Japanese navy in 1904–5 depended on Britain to supply it with capital ships: if the lenders cut off the flow of warships, Japan's capacity to wage war would be seriously reduced.[35] Without British and American technology, raw materials (petroleum from Marcus Samuel's Shell Oil, for example), and capital, Japan would not have won the Russo-Japanese War.

Finally, Takahashi, because of his direct experience with Shand, Revelstoke, Cassel, and Schiff, recognized the growing Anglo-American rapprochement of the early twentieth century—from this point on, and especially from the end of World War I, Britain and America acted in financial and diplomatic harmony more often than not. To a pragmatist such as Takahashi, it made sense to ally oneself with the winning team.

The Second Russo-Japanese War Loans, November 1904

Takahashi, thinking he had completed the task for which he had been sent abroad, expected to return home in the spring of 1904, but Tokyo asked him to remain in London until the summer so he could oversee the transfer of the loan funds from the British issuing houses to Japan's account at the Bank of England. Takahashi believed from this time forward that Japan would succeed in raising money abroad only if its leaders followed the generally accepted Anglo-American standards of judicious financial probity. One can imagine how pleased he must have been to read later in the London *Standard* of March 23, 1905, that the Japanese government was as "highly civilized in matters pertaining to finance as those concerning military affairs."[36] Takahashi also realized that the best way to assure that Japanese officials understood these standards was for its bankers and financial leaders to join an international network of like-minded men. He worked hard at establishing and maintaining contacts in London, New York, and Europe, and when he returned to Japan he began to send young officials abroad to nurture and expand his network and to learn about the importance of personal contacts in maintaining Japan's credit in London and New York.[37]

A list of the men and women he met, helped, or corresponded with over the next few months in London shows Takahashi hard at work building his network of international financiers: On May 13 Takahashi met Otto Kahn of Kuhn, Loeb, and Koch and Levita of Panmure Gordon (both close to the Rothschilds); on May 15, Shand and Cameron (HSBC). On May 18, he received a cable from Schiff in New York. On May 19, he received another cable from Schiff, sent Lady Cameron a roll of Japanese silk, and met Shand and Whalley (Parr's). On May 24, he conferred with Levita and Shand. Levita proposed that Japan purchase two warships from Chile, which were originally to be sold to Russia. On May 25, Takahashi took lunch at Parr's country home with Mrs. Parr and "other ladies." From May 30 to June 6, Takahashi, with the permission of Tokyo, traveled to Inverness, Glasgow, and Edinburgh, where he visited the famed railroad bridge over the Firth of Forth. On June 13, he dined with Mr. and Mrs. Carl Meyer (Cassel associate, former chief clerk for the Rothschilds, and member of the HSBC board), Sir Marcus and Lady Samuel, Mr. and Mrs. Mitchell (Samuel, Samuel), and Mr. and Mrs. Hill (at whose home Takahashi had met Schiff for the first time).

The networking and Takahashi's education in financial reality continued seven days a week. On Sunday, June 19, Takahashi met Koch and Levita of Panmure Gordon, and broached the idea of a second Japanese tranche. They told him that Japan could not sell bonds at this time unless the "issuing price [was] a great deal below the [current] price quoted for the existing bonds." Japan "must sell and buy according to the circumstances of the market." Moreover, Japan must wait to issue its bonds in London until after the Russians sold theirs in Berlin—this would "give more spirit to the people here." The next day, Takahashi met Frasier of HSBC, who reiterated this. He told Takahashi that Japan must postpone its next issue until the end of October, or until after Japan had collected all the funds from its May loans, and that the Japanese should not think a military victory at Port Arthur or elsewhere would improve market conditions for their bonds. Takahashi noted in his diary, "Japan must act with dignity in finance matter[s] as she does in war and politics. Try French market when the war was over and because the French will get sick of the Russian bonds. *Japan must give profit and then the people will follow* [italics added]. From this point of view, the new loan was a splendid success."

On Saturday, June 25, Takahashi had tea at Mr. Oppenheimer's with Otto Kahn and his wife. After tea, everyone went to the Burlington Fine Arts exhibit where Takahashi spent almost three hours looking at medieval and Renaissance Italian paintings. On the following Monday, Takahashi lunched with Koch and Kahn. The two spoke of a loan Cassel and they proposed to underwrite for the Brazilian government. Kahn said that the issuers would receive 3½ percent of the price—2½ percent for underwriting and 1 percent for issuing. Takahashi, who had received similar terms in May, learned a hard lesson about Japan's place in the world's financial pecking order.[38]

As Takahashi made his seemingly endless rounds of luncheons, teas, art shows, and trips to the country with financiers and their wives, he never lost sight of his primary short-term goal: finding the most propitious time and best terms for floating another set of Japanese bonds to pay for the escalating costs of defeating Russia. Whereas his allies such as Shand, Schiff, Revelstoke, Cassel, and Kahn were prepared to help Japan as before, they were also prudent investors who would not undertake investing in Japan for themselves or their clients until they had assurance that the market could absorb the new bonds profitably. At this point, Takahashi showed that he had the savvy and the nerve to try to manipulate the financiers and the markets in his favor. First, on June 30, he arranged for Cameron of HSBC, Dun, Whalley, Fraser, and Shand of Parr's, and Koch of Panmure Gordon to receive decorations from the Japanese finance ministry. Cameron also received a photograph of the Meiji Emperor and three gold sake cups. These were the first of several sets of government and imperial decorations awarded to Japan's primary wartime helpers in the London and New York financial worlds. Second, Takahashi demonstrated for the first time a skill he would display several more times before he left London: an ability to provide "spin" to London newspaper reporters. On Friday, July 1, he wrote in his diary that Arthur Kiddy of the London *Standard* "came to see me according to the previous arrangement." He "wished to know whether the Jap. government wants to bring out another loan in a few months time." Although Takahashi knew that the government did, he replied that it did not.[39]

As the summer dragged on, Takahashi continued to make the rounds of meetings with financiers and of social occasions with them and their wives. He took trips to the country both with other members of the London Japanese community and to visit his various City acquaintances. On August 3, Takahashi received a cable from Tokyo again raising the question of a new issue of 10,000,000 pounds of treasury bills. On August 12, a reporter from *Bankers Magazine* visited to ask for a photograph and short biography of Takahashi to publish in the journal. On Monday, August 15, Levita came to see him and reported that the Rothschilds were elated over Japan's victories at Port Arthur and Vladivostok, but were surprised that in their wake the price of Japanese bonds had risen so little. London investors, Lord Rothschild thought, feared Russia would not make peace without victory, and that accordingly Japan would soon have to issue more bonds to pay for its ongoing war expenses.[40]

Finally, in September, negotiations for a second Japanese loan began in earnest. Takahashi reported in his diary that on Thursday, September 8, Levita came to see him again: "Levita . . . thinks Japanese loan if wanted should be placed before the iron gets cool. When the prospect of war begins to seem very dull, the people will not take interest as they do now. Require security. Interest no less than the previous six percent." On Saturday, Cameron of HSBC came to say that Japan's credit had not improved with the investing public because they could not yet foresee a successful outcome of the war for Japan. In order to get good terms for another loan, Japan needed a significant victory, for example, at Mukden. Two days later Cameron visited once more and said the same thing. Then on Tuesday, September 13, Levita returned and suggested a 6 percent loan with security. He said that the king had heard that the czar intended to continue the war with Japan "as long as he has left a ruble and a man." On September 15, Cameron reported to Takahashi that Shand and Whalley of Parr's wanted Takahashi's permission to contact Kuhn, Loeb about a new loan. Needless to say, he consented. Later in the day, Levita visited to report that the price of Japanese bonds had risen a bit that day. He blamed the downturn on Russian efforts to depress Japanese bonds. Levita also reported that for the first time the Rothschilds had expressed an interest in underwriting Japanese bonds. But in spite of Takahashi's blooming friendship with Alfred Rothschild and Levita's influence with Lord Rothschild, the Rothschilds equivocated again. Levita reported a week later that they would not issue Japanese bonds at that time.[41]

Not surprisingly, given this flurry of discussion, the question of Japanese loans reappears in Parr's documents. On September 17, Whalley, Parr's general manager, wrote Kuhn, Loeb in New York with a proposition, which I paraphrase as follows: Although the Japanese government has not approached us [officially?] Japan's special financial commissioner [Takahashi] has stayed in London. Parr's thinks the time has come to prepare in case Takahashi asks to arrange a second loan. Thus, Whalley and his colleagues want to exchange ideas with Schiff. They propose more or less the same terms as the first loan. Whalley then adds that he has not conferred with Revelstoke and Baring Brothers yet, and concludes by stating that "Durham" will be the cable cipher for the Japanese government, and "Surrey" for the British banks in the loan syndicate.

A few days later, Schiff replied that strong hypothecation would be necessary for this loan, explaining that using customs duties as security will not satisfy the American public. Japan may have to use railroads (which were privately owned at the time) as well. Baring Brothers should also be brought into the picture. Kuhn, Loeb will inform them from New York, but Parr's must show Revelstoke and his colleagues the relevant documents. The price of the issue will depend on the New York market, which is depressed, and on the state of the war. The code is acceptable.[42] Japan's ally in New York drove a harder bargain than Japan's friends at Parr's Bank.

Takahashi reported in his diary that Shand and Whalley, after receiving word from New York, visited him on Monday, September 28, to report that it would be hopeless to bring out a loan without security. Japanese public opinion and even some government officials in Tokyo, buoyed by military victories, expected to offer no hypothecation at all, but Takahashi, who talked daily to hard-nosed London and New York "pockets," realized that in a new loan issue, Japan might have to offer even greater security than it had in May.

A new factor entered the picture the next day, one that did not help this time, but that would give Takahashi leverage vis-à-vis New York and London in loan negotiations in 1905. A Berlin sugar merchant named Ludwig Burchard, who did business with Japan, came to tell Takahashi that smaller German financiers, especially those who supported the liberal party, were sympathetic to Japan and wanted to invest in Japanese bonds. Takahashi replied that because of the situation in London, it was diplomatically impossible to issue bonds in Germany at this time. But Takahashi, thinking ahead, gave Burchard English and French translations of Japan's financial reports, and cabled Matsuo in Tokyo about the meeting. The same day, Hill explained to Takahashi that Kuhn, Loeb wanted railroad revenue as security if new bonds were issued in New York. On October 1, as these desultory and disadvantageous talks continued, Takahashi received a telegram from Tokyo informing him that the Japanese government's shortages of funds were even greater than he had been told: Tokyo needed to raise 20,000,000, not 10,000,000 pounds. The following day, Takahashi reported this to Shand, along with the Japanese government's reluctant willingness to provide security, as long as railroad revenues were not involved. Shand replied that he did not think the London market could handle a sum this large. On October 4, Cameron met with Takahashi, who reported to the HSBC officer that the Japanese government had agreed to "give security" (customs duty revenues), but would "require better terms and £20,000,000 to be raised in conjunction with America." Cameron agreed that using railroad revenues as hypothecation, which some Americans wanted, "must be put off." But Cameron added that the final terms of the bonds depended on Kuhn, Loeb's response from New York.[43]

On October 6 and 7, negotiations grew even bleaker, according to Takahashi's daily diary accounts of the protracted discussions with Cameron, Whalley, Shand, and Levita. Not only did the British bankers reintroduce railroad profits as security, but they also wanted this condition clearly presented in the prospectus accompanying the bond issue. Furthermore, they told Takahashi that the New York and London markets could not absorb even 15,000,000 pounds. But on October 11, Cameron, Whalley, and Shand, on the basis of discussions with Revelstoke, proposed what a month later would become the final version (with the exception of price) of the Second Japanese Loans: 12,000,000 pounds at 6 percent with customs duties as security. Yet on the following day, affairs soured once again, as Takahashi reports: "Mr. Shand came in . . . with telegram to be sent to Kuhn Loeb. He met Revelstoke and astonished to find him changed. He fears Kuhn Loeb will require other security. . . . A little anxiety about American attitude." October 15: "Mr. Shand brought telegram and says Barings are quite in agreement with views so he thinks Kuhn Loeb will agree." And finally on October 17, Kuhn, Loeb agreed to the conditions laid out by HSBC, Parr's, and Baring Brothers; they were even more "colonial" than the ones Japan accepted in the first loan issue, but at least Takahashi would not have to accept railroad profits as hypothecation, which would have shocked a Japanese public swept up in a nationalistic fervor by its military's battlefield victories over the Russians. On October 17, Schiff cabled Parr's Bank as follows: "While we wish to make negotiations on satisfactory reasonable terms, our main desire is to again aid in sustaining Japanese government which will be the surest way to bring this appalling war to early termination—Please say this on my behalf to the special commissioner."[44]

Yet the following day, a new bombshell exploded, which Takahashi absorbed into his expanding financial education. The incident was recounted in both Takahashi's diary and in the Baring Journals. Although Western financial houses emphasized prudence over sentiment in investing their money in risky ventures, they also turned out to have rivalries and enmities that affected their decisions. Takahashi reported on Tuesday, October 18, that he was pleased with Kuhn, Loeb's answer, "but there was something that can not be understood well." Speyer Brothers, a New York competitor of Kuhn, Loeb, wanted part of the action. While the London banks seemed willing to let the Speyers in, they decided to ask Schiff before making a decision. On October 17, Revelstoke cabled New York that Speyer Brothers had approached HSBC "demanding ground floor participation. They threaten outbidding our group for the whole amount, inspiration is from New York. Hong Kong Bank enquires your wishes." Schiff's answer came swiftly, the very next day: "Speyer and Co's highwaymen's methods don't surprise us."[45] The cable then advised Revelstoke to contact Cassel for advice. Takahashi faced yet another dilemma: should he negotiate with the Speyers and endanger his relationship with Kuhn, Loeb, or should he stick with the syndicate from the first set of war bonds?

While Takahashi had to deal with the caution of his Wall Street and City backers and their clients, his bosses in Japan had to contend with another problem: Japanese public opinion. As negotiations advanced, it became clear that the price of the second set of Japanese war bonds would be less generous to Japan than even the 90 pounds it had received in May—87½ was what Schiff, Parr's, and HSBC offered in mid-October. The government in Tokyo contacted their diplomatic agent in London, Minister Hayashi, and asked him to use his influence to persuade the British government to pressure the bankers into accepting better terms. Takahashi reported on October 19, "telegram from Japan to Minister Hayashi asking him to make British government's influence on loan. The [Japanese] public will not satisfy at 87½ after such continued victories."

Moreover, Tokyo's fears had consequences in finance, as well as in sentiment, as Takahashi recorded in his diary on October 22: the Japanese government, desperately in need of funds, decided to float a domestic bond issue for 80,000,000 yen (equivalent to 8,000,000 pounds). Since the foreign and domestic issues could not go on offer simultaneously without affecting both markets, the government in Tokyo contacted Takahashi about postponing the London/New York issue. Takahashi contacted his London bankers, who met and told him that the market "will be just as good as now after three weeks. But if political or economical unforeseen events occur, the risk of the delay will be on the part of [your] government. [The London bankers] wired Schiff, which answer they will have on Monday." The Baring Archive also documents Takahashi's request for a postponement in issuing the bonds, and Schiff's answer, "that delay would not be prejudicial in New York."[46]

The Japanese government, still desperately in need of funds, accepted the offer on October 26 to issue 12,000,000 pounds of bonds at 87½, two and a half points less than the loans of six months earlier. But the negotiations were not yet complete. On November 1, Kuhn, Loeb cabled from New York that it could not give more than 86½, terms even worse than those of October 26. Takahashi informed his government of this, and on November 2, he received a cable from Japan that the government accepted Schiff's offer as a "last resort." On November 3, Takahashi wrote to Baring Brothers and Revelstoke to inform him that the Japanese government accepted the second loan offer under these conditions. On November 12, 12,000,000 pounds of 6 percent Japanese government bonds, secured by customs revenue receipts and to be repaid in seven years, with Japan to receive 86½ pounds for every 100 it must repay, went on sale.[47] A small, upstart nation that had undertaken a war with a larger and richer power had few favorable financial options, and at the time, it had no alternatives to the hard loan conditions offered by London and New York bankers.

NINE

Fundraising During
the Russo-Japanese War: 1905

Takahashi Goes Home Briefly

On November 11, Takahashi telegraphed Tokyo from London to ask "for return," which was accepted, and on December 8, en route to Japan, he arrived in New York. At the dock, Takahashi received a message from Jacob and Therese Schiff inviting him to dinner and the opera on December 14. Schiff sent apologies for not meeting him at the ship—the New York financier was traveling with Cassel, who was in the United States at the time—but he did send his son Mortimer and his partner Otto Kahn to meet Takahashi at his hotel, the Waldorf-Astoria. As soon as he returned to town, on Saturday, December 10, Schiff himself came to the hotel to call.[1]

Takahashi's lessons continued in New York about the realities of international finance, of pockets and sympathy, and of the role that prejudice could play in financial decision making. On Tuesday, December 13, Takahashi recorded in his diary that J. P. Morgan is "antagonistic to Japan. So is also [James Buchanan] Duke of the tobacco trust . . . According to Kaneko [Kentarō], Morgan, James Hill [railroad tycoon and Morgan ally], Speyer, Charles Lanier are against Japan and tried for Russia loan here." The choice was not just between pockets and sympathy; at times, antipathy also seemed to play a role. But fortunately,

Takahashi told Kaneko, "Kuhn, Loeb is strong enough to prevent any mischief that might come from Morgan."[2]

If Kuhn, Loeb's demand for 86½ was not a strong enough dose of financial reality for Takahashi, Schiff soon gave him another. Takahashi, while in New York, took charge of receiving for the Japanese government the American funds from the second loan. Since Tokyo wanted to keep the money in New York so it could be sent quickly to London to purchase British weapons, Takahashi asked Schiff about a place to deposit the money from which it could be easily withdrawn by Japan. Schiff recommended the money be placed in a trust company rather than in a regular bank because Japan would receive better interest, probably 3 percent. When Takahashi asked Schiff whether the chosen company, Guaranty Trust, could provide equities as security for the large deposit of Japanese specie, "Schiff's eyes grew wide with surprise. He laughed and said, 'What, give security? In America, we never receive security when we entrust money to a trust bank. But if you are worried, I'll guarantee the money to satisfy the Japanese government. Of course, we'll charge half a percent interest for the trouble.'"[3] On December 16, Takahashi met Sir Ernest Cassel for the first time at a dinner party at Schiff's, and on December 18, he departed New York for San Francisco and home.

Takahashi arrived in Yokohama on January 10, 1905, and the next day began to make a series of reports to the top officials of the government on his activities in London and New York: January 10, Bank of Japan Governor Matsuo; January 12, Finance Minister Sone; January 13, Count Matsukata; January 14, Count Inoue; January 15, Prime Minister Katsura; and January 16, the emperor. Through these meetings, Takahashi convinced government officials to grant Japanese decorations to Japan's primary financial supporters in London and New York. The government agreed to award the First Class Order of the Sacred Treasure of the Japanese Empire to Revelstoke, Second Class Order to Schiff, Third Class Order to Jackson (HSBC) and Parr, and Fourth Class Order to Townsend (HSBC). On January 28, Takahashi wired Yamakawa Yūki, head of the Specie Bank office in London:

Contact Revelstoke, Jackson, Schiff, and Parr in English over my name, and tell them that on my return home I had an audience with the Emperor who instructed me to thank them for their efforts in the first two bond issues and to present them with decorations. Tell them that these are not only because of their past efforts, *but also because it signifies reliance and confidence in their ability to render any further similar services that the future may require* [italics added].

Hayashi, the Japanese minister, will present the decorations to them. I congratulate them for their efforts. The Japanese government is following the British and American markets to issue more bonds. I would like to know their views on timing and conditions for such an issue.

On February 1, Baring Brothers cabled Kuhn, Loeb about this. Kuhn, Loeb replied the next day that such a loan was feasible. Revelstoke replied to Schiff the same day about security: "preferably tobacco or saki [*sic*]."[4]

In the midst of this activity, Katsura called Takahashi to the prime minister's residence. When he arrived, much to his surprise Takahashi found all four elder statesmen—Itō, Yamagata, Matsukata, and Inoue—present. Katsura looked at Takahashi and asked, "We want to raise 200–250 million yen more right now. Do you think this is possible?" Takahashi replied, "250 million yen would be no problem. I could do it with one cable." Inoue then interposed, "We don't want this done by cable. You must go again." Itō looked at Yamagata over his shoulder and said, "Didn't Takahashi say he could get the money!" Yamagata stood, thrust both hands into his pockets, and without looking up paced the room. Then as if talking to himself, the field marshal said, "Finances can be done by telegraph, but not war." Katsura suddenly interjected, "Even if we are losing the war, could you do it?" Takahashi answered, "It depends on how we lose the war. I can't raise money while we are losing. But if we could stop the losses temporarily, I could negotiate loans. Of course, in such a situation the terms might not be very good." Takahashi, having completed what he had been summoned for, left the meeting at this point. But since Inoue had said, "You must go again," Takahashi prepared to return to London. On February 5, he cabled Yamakawa, "Although I recently returned home, I have been ordered abroad again. I shall sail from Yokohama on February 17 on the Empress of India. Please pass this information on to the issuing banks. Let Revelstoke have this information. Tell him I had planned to send a letter, but won't since I am on my way to London again." On February 11, the Baring Journals record that Takahashi sails February 17 for America.[5]

In the few weeks prior to his departure, Takahashi entered into a flurry of activity. On January 29, the 50-year-old Takahashi received an imperial appointment to the House of Peers. On February 7, the Emperor presented him with court rank. The cabinet appointed Takahashi "Special Financial Commissioner of the Imperial Japanese Government." On February 11, Takahashi visited Prime Minister Katsura and received his official orders to travel abroad to raise money. The same day, he met the American Minister to Japan, L. C. Griscom, who asked him if he planned to change his base of operations from London to New York. Takahashi replied that he did not. That evening Count Inoue held a dinner party in Takahashi's honor and composed a poem for him:

> For better or worse, we cross the high bridge [*takahashi*]—
> the cry of the wild goose.
> [*karikane*, a homonym for "to borrow money."]

The next day, Takahashi was invited to lunch by Itō Hirobumi, who presented at length his views on the current Japanese economic situation. Itō's central message was a warning that Takahashi reiterated in his communiqués from London to the prime minister, finance minister, elder statesman Inoue, and Governor Matsuo later in the year: Japan's extensive borrowing both at home and abroad during the war endangered the nation's fiscal health. If Japan could not increase production and exports and restrain spending, it would fall into the dilemma of 1881: rampant inflation. Two days later on February 14, Governor Matsuo held a farewell dinner party for Takahashi at the Mitsui Club. Prime Minister Katsura, elder statesmen Inoue and Matsukata, Foreign Minister Komura, Finance Minister Sone, the financier Baron Shibusawa Eiichi, and all of the directors of the Bank of Japan attended. Matsukata underlined Itō's fears when he told Takahashi, "If the war goes on beyond the end of the third foreign bond issue, we shall have to abandon convertibility [of paper money for gold] at home." Then Shibusawa composed a farewell poem for Takahashi:

> In a foreign country where the colors and aromas of spring are about
> to burst forth, you will break off flowers of bright yellow.
> [*yamabuki*, the yellow flowers of the wild rose, and also the color of
> Edo period gold coins, meaning by extension, money.][6]

Takahashi Returns to Europe:
The Third Russo-Japanese War Bonds

Takahashi's ship left Yokohama on February 17 and arrived in Vancouver eleven days later. By March 6, Takahashi was back in New York after less than three months' absence. News, most of it good, awaited him. To begin with, the war had taken a turn for the better. So had the New York and London markets, which was advantageous to Japan. Furthermore, new financial houses, particularly in Germany, wanted a share of the Japanese business, giving Japan increased leverage vis-à-vis its old syndicate members. Takahashi immediately went to see Schiff. Their first job was to get the Japanese money held in New York transferred to London where it was needed to pay for ships and other war materials. Takahashi took the opportunity while in New York to talk to Schiff about a third bond issue. Takahashi told Schiff that his government had asked him to raise 200,000,000 or 250,000,000 yen, but that he himself wanted 300,000,000. Schiff immediately agreed, said he would underwrite half in the United States, and would also bring his son-in-law Max Warburg's company in Hamburg and other German capital into the syndicate. On March 11, after less than a week in New York, Takahashi departed for London.[7]

With Schiff's prior approval and in the glow of Japan's victory at Mukden, Takahashi quickly completed negotiations with the London banks to issue the third set of Russo-Japanese War bonds. Moreover, the terms improved over the 1904 loans: 30,000,000 pounds (compared to 22,000,000 for the two 1904 issues combined), at 4½ percent interest rather than 6, repaid in 20 years rather than seven, with tobacco monopoly revenues as security and a price of 90 pounds. Given Japan's successive military victories, one would expect its government to receive better terms—the triumphs on the battlefield reduced the investors' risk.

There was another reason, however, for Takahashi's success: Speyer Brothers in New York and various German banking houses wanted to join the loan consortium. As Takahashi wrote in his memoirs:

At this time Speyer Brothers had gone so far as to present terms and to pressure important members of our government [in Tokyo]. While this helped keep the British and American bankers in line, participation by Speyers and German banks would most likely lead the British bankers who had supported us before to withdraw from the issue. In the end, we allocated one million pounds to Speyers and three million to the German banks, but they did not become direct issuers of bonds. Although our efforts to include German banks failed on this occasion, two German bankers visited me to ask if they could be included the next time. I informed the governor of this.

Discussions of both the Speyer Brothers' and the Germans' efforts to gain a part of the Japanese bond business also appear in the Baring Brothers archives. They report, for example, that Kuhn, Loeb wanted to issue the bonds "through former channels" without letting the Speyers in; Takahashi agreed because he was annoyed that the Speyers went directly to the Tokyo government without contacting him. Foreign Secretary Landsdowne contacted Revelstoke about his ambivalence over possible German participation.

The bonds went on sale on March 29. The banks opened their doors for business at 9:00 AM and because of the high demand, were forced to close by 2:30. Orders amounting to 100,000,000 pounds (of an available 15,000,000 pounds for sale in London) came from the continent. North American bonds sold not only in New York, but also in Boston, Philadelphia, Chicago, St. Louis, San Francisco, and Montreal. An important new phenomenon appeared in this issuance: many small investors bought bonds. In the end, 50,000 investors made offers totaling 500,000,000 dollars, over six times the 75,000,000 in bonds available; of this number, 43,000 applied for bonds of 2,000 dollars or less. Moreover, the Foreign Secretary was pleased with the outcome, especially the exclusion of the Germans. Landsdowne wrote Lord Revelstoke to say:

My Dear John

I am delighted to hear that the loan has been arranged and that we have got it without assistance from the "salt of the earth."

Yours ever,

L.[8]

Takahashi has often been described as having had a one-track approach to Japanese fiscal policy and international finance. Many scholars see him only as an advocate of "positive" finance, that is, of a fiscal policy that emphasized government spending to stimulate economic growth and other state needs, even if it required unbalanced budgets and extensive borrowing abroad. Takahashi's role in raising large sums of money abroad in 1904–7 in spite of the risks for Japan of over-borrowing and defaulting is held up as evidence of his commitment to a "loose" fiscal policy (*hōmanshugi*) even before he became Governor of the Bank of Japan in 1911 and finance minister in 1913. In this light, he has been called an economic nationalist who put the funding of building Japan's nascent empire ahead of balanced budgets and international cooperation.[9]

I disagree with this interpretation of Takahashi's views. While he indeed was a nationalist whose primary goal throughout his adult career was to grow Japan's economy and to increase the livelihoods of its citizens, Takahashi also knew that, depending on the situation, this required using fiscal policy either to expand or to slow the economy. His willingness to go both ways makes Takahashi unusual among prewar Japanese financial statesmen. He knew that Japan would prosper most by working within the framework of international trade and finance, although this did not mean that Japan must eschew legitimate economic competition with other nations. He understood the importance of prudence and transparency when dealing with large sums of other people's money. The origins of his developing economic philosophy predate 1904–5, but he was clearly influenced by his dealings with British and American financiers during the Russo-Japanese War.

Having spent more than a year in New York and London, Takahashi understood the facts of international financial life more than did most Japanese leaders of his generation. His lessons derived not only from hard negotiations with risk-averse foreign investors, but also from his general discussions with these men. Two weeks after the fall of Mukden and just three days before the third loan issue went on sale, Takahashi met with Alfred Rothschild and his elder brother, Lord (Nathaniel) Rothschild, in their office. Alfred told him that Japan, in spite of its military victories, must be moderate in its demands on Russia. While he did not tell Takahashi what Schiff would tell him a few months later, that Japan should altogether avoid demands for reparations in the peace talks, Rothschild warned, "Even if you try to make peace now, if Japan demands too much in reparations, there will be no peace." Moreover, he warned, Russia will not pay cash, so any payment must be in bonds, to be paid over 20 years. He added an important lesson for Takahashi: "If you follow my recommendation, the Rothschilds will help you all they can." In other words, playing by the rules brings rewards. Lord Rothschild then chimed in: "What Alfred says is correct. Japan must have a financial specialist among the peace negotiators. You should be a member of the peace conference team."[10]

It is apparent from reading Takahashi's correspondence with the Tokyo leaders in 1905 that he had a clearer understanding of the realities of international finance than they did, as Lord Rothschild seemed to have realized. On April 10, the price of Japanese bonds fell sharply on the London market. The reason for the drop, Reuters reported, was twofold. The Russian Baltic Fleet, on its way to join Russia's war effort, passed through Singapore, and more importantly, the government in Tokyo erred in announcing almost simultaneously forthcoming domestic bonds to be sold at better terms than the London ones. When the British and American bankers heard about the domestic bond issue, they were outraged. The financiers told Takahashi they did not believe the news. A country that issued two sets of its bonds at the same time, but with different terms, was not acting honorably. Did Tokyo not know, the bankers asked, that non-Japanese could buy bonds on the Japanese market? The men who underwrote the London and New York bonds had put their money, and their customers' money, at risk. Koch told Takahashi to instruct his government to cancel the domestic bond issue. Takahashi agreed with the Anglo-American bankers and cabled Tokyo along the lines proposed by Koch. But the Tokyo government replied that it had mounting bills at home as well as abroad and could not postpone the domestic bonds. Takahashi wired back, "Since the government cannot change the conditions that necessitate a bond issuance, issue the bonds as soon as possible so the bond issuance is completed quickly. Furthermore, publish the amounts each domestic bank has agreed to buy, and announce that the bonds have not been issued for foreign buyers. Make sure you publish this in domestic and foreign newspapers." But Takahashi knew that in the real world of international finance announcements of this sort would not prevent money from flowing to the best investment. He explained the circumstances to the British bankers and Kuhn, Loeb in New York as best he could, and they accepted his explanation.[11]

Takahashi outlined his realistic views both of Japan's position in the world of finance, and of its need for industrial development, in two bold letters he sent from London to Prime Minister Katsura and Finance Minister Sone, the first two days after the third issue of bonds, on April 1, 1905, and the second two months later, on June 6. The first letter warrants quotation at length, not only because Takahashi had brazenly written to the prime minister without even sending a copy to his superior, Governor Matsuo, but also because the letter encapsulates Takahashi's developing financial and economic views for the first time.

Takahashi opened the letter with laudatory words about the war, and a bit of self-congratulation: "The war progresses well. Our imperial army's wonderful victory at Mukden is unprecedented. Our country's greatness shakes the whole world. We should drink congratulatory sake time and again over such a thrilling result. You have probably heard from Governor Matsuo about my fulfillment of my duty to sell bonds abroad." He then addresses the purpose of the letter, conveying the importance of fiscal responsibility and economic development in the future:

Because of our victories, we have been able to raise funds abroad by providing security. . . . When the war ends, we must worry about our fiscal base in order to create trust for ourselves abroad. At that time, excitement about Japan will quiet and international markets will look at Japanese fiscal policy soberly. They will investigate matters in a more conventional manner. If we want to have a fiscal policy that does not hinder our international borrowing, we must meet the conditions of the major powers. If we do not firm up our fiscal base, we will have difficulty winning trust abroad. Our country will lose face and not gain the benefits of the renown of its victory. We will regret this for all time. All true financiers understand this, and Schiff of Kuhn, Loeb in New York said to me, "At present your country must concern itself with making interest and capital payments on secured loans. The key is not to cause your creditors to worry. Then you can restructure your bonds after the war. You should pay back government expenditures raised through taxes and loans secured by customs duties and monopoly revenues."

Takahashi then introduced industrial development as the best method for achieving fiscal responsibility, as a growing economy would increase government revenues to help it balance its budgets:

We have increased taxes during the war by 170,000,000 yen, but this is not a burden on our people. We have some margin in our finances. So even if we do not receive an indemnity from Russia right away, we can continue domestically. We must apply part of these revenues to paying interest, but most of it for investment to stimulate industrial development. . . . Not only will industrial development allow us to repay our debts, but also it will add to our future economic strength. If we encourage economic growth, we shall strengthen our industry, stimulate foreign trade, increase our revenue surplus, and make restructuring our debts easier.

Takahashi then returned to fiscal responsibility and international financial standards:

Warburg of Hamburg, who sold one million pounds of our loans in this current issue, said, "People who apply to trade stocks and bonds on the German market have a great responsibility. In the first five years of trading on the exchange, one's ability to pay interest on the securities and to make accurate reports about one's finances affects the market value of the bonds. When borrowing on a foreign market, one must study the country's laws, ways of soliciting money, and ways of repaying it. We worked for the first issuance of your country's bonds in Germany. If, in the future, you want to use the Berlin market, you must be willing to have your fiscal policies and economy investigated. We may submit written questions to you. The Berlin bankers will want to publish newspaper articles about these matters. They will investigate your country's fiscal reality closely and look to see if it has a solid foundation."

In the following section, Takahashi tied the two themes, financial reliability and economic development, together:

To summarize, after the war Japanese government bonds will circulate under the same conditions in both domestic and foreign markets. We can use this opportunity for our country's economic development. Our primary task is to build a strong fiscal structure. . . . To develop a firm basis for our finances, we must work hard to develop those industries that provide our nation's lifeblood, that is, export industries. Accordingly, I propose for your consideration four industries to develop further: silkworm egg cards, raw silk, mining, and foreign tourism to Japan.

Takahashi then proceeded to lecture the prime minister and finance minister in some detail on how best to use modern technology to improve Japan's sericulture industry, and concluded, "By encouraging industry in this way, we shall not have to worry when the time comes to redeem our wartime bonds. I hope the cabinet will follow my suggestions."

In the second letter, which reads almost as a continuation of the first, Takahashi wrote of the key to developing Japan's export industries: inexpensive capital. He proposed three ways of raising such funds. First, the use of foreign borrowing to repay domestic war loans and thereby create free low-interest capital in Japan for industrial development, especially for investment in infrastructure such as railroads. Second, the use of the Industrial Bank of Japan to sell its own bonds abroad in order to import capital for economic development. This would require the Industrial Bank to work in partnership with foreigners, which would mean that the bank would have to become more open and transparent in its methods of operating and accounting. Third, the use of the Industrial Bank to sell abroad bonds of domestic companies such as railroads. By proposing the use of foreign capital for industrial development and the reorganization of the Industrial Bank as a joint Japanese-foreign venture, Takahashi made a radical proposal; one can see why, on his return to Japan in early 1906, Takahashi would oppose the plan to nationalize the privately owned railroad system. To him, the government's job was to encourage economic development through privately owned companies, not to manage enterprises itself.[12]

The Fourth Russo-Japanese War Bonds

On April 30, Takahashi returned to New York from London to arrange for the deposit of the American money raised in the third bond issue. On Schiff's advice, Takahashi put the money, 56,000,000 dollars, in fifteen different banks in New York and Philadelphia. The largest deposit, 10,000,000 dollars, went to the National City Bank—despite Stillman's sympathy for Russia in the war, it did not interfere with his business. Tokyo almost immediately informed Takahashi that they wanted him to stay in New York to transfer the money to London to pay for war materiel purchased in Britain. Then on May 31, Takahashi received a shocking cable from Governor Matsuo: "Our navy has destroyed the Russian fleet in the Tsushima Straits and has captured three enemy commanders. Can you use our victory to raise three hundred million yen more so we can rationalize our debts?" Takahashi responded immediately that given the market conditions for Japanese bonds it would be best to wait until at least fall, and maybe even the spring of 1906, to issue bonds to rearrange Japan's indebtedness: "The Europeans and Americans overwhelmingly want peace after our victory at Tsushima. . . . They think it better for us to consolidate our debts after peace has been concluded. We have just raised three hundred million yen and it is well known that the Japanese government has large specie reserves abroad. The time to issue more bonds is after the restoration of peace or if the war begins again. We must wait until that is decided. There is no reason for a foreign loan now." On June 3, Matsuo cabled to repeat his request, stating that Japan needed the funds immediately; Takahashi, with his knowledge of European and North American financial markets, again replied that the time was not right for more bonds.[13]

In early June 1905, President Theodore Roosevelt offered to mediate between Japan and Russia, and the two antagonists warily accepted. Matsuo almost immediately sent Takahashi a long cable reiterating his message of Tokyo's dire financial straits: the government had spent heavily on the war, taxes had been raised to the breaking point, domestic lending markets were overburdened, etc. Tokyo needed 300,000,000 yen from foreign sources by September at the latest and ordered Takahashi to begin talks with the London and New York syndicate. Elder statesman Inoue Kaoru also telegraphed Takahashi in New York reiterating Matsuo's call to negotiate another loan. Two American financial houses, M. R. Morse and Speyer Brothers, had approached him about selling Japanese domestic bonds on the international market to open the way for more domestic borrowing. On the 16th, Matsuo wired again to re-emphasize the government's needs. Tokyo questioned the sincerity of Russia's desire for peace. If the war continued, the army and navy needed to be prepared. The 300,000,000 yen was necessary as soon as possible. The Governor instructed Takahashi to raise the money by re-selling domestic bonds, or by using tobacco monopoly or railroad profits as hypothecation for new loans. Takahashi was told to talk to the current syndicate. If it would not help out, the government would have no choice but to turn to Speyer Brothers.[14]

Takahashi, understanding the reluctance his New York and London friends might feel in undertaking another large Japanese loan so soon, went immediately to see Schiff. Takahashi opened the conversation with, "The government has ordered me to raise another three hundred million yen, but I personally think this is a bit much. What do you think our prospects are right now?"

Schiff showed surprise and replied, "You collected thirty million pounds by saying it would pay for the war for one year, and you have not yet collected all your money in London. Why do you want another thirty million now? Isn't the peace conference about to open?"

Takahashi, increasingly adept at dealing with foreign bankers and reporters, replied at length:

The Japanese government has no notion of continuing the war or rejecting the peace. But we must think about the future and plan with care. We have no guarantee that the peace negotiations will lead to a harmonious conclusion. Accordingly, we don't know what our expenses will be until the peace is concluded. We have a truce during the negotiations, but a truce means only that we do not hear the sound of guns. We must leave two hundred thousand soldiers in the field. Thus, we spend a large sum of money each day. If peace negotiations break down, the Western financiers who have supported us may be disappointed and we may not be successful at raising more funds. Moreover, the militarists who hold sway in Russia think Japan has fallen into a financial morass and thus may opt to continue the war. A new loan during the peace negotiations would allow us to prove the Russian propaganda about Japan's financial difficulties wrong. If peace does come and we have too much money, Japan can use the surplus to repay our domestic loans. This would help create liquidity and revive the domestic economy. Thus, I have come to ask your opinion.

Schiff answered, "You are right. Your idea is good. We should do the loans exactly as the last ones. The bankers have all gone off to their villas, which makes things difficult right now. Autumn would be better."

Schiff then cabled the Warburgs in Hamburg, and they quickly put together a syndicate of thirteen German banks willing to underwrite Japanese bonds.[15]

The possibility of a new loan looked good in New York, but Takahashi faced problems in both Tokyo and London. Public opinion in Japan, inflamed by the press, and even some officials did not see why Japan should pay collateral after its triumphant military victories, especially the defeat of the Russian Baltic Fleet at Tsushima. Inoue Kaoru wrote to Takahashi about this, who answered in two letters in early July, one written the day he returned to London on July 3, and the other written eight days later. Takahashi told Inoue that in a perfect world Japan would not have to hypothecate its foreign loans. However, if it did not hypothecate, it would have to pay a higher interest rate, probably 5 percent rather than 4½, market the bonds at a sharply discounted price, and repay them in a much shorter time than in the third issue— if the London and New York financiers would agree to underwrite the bonds at all. Better to put up tobacco monopoly revenues or some other security than to face the dishonor of rejection or terms similar to those Japan received for the 1904 loans. He further explained:

We must not forget our long-term advantage in the pursuit of temporary benefits. We have learned that even if markets allow us great short-term advantages, we cannot feel safe. Conditions can change quickly. If one does not prepare for downturns he does not expect, he will come face-to-face with severe setbacks. If we borrow money without collateral because of temporarily good market conditions, we shall certainly try in the future to borrow under less favorable market conditions and inevitably have to offer collateral. Such a situation would damage our nation's credit severely—brought about by the temporary glory of borrowing money without hypothecation. We must show extreme caution in managing our nation's fiscal affairs during wartime. We must move forward without misjudging market conditions. This is our most important task. We must not begrudge pledging collateral, but focus on our real benefits like interest rates and issuing price.[16]

At the same time as many in Tokyo thought that the national glory of Japan's victories should win better terms than before, the risk-averse London syndicate members thought otherwise. They conferred and wired Takahashi and Schiff that "the plan is impossible right now." Takahashi replied that this time underwriting could be split three ways—London, New York, and Germany—rather than two as before, and that Schiff, whose daughter Frieda had married into the Warburg family, supported his proposal. Koch, an important Takahashi ally in London with close connections to Paris, reacted negatively to German participation. When London continued to drag its heels, Schiff suggested a new approach to Takahashi: "I am sure the London bankers will underwrite the bonds as before. But if they will not, we can split the issuance between New York and Germany. Hurry to London to tell them this. I will make no objections while you are in London to make negotiations more difficult for you."[17] Takahashi followed Schiff's suggestion and for the first time played the German card in his dealings with British bankers.

Takahashi decided to return to London to meet his contacts face-to-face and cabled Yamakawa that he would depart New York on June 24 to arrive in London on July 3. But before Takahashi left New York, he had another introduction to deep Wall Street pockets. E. H. Harriman, the railroad baron who visited Japan in late 1905 to propose joint Japanese-American development of the Manchurian railroad system, held a dinner party in Takahashi's honor and invited 20 or so of New York's leading financiers. According to Takahashi, they praised Japan, saying, "The Japanese government has issued a large amount of bonds on the New York market, but has been careful not to upset financial markets here." Takahashi, bold in dealing in English with powerful foreign financiers and politicians, also had the shrewdness to understand that Harriman had not invited him to dinner out of admiration or even curiosity. Harriman, knowing that Japan's influence in Manchuria would increase with the end of the Russo-Japanese War, had already begun to think about investing in Manchuria.[18]

Shand and Yamakawa arranged to board Takahashi's ship before it reached Liverpool, and told him that his plan to issue more bonds so quickly after the last set was not a good idea. Not only were his British bankers apprehensive, but the London financial newspapers also opposed the idea. Shand told Takahashi that the press had agreed, however, not to file their stories until after they had met with him. At 8:00 AM on July 3, his first day back in London, Takahashi held a press conference in which he used the same line of argument he had used with Schiff, and added that if the British did not participate, Japan would divide the bonds between America and Germany. "Wouldn't it look odd if those two countries underwrote our bonds, but our ally did not?" Shortly after the reporters departed, the bankers arrived. Again, Takahashi used the same approach. The Japanese government felt it necessary to go ahead with a fourth bond issue. If London would not join in with New York, Japan must look elsewhere. Given the willingness of the Warburgs and their compatriots to underwrite the bonds (with the approval of Kaiser Wilhelm), Germany was the obvious place to turn. By evening an agreement had been reached to issue bonds in London, New York, and Germany; on July 6, all the parties had signed the contracts, and on July 11, only eight days after Takahashi's return to Britain, the fourth Russo-Japanese War issue went on sale: 30,000,000 pounds, one-third each in London, New York, and Germany, with 4½ percent interest for 20 years, at a price of 90 pounds with Japan receiving 86¾, and tobacco monopoly revenues as collateral.[19]

Takahashi's triumphant march through New York and London reached another high point on July 31: through the intercession of Sir Ernest Cassel, Takahashi had an audience with King Edward VII. Takahashi reported that he and Minister Hayashi were met at Buckingham Palace by a man who led them into a large, cathedral-like room with no furniture other than three chairs in the middle. When they got there, the guide invited Hayashi and Takahashi to sit in the seats on either side and then proceeded to sit between them. "For the first time, I realized that our guide was the king himself." The king shook hands with the two Japanese, who had begun their English-language studies together as children in Yokohama 40 years earlier, and then asked Takahashi, "You came to England to sell Japanese bonds. How did it work out?" Takahashi replied, "The outcome was excellent and I am greatly pleased," to which Hayashi added, "Takahashi had a great success in the bond issuance and we congratulate him." The king then said, "I am highly gratified," and asked Hayashi about the prospects for peace.

Around the same time, Takahashi had another dealing with the British royal family. Cassel informed him that Prince and Princess Arisugawa, who had represented Japan at the king's coronation, had presented the queen with a small Japanese spaniel (*chin*). But her dog was male, and she wanted a mate for it. When she heard that Cassel had befriended the Japanese financial commissioner, she asked him to contact Takahashi about finding another spaniel. Takahashi immediately cabled Governor Matsuo, who found appropriate dogs in Nagoya. The Bank of Japan dispatched someone to pick four dogs to fill the queen's request. But, of course, one could not just give any dog to a queen, particularly when she was the consort to the monarch of the world's richest and most powerful nation. So the Bank of Japan found a dog specialist who spent six months training the spaniels. Finally, early in 1906, the Japanese government shipped the dogs to England. Takahashi had already left for New York and home, but he heard that the dogs had reached Cassel and the queen.[20]

A Peace Treaty Is Negotiated: One More Set of Bonds

While Takahashi had an audience with the King of England and arranged for spaniels to be sent to his queen, the two peace negotiators, Komura Jutarō and Sergei Witte, sat day after day in Portsmouth, New Hampshire, trying to iron out peace conditions acceptable to both parties and to world opinion. The primary sticking point was over an indemnity. In virtually every imperialist war of the late nineteenth century, that is, all of those fought between post-Industrial-Revolution Western powers and militarily weaker Asian nations, the European victor received a large sum of money to cover the costs of its war effort. Japan, which became the first Asian country to receive such an indemnity, from China after the Sino-Japanese War in 1895, expected Russia to pay in 1905. But Russia, the first European country to lose an imperialist war, was not about to become the first to have to finance the victor's war effort. The Japanese government found itself in a difficult position: on the one hand it had won the war on the battlefield decisively, and its public opinion adamantly demanded reparations from Russia. On the other, Japan was at the end of its military and financial rope: 75,000 soldiers had died in Korea and Manchuria, and Japan was deeply in debt, both at home and abroad. The war party in the Russian government let it be known that they would most likely continue the war if Japan did not withdraw its demand for an indemnity.

Takahashi, influenced by the views of his financial backers in New York, London, and Germany, urged this view on the government in Tokyo: not only might the war continue if Japan did not back down, but foreign bankers would be less likely to lend Japan money in the future. As a Japanese nationalist, Takahashi resented Russia's refusal to pay an indemnity, but as a realist, he understood Japan's financial position vis-à-vis its richer enemy.

On August 29, Komura and Witte agreed to a peace treaty that ceded to Japan Russia's leasehold in Manchuria's Liaodong Peninsula and the southern half of the island of Sakhalin, but that included no indemnity. Schiff wired Takahashi from his villa in Bar Harbor: "Banzai. Your modesty has been rewarded. I am struck with admiration. Well done." Warburg cabled congratulations from Hamburg as well. Takahashi in turn wired Foreign Minister Komura in Portsmouth, "I am moved to tears by the Emperor's wise decision. Congratulations on making peace. I admire your patience and sincerity." Takahashi, in a cable to Governor Matsuo, wrote that French and German financiers had told him that there would have been no peace if Japan had continued to demand an indemnity. The war faction in the czar's court had to be pacified to bring peace. Europeans universally praised Japan for not insisting on an indemnity and thus bringing an end to the war. Japan, in rocky financial straits, decided not to gamble.

No sooner was the treaty conference completed than Tokyo cabled Takahashi with what by now must have seemed a familiar message. "The peace negotiations are completed without an indemnity. We shall need to issue two or three hundred million yen in bonds to reorganize our outstanding bonds. Please gather the views of the financiers while our popularity is high, and report to us." Takahashi replied that the time was good for new bonds. He thought he could even get 4 percent at a price of 90 without security. This would allow Japan to adjust the onerous 6 percent bonds of 1904 into a new, less costly issue. Matsuo replied that specie reserves were low and would not last two years. The problem was exacerbated by the need for rice imports because of a poor harvest. Takahashi then answered that he could raise the money, but that Tokyo needed to limit unessential expenditures to as great an extent as possible:

The government must insure that imports are limited to productive goods and capital. . . . It must open the way to find capital for productive enterprise. . . . Each minister, and especially the army and navy minister, must consider what facilities are most important to him, and whether or not the nation's wealth is adequate to support them. Tell this to all of the ministers. Each individual allocation must be decided on the basis of a unified national fiscal policy. If we act hastily beyond our national power and do not think out and plan what we do, we shall fall into the tragedy of national bankruptcy. . . .

Bankruptcy would cost Japan the trust of the New York and European bankers.[21]

Yet before Takahashi could commence negotiations for yet another Japanese bond issue abroad, he had to deal with the fallout of his country's failure to garner reparations from Russia. His problem was twofold. First, the price of Japanese bonds in London, New York, and Germany fell sharply at the beginning of September: investors believed that Japan would need to borrow money again soon to make up for the lost indemnity and would flood the market with Japanese securities. Takahashi called in his press contacts at Reuters and elsewhere to tell them that Japan had adequate funds to bring its troops home from Manchuria and to conclude the war. If it floated new foreign loans, it would only be to restructure the 1904 issues. The absence of an indemnity was therefore not a major problem for Japan. The reporters published stories about their interview with Takahashi, which stemmed the run on Japanese bonds. Second, riots broke out in Tokyo over the peace terms. Elements of the Japanese public, enraged that Japan had not received an indemnity in spite of its overwhelming military victory (and apparently unaware of its financial straits), attacked police stations and other government facilities in the capital. When London newspapers reported the unrest in their September 7 editions, Japanese bond prices again fell. Takahashi called a press conference to tell the reporters that the riots were the actions of a few malcontents and that the situation would have no effect on the ratification of the peace treaty.[22]

Even as Takahashi put out brush fires through the press, Tokyo cabled to reiterate its need for money: "In order to restructure the first two 6 percent loans of 22 million pounds and the fourth 5.6 percent domestic loan of 200 million yen, we would like to float in foreign markets a 4 percent unsecured, long-term loan at 90 or more; we want to raise 300–400 million yen." Takahashi conferred with Revelstoke, Cassel, and Schiff, and all recommended postponing a new bond issue. Revelstoke worried that Japan already had too much capital in the market. Cassel feared that speculators held too much of Japan's earlier bond issues. Until "real investors" gained control of the bonds, it was best to postpone issuing new bonds. If the Japanese government needed money immediately, it could issue 12-month, 5 percent bonds to rich investors like himself now, and turn them into long-term bonds in the spring. Takahashi cabled Tokyo that his advisors told him that selling the bonds now would be difficult. On September 9, Matsuo replied,

We cannot wait until spring. We want to move ahead now. Since yesterday, the city has been quiet. The people opposed to peace regret the riots. Everything is secure. But until peace is restored and our soldiers brought home, there will be huge expenses. To meet them through next March, we need to issue 200,000,000 yen in domestic bonds, but because of the unpopularity of the peace settlement, doing so will be difficult. Thus, we need to restore confidence by restructuring the domestic loans.

And then Matsuo gave Takahashi a new arrow for his quiver: "Sauerbach of the Paris bank Sauerbach-Tarman has approached the finance minister about underwriting bonds. If it is convenient for you to meet him, we can arrange it. If you need help with the French government, let us know." Within a week, on September 15, Takahashi left for Paris, quietly so as not to alarm his British financial supporters.[23]

The next morning Takahashi met with Koch, his French connection from London, and two French financiers, M. de Verneuil and Gunsburg. Takahashi proposed a bond issue of 50,000,000 pounds, half to convert the 6 percent bonds of 1904, half to redeem domestic bonds. The bonds would be unsecured and issued in France, Britain, and the United States. The French bankers replied that they would have no problem with 4 percent unsecured bonds, but that they could not set a price while Japanese bonds were listed on the London exchange— the British market value at the time of issuance would become the price for the new issue. On September 19, Takahashi's three French sponsors took him to meet Finance Minister Rouvier, who gave his stamp of approval: "The Japanese government has shown wisdom in signing the peace treaty. I think it is a good idea to issue bonds on the French market. . . . Negotiate with the Bank of France, which is the bank of issuance." To which Takahashi replied, "The Japanese government has long wanted to issue bonds on the French market. I am happy with your Excellency's words. Since in France, unlike Britain and other countries, the government has a major influence on financial markets, I expect great results."[24]

Takahashi once again found himself involved in a delicate international question. Could the Germans and the French participate in the same consortium? The British had come to accept both German and French participation in Japanese loans, but the French equivocated. In Takahashi's words, "Verneuil and Rouvier said not a word about the Germans. There was a strange hostility here. Each side felt that if it spoke first it would win the enmity of the other. . . . Including the Germans would hurt the feelings of the French. Excluding them would do the same to the Americans, and win the anger of the Germans." Another problem arose at the same time: whether to include the Paris Rothschilds in the French consortium. Before leaving for France, Takahashi had met with his London friends, the Rothschild brothers, and they had agreed to introduce him to their continental cousins. The Paris branch agreed to join the issuers only if the London house did. But Lord Rothschild was miffed because "during the war, the London bankers did not include us in their group and floated large issues successfully. Now the Japanese have come to us because they seem to need us." He sent such a message to Paris. Arthur Levita, a close associate of the

Rothschilds and one of Takahashi's best contacts in London, intervened, and both Rothschild houses agreed to participate. On September 28, this was confirmed by a letter from Takahashi to Lord Rothschild thanking him for taking the Japanese loan "in hand."[25] Still, the road to a final arrangement was not without its rough spots: Lord Rothschild insisted that he replace the chairman of the old standby, Parr's Bank, as the head of the group. Takahashi conferred with Revelstoke over this, and he in turn brought Rothschild around. Takahashi later heard about a gratifying incident of September 1905. When Count Witte, on his way home from Portsmouth, called on the Paris Rothschilds and asked them to front a loan to the Russian government, they turned him down.[26]

Other problems emerged in October and November 1905 to vex Takahashi before the fifth set of Japanese bonds went on the market in late November. To begin with, New York and European markets contracted and capital costs rose sharply. Second, in mid-October the czar's government tried to raise money in France and Germany, an effort that failed in the end because of the bankers' fears of the revolutionary unrest in Russia. Third, Reuters reported from Tokyo that Count Ōkuma Shigenobu, who had already been prime minister once and would be again in the future, had written that Japan was unsafely in debt. Takahashi called in his press contacts and explained that the debt burden was heavy, but neither unexpected nor unmanageable. Fourth, Takahashi found that while the French bankers had no objection to underwriting bonds to restructure Japanese domestic securities, they disliked the idea of their money being used to redeem British and American 6 percent bonds. Ultimately, Takahashi devised an ingenious solution: the financial houses would issue the bonds in two tranches. The first set, 25,000,000 pounds, would be issued in November 1905 in London, New York, Paris, and Germany, and be used to redeem domestic bonds; the second set, also 25,000,000 pounds, would be issued later in London and Paris (and was issued in March 1907, although at different terms), and go toward restructuring the 6 percent 1904 foreign bonds. The Rothschilds in Paris underwrote all of the French 12,000,000 pound allocation in the first 25,000,000, the British 6,500,000 (split among the former issuing houses and the London Rothschilds), and the Americans (Kuhn, Loeb)[27] and Germans (for the most part, split between M. M. Warburg and Company in Hamburg and the Deutsch-Asiatische Bank in Berlin) 3,250,000 each; the second 23,000,000 (not 25,000,000 as it turned out) would be divided equally between the City of London and Paris. The November 1905 bonds were issued with 4 percent interest, no security, for 25 years, at a price of 90 pounds with the Japanese receiving 88.[28] On November 28, 1905, Takahashi's fifth bond issue went on the market. The London allocation was oversubscribed by 27 times, the French by 20, the German by 10, and the American by 4. On November 30, the finance minister cabled Takahashi his congratulations. Takahashi cabled Governor Matsuo for permission to return home. On December 20, 1905, Takahashi left London and returned to Japan via New York and San Francisco.[29]

Prior to his departure on December 14, his primary London sponsors, Parr's Bank, the Hongkong and Shanghai Banking Corporation, and the Yokohama Specie Bank, held a farewell dinner for Takahashi at the Savoy Hotel. Although we do not have an account of the dinner, we have a photograph of the attendees, splendid in white tie and tails, taken just after the meal. Spread around the table are dozens of chrysanthemums and other flowers, and many bottles of wine, champagne, and Perrier in bottles shaped exactly like those of today. In attendance were many of the most prominent bankers in the City of London: Shand, Whalley, Dun, Fraser, and the other top officers of Parr's Bank; Sir Thomas Jackson, Cameron, Charles Addis, and Townsend of HSBC; Koch; Carl Meyer, Arthur Stanley M.P.; a variety of Takahashi's Japanese assistants and associates such as Yamakawa and Fukai; and the four primary guests, sitting in the central seats: the host, Cecil F. Parr, Chairman of Parr's Bank, a rather pompous looking Takahashi, and two tall, white-bearded, and very distinguished looking gentlemen, Japanese Minister Hayashi and Lord Rothschild.[30]

TEN

The Lessons of Wars,
1906–18

Takahashi returned home in January 1906 having learned important lessons from his wartime and immediate postwar experiences in Europe and the United States. First, Japan could not have defeated Russia without European and American capital. The Americans and their German in-laws alone, that is, Jacob Schiff and the Warburgs, underwrote half of Japan's wartime foreign borrowing; their role and that of the London and Paris Rothschilds after the peace, although rarely mentioned in later Japanese accounts of the war, were at least as important to Japan's victory as that of either the imperial army or navy. Second, Japan could not have won the war without British-made warships and Shell Oil's petroleum—technology and raw materials were as crucial to military victory as were soldiers' courage and their officers' skill—although Japanese memory of the war has deified Admiral Tōgō Heihachirō and General Nogi Maresuke, while ignoring the contribution of foreign technology and raw materials.[1] Third, foreign investors demanded transparency: they would not lend money to Japan or anyone else without detailed knowledge of the borrower's financial status. Fourth, borrowing beyond one's capacity to maintain interest payments and repay the principal on loans was dangerous. In fact, as Takahashi wrote and cabled from London in 1905, as the war ended, Japan needed to control military spending or risk endangering its access to foreign capital markets. Fifth, the safest place for a developing country like Japan to ensconce itself was in the Anglo-American world order, which required both fiscal rectitude and military self-control. But sixth, Takahashi also thought that Japan could pay back its indebtedness not only by savings garnered through retrenchment and restraint, but also by economic growth generated by macroeconomic fiscal stimulation.

Many writers on Takahashi, both contemporarily and historically, view him only as a spender, and not as a saver. One frequently sees his name linked with that of Hara Takashi, whose political party, the Seiyūkai, Takahashi joined in 1913, as an advocate of a positive fiscal policy. Takahashi encouraged government spending to stimulate economic growth; Hara used the "pork barrel" to solidify his party's regional base. However, this view oversimplifies Takahashi's economic philosophy. Although since 1885 Takahashi had emphasized that the government's primary role was to promote economic development by raising the people's standards of living to stimulate consumption and demand, he also understood that there were times when one must rein in expenditures, including consumption and demand. The government could not continually borrow money to spend over long periods of time without endangering Japan's fiscal health, and thus its access to international, and even domestic, credit. Takahashi returned home from London in 1906 knowing that Japan had in less than two years borrowed more than 2,000,000,000 yen, half of it abroad, an amount seven times larger than all of the central government's tax revenues in fiscal year 1905. Japan, throughout the decade between the Russo-Japanese War and World War I, was highly leveraged.[2] Takahashi understood the dangers of this, and regularly called for fiscal restraint.

The Nationalization of Japan's Railroads

Takahashi arrived in Tokyo from London and New York on January 10, in the midst of a political debate over nationalization of Japan's railroads. Although Japan's first railroad lines had been laid down by the government, from the 1880s on, during a railroad-building "frenzy," private capital took over. Entrepreneurs constructed most of the trunk lines in the nationwide rail network that came into existence in the last two decades of the nineteenth century. But by the early twentieth century, fears of foreign control of Japan's railways, and the military's desire to have unified management of what it valued as an important strategic asset, led more and more people to advocate government ownership of the railroad system. The army, as one might expect, stood in the vanguard of the nationalization movement. As one might also expect, the army did not worry about finance, even though the government could not afford to buy the railroads from their private owners without borrowing money. One should bear in mind, however, that the army did not stand alone in touting nationalization. It had many supporters, for example, the relatively liberal prime minister, Prince Saionji Kinmochi, and the advocate of party government, Hara, who saw an opportunity to create a regional base for his Seiyūkai party through government control of railroad-building.

Opponents of government ownership of the national rail network were few but influential: Saionji's foreign minister, Katō Takaaki, who opposed it as an "invasion of private rights," Takahashi, and under his influence, the elder statesman Inoue Kaoru. Takahashi called nationalization a "plan for destroying the country" (*bōkokuan*) because he feared further borrowing abroad would lead to a decline in the price of the Russo-Japanese War bonds, and a loss of Japan's credit abroad. Takahashi stated his opposition as follows:

Because we borrowed so much money abroad during the war, we need to think of how to manage our funds in the aftermath. We have a great deal of principal and interest to repay, and it will not be easy. At the same time as the Japanese people must practice frugality, we need to develop industry fully. So we must avoid unnecessary spending and support increasing the people's wealth. But if we nationalize the railroad system now we must increase government appropriations accordingly. Of course, railroads are not unproductive, but nationalization should be carried out at the appropriate time. To nationalize the railroads, we will have to borrow money at home and abroad, and the value of our wartime bonds will fall. This will endanger our creditor nations' confidence in us.[3]

Takahashi seemed to read his new European acquaintances' views correctly, and they seemed to trust his influence in Tokyo. On March 6, James de Rothschild wrote from Paris to his cousin Nathaniel in London that he hoped the Japanese would not nationalize their railroads. Lord Rothschild replied, "I confess I am not much alarmed, as it is very doubtful this proposal will become law."[4]

Takahashi returned to Japan a hero in the eyes of many in high government circles for his success in raising money abroad, and his views were persuasive. In addition to Inoue, who came out against nationalization, many others, particularly Finance Minister Sakatani Yoshio and some of his subordinates in the ministry, who feared that the railroads would lose rather than make money, followed suit. Prime Minister Saionji, who worried that his cabinet might fall if nationalization failed, called a meeting of Takahashi, Inoue, Sakatani, Army Minister Terauchi Masatake, Transportation Minister Yamagata Isaburō (who was the nephew and adopted son of the field marshal), and various ministry subordinates to make the case for nationalization. Nakashōji Ren, the Deputy Minister of Transportation, told Takahashi that bonds for infrastructure projects such as railroads were not "unproductive," and then argued, "Public bonds for nationalizing railroads are different from other government bonds. They will replace 225,000,000 yen worth of company stocks and bonds, and thus do not affect the ability of the market to absorb them." In other words, the government would issue bonds to buy the outstanding shares and bonds of the private railroads, thereby merely maintaining the same overall level of indebtedness in financial markets. This explanation seemed to persuade Takahashi to end his resistance, and when he and Inoue agreed not to contest nationalization, the opposition fell away—except that of Foreign Minister Katō, who resigned over the issue. One can only speculate on why Takahashi shifted his position. Was he, home from two years of "study" in the economic *realpolitik* of the citadels of international finance, actually convinced by Nakashōji's arguments (after all, railroads were clearly productive and helpful in economic development), or did he have other motivations? It is not hard to imagine, for example, that an ambitious 51-year-old national bank vice governor, when faced with pressure from some of the most powerful men in Japan—including Prime Minister Saionji, who had made the issue the primary one of his first cabinet, Yamagata's protégé, General Terauchi, and adopted son Isaburō—decided that advancement to the highest levels of government might take place more smoothly if he did not resist. Just as likely, however, if not more so, is that Takahashi compromised on railroad nationalization so as not to lose his ability to influence the government in other policy areas.

Jacob Schiff arrived on his triumphal visit to Japan on March 25, and Takahashi used the opportunity to preach fiscal self-control and cooperation with the Anglo-Americans. Shortly after Schiff landed in Tokyo, on March 27, 1906, parliament passed a bill to nationalize the railroads. In fact, Schiff wrote that on his visit to the Diet, he watched from the gallery of the House of Peers as the members voted on the bill. The government subsequently bought seventeen privately owned railroads at a cost of 456,000,000 yen, most of it raised in the domestic market.[5]

Jacob Schiff Visits Japan

The Japanese government invited Schiff to Japan in 1906, and his account of the journey makes it sound like a progression of royalty, which it was: financial royalty. Schiff traveled across America in a private train on a series of railroad lines that he had helped finance; the president or vice-president of each one boarded the train as it entered his territory and exited as it left.[6] He sailed luxuriously across the Pacific to Yokohama, pausing only in Hawai'i to meet Lili'uokalani, the deposed queen. Over the course of his two months in Japan, Schiff met with most of Japan's major leaders and many lesser ones: Itō Hirobumi, who came from Korea expressly to meet Schiff on his last day in Japan; Yamagata; Inoue; and Matsukata; the wartime prime minister General Katsura; his successor Prince Saionji; and the commanding general of the Manchurian front during the war, Field Marshal Ōyama Iwao—in other words, all seven living current and future elder statesmen (*genrō*). Schiff met Admiral Tōgō Heihachirō, whose British-made ships had defeated the Russian Baltic Fleet at the Battle of Tsushima. Schiff reports that during one of his long conversations on finance with Matsukata, the admiral, who had also joined the talk, wandered off, seemingly bored. "When we later rejoined [Tōgō] and the others, I remarked to the Admiral that I have apparently succeeded in doing what the Russians had never been able to do—to drive him away."

Schiff met key members of Japan's "money aristocracy," to borrow his own phrase, such as Baron Mitsui Takayasu and his three sons; Masuda Takashi of the Mitsui Trading Company; Baron Iwasaki Hisaya, the son of Yatarō, the founder of Mitsubishi, and a graduate of the University of Pennsylvania; Shibusawa Eiichi, the maverick entrepreneur; Ōkura Kihachirō, "the merchant prince of Japan"; Baron Asano Sōichirō of the Asano and Yasuda enterprises; and Sonoda Kōkichi, president of the Peers' Bank. Schiff also met various government ministers, both past and present: Ōkuma Shigenobu, who had been and would again become prime minister; Katō Takaaki, recently resigned as foreign minister to protest railroad nationalization, but who would serve again in that post and as a democratizing prime minister; and Komura Jutarō, Japan's wartime foreign minister and principal negotiator at the peace conference in Portsmouth. In fact, during his trip Schiff spoke at least once with eight of the thirteen men who served as prime minister between 1885 and 1925.

Schiff also met with many of the government's financial leaders, such as Sone Arasuke and Sakatani Yoshio, the former and present finance ministers respectively; Governor Matsuo Shigeyoshi of the Bank of Japan; and naturally the finance ministry and central bank officials who spoke English: Mori Kengo, Fukai Eigo, Kitajima Kenjirō, Soeda Juichi (later the Japanese correspondent for Keynes's *Economic Journal*), Inoue Junnosuke, and Takahashi. At one time or another during his stay, Schiff spoke with half of the fourteen men who had served or would serve as finance minister between 1885 and 1925. Schiff met Ozaki Yukio, the mayor of Tokyo, who wrote in his memoir that his gratitude for Schiff's help to Japan was the impetus for his decision to give 3,000 cherry trees to Washington, DC.[7] Schiff's hosts arranged for Kawabata Gyokushō, one of the leading artists of traditional Japanese painting (*nihonga*) at the turn of the twentieth century, to give the Schiffs a demonstration of his artistic skill. The names of few major early-twentieth-century Japanese leaders do not appear in Schiff's travel diary. The only prominent figures he seems not to have encountered are the financier Yasuda Zenjirō; General Nogi Maresuke; Foreign Minister Hayashi Tadasu (who was returning from London during much of Schiff's stay); members of the Sumitomo family; and the interior minister and head of the Seiyūkai political party, Hara Takashi.

During their stay in Japan, the Schiffs and their entourage were invited to many luncheons and dinners. On March 28, the emperor entertained the financier at a Western-style banquet, and when Schiff toasted the emperor, he borrowed Harry Lee's words about George Washington: "First in war, first in peace, first in the hearts of his countrymen." The emperor returned the toast, thanking Schiff for his services to Japan during the recent war. Schiff replied, "I feel my services have been overestimated, but from the start my associates and I, believing in the righteousness of the cause of Japan, gladly embraced it." The emperor presented Schiff with the Order of the Rising Sun, Second Grade, the same decoration the emperor wore during the ceremony, which obviously flattered Schiff. He was entertained by elder statesmen Matsukata and Inoue; Ōkuma; Finance Minister Sakatani; Bank of Japan Governor Matsuo; the trio of entrepreneurs, Ōkura, Shibusawa, and Iwasaki; Takahashi; Soeda; Inoue Junnosuke in the Osaka offices of the Bank of Japan; and Field Marshal Ōyama (whose wife was a graduate of Vassar College and spoke fluent English). Schiff visited most of the primary tourist sites: Yasukuni Shrine, dedicated to the war dead, and the Yūshūkan, its attached war museum; Hakone, where he viewed Mount Fuji and stayed at the Fujiya Hotel, a stunning example of late-nineteenth-century Anglo-Japanese architecture; the mausoleum of the first Tokugawa shogun, Ieyasu, at Nikkō, and the nearby Kegon waterfall; Nagoya Castle; some of the temples of Kyoto; and the island shrine at Miyajima near Hiroshima. He also traveled to places one might not expect a Westerner to go in 1906, particularly Korea, where in the run-up to its annexation by Japan in 1910, Schiff was entertained by Korean royalty and Japanese and American diplomats. He also held a Passover Seder in his suite in the Imperial Hotel for his family and other traveling companions.

On May 14, just before Schiff departed Tokyo for Yokohama and home, he entertained most of his new acquaintances at a dinner in his hotel. "Carte blanche having been given by us to the manager of the Imperial Hotel, the banquet hall had been splendidly decorated with flowers, American and Japanese flags, etc., the dinner itself being very credible. Mother was seated between Count Matsukata and Count Inouyé, my own seat being between the Marchioness Oyama and Countess Matsukata." Toward the close of dinner, Schiff rose and in thanking his hosts, left a gentle message, one that must have overjoyed his friend Takahashi:

While here I have been asked repeatedly what impressions we were receiving, but not wishing to express prematurely formed views, I rather sought until now to avoid a reply. I know, however, I shall be asked the same question as soon as we land upon our own shores, and in parting from you I think I may tell you what my reply will be. I shall say that the inherent characteristics of the people of Japan appear to be simplicity, frugality, and loyalty—loyalty to their sovereign, loyalty to their country, loyalty to one another. I shall speak of your piety and of the touching reverence the young have for the aged, of the love with which the aged dote upon the young. I shall say that in my opinion your people derive their strength and self-reliance from their early training and systematic practice of manly sports, developing themselves physically and at the same time becoming accustomed to control and to subjugate their passions, and from thirst for learning, education having been made almost as accessible and as free as the air they live in.

Having flattered his guests, Schiff then proceeded to the center-piece of his message, his advice, I think, to the prominent Japanese in attendance:

I shall also feel justified in saying that Japan having just been victorious in one of the greatest wars in history, its people have not become overbearing, but have modestly returned to their daily occupations, evidently resolved to secure by peaceful means compensation for the sacrifices which have been brought, by opening new markets for their commerce and industry—*willing, however, to share these markets with the other nations of the world, and that because of this, Japan should have the good will of the other nations and the recognition of leadership in this hemisphere, which now of right belongs to it* [italics added].

In his long conversations with Matsukata, Inoue, Itō, and others in the highest levels of Japanese government, Schiff had clearly spoken of the advice he urged upon Takahashi in London and New York. Japan was now a member of the Anglo-American economic order, and was in fact the East Asian leader in that system, and should therefore have a commitment to its values: economic development, open markets, and the free flow of capital and goods. Whether the Japanese men who believed in these values, Takahashi (for the most part), Katō, the young financiers such as Inoue Junnosuke, and to some extent Matsukata, Itō, Katsura, and Saionji, would prevail, remained to be seen.

Another point should be made before we close our discussion of Schiff's trip to Japan. In 1906, everyone, whether they represented Anglo-American liberalism like Katō Takaaki or military values like Yamagata Aritomo, recognized an important lesson from the war. Japan could not have defeated Russia without British and American capital, technology, and raw materials. The men who met Schiff during his two months in Japan in the spring of 1906, the cream of Japan's government and business world, recognized what he and Lord Revelstoke, HSBC, Parr's Bank, Sir Ernest Cassel, Shell Oil, the British shipyards, and the Rothschilds had done for them. This is why they turned out to meet Schiff. This is why Admiral Tōgō would tell the workers of

Barr and Stroud in Glasgow in July 1911, "You won the battle of Tsushima for me."[8] This is also why Japan's leaders reluctantly withdrew their demand for a Russian indemnity at Portsmouth in 1905. But not all of these men recognized, as Takahashi did, that Japan should build its empire within the framework of what was acceptable to the British and American imperialists.

The Schiffs' ship left Yokohama for Vancouver on May 18, and on the morning of their departure, Takahashi and his wife came to the pier to deliver their daughter Wakiko, who was to live with the Schiffs in New York for three years. Schiff wrote about Wakiko,

She is just fifteen years old, knows no English or other foreign language, and is a typical Japanese maiden. Mother believes it somewhat of a responsibility we are undertaking in assuming charge of the girl and her education, but Mr. Takahashi has shown himself so good a friend, and it appears so tempting a problem to introduce this young Japanese maiden into a new world of speech and thought, that we have decided to endeavor to assume the responsibility.

Wakiko left for North America just shy of 40 years after her father had made his first trip, but she sailed on a higher deck.[9]

Takahashi Returns to London Once More

Four months after Schiff sailed for America with Wakiko in tow, the government sent Takahashi abroad to complete the job he had started in the fall of 1905, to issue bonds to redeem Japan's first wartime borrowing, the 22,000,000 pounds of expensive 6 percent 1904 bonds, due to be repaid by 1911. The cost of servicing these short-term bonds weighed heavily on a highly leveraged exchequer. Takahashi's task was to issue a new set of less expensive, longer-term bonds to buy back the earlier ones and to reduce Japan's financial liability. Both bad and good news awaited him in London. On the negative side, the United States in late 1906 was going into recession, and Schiff and his New York colleagues were not in a position to help Japan directly. On the positive side, the London and Paris Rothschilds, miffed that Schiff's 1904 gamble had succeeded, decided to help Japan again in 1906–7 as they had in November 1905. Lord Rothschild demonstrated his feelings toward Schiff and his German in-laws when he wrote to his Paris cousins on May 7, 1906:

You no doubt are aware that Mr. Jacob Schiff left New York some time ago to take a well earned holiday, or perhaps to be absent from New York pending the railroad inquiries President Roosevelt was making. Be that as it may, Mr. Schiff had a triumphal journey in a private car, with every kind of luxury over the various railroads he is interested in, sailed in a large steamer to Yokohama & has been a welcome & much honoured guest at Tokio. Naturally, in the midst of the incense which was poured on his devoted head, he is quite ignorant of what has gone on at home or in Europe, & probably the only person he hears from is his dear nephew Warburg at Hamburg who resembles the frog in the fable & is swollen up with vanity & the belief in his own power over the European markets. . . .

But at the same time (perhaps in an attempt to rival Schiff's influence), Lord Rothschild's letters express a sincere trust in Takahashi and an almost naïve belief in the Japanese government. Lord Rothschild continually attempted to allay any misgivings his Paris cousins might have had toward the financial dependability of Japan, so that under his leadership, both sets of Rothschilds took the lead in what would become the March 1907 loans.[10]

Correspondence between the two branches of the Rothschild family over the Japanese bonds continued for almost a year before their final issue in 1907. On May 8, 1906, for example, Lord Rothschild wrote to say that he had told Takahashi that they will act when the "propitious moment arises," but that such a moment was unlikely before "April next." Only beginning in February 1907, after Takahashi has been in Europe for more than six months, does the correspondence show the bond issue beginning to take shape. Takahashi insists on 4 percent bonds, but the Rothschilds counter with 5 percent. Takahashi asks why Japan should pay 5 percent, but China and Siam less. The French Minister of Foreign Affairs tells Takahashi that he worries about tensions between Japan and Russia. Paris wants the interest rate and price of the bonds set in London. The Japanese government wants New York and Germany involved too. By February 28, negotiations seem to be approaching fruition: it would be 5 percent bonds, but with a lower underwriter's commission and a higher price than Japan's earlier bonds. And finally on March 1, Lord Rothschild reports that "Mr. Takahashi as usual behaved admirably; naturally the objections he raised at first were fully justified." On March 7 he continues that "The Japanese are a remarkable nation, they have proven themselves on land and sea and their financial representative Mr. Takahashi deserves the highest praise for having placed the finance of the country on so firm and stable a basis," and on March 8, that "all preparations are made for the Japanese Loan and the prospectuses will be issued this afternoon and judging from appearances I expect the loan to be a great success."[11]

On March 6, 1907, Arthur J. Fraser of Parr's Bank, A. M. Townsend of HSBC, T. S. Nishimaki of the Yokohama Specie Bank, Albert Bright for the London Rothschilds, F. Heinrich for the Paris Rothschilds, and Takahashi for the Japanese government signed an agreement to issue 23,000,000 pounds of treasury bonds, half in London and half in Paris, at 5 percent, with an issuing price of 98½ pounds—almost parity—and without security. The usual consortium plus the Rothschilds issued the 11,500,000 pounds in London; the Paris Rothschilds underwrote the entire Paris issue. Since the banks had issued the 1904 bonds at 6 percent and at selling prices of 92 and 90½, the savings were enormous. Suzuki Toshio estimates that the Japanese government reduced its interest payments alone by 220,000 pounds (more than 2,000,000 yen) per year through this bond issue.[12]

On May 7, Lord Rothschild, almost gloating, wrote to Paris that, "We can heartily congratulate you upon the expected satisfactory conclusion of a Franco-Japanese arrangement. We have always had great faith in Japan, faith in their military and naval prowess which the late war amply justified, faith in the resources of their country and still greater faith in the wisdom of the Japanese rulers. . . ."[13] The "always," of course, had not begun until November 1905, that is, after the peace, when the risk of lending to Japan had been greatly reduced.

Schiff, the hero of 1904–5 and Lord Rothschild's straw man in 1906–7, was not involved in the March 1907 bond issue. But given the speed by which information traveled in the world of high finance at the turn of the century, he had no trouble staying informed of its progress. On March 6, he wrote to Takahashi in London, sounding defensive and including his own barb for the current issuing houses:

You appear to have made very considerable progress during the past week or two in coming to an arrangement through which the redemption of the 6 per cent War Bonds can be secured. While the proposed negotiation of 5 per cent Bonds in Paris and London is naturally not as advantageous to your Government as had been hoped, yet with the great change which has come over the international money markets, and which for the time being has practically closed the American market not only to foreign, but also to the best home investments, I think it is an accomplishment that you can be proud of to float £23,000,000 of 5 per cent Japanese Bonds at almost par. This accomplishment is perhaps even greater than your earlier negotiations, made at a time when both the markets of Europe and America were eager for investments, in strong contrast to the conditions which exist now.

Schiff went on to write that he and his partners, to the extent possible under present business conditions, had tried to help the Japanese government.

We have . . . as you already know, arranged to receive subscriptions here for the new 5 per cent Bonds, in the hope that the American holders of the 6 per cent Bonds may conclude to continue their investment by subscribing to the 5 per cent Bonds. How successful we may be in this effort we cannot tell in advance, as we have no data from which we can judge of the amount of 6 per cent Bonds still held here and of the manner in which these may be held. . . . We thought we owed it to you and your Government to officially receive subscriptions here, even without the possibility that profit accrue to us from this.[14]

In spite of the difficulties, Takahashi returned in triumph to Japan on May 10, 1907, from what would be his last trip abroad. On March 23, before he left London, the government in Tokyo dubbed him Baron Takahashi. From that time on, Schiff, in his frequent letters to his Tokyo friend, always addressed him, "Dear Baron Takahashi." Between 1907 and 1911, the governments of France, Korea, and China bestowed decorations upon Takahashi, with the last, from the Emperor of China, granted on October 31, 1911, in the final months of the Qing Dynasty.

Harsh Contraction Versus Controlled Growth

The economic policies Takahashi advocated between 1907 and 1914, while he served successively as vice governor and governor of the Bank of Japan, and then as finance minister, have been described as "positive" in contrast to the "negative" policies of men such as Yamamoto Tatsuo and Wakatsuki Reijirō, also finance ministers in this period, but as noted above, this characterization misses some of the nuances of Takahashi's economic thinking.[15] The imputed "positivists" are understood as advocating a policy to stimulate economic growth through low interest rates, foreign borrowing for productive purposes, lower taxes to encourage demand and business investment, and the use of government funds for infrastructure projects such as upgrading harbors, building railroads, and improving irrigation and riparian facilities, combined with a willingness to fund military expansion. The "negativists" feared that excessive spending, especially on the army and navy, foreign borrowing, and low interest rates would overheat the economy and lead to inflation, which they feared far more than deflation (actually, they did not seem to fear deflation at all). A stagnant economy and some bankruptcies were a small price to pay in order to rest safely in the bosom of the "self-regulating gold-standard system"—thus my use of the term "harsh contraction." While these descriptions set out the polar distinctions between the two positions, Takahashi himself was not an out-and-out positivist. Although he believed that the government had a primary duty to expand Japan's economy and to raise its citizens' standards of living, he also understood that there were circumstances for implementing the negative approach—cutting government spending, reducing foreign borrowing, and raising interest rates—and he was an opponent of excessive military spending.[16]

Takahashi recognized in the wake of the Russo-Japanese War that Japan had a large external debt: in 1908, debt service comprised a full quarter of all government expenditures, compared to 15 percent before the war in 1903. Accordingly, he looked for ways to stimulate economic growth both to increase exports and thereby reduce Japan's loss of gold reserves and specie, and to increase tax revenues to contribute to foreign debt repayment. It is fair to say that Takahashi proposed to balance the budget through the positivist method of growing the income side of the ledger, while his negativist opponents proposed doing so through reducing expenditures. But in his positive approach, Takahashi made a clear distinction between productive and non-productive government spending and tried to encourage the former, which would help stimulate economic growth, over the latter, such as military spending, which would not. This was difficult to do in the postwar decade, because the military, with its increased popularity and newly enlarged empire, made greater and greater demands on the government: military spending grew by 2.5 times between 1903 and 1908, from 2.3 to 6.3 percent of national income. It is fair to say, as Masazo Ohkawa writes, that, "the Japanese Government after the Russo-Japanese War had given priority to armaments expenditures over capital accumulation. The military's control over government finance could not be removed even with the united strength of the economic circles," of which Takahashi was an increasingly important member.[17]

Takahashi not only opposed excessive military spending, but also as vice governor, and after June 1, 1911, as governor of the Bank of Japan, he realized that there were times when one simply had to bite the bullet and raise interest rates. Whereas Takahashi feared making capital too expensive for business investors, he also understood that sometimes one had to cool the economy. He therefore agreed to the proposal by Finance Minister Yamamoto Tatsuo of the second Saionji Cabinet in 1911–12 to raise the prime rate to discourage imports and slow the outflow of specie. Normally Takahashi thought of imports of machinery and raw materials as a sign of a healthy, growing economy, but in the 1911 specie crisis, he agreed to raise interest rates. At the same time, unlike Yamamoto and Wakatsuki, he saw the increase in interest rates as temporary, to "warn" the private sector not to import excessively.[18] Takahashi, after all, was an advocate of controlled growth, not negativism.

Takahashi Joins the Yamamoto Cabinet as Finance Minister

The Japanese polity in the first three decades of the twentieth century experienced gradual democratization. Whether one can speak of something called "Taishō democracy," as some writers have, to describe the system of quasi-party and party governments that ruled Japan between 1912 and 1932, there is no doubt that by the end of World War I, more Japanese citizens had a greater influence over how they were governed than ever before.[19] For most of the period between 1918 and 1932, the head of the party that held a majority of seats in the House of Representatives, the lower house of the parliament, served as prime minister. The process of democratization began with the first Diet election in 1890, and gradually accelerated after that: the Yamamoto Gonnohyōe cabinet that Takahashi joined as finance minister on February 20, 1913, was not officially a party government, but it could not have been formed without the support of the strongest of Japan's political parties, Hara Takashi's Seiyūkai. The negotiations that would form the government required that Takahashi join the Seiyūkai, along with two other former bureaucrats who became ministers. In 1913, Takahashi became a leading member of a democratizing political party.

The Meiji Constitution of 1889, which posited imperial sovereignty and was given to the people as a gift from their emperor, was far from a democratic document. It gave the army and navy the "right of supreme command," the right under certain circumstances to report directly to the emperor and in so doing, to operate independently of the prime minister. Citizens received the rights to free speech, assembly, and religion, but these rights were subject to the needs of the government. The Privy Council, an appointed body, ratified treaties with foreign countries. The constitution did set up a bicameral legislature, the lower elected and the upper made up of members of the nobility and persons appointed by the government. But even voting for the lower House of Representatives was limited by extra-constitutional regulations to men who were substantial taxpayers; a little more than 1 percent of the total population of Japan voted in the first election in 1890. The Meiji constitution did not establish an auspicious framework for the rise of a democratic polity. But it did give democratizing politicians one important lever: the lower house alone had the authority to approve the government's annual budget. Here the oligarchs who wrote the constitution had miscalculated. Rich people voted because they paid high taxes. As Japan fought successive wars against China and Russia and created an empire, military spending skyrocketed, by over six times between 1890 and 1912 after adjustment for inflation. The rich voters objected because they bore most of this growing tax burden, and they joined political parties to gain political influence. By 1912, governments found themselves in need of support from political parties in order to pass budgets to obtain money to operate.

Meanwhile, other policies of the Meiji government also began to bear democratizing fruit. Real per capita income doubled between 1880 and 1910, and grew by another 40 percent by 1920. In 1879, six years after the government promulgated compulsory primary school education, only 41 percent of eligible children went to school; by 1912, 98 percent attended. These newly educated citizens gained the ability to read a plethora of magazines and newspapers written to appeal to those with only a primary-school education. While in the late feudal period few peasants left their home villages, by 1912 trains, factories, and the army drew millions of people to other regions of the country. Health care improved, and people used an abundance of modern devices, including bicycles and electric lights, to mention only two. Higher standards of living, education, and literacy and increasing cosmopolitanism were the hallmarks of a new kind of worker and farmer in early-twentieth-century Japan. A greater role in determining the nature of his government was both his demand and his reward. Gradually in the three decades after the first election in 1890 the government reduced the level of tax payments necessary to be eligible to vote until, in 1925, a parliament in which Takahashi sat legislated universal manhood suffrage. Rich people began the democratizing process, but eventually all economic classes joined in. It was in the midst of this process that Takahashi joined the Seiyūkai and the Yamamoto government in 1913.[20]

Yamamoto Gonnohyōe became prime minister in the wake of what is viewed as one of the major events in the rise of party government in Japan: the Taishō Political Crisis. In November 1912, Army Minister Uehara Yūsaku presented the Saionji cabinet with a demand for two additional army divisions to "maintain order" in Japan's new colony in Korea (essentially to quell independence movements) and to protect Japan's growing interests in Manchuria. The cabinet, in the process of contracting the economy and supported by the Seiyūkai's absolute majority in the House of Representatives, voted unanimously to reject the demand. Uehara did not give in, however, because he had the backing of the army's own elder statesman, Field Marshal Yamagata. The marshal made the rounds of his fellow *genrō* in an attempt to bring them aboard, but all either opposed his efforts, as did Bank of Japan Governor Takahashi, or were at best lukewarm.

When the cabinet refused to capitulate, Uehara resigned as minister and all of the army officers eligible to serve refused to replace him. Since a cabinet needed to have all of its portfolios filled to continue to exist, and Saionji could not find a replacement for Uehara, the cabinet fell on December 5, outraging both public opinion and the Seiyūkai party. General Katsura, who replaced Saionji, agreed to continue the former cabinet's retrenchment policies, upsetting the navy as well as the army. When the navy also refused to provide an officer to serve as minister, Katsura attempted to force its hand by using an imperial rescript. Furthermore, he decided to form his own political party to provide a basis of parliamentary support for his cabinet. Even though Katsura, in agreement with the Seiyūkai, opposed increased military spending, his actions enraged the public and the Seiyūkai: the former because such actions seemed high-handed, the latter because a new party would threaten its increasing power. The first "Movement to Protect Constitutional Governments," undertaken for the purpose of establishing governments responsible to the parliament, spread, culminating in riots on February 10, 1913, during which thousands of protesters surrounded the parliament and set fire to police stations. On February 20, after less than two months in office, Katsura resigned as prime minister. This was a momentous event in the transition from oligarchic to parliamentary government: from the establishment of the first cabinet in 1885 until 1913, every prime minister, with only one exception during five months in 1898, had been a current or future elder statesman—Katsura was the last *genrō* to serve as premier.

Oligarchs such as Field Marshal Yamagata, who detested political parties, were on the horns of a dilemma. Yamagata could neither bring himself to approve Hara, the head of the Seiyūkai, as prime minister, nor could he ignore Hara's party and public opinion. Therefore, after much discussion behind the scenes, a compromise was reached: Admiral Yamamoto would become prime minister. To obtain the support of the Seiyūkai, he agreed to include Hara and two other party members in his cabinet; he also agreed that several of the bureaucrats who joined the government could do so only if they enrolled in Hara's party. Takahashi, with the support of Matsukata, who called him the "number one fiscal and financial person" at the time, became finance minister and a Seiyūkai member.[21]

Although the Yamamoto Cabinet lasted only fourteen months, it made significant contributions in the transition from oligarchic to party government. First, it made a decision to allow retired officers to serve as army and navy ministers. With this reform, the military lost its ability to topple or prevent the formation of cabinets by refusing to assign officers to serve as ministers. Second, the government reduced the size of the Privy Council from 28 to 24. Third, the cabinet changed the civil-service regulations to allow party politicians to serve in high-ranking, sub-ministerial positions, in an attempt to bring the bureaucracy under democratic control. Yamagata opposed all of these changes, and tried to block their approval by using a decidedly undemocratic organ, the Privy Council, to defeat Yamamoto's plans. The prime minister countered with a threat to dismiss all of the privy councilors and appoint new ones if Yamagata persisted.[22]

The Yamamoto cabinet fell in February 1914 over a naval procurement scandal in which the Siemens company bribed Japanese naval officers to purchase its equipment. Although there was no evidence that Prime Minister Yamamoto himself was involved, the opposition Dōshikai party, founded by Katsura, and after his premature death in 1913, led by former foreign minister Katō Takaaki, saw the scandal as an opportunity to attack Hara's Seiyūkai. The public, outraged by what it saw as another example of oligarchic control of government, and by the Seiyūkai's complicity, took to the streets again. Strange bedfellows, including genuine advocates of party politics such as Katō and elder statesmen such as Yamagata, who did not want to give up oligarchic control of government, joined forces to oust a cabinet supported by Hara's party. The old warhorse Ōkuma Shigenobu, who had entertained Jacob Schiff at his mansion at Waseda University, became premier with the support of the Dōshikai, and Katō became foreign minister. In the March 1915 election, the Seiyūkai lost 92 of its 207 seats, while the Dōshikai won 151. Wakatsuki Reijirō became finance minister and introduced a harshly negative fiscal and monetary policy: this led to a sharp decline in Japan's trade deficit, for which Wakatsuki took credit. Wakatsuki's bragging—similar to Inoue Junnosuke's eighteen years later—was technically valid: he did reduce the imbalance of imports over exports, but he did it by reducing trade altogether, that is, exports as well as imports. Japan, on the eve of World War I, descended into recession: in 1914, national income fell by 7 percent from its all-time high in 1913.[23]

Because the cabinet fell amid a furor over naval spending and the Siemens scandal, Takahashi in his fourteen months as finance minister never passed a budget, but his proposals clearly demonstrate that he did not, in cooperation with Hara, put forward an expansionary, positive fiscal policy. His budget target for 1914 was 640,000,000 yen, only 10,000,000 more than Yamamoto Tatsuo's negative 1913 budget. In preparing his budget, Takahashi advocated government frugality and rationality; in fact, two of the cabinet's primary goals were to reduce the size of the bureaucracy and to introduce a system to promote officials on the basis of merit, not seniority. The army's two proposed divisions disappeared entirely. Takahashi even resisted Hara's proposal to use government funds for railroad development, although he was willing to borrow abroad for the purpose. He expected that increased revenues from government enterprises and taxes would provide a budget surplus of 50,000,000 yen, which he wanted to use for naval expansion, the stimulation of industry, and tax relief. The budget contained a proposal to reform the tax laws, in which Takahashi proposed lowering inheritance and business taxes, and reducing income taxes by allowing various deductions from earned income. Does this indicate that Takahashi, well ahead of his time, understood that government spending was not the only way to encourage economic development? He seems to have recognized that reducing taxes so that people have more money to spend could also stimulate demand and growth.[24]

Takahashi in his short term of office, as always, emphasized productive as opposed to unproductive spending and borrowing. He believed that Japan should redeem bonds for unproductive purposes, such as his wartime borrowing, and replace them with productive ones for building railroads, other infrastructure, or for private industrial development. Between 1906 and 1914, the cities of Tokyo, Yokohama, Nagoya, Osaka, and Kyoto borrowed money abroad, largely in London and Paris, but also in New York, for the improvement of harbors, roads, gasworks, waterworks, and electric works. Private companies also raised money in London and Paris. So even while Takahashi tried to control government spending, he encouraged local government and entrepreneurs to borrow abroad for economic development. I have therefore used the phrase "controlled growth" rather than "positivism" to characterize Takahashi's thinking.

World War I and China Policy

World War I broke out in Europe in early August 1914, and by the end of the month Japan had joined its ally, Great Britain, to neutralize German power in China and the Pacific. The Japanese military took the opportunity to seize the German naval base at Qingdao on the Shandong Peninsula in China, and the German island chains (the Mariana, Caroline, and Marshall Islands, scenes of bitter fighting in the next world war) to the north of the equator. The war presented Japan with a twofold opportunity. For the military and certain civilian foreign-policy makers such as Katō, it allowed Japan, in the absence of the European and North American powers, a unique opportunity to expand its influence over China. For Takahashi and his ilk, interested in economic growth, it gave Japanese exporters the opportunity to move into British colonial markets in South and Southeast Asia. Japan's recession, export deficit, and specie crisis disappeared during a five-year economic expansion from 1914 to 1919.

On January 18, 1915, only two months after the seizure of Qingdao, Foreign Minister Katō presented the Chinese government of Yuan Shikai with the infamous "Twenty-One Demands," a brazen Japanese attempt to become the dominant imperialist power in China, while Great Britain was involved in a war nearer to home. In a five-article diplomatic memorandum, the Japanese demanded the Shandong Peninsula as a Japanese "sphere of influence"; an extension of Japan's various railroad and leasehold rights in South Manchuria until at least the end of the twentieth century; joint ownership of a mining and metallurgical complex in central China; no further cessions or leases of coastal harbors to any country other than Japan; and in the fifth section, which Katō did not reveal even to his British allies, the appointment of Japanese advisors to the Chinese government and Japanese participation in Chinese police forces. Yuan's government, under the threat of Japanese military intervention, attempted to use British and American pressure to force the Japanese to back down. The Anglo-Americans, unfortunately for China, offered very little support, and in the end, Yuan had no choice but to give the Japanese everything they requested except the demands in the fifth section. Chinese public opinion, on the other hand, not required to concern itself with the realities of possible military intervention, vented its outrage.[25]

It has been argued that the Twenty-One Demands were in keeping with the imperialist tradition of great power intervention in China, and this is certainly true. The powers, particularly the British and the French, had increased their dominance over the economics and politics of regions of China, and of the central government as well, since the Opium War in the 1840s. Foreign Minister Katō, fluent in English and a long-time diplomat with close ties to Britain, had studied Western imperialism carefully and saw his Twenty-One Demands as a Japanese version of what his British friends had been doing for a century.[26] But there were problems with Katō's view, and with this mode of analysis. First, Japan in 1915 was not Great Britain in the nineteenth century, or the United States in the twentieth: it did not come close to matching the Anglo-Americans in national wealth, industrial capacity, access to natural resources, or technology. In fact, one of the dilemmas of Japanese foreign policy in the pre–World War II twentieth century is that few government leaders recognized, as Takahashi did clearly, that Japan was more of a paper tiger than a real one. Second, Japan entered into serious expansion in China when the Western imperialist game was winding down. While there is some truth to Matsuoka Yōsuke's pithy quip that "the Western Powers taught Japan the game of poker, but after acquiring most of the chips they pronounced the game immoral and took up contract bridge," nonetheless Japan did not have the wealth or power to force the Westerners back to the poker table.[27] Third, a new force, Chinese nationalism, began to intensify in the first two decades of the twentieth century, and from the seizure of Qingdao on, Chinese public opinion began to see Japan, not the Westerners, as China's primary enemy. Fourth, rising literacy in Japan was a two-edged sword: it encouraged mass political participation and at the same time turned peasants into Japanese citizens, with a concomitant rise of Japanese nationalism, part of which included a collective denigration of China and thumbing of Japanese noses at the Western powers. In the early twentieth century, Japanese nationalism, which cheered the seizure of Qingdao and the Twenty-One Demands, was on a collision course with Chinese nationalism and Anglo-American power.

Takahashi, unusual among Japanese politicians at the time, understood the dangers of using force or threats of force in China outside the framework of the British and American world order. As early as May 1911, mere days before his promotion to Bank of Japan governor, Takahashi, in a speech in English, told an audience of Americans and Japanese in Tokyo that Japan did not have the resources to act independently in China, but should cooperate with the British and Americans in its economic development.

Japan is by no means in a position to take any undue advantage on account of the development of China. What are required in China most urgently and in the largest scale are doubtless capital, steel, and machinery. But Japan cannot hope, for a long time to come at any rate, to compete with the Western nations in the contribution of these elements. Japan will only share in the benefit resulting from the development of China, which is at first instance mainly dependent upon the enterprise and resources of the Western nations.

Takahashi, who consistently emphasized pragmatic solutions over those predicated on national pride, understood the cold reality: Japan was poorer than its European and North American allies/rivals. In 1913, Japan provided 13.6 percent of all foreign investment in China, ranking fourth behind Great Britain (37.7 percent), Russia (16.7), and Germany (16.4). Even in 1936, five years after the seizure of Manchuria, Japan trailed Great Britain in the amount of foreign investment in manufacturing on the mainland.[28]

In 1915, Takahashi criticized Katō's handling of the Twenty-One Demands as "absurd" because of his fear that bungled Japanese involvement in China would stimulate military demands for larger budgets, unduly antagonize the Chinese people, and bring Japan's foreign policy into conflict with those of the United States and Great Britain. As Takahashi wrote to Jacob Schiff in New York on April 20, 1915:

I have little personal concern in the vicissitudes of our home politics, only I am constrained to feel some anxiety about the trend of diplomatic dealings of the present cabinet, especially in regard to the negotiations with China. As Baron Kato keeps secret all matters in this respect, even those already events of the past, we are driven to conjecture by means of reports circulated abroad. It would be fortunate if my anxiety should prove groundless. If on the contrary, the reports sent back here from abroad be not wide of the mark, there are in store many causes of anxiety, because our diplomacy seems to be conducted in a too light-hearted manner. . . . Your view that the relations between Japan and China must be a natural alliance has my warm endorsement; but I rather fear that the way in which the present Cabinet approaches China may tend to alienate the Chinese people from us and to engender their dread and hatred toward us.

Takahashi reiterated these sentiments a few years later when he wrote, "We have hurt China's self-respect and pride. . . . The group five articles of the Twenty-One Demands almost intruded on China's sovereignty."[29]

In 1916, General Terauchi Masatake replaced Ōkuma as prime minister, and his cabinet continued his predecessor's efforts to expand Japan's influence piecemeal in China. Takahashi, still out of power, continued to oppose such efforts. In 1917–18, Takahashi opposed the Nishihara loans, an effort by Terauchi's cabinet to extend loans to the Chinese warlord Duan Qirui in order to advance Japan's claims in Manchuria by making the yen the currency of China's northeast provinces. Takahashi attacked the concept of using loans granted to various warlords to gain specific rights in China. Since 1907, when he met the modernizing Qing Dynasty official Zhang Zhidong, Takahashi argued that Japan benefited more from the creation of an independent, stable, and unified China than from its dismemberment.

World War I and the Military

Throughout his mature career, Takahashi cast a jaundiced eye on excessive military spending, both because he feared it could lead to military adventurism in China and also to expenditures Japan could not afford. As noted, to Takahashi, economic development came first, national defense afterward. This is not to suggest, however, that Takahashi was a pacifist who believed national defense was unnecessary. He understood that a nation would be foolish not to prepare to defend itself. Takahashi, while serving as finance minister in the wake of the Taishō Political Crisis, expressed both his recognition of the need for national defense, and of the need to keep military spending under control, in a letter to Jacob Schiff, dated January 24, 1914:

Of late, there is a trend of public opinion here, which I fear might cause some misunderstanding abroad—the growth of an extreme form of anti-militarism. It is hardly necessary to assure you that the advocacy of international peace by men like Dr. Eliot and Dr. Jordan is heartily endorsed by us. . . .[30] But now some people [in Japan] have gone to the extreme and talk as if armaments can be dispensed with at once. . . . They oppose even the replenishment of the armaments which are necessary for national defence. They . . . often declare that the country is being ruined by the financial burden of armaments. What I fear is that the exaggerated picture drawn by them may disquiet the foreign public. But I believe you know nothing is farther from the truth than their allegation. The prevalence of militarism here is a mere bogey. It is agreed on all hands that the future of the country depends on our economic development and that peace is the desideratum of the economic development. Only the lofty ideal of permanent international peace can not be realized in a day, and meanwhile every nation must take measures of national defence to meet the cold realities of the present moment. But you may rest assured that we shall never pass the limit of financial capacity. What we must look after is only the replenishment of the armaments necessary for defence.[31]

Takahashi not only understood that national defense was essential, so long as it was carried out within the limits of what Japan could afford, but also that diplomacy and economic development should lead and the military follow, and that ultimate military success depended on technology, not spirit. In December 1916, Takahashi wrote an article entitled "National Defense and Foreign Policy," in which he stated his views about national defense, its cost, and diplomacy, which I have paraphrased as follows. National defense is vital for a people, but national defense spending that exceeds the nation's capacity to pay for it is not effective defense, and establishing one's country as a world power is expensive. In the past, the army and navy competed for resources unproductively. During World War I, the Western powers developed highly technical and costly weapons, and therefore a soldier's bravery counts for less than in the past, and machines count for more. Given the price of new technology, unbridled competition between the services will not work. As a result we require a national defense policy based on peace. Diplomacy should formulate the agenda for relations with other countries and the military should follow. We cannot plan a national defense that takes on the whole world as our enemy. An important goal of foreign policy is to increase the nation's wealth. In the past, foreign-policy makers did not concern themselves with economics, but now they must do so. When the war ends, economic competition will become the primary mode of competition among nations. Until now the military has not thought about diplomacy and economics in developing its plans. Soldiers dislike looking at matters from other than a military point of view, yet it is crucial for them to remember that defense planning must not hinder economic growth.[32]

Takahashi, prior to his return to the finance portfolio in September 1918, had already developed a coherent view of the role of national defense within a context of foreign and economic policy.

World War I and Japan's Economic Development

On the brink of World War I, Japan was heavily leveraged. In 1914, total national government debt reached 2,650,000,000 yen, of which 1,500,000,000 was foreign debt, against tax revenues of 344,000,000 yen and a total national income of 4,000,000,000 yen: in other words, total debt reached two-thirds, and foreign debt over one-third of national income in that year. Japan's specie reserves fell to 341,000,000 yen, their lowest level since 1905.[33] Japan's credit abroad fell precipitously, and it faced the possibility of defaulting on its foreign debt payments.

World War I brought Japan "divine providence," in two forms.[34] As the British and other European countries shifted their industrial production to war goods, Japan moved into British export markets, especially in South and Southeast Asia. The value of Japanese textile exports in constant yen increased by 64.6 percent from 1914 to 1918, and total manufactures by 61.8 percent. Japan, which ran a trade deficit of 97,000,000 yen in 1913, and of 4,600,000 yen even in 1914, had a trade surplus of 371,000,000 yen in 1916. The period between 1915 and 1918 was the only time in Japan's pre–World War II history that it had a surplus of exports over imports for four years running. Japan's specie reserves grew to almost 1,600,000,000 yen in 1918, and almost 2,200,000,000 yen in 1919. Japan, a debtor nation on the verge of bankruptcy in 1914, ranked second only to the United States among the world's creditor nations by the end of the war. During the war, Japan had to learn to produce many of the heavy industrial goods—for example, steel and ships—that it had imported from Great Britain prior to the war. Accordingly, the structure of the Japanese economy shifted dramatically toward industry. In 1914, 61.7 percent of the labor force was engaged in agriculture and forestry; by 1918, the percentage had fallen sharply, to only 53.3 percent, and in 1923, a few years after the end of the war, non-agricultural workers surpassed agricultural workers in number for the first time. One could argue that World War I provided the impetus for Japan's transformation into an industrial society.[35]

The war and the industrial transformation brought with it difficulties as well as providence. The most dangerous of these was inflation, generated as a result of the overheated economy during the wartime boom. Although real wages for every category of worker—including those in both the agricultural and manufacturing sectors, and regardless of gender—outran inflation, they rose much more slowly than the economy expanded. Real wages for agricultural workers grew by 36 percent, for male manufacturing workers by 38 percent, and for female manufacturing workers, largely textile workers, by only 15 percent, over the four years from 1914 through 1918. During the same period, consumer prices rose by 74 percent, and from 1918 to 1920, by an additional 36 percent. But certain commodities spiraled upward in price more sharply than others, and one was the staple rice: between 1914 and 1918, the price of rice increased by 2.5 times, and in one year, 1917–18, by 65 percent.[36] In August and September of 1918, violent rice riots broke out in cities, towns, and villages all over Japan. Some Japanese historians interpret these riots, in which workers and farmers destroyed government and company offices, attacked rice warehouses and even the homes of the rich, destroyed police boxes, and generally looted and burned, as an indication of the revolutionary potential of the Japanese masses.[37] The premier, General Terauchi, was forced to resign over the riots, and he was replaced by Hara Takashi, the leader of the Seiyūkai, who formed what is widely regarded as Japan's first real party government. The violence of the Rice Riots, like that of the Taishō Political Crisis five years earlier, played a major role in Japan's democratizing trend during and after World War I.

ELEVEN

Taishō Democracy, 1918–27

Takahashi returned to the finance portfolio at a major turning point in Japanese history. The wartime expansion of the Japanese economy raised national income dramatically. The concomitant rise in standards of living and in levels of education, literacy, and cosmopolitanism stimulated widespread demand for greater popular participation in the political process. Japan's enlistment on the Allied side in the war brought Japan new territories and recognition as one of the powers, and in the minds of many Japanese at least, as *the* power in East Asia. The head of the Seiyūkai, Hara Takashi, who became Japan's first party prime minister in September 1918, exploited these trends brilliantly to bring his party into office. Japan in 1918 began the most democratic epoch of its pre–World War II modern history. The rise of Hara to power seemed to mark the dawn of a new Japan.

But with sunrise emerged dangers, some of which prefigured democracy's sunset fewer than fifteen years later. Rapid wartime economic growth produced dangerous inflation. Wartime success gave rise to a new and widespread nationalism and national self-confidence: the same era in which Japan democratized was also marked by the successful transition of a nation of parochial peasants into one of Japanese citizens. The military, emboldened by its new territories, its increasingly predominant position in northeast China, and the swift development in Europe and North America of new, technologically advanced weapons, demanded ever-increasing sums of money. It also used the opportunity of Allied intervention in Siberia in 1917 to embark on an expensive and dangerous five-year adventure there. Civilian as well as military leaders saw the absence of the Europeans and Americans from East Asia during the war as a chance to increase Japan's influence over a fragmented China. Japanese policy toward China, as symbolized by the Twenty-One Demands and the Nishihara loans, triggered alarm bells in London, New York, and Washington. While Japan's recognition as a power stimulated a solipsistic, nationalistic pride among Japan's leaders and populace, the Westerners, and especially the United States, significantly tempered such recognition. They limited, and later in the case of the United States, prohibited Japanese immigration into their countries, refused to approve a racial equality clause in the Treaty of Versailles that established the League of Nations, forced Japan, but not the British, to relinquish its naval base in China, limited the size of the Japanese navy to three-fifths of either the American or British one, and finally dissolved the symbol of Japan's international status, the Anglo-Japanese Alliance. Within this milieu, Hara's party came to power not only because of the growth of a mass society, but also because he made compromises with less liberal *genrō* and military leaders, compromises that limited his freedom of democratic action once in power. In fact, one of Hara's major tasks as prime minister was preventing his more liberal, but less politically savvy, subordinates such as Takahashi from rocking the Seiyūkai's precariously balanced boat.

Between September 1918 and June 1927, Takahashi served as prime minister, finance minister three times, and agriculture and commerce minister. This decade encompasses both the high and low points in Takahashi's career at the top levels of government. On the one hand, the policies Takahashi advocated in this period demonstrate that he was one of the most progressive major politicians in prewar Japan. He advocated a shift in the focus of Japan's foreign policy away from military expansion and toward trade competition within a framework of international economic cooperation. He argued for the abolition of the general staff system in 1920 and headed the Japanese government that enlisted in the Washington Treaty system in 1921–22. He succeeded Hara as head of Seiyūkai, and together with his own desired successor, Yokota Sennosuke, proposed the most progressive party platform in pre–World War II history: peaceful diplomacy, abrogation of Japan's unequal treaty rights in China, establishment of trade relations with the

Soviet Union, major cuts in military spending, civilian control of the army and navy, devolution of certain central tax and spending authority to local governments, election rather than appointment of prefectural governors, decentralization of education, universal suffrage, recognition of the right of workers to bargain collectively, and a graduated income tax. In 1924, he resigned his peerage and ran as a commoner for election to the House of Representatives. He played an important role in the establishment of universal manhood suffrage in 1925.

Yet on the other hand, he mistimed efforts to provide Japan with a soft landing at the end of its long wartime and postwar boom, and thus played a role in the onset of a recession in 1920. He also failed as his party's leader, not only because he lacked Hara's skills as a politician, but also because the liberal platform he and Yokota proposed for their party ignored the needs of Seiyūkai's power base and antagonized some of its more nationalistic members. By advancing his forward-looking proposals, he overlooked political reality, and under his leadership the party split in two.

Takahashi and the Postwar Hard Landing

The Japanese economy grew during World War I largely because the European combatants shifted production from exports to war goods. Japan's exports to British and French colonial markets in Asia expanded dramatically. At the same time, in light of reduced imports of advanced machinery and technology from the European powers, which they needed for their own war effort, import-substitution production spurred the growth of Japan's heavy industrial enterprises at home. National income doubled from 1914 until 1918, and grew by another 50 percent by 1920. But consumer prices shot up as well, by 74 percent until 1918, and by another 36 percent from then until 1920. In fact, when looked at in real rather than nominal terms, the wartime expansion looks less impressive: the economy grew by only one-third from 1914 to 1920. Takahashi returned to the finance portfolio in late September 1918, just as the war was coming to a close and the British and French were poised to reenter their prewar markets. Within the current context, Takahashi faced two risks: increased competition in Asian markets from the returning Europeans, and dangerous inflation.[1] If ever there was a time for a gradual budgetary contraction and increase in interest rates to bring about a soft landing from the wartime boom and cool inflation, the autumn of 1918 was that time, yet the government moved in the opposite direction.

The fiscal policy of the Hara cabinet in 1918–21 was one of steady expansion. Government spending increased by 15 percent in 1919, another 17 percent in 1920, and nearly 10 percent in 1921. Most expenditures went to the military: 48 percent of the regular 1920 budget, and this excluded the additional costs of the Siberian intervention. Army spending in 1921 was 2.6 times higher than in 1915, navy spending 5.7 times higher; military spending from 1915–21 increased by 75 percent even when adjusted for rampant inflation. Furthermore, spending for the construction of railroad lines, port facilities, roads, and communications networks, and for the expansion of higher education facilities, all grew dramatically. Indeed, the transportation ministry's budget in 1921 was third only to those of the navy and the army. In a period when the government should have tried to bring spending under control to stem inflation, Hara's government increased government spending by almost 50 percent.[2]

Panic and recession hit Japan in March of 1920, and its economy quickly fell into disarray. "Bubbles had arisen on top of bubbles in 1919, and most of them burst in 1920."[3] Consumer prices fell by 7.5 percent in 1921, and continued to decline more or less steadily until the Takahashi reflation took effect in 1932, after which prices would not surpass their 1920 level until the beginning of the World War II inflation in 1939–40. Nominal national income also declined, by 8 percent in one year, and only recovered slowly through the 1920s: it would be only 15.6 percent higher in 1929 than it had been in 1921. However, because of steadily declining prices throughout the decade, real national income rose by almost one-third in eight years. In fact, when calculated in real terms, the economic expansion following the 1920–21 recession was nearly equal to that of the World War I boom. But in spite of the seeming short-term nature of the recession in macroeconomic terms, some sectors of the economy, particularly export industries such as raw silk and cotton textiles, and the farmers who specialized in sericulture, suffered greatly. The financial sector also suffered: many banks that provided export or rural capital either failed or were absorbed by larger banks in 1920–21.[4]

Why did Takahashi persist in his big-spending and low-interest-rate policies when critics such as future prime minister Hamaguchi Osachi, allies such as Bank of Japan Governor Inoue Junnosuke, and common sense recommended otherwise? First, Takahashi continued to believe that the way to solve economic problems was to increase productivity and production in order to increase demand, rather than to contract the economy by cutting government spending and raising interest rates. The government, by building railroads, roads, and schools, developed infrastructure for future economic growth and at the same time created jobs. By keeping interest rates low, the government also encouraged entrepreneurs to borrow to build new facilities and generate jobs. Takahashi also understood, and admitted publicly, that it was necessary to cool the economy by contracting the money supply at the end of the wartime boom, but he equivocated on how and when to do it. Takahashi feared that stepping too hard on the brakes would create a recession and unemployment, but ironically by doing little he would help to create the very recession he sought to avoid.[5]

Second, Takahashi did not have a free hand in dealing with the army and navy; in fact, his only weapon in controlling military spending was persuasion. To complete a budget, the government needed the unanimous approval of all cabinet members, including Army Minister General Tanaka Giichi and Navy Minister Katō Tomosaburō. Prime Minister Hara, who had come to power with the reluctant support of Field Marshal Yamagata and the military, advocated providing the services with as much as (or indeed more than) the government could afford. The Ōkuma and Terauchi cabinets during the war made large, multiyear military appropriations, especially to the navy, which Takahashi inherited. In the words of Imamura Takeo, "That which vexed Takahashi most in formation of the 1920 budget was managing the military's demands," and in the words of Charles Schenking, "Takahashi shuddered over the requests presented by the navy and the army, but Hara encouraged him to find a way to provide funds to support both, claiming that national defense was the first priority of the budget." Therefore one cannot, as Hamaguchi did on the floor of the Diet on January 22, 1920, place the primary blame for the government's spending policy on Takahashi. In a meeting with Tanaka and Katō in an attempt to persuade them to reduce their demands, Takahashi presented his recurrent mantra, "Of course, we must have a strong national defense, but we must consider our national wealth at the same time. . . . The army and navy have put forward these large plans, both at the same time. Some of their demands must be more, and some less, important. Why have they not indicated that here?" Tanaka compromised and gave spending precedence to the navy, which impressed Takahashi very much. But the whole incident doubtless played a role in Takahashi's memorandum, presented to Hara the following year, to abolish the general staff system. Takahashi was an advocate of fiscal and monetary policies that encouraged "controlled growth"; he was not a "reckless spender." Moreover, far from being a free agent, he operated in a constraining milieu.[6]

"A Personal View of National Policies at Home and Abroad"

In the autumn of 1917, the Bolshevik Revolution took place, and the Soviet government came to power. Since large amounts of Allied munitions were stockpiled in Vladivostok, some 50,000 Czechoslovak troops remained in Siberia, and the United States feared unilateral Japanese intervention in the Russian Far East, the Allies, under the direction of American President Woodrow Wilson, decided to send a contingent of 25,000 troops to the area. Wilson asked the Japanese to provide 7,000 troops, and the Japanese cabinet, under the leadership of Prime Minister General Terauchi, overruling the army's general staff, which wanted to act independently of the Allies, agreed to contribute 12,000 troops to the joint venture. After the campaign began, however, the general staff, acting independently of both the Allies and the premier, took command of Japanese operations, and by November 1918, had 70,000 troops in the Amur River valley. In June of 1920, all of the Allies except the Japanese pulled their troops out of Siberia. The Japanese would remain for another two years before finally withdrawing in October 1922. The Siberian intervention was pointless, costly in terms of money (1,000,000,000 yen) and lives (3,000 men), and strained Japan's relations with Great Britain and the United States. At the end of September 1918, just as General Uehara Yūsaku (who ironically would be promoted to field marshal in 1921, while the operation was underway) and his subordinates in general staff headquarters were in the process of sextupling Japan's troop commitment in Siberia, the Hara government came to power.

The army's intransigence over Siberia outraged Takahashi. The dispatch of troops there was expensive, threatened Japan's relations with the countries Takahashi saw as its primary allies, and most dangerously in his view, revealed the army's unwillingness to follow the lead of the prime minister and his cabinet. Once troops were in the field, Uehara argued that the "right of supreme command" had set in—that is, the emperor, not the prime minister, commanded the army. In other words, the army reported to itself, and Hara did not have the authority to influence or terminate the operation.

In September 1920, Takahashi sent a memorandum to Hara entitled, "A Personal View of National Policies at Home and Abroad," in which he wrote:

The Japanese organization which gives foreigners the impression that our country is militaristic is the army's general staff. . . . Because of our general staff system, military organizations are not subordinated to the cabinet, but are independent of the nation's political structure. The army does not stop at planning to send troops abroad for military reasons, but interferes in diplomatic and economic decision making as well, so that our country does not have a unified foreign policy. . . . Because the army's general staff interferes with other state organs, we should abolish it and unify the army's administration [under the army ministry, part of the cabinet]. The navy's general staff happily does not have the same invidious effects as the army's, but it is an unnecessary organ. We should abolish both general staffs at the same time.

Hara shared Takahashi's aggravation over the Siberian intervention, but also understood that progress toward a system of governance by political parties depended on the goodwill of Yamagata and the military: "Since the proposal is unrealistic, it will needlessly make enemies for us." Accordingly, he suppressed publication of the memorandum as inflammatory, but not before word of it got out to Yamagata and Uehara, who were not amused. Takahashi would reveal his anger over the army's use of the so-called right of supreme command to avoid government control again in the 1930s. Takahashi was a politician who was committed, in the words of the dean of Marxist historians of Taishō democracy, Shinobu Seizaburō, to the "bourgeois principle of civilian control of the military." Even Hara wrote in his diary, "Naturally, should Yamagata die, there would be a chance of abolishing the General Staff as well as the world's misunderstanding of [our] militarism."[7]

"An Opinion Concerning the Establishment of East Asian Economic Power"

Takahashi not only distrusted an overly powerful military, but also an overly aggressive China policy as it too endangered Japan's peaceful economic development. Takahashi, as discussed above, believed that Japan should encourage the formation of a unified China, and should cooperate with its national government, based on the will of the Chinese people, to create a Chinese-Japanese economic alliance. While he saw one purpose of this new Chinese-Japanese union as creating a "third" economic force to compete in trade with the two major Western nations, he also believed Japan should act within the framework of what was acceptable to the richer and more powerful British and Americans. He therefore opposed the Twenty-One Demands, the Nishihara loans, and any form of military intervention on the mainland as they all stirred anti-Japanese feeling in China, antagonized the powers, and increased the Japanese military's demands for additional funds.[8] He feared a vicious circle of Chinese anti-Japanese nationalism, Japanese military intervention, and Anglo-American resistance.[9]

In May 1921, Takahashi sent Hara a memorandum entitled, "An Opinion Concerning the Establishment of East Asian Economic Power," in which he drew together the various threads of his thinking on China. He argued that Japan should withdraw all Japanese troops and military installations in China; end the use of loans to gain railroad, mining, and other rights there or as levers to force the Chinese to employ Japanese technicians and advisors; reverse the requirement that China provide current or future government income from increased taxes as security for the loans; and limit one-sided lending to regional and other special interest groups on the mainland. He rejected the idea that Manchuria was a separate entity from the rest of China, and that Japan had special interests and rights there. Takahashi reiterated that Japan benefited more from a strong, industrializing, and allied China than from a weak, decentralized one that could be picked apart by Japanese yen diplomacy and military intervention. He believed that the rise of Chinese nationalism would soon lead to the creation of a unified China, and that the two East Asian powers, working in unity, could create a new economic force to resist Anglo-American economic power. But he emphasized that the East Asian coalition he wanted to create should be an economic, not a military one, that it should compete economically with the powers within the internationally accepted framework for international trade, and that Japan's China policy should focus on a centralized China, not on one part, like Manchuria. He also welcomed European and North American capital in such a venture, although he added that if it were not forthcoming, Japan should act alone. His views ran counter to the ideas of the military, most civilian leaders, and much of public opinion at the time. In fact, his own prime minister labeled Takahashi's memorandum a "schoolboy theory that must be suppressed. We must be alert against its leaking out."[10]

Historians differ over whether this document was a prescient insight about the benefits of working with China both to cooperate and to compete economically with the Anglo-Americans, or a naïve and maybe even pan-Asian vision of an economic system in which Japanese capital used Chinese natural resources for Japanese economic growth. Three leading scholars of modern Japanese history, Mitani Taichirō, Banno Junji, and Itō Yukio, offer strikingly different interpretations of Takahashi's memorandum. Mitani writes that Takahashi's view was in the mercantilist tradition of Ōkubo Toshimichi, the doyen of early-Meiji industrialization, which held that Japan should industrialize without foreign borrowing. In Mitani's view, Takahashi advocated the use of the gold and specie garnered by a five-year period of trade surpluses during World War I as investment for the exploitation of Chinese natural resources to produce goods for a growing Japanese domestic market.

Banno's interpretation is that Takahashi wanted to attract, not exclude, foreign capital and use it along with Chinese natural resources to increase Japanese exports. Banno goes so far as to say, even though Takahashi says otherwise in his memorandum, that the finance minister created here a concept for the economic development of Manchuria; his views differed from those espoused later by Prime Minister General Tanaka Giichi (1927–29) only in that Takahashi advocated an economic approach and rejected military intervention.

Itō Yukio criticizes Banno's interpretation, and argues that Takahashi disagreed with the China policy of the Hara cabinet in which he served, which would explain Hara's rejoinder. The prime minister, in the context of what was generally advocated as China policy during and after World War I, used loans and military support, especially to the Chinese warlord

Zhang Zuolin, to advance Japanese influence and interests in southern Manchuria. Takahashi rejected this approach, which had been urged on Hara by the Kwantung Army, the Japanese force in the leased regions of northeast China, and instead proposed a policy of encouraging the creation of a unified, national government in China with which Japan could cooperate to resist the Anglo-American domination of East Asia. Kobayashi Michihiko, expanding on Itō's view, writes that Takahashi's proposal also differed from that of his close associate, Bank of Japan Governor Inoue Junnosuke, who preferred greater reliance on British and American capital. As Takahashi wrote in his memorandum, "If China and Japan do not develop cooperatively their latent economic potential, the British and Americans will invade East Asia economically, and we will have no choice but to capitulate under that power." Or as he told an interviewer in 1928, "If Great Britain and the United States conquer China economically, unlike a conquest by military force, such an economic conquest is not easily reversed."[11]

Itō's and Kobayashi's interpretations fit well with other aspects of Takahashi's perspective on economic development, and with what scholars such as Mark Metzler have written about Inoue. Takahashi's primary goal was Japan's economic development. This would best be accomplished in ways that avoided antagonizing the world's two major powers of the time, as they had capital, markets, raw materials, and technology that Japan needed. But this did not preclude economic competition with the Anglo-Americans, nor did it require Japan to accept every part of their system all of the time. While Inoue believed the Anglo-American system, including the gold standard, attained the level of an ideal model, to which Japan should conform, Takahashi saw it as a means to an end, which could be discarded if no longer useful. As for the question of whether Takahashi was a pan-Asianist, the answer is simply no. Contrary to true pan-Asianists, Takahashi spurned the idea of an emperor-centric, Japan-led mission to liberate Asia, opposed the use of military force on the mainland, and advocated an equal partnership between China and Japan. But whether his thinking would have changed if anti-Japanese nationalism and difficulties in creating a unified state in China had persisted and intensified is difficult to say. Takahashi, in one of his last statements before resigning the finance portfolio, opposed Tanaka Giichi's dispatch of troops to China in 1927, and disapproved of Japanese unilateralism in Manchuria and its military conquest in 1931–32, although he would come to live with the latter out of necessity. Luckily for his reputation, he was killed before the full-scale invasion of China in the summer of 1937, and thus did not have to make a bitter choice.

The Takahashi Government, November 13, 1921–June 12, 1922

On November 13, 1921, Takahashi became prime minister of Japan. Hara, on his way to make a political speech in western Japan, was stabbed to death on November 4 in Tokyo Station by a right-wing ideologue. Two of the *genrō*, Princes Matsukata and Saionji, conferred, decided that continuity was important since the Washington Naval Disarmament Conference was about to begin, recommended the cabinet go on with the finance minister as premier, and sent a messenger to secure the agreement of the ailing third *genrō*, Yamagata. Takahashi served as the head of the cabinet for seven months, one of the shortest tenures in history. Most historians see Takahashi as an inept politician, who lacked the necessary skills to run a political party government.[12] Takahashi himself believed this, and in 1934, looking back on his half year in office, offered the following analysis of his own term of service:

I entered the Seiyūkai because Count Yamamoto asked me to. I found that the party was complex and not the right organization for a person like me. I admired Hara for the way he ran the party so well. He was enthusiastic and had a great interest in the great and small, the significant and insignificant when it came to his party. He knew the names, faces, histories, and strengths of the party's members. He listened to each person's appeal individually and talked to each equally. I had no interest in such things, and didn't know who was who, and whose face was whose. I was an inappropriate person to be a party president and did not want to succeed Hara. When I was recommended as prime minister, I tried to refuse, but it was just at the time of the opening of the Washington Conference and we needed a government as soon as possible. We worried that if the Hara government did not continue, we would have to send new instructions to the delegation in Washington. . . . So I had no choice but to become prime minister.[13]

Imamura Takeo, Takahashi's preeminent Japanese biographer, thinks that Takahashi didst protest a bit too much when at the age of 80 he wrote this statement twelve years after the event. While it is true that Takahashi did not have Hara's political skills, Takahashi was without a doubt an ambitious man who enjoyed the prestige, if not the tribulations, of performing on center stage. But at the same time, Takahashi was a rationalist, who hated the traditional boss-patron type of relationship that Hara had developed with his party followers. Takahashi undoubtedly told the truth when he said he had little interest in people; in fact he was famous for forgetting the names of his subordinates in the finance ministry. Instead, he simply called them "Mr. Tax" or "Mr. Budget."

Not only did Takahashi lack Hara's political skills, he also lacked his long-standing status as Seiyūkai leader. A number of Takahashi's fellow party leaders, including for example Yamamoto Tatsuo, who had preceded Takahashi both as Governor of the Bank of Japan and as finance minister, were not happy that "the goose that followed became the first goose." In Imamura's words, "Takahashi was a party first grader who tried to win people over with reason and frankness." But those who had preceded him into the party were not ready to be won over easily, especially since Takahashi was in political primary school, while Hara had had a Ph.D.[14]

Takahashi failed as Seiyūkai prime minister for another, perhaps more important reason: policy. With his closest party colleague, Yokota Sennosuke, he proposed what in the context of 1921–22 must have seemed like a radical party platform. The following document, "A Private Proposal to Restructure the Takahashi Cabinet," lays out Takahashi's and Yokota's goals:

1. Cut the power of the Privy Council [a non-elected group that had sole authority to ratify treaties] drastically.
2. Abolish the Foreign Policy Research Council [a group set up to take control of foreign policy away from the larger cabinet].
3. Allow civilians to head the army and navy ministries, and place the two general staffs under ministry control.
4. Cut the army's armaments in half.
5. Establish universal suffrage.
6. Lower consumer prices.
7. Transfer the land tax and the business tax to local governments, and allow them to use the revenues to help pay local school costs.
8. Revise the public safety police [anti-radical activity] law and give workers the right to bargain collectively.

9. Choose prefectural governors by election.
10. Withdraw troops from Siberia completely, and open trade relations with the Soviet Union.
11. Act in advance of the [Anglo-American] powers in abolishing the unequal treaties in China, and stop acting like a stepmother toward China.
12. Try to bring the public to our position by acting with enthusiasm.
13. Carry out other social policies to the extent that it is possible.

Why Prime Minister Takahashi is the proper person for the job

1. He has served as prime minister and feels deeply about his long-term duty to his country.
2. He does not belong to any party faction, and will not play favorites.
3. He is impartial and not covetous.
4. If Count Yamamoto [Tatsuo] or others come to power, they will swim against the tide of the times.[15]

While Takahashi was prime minister, Japan joined the Washington Treaty system, the most comprehensive plan until that time to create a structure that would replace military with economic competition in East Asia. Although the negotiations that led up to the Washington Conference had begun before Hara's assassination, Takahashi enthusiastically supported these efforts for several reasons. First, naval armaments' limitations would reduce military spending, thus freeing government funds to be redirected toward areas Takahashi considered "productive," particularly the creation of infrastructure that would help in economic development. Second, the treaties that were signed in Washington established the principle of respect for the "territorial integrity of China," which meant no additional acquisitions of territory in China, and also required Japan to give up its newly acquired naval base at Qingdao on the Shandong Peninsula. Given Takahashi's commitment to an economic alliance with a unified China, his opposition to the use of loans and military force to gain special rights in Shandong and Manchuria, and his desire to prevent Chinese nationalism from segueing into anti-Japanese nationalism, the Nine Power Treaty over China was a godsend. But third and also important, the treaties signed in Washington brought Japan into an Anglo-American-Japanese alliance. While on the one hand, the agreements ended the bilateral Anglo-Japanese Alliance, a point of great pride to many Japanese, they helped dispel rising tensions between Japan and the United States, which after World War I had replaced Great

Britain as the world's dominant military and economic power. Membership in the Washington system allowed Japan to benefit from Anglo-American capital, markets, raw materials, and technology, while at the same time allowed it to free up domestic capital and make Japanese industry more productive and thus more competitive with the British and Americans. Cooperation, to Takahashi, did not require subservience or preclude economic competition.

Takahashi advocated reduced government spending, although in line with his principle of encouraging controlled growth, not to the extent that contractionists such as Hamaguchi approved. At a meeting to discuss the 1922 budget, Takahashi said, "Because of the economic situation, we must control the expansion of government expenditures. We must be frugal where we can be frugal . . . and postpone all expenditures that can be put off to the future." On January 21, 1922, he told the Diet, "Because of the Washington Conference, we can reduce military expenditures and have a little surplus for the future. I would like to increase money for elementary education and flood control." In spite of intense pressure from Army Minister Yamanashi Hanzō, the Seiyūkai, with the support of the opposition Kenseikai, passed a bill to reduce the size of the army and shorten the term of service for draftees by one-third to sixteen months. Takahashi also advanced a proposal to reorganize the bureaucracy to reduce government costs. In other words, Takahashi characteristically tried to cut in areas he saw as unproductive, but where possible to maintain spending on productive infrastructure.[16]

Takahashi called for Japan, as best it could with its smaller and more primitive industrial base, to imitate the increased productivity of American industry. He advocated larger and more efficient factories, which would use new forms of inanimate energy like electricity, to lower production costs and benefit consumers. He strove to rationalize industry, not in the manner of Hamaguchi and other Kenseikai financial leaders by reducing wages, laying off workers, and keeping interest rates high, but by increasing efficiency and investment, and thus production. Furthermore, unlike most economic leaders of the time, he wanted workers to benefit in the process through higher wages.[17] In a statement entitled "Speaking of First Principles of Economics: Concerning Our Country's Production," written in October 1925, three years after he had resigned as prime minister, he laid out his views on increasing productivity and sharing the benefits of efficiency with workers:

Everyone says that prices are high because wages are high. They say that wages must come down. But since the recipients of the so-called high wages are carpenters and skilled factory workers, we cannot simply conclude that prices are high or low because wages are high or low. We are in the process of creating a system that produces high quality goods in great quantities. In this system, the cost of capital is also one of the factors of production. There is no reason to posit that wages of each individual worker determine prices, because if his efficiency improves (through the use of capital), his wages will rise and the prices charged to the consumer will fall at the same time. Let me repeat: one cannot discuss prices by looking only at wages.

For example, posit that it takes ten workers to build something in a fixed period of time. But, because of increases in efficiency, six men can make the same product in the same time, thus saving four men's wages. The cost of production falls by the wages of four workers. Managers then must decide how to distribute the savings. It would be fair to increase the wages of the six remaining workers by half the savings. At the same time, as the cost of production declines by the wages of two workers, the product becomes cheaper, and consumers benefit. If managers operate their businesses in this way, we would have no reason for conflict between labor and capital, and no strikes.

Today's managers blame low efficiency on their workers. But I think the companies have a duty to raise the productivity of their workers. To make no attempt to do this, and to blame the workers is wrong. It is not enough for capitalists to talk about a general increase in productivity. They must invest new capital.

Takahashi then proceeded to criticize the Kenseikai government for its tight-money policies that kept interest rates high and thus deterred business investment:

One has difficulty finding new capital today. Banks even call in money they lent in the past. They invest in few new projects and do not expand old ones. Private entrepreneurs and railroads follow the government's tight fiscal and monetary policies and retrench.

The problem is high interest rates. No matter how efficient a business, it is almost impossible to show a 10 percent return on investment these days. Our businessmen are powerless in the face of these [high interest rates]. It is impossible to use capital profitably. They need to improve the efficiency of their capital as well as of their workers, but the higher interest rates are, the more the efficiency of capital declines. If interest rates fell, capital could be used more efficiently.[18]

One can only be struck by the transformation of Takahashi's ideas about economic development from an emphasis on rural, traditional industries, à la his mentor Maeda Masana in the 1880s, to one focused on urban, modern industries in the 1920s. As the structure of Japan's economy changed, so too did Takahashi's empirically based ideas about growth, which would ultimately undermine his support in his own political party.

But at the same time that Takahashi came to realize that Japan's economic development depended more on modern, heavy industry than on its traditional, rural counterpart, he also advocated, in the Maeda tradition, decentralization of government because he believed that institutions such as education should fit local customs and needs. He also advocated reducing the heavy tax burden on middle and poorer farmers since they particularly suffered as the structure of the economy shifted toward an urban focus.[19] Takahashi explained this as follows in the *Asahi shinbun*:

In 1919, while Hara was prime minister, I proposed local autonomy and transfer of the land tax to local authorities. We would turn education, public works, and public health over to the regions. Thus, they needed their own fiscal base, and I proposed the land tax as the answer. But Hara did not carry this forward. Why not? Because at that time—and it's still true—we do not have a tax as reliable as the land tax. On top of that, Matsukata opposed it. He said, "Takahashi's proposal is outrageous. We are in a fix to have that person as finance minister." Hara knew that the *genrō* opposed the idea. Regional autonomy was all right, but he did not agree to the transfer of the land tax.

I visited Prince Matsukata in Kamakura and explained my proposal. Matsukata replied, "in times of national emergency, one can increase taxes mostly rapidly using the land tax. There is no other tax as solid. We cannot turn it over to local government."

I argued that regional people were suffering under the land tax and other add-on taxes.... But the old prince did not agree. He said, "I completely agree about rural autonomy. We must do it. But I cannot agree with you about transferring the land tax." Then Matsukata told stories about the old days. "I risked my life on collecting the land tax in money. We had to face rebellion to collect the land tax in money. I expected to be killed over that enterprise. . . ." So thinking there is nothing I could say to persuade the old man, I said, "your achievement was a great one, but today, if we do not distribute taxes equitably, we cannot induce people to pay their taxes. . . ." When I came to see him again, he compromised and said there was nothing to do but transfer the tax. . . . But Hara would not agree to giving local regions control over the land tax. At the same time, he approved of giving regions control over schools because (like me) he did not approve of nationally uniform education, and wanted to encourage education suited to each region.[20]

Finally, Prime Minister Takahashi attempted to reverse three more of the party's positions. He advocated a graduated income tax to reduce the growing gap between the incomes of the rich and poor. He supported the establishment of universal manhood suffrage, which Hara had opposed. Takahashi was lukewarm at best toward the passage of a law to control radical social movements, which was a pet project of Hara and Tokonami Takejirō, who was home minister for both Hara and Takahashi. In 1922, Takahashi killed the "Bill to Control Extreme Social Movements," by refusing to call a special, extended session of the Diet so the House of Peers could vote on the bill.[21]

Takahashi failed as prime minister and leader of the Seiyūkai not only because he lacked Hara's skills in dealing with party members, but also because he proposed a platform that challenged long-standing party policies and threatened the party's support bases, regardless of how forward-looking and rational the platform appears in retrospect. Takahashi also failed because in the minds of other party leaders, and for that matter much of the public, he did not have the authority to modify Hara's policies: to them, Takahashi was "Prime Minister pro tem," as the *genrō* Saionji later said, not a legitimate prime minister in his own right. Since the Seiyūkai's primary electoral backing came from the countryside, a shift to a focus on city-based modern industry and even Takahashi's moderate efforts to control spending (which doubled between 1917 and 1920, but remained more or less the same through the final two Takahashi budgets) threatened his party's base. His adamant support for universal suffrage not only contradicted Hara's position, but also endangered the rural elites' control of their towns and villages; these men were the backbone of the Seiyūkai's regional power structure. His opposition to laws to control radical activity reversed Hara's position, and, at the same time, angered important party leaders such as Tokonami and Nakahashi Tokugorō, the education minister. Takahashi's advocacy of dealing with a centralized China and his opposition to loans to regional warlords also reversed Hara's policies and angered party leaders or potential party leaders such as the industrialist Den Kenjirō or General Tanaka Giichi, who wanted a more aggressive China policy. Takahashi's continued belief that Japan should increase productivity and export capacity before returning to the gold standard (Japan, like the other major industrial nations, had left the gold standard during the World War I inflation) irritated men such as Agriculture and Commerce Minister Yamamoto, with whom Takahashi's relations had been strained since their service together in the Bank of Japan.[22]

Frustrated by his inability to win party support for his policies, Takahashi and his primary advisor, Yokota, decided to reorganize the cabinet to divest it of their opponents. On May 2, the prime minister announced at a cabinet meeting that he wanted to restructure the cabinet, and called for everyone's resignation. But the men he wanted to get rid of, including Home Minister Tokonami, Agriculture and Commerce Minister Yamamoto, Education Minister Nakahashi, and Railroad Minister Motoda Hajime, fought back and mobilized their supporters to oppose reform. Unfortunately for Takahashi, the press did not come to his side: they saw his government as merely the continuation of Hara's, and thus without the political stature to carry out political reorganization. On June 12, after only seven months in office, Takahashi resigned as prime minister. His primary political failing was biting off a bigger mouthful than he could chew, not an inability to stroke his fellow party members. Itō Yukio also suggests that Takahashi was not tough enough: he did not pressure recalcitrant ministers to fall into line.[23] Nevertheless, on the basis of the reforms it attempted, Takahashi's government in 1921–22 stands with the opposition Minseitō's in 1929–30 as one of the twin peaks of prewar liberalism.

The Movement to Protect Constitutional Government

Three non-party cabinets held power from June 1922 until June 1924. The first two, headed by retired admirals Katō Tomosaburō and Yamamoto Gonnohyōe, in whose cabinet Takahashi had served in 1913, passed relatively uneventfully, but the formation of the third, headed by Kiyoura Keigo, a former home ministry bureaucrat and Yamagata Aritomo protégé, gave rise to a powerful democratizing movement,

"The Movement to Protect Constitutional Government," which formed in January 1924 to oppose the third successive non-party government. As each of these cabinets formed, Takahashi and other Seiyūkai members expected their party to be asked to govern, but Saionji, who at this time preferred neutral governments, did not choose them. Finally, after they were passed over for the third time, Takahashi's wing of the Seiyūkai joined forces with two other parties, the Kenseikai and the Kakushin Kurabu (Reform Club), to oppose Kiyoura. The anti-Takahashi faction of his party broke away, decided to support the Kiyoura government, and renamed themselves Seiyū Hontō (Real Seiyū Party). To face down the opposition, the new prime minister dissolved the parliament and called for a new election. When the votes had been counted in May, the Kenseikai had won the most seats, the opposition Seiyū Hontō the second most, and Takahashi's Seiyūkai came in third. Nonetheless the three parties in the anti-Kiyoura coalition held a solid majority of the seats in the Diet, and in June, Saionji, by this time the only active *genrō*, had no choice but to ask them to form a government.[24]

When the new parliament met, the lower house of the Diet had a new member: Takahashi Korekiyo. In an emotional speech on January 15, before his party split over whether to support Kiyoura, Takahashi announced, "To serve the state, I have decided to resign my peerage to run for the House of Representatives in the next election" (in 1920, Takahashi had been promoted from baron to viscount). The city council of Morioka, the former castle town of Nanbu domain in the northeast, asked Takahashi to run for Hara's former seat, and Takahashi accepted. In spite of his having the chance to run in what seemed a safe district, however, the election was closely contested. The breakaway wing of Takahashi's own party put up a local candidate to oppose him. Former Home Minister Tokonami, who had broken with Takahashi over his opposition to the law to suppress radical activity, went to Morioka to direct the Seiyū Hontō candidate's campaign, and the Kiyoura government paid 60 bureaucrats to return home to Morioka to vote for him. Takahashi, in the last election before universal manhood suffrage, won a close election by a vote of 859 to 810.[25]

Fukai Eigo, in a letter to Paul Warburg, the brother-in-law of Frieda Schiff Warburg, dated August 7, 1924, described Takahashi's electoral victory as follows:

I think Mr. Takahashi's new political career will be of particular interest to you. His resignation of the peerage was a vindication of principle, because the Kiyoura Cabinet was formed mainly by members of the House of Peers in disregard of powerful parties in the House of Representatives. The then Viscount Takahashi was the leader of the biggest of those parties. When he declared himself against the so-called "peers' cabinet," a large portion of his followers seceded; but he was a veritable hero of the day. In the general election, he was newly elected as a commoner. The parties in opposition commanded the majority, and the resignation of the Kiyoura Cabinet ensued. But Mr. Takahashi's party had ceased to be the biggest one. Then public attention was focused on the question whether Mr. Takahashi, who had been in a commanding position as ex-premier and leader of the majority in the House, would take a secondary post in the coming cabinet, which Viscount Kato, leader of the biggest party after the election, was summoned to form. Personal considerations appeared to command [Takahashi's] standing aside. But he joined the Cabinet with all of his heart, because as he said in a brief statement, a strong cabinet was required in order to give effect to the political principle entertained by him and his friends. The public-spiritedness has been appreciated by his colleagues and widely recognized by the public. In a position likely to be a little awkward, his actions and speeches have been full of admirable grace and unaffected self-confidence. He is uncommonly popular at present and is admittedly a very interesting figure in our political arena.[26]

Saionji asked Katō Takaaki, the head of the Kenseikai, to form a new three-party government, and after intense negotiations over which cabinet positions would go to the two junior parties in the coalition, Takahashi agreed to serve as Minister of Agriculture and Commerce. Takahashi became the minister in charge of economic development in a cabinet in which his policy nemesis, the budget-slashing contractionist Hamaguchi Osachi, served as finance minister. Takahashi's closest associate in the Seiyūkai, Yokota Sennosuke, became justice minister.[27]

From Takahashi's point of view, the government achieved two major goals during his ten months in office. First, it passed the universal suffrage law. From 1925 on, almost all men over the age of 25, rich or poor (with those on welfare excluded), had the right to vote. Second, reflecting Takahashi's commitment to increasing industrial productivity to make the country and its citizens richer, he proposed and successfully brought to fruition the division of the Agriculture and Commerce Ministry into two separate ministries. He thought that the government organization in charge of encouraging industrial development should be separate from that which handled agriculture. In April, following the successful separation of the two ministries, and after General Tanaka Giichi succeeded to the leadership of the Seiyūkai, Takahashi submitted his resignation from both the government and the party chairmanship. At age 70, he went into retirement to tend his bonsai, appreciate his Buddhist statues, and play with his grandchildren.[28]

On May 5, 1925, Fukai wrote once more of Takahashi to Paul Warburg:

Your friend Mr. Korekiyo Takahashi has recently resigned his portfolio in the Cabinet as well as the leadership of the Seiyukai Party. As I told you before, it must have been a great sacrifice on his part to join the present Cabinet. The main purpose for which the coalition of the "three parties"—of which his party was one—was effected were the adoption of universal suffrage and the reform of the House of Peers. It may be fairly said that the former was accomplished in the last session of the Diet. In regard to the latter, some changes were initiated in the contemplated direction. Considering his advanced age, I think it is quite natural for him to desire at this juncture to return to a more quiet life. So, I think, the resignation came soon after the close of the Diet's session. Everyone thinks he chose the right moment and now that his part of active political strife is at an end, high tributes of respect and sympathy are paid him from all quarters. The Imperial Regent [who would become emperor the next year] especially ordained that in the Court he shall be accorded honours attached to a Prime Minister, which office he held.[29]

Fukai could not know in May 1925 that Takahashi would shun the quiet life and go on to serve four more terms as finance minister.

Given the policy positions of Takahashi's and Yokota's wing of the Seiyūkai, which opposed both an aggressive foreign policy toward China and harsh legislation to control radical thought, the choice of Tanaka as Takahashi's successor seems an odd one; indeed, the two men had locked horns over the Siberian intervention and the military budget when both served in the Hara Cabinet in 1918–21. But when Justice Minister Yokota, Takahashi's preferred successor, died in February 1925, Takahashi, who very much wanted to retire, repeatedly urged the party leaders to find a new leader, and they finally turned to Tanaka, who had the advantage over other candidates of being a nationally known figure. When he became prime minister in April 1927, Tanaka chose to reject a foreign policy of cooperation with the British and Americans, to emphasize Japan's special position in southern Manchuria, to extend Japanese influence into northern Manchuria, to use military force to intervene in China's efforts to create a unified, nationalist government, and to crack down harshly on the Japan Communist Party.[30] In the space of two years, Takahashi's "liberal" Seiyūkai segued into a far more conservative party. But to give added support to the dictum that politics creates strange bedfellows, on June 1, 1927, the Seiyū Hontō, which supported the views espoused by Tanaka, merged with the Kenseikai, which like Takahashi and Yokota, opposed them.

The Financial Panic of 1927

Many corporations that expanded their business during the World War I boom suffered during the postwar contraction, and were saved from bankruptcy only when the finance ministry under Takahashi and the Bank of Japan under its governor at the time, Inoue Junnosuke, provided them with government-backed loans. Many of these postwar loans had not been repaid when the Great Kantō Earthquake occurred in September 1923. After the natural disaster, the Bank of Japan issued loans known as "earthquake bills" (*shinsai tegata*) to help companies rebuild that had suffered serious damage to their facilities, and many of these loans went to companies such as Suzuki Shōten, which was already highly leveraged from its rapid wartime expansion. Since Suzuki, under the direction of an aggressive financier named Kaneko Naokichi, owned a number of efficient companies that produced goods such as textiles, steel, and ships, the government was concerned about their solvency. At the same time, the Kenseikai government in 1926–27, headed by Wakatsuki Reijirō, a former contractionist finance minister, wanted to return Japan to the gold standard as soon as possible. As a result, in January 1927, Finance Minister Kataoka Naoharu proposed a plan to use low-interest loans to redeem the outstanding earthquake bills as part of an effort to restore order to the financial world.

Kataoka, understanding the delicacy of what he proposed, talked to the leaders of all three major opposition parties about the need for restraint in attacking the government over this issue. Even General Tanaka, the blunt-speaking leader of the Seiyūkai, agreed to support the government. But just as the Diet began to discuss the question, the press reported that the government party was negotiating with the Seiyū Hontō over the possibility of a merger. The Seiyūkai's leadership, clearly understanding that such a move would give the new party a clear majority in the House of Representatives, decided the agreement was off and began to question Kataoka aggressively. Under belligerent interrogation in the Diet, Kataoka, on March 14, 1927, made his famous "slip of the tongue," in which he told the Diet incorrectly that the Watanabe Bank had failed that morning. Soon thereafter the Watanabe and five other banks did go bankrupt, and the members of the Seiyūkai, smelling an issue to bring them back into the majority, continued to attack Kataoka and the government mercilessly.

Suzuki's largest creditor was the Taiwan Bank, a joint government-private bank that served as the primary bank in one of Japan's major colonies. During World War I, the bank had begun lending to Suzuki, which produced camphor and sugar in Taiwan, and as the company faced bankruptcy after the war, it poured millions of additional yen into the enterprise to stave off failure—good yen after bad. By April 1, word leaked out that Suzuki and the Taiwan Bank were in deep financial trouble, and the latter turned to the Bank of Japan for emergency funds for protection against bankruptcy. Kataoka proposed that the central bank provide 200,000,000 yen without security to the Taiwan Bank, but the Bank of Japan refused to make the funds available without legislation to permit it. The Diet session having ended, the government sent the proposal to the Privy Council for approval, but the council rejected it. On April 17, the Wakatsuki cabinet resigned. The next day the Taiwan Bank closed, many small and medium banks followed suit, and a financial panic threatened in which dozens of bankruptcies appeared likely.[31]

On April 20, Saionji asked Tanaka to form a Seiyūkai government, and the general quickly asked Takahashi to come out of retirement to serve as finance minister. Takahashi, concerned about Japan's credit abroad, immediately agreed to take on the job long enough to find a solution to the crisis; in the end, his fourth term as finance minister lasted six weeks. He proposed two measures: first, a bank moratorium to end runs on healthy banks until stability in financial markets could be re-established; second, a special session of the Diet to discuss how to save the Taiwan Bank. The Privy Council, which had rejected Kataoka's proposal less than a week earlier, immediately approved a three-week bank moratorium; only money to pay wages or withdrawals of 500 yen or less were permitted.

On the surface, the proposal to the Diet seemed to face a greater danger. The Seiyūkai was a minority party and had only 160 seats versus 232 for its rivals. When the Diet met for a four-day session on May 5, Takahashi proposed that the Bank of Japan provide up to 500,000,000 yen in guarantees to the Bank of Taiwan and other financial institutions. The measure passed easily, because in his speech Takahashi emphasized the nation's needs, and the Kenseikai members, apparently less partisan than their rivals, voted for Takahashi's proposed legislation, which was more or less the same as that proposed by Kataoka a month earlier. Although in the end, the Bank of Japan provided 879,000,000 yen in loans to banks, substantially more than the legislation provided for, the bank crisis was solved. On June 2, Takahashi retired yet again and returned home to his house and garden in Omote-machi. His parting contribution to the government was to criticize Tanaka's dispatch of troops to Qingdao and north China in May.[32]

TWELVE

"Japan's Keynes":
Japan and the World Depression, 1929–34

Takahashi became finance minister for the fifth of what would be
seven times in December 1931, at the age of 77—during the depths of
the world depression—and implemented the countercyclical "Keynesian" economic policies for which he became famous. Prices were falling
sharply, unemployment rising, farmers suffering from the collapse of
agricultural commodity prices, industrial production stagnating, factories under- or unutilized, and investment in new plants and equipment
evaporating. To counter these problems, within a little more than half
a year of coming to office, Takahashi engineered Japan's recovery by
introducing a series of unorthodox, reflationary monetary and fiscal
policies that radically reversed his predecessor's conservative, deflationary policies.[1]

In monetary policy, Takahashi removed Japan from the gold standard, ended the convertibility of paper money for gold, devalued the
yen vis-à-vis the dollar and pound, reduced the Bank of Japan's prime
rate to further encourage lower interest rates, and introduced legislation
to raise the limit on the Bank of Japan's issuance of bank notes. With
the impact of cheaper currency, Japan's exports boomed even while
the rest of the world's trade contracted. The value of Japanese exports
in constant yen increased by almost 2.5 times between 1931 and 1937.

Takahashi then introduced a countercyclical fiscal policy by increasing government spending to stimulate demand. He made up the differ-

ence between expenditures and income not by raising taxes, but by selling low-interest government bonds directly to the Bank of Japan—the so-called "undertaking (*hikiuke*) system." Government spending increased the amount of money in circulation and thereby increased effective demand. Along with expanding exports, this stimulated production and re-employment: people had more money to spend and Japan began to recover from the depression. Takahashi's policies worked, and by 1935–36, half a decade before the United States would, Japan returned to complete utilization of capacity and to full employment, and did so with an inflation rate of less than 3 percent per year.[2]

Although to many scholars, Takahashi carried out "one of the most successful combinations of fiscal, monetary, and foreign exchange rate policies, in an adverse international environment, the world has ever seen," other contemporary and later economists, historians, and journalists have criticized his performance.[3] Although going off the gold standard and devaluing the yen led to an upsurge in Japan's exports, was this not a case of social dumping or "beggaring thy neighbor," that is, saving your own trade ship at the expense of others?[4] Was Takahashi guilty of a "reckless fiscal policy" because his introduction of the sale of treasury bonds to the central bank rather than directly on the open market would lead to dangerous inflation after his assassination in 1936? Was not the policy of selling treasury bonds to the Bank of Japan rather than to the public dangerous because it gave finance ministry bureaucrats and central bankers the power to expand the money supply free from market constraints?[5] Did not Takahashi's spending, which went primarily to rural relief and the military, play a vital role in the rise of militarism and the road to Japan's aggressive war against China, the United States, and their allies?[6] Did not rural relief expenditures fail to bring any significant help to poor farmers?[7] And even had they done so in 1932–34, why did Takahashi's rural relief spending end after 1934?[8]

The Onset of the Shōwa Depression:
Japan's Return to the Gold Standard, 1929–31

Japan fell into depression at the midpoint of the interwar decades for two reasons: the impact of the world depression, signaled by the collapse of the New York stock market in October 1929, and the Japanese government's decision earlier in the same year to return to the gold standard

at the pre–World War I price of gold. Like most other industrial or industrializing nations, Japan left the gold standard during the war, in September 1917, the same time as did the United States. In April 1919, the
United States became the first of the combatant nations to lift the embargo on the export of gold, in essence returning to the gold standard,
but Japan did not follow suit. Even in the following decade, when most
Japanese financial leaders supported going back to gold, and doing so
at the prewar parity, Japan equivocated. In 1919, as finance minister in
the Hara government, Takahashi resisted following the United States
because he believed Japan should store gold and specie for investment to
help China in its future economic development. In September 1923, as a
new government planned to return to the gold standard, the devastating
Kantō Earthquake intervened, and the inflationary fiscal and monetary
policies necessary for reconstruction devalued the yen and precluded
ending the embargo on the export of gold. Again in 1927, a fiscal crisis
that had been produced by an attempt to return to the gold standard by
liquidating earthquake bills—essentially easy money lent in the aftermath
of the 1923 disaster to major banks and corporations, some of which
were already on the brink of bankruptcy—intervened.

Although Japan did not make a firm decision to return to gold until
the contractionist Hamaguchi Osachi became prime minister in July 1929
and appointed Inoue Junnosuke as his finance minister, the consensus
among financial leaders in the 1920s was that Japan, the only "power"
not back on the gold standard, should return to it as soon as possible—
and nearly everyone recommended going back at the pre–World War I
price of gold. In fact, this widely held view caused most cabinets to pursue tight monetary and fiscal policies during the decade, a strategy that
not only inhibited exports, but also deflated consumer prices (which fell
by 18.7 percent between their post–World War I high in 1920 and their
pre-depression low in 1929) and lessened domestic demand. Japan's economic stagnation in the 1920s is partly attributable to the aspiration of
most of its leaders to return to the gold standard at the prewar parity.
Satō Kazuo has suggested that what Japan needed in the 1920s was the
opposite, that is, the policies Takahashi introduced in 1932, which would
have brought "recovery from stagnation without military fervor."[9]

The 1920s were also the high point of democratization in Japan.
From the time Hara took office in September 1918 until Inukai Tsuyo-

shi was assassinated on May 15, 1932 (with the exception of a short interregnum of bureaucratic governments in 1922–24), two political parties dominated Tokyo's political scene: the Minseitō (Kenseikai before 1927) and the Seiyūkai. Members of parliament were selected in general elections (and after 1925, by universal manhood suffrage), and the head of the victorious party served as prime minister. Although some have argued that the two parties were much like tweedledum and tweedledee in the sense that both were bourgeois parties that did little to help the urban and rural poor, in fact by the end of the 1920s they came to advocate quite different policies. The Minseitō, led during this period by two ex-finance ministry bureaucrats, Hamaguchi Osachi and Wakatsuki Reijirō, advocated fiscal retrenchment, disarmament, and cooperation with the powers over China. The Seiyūkai, led by Takahashi and then his successor, retired General Tanaka Giichi, advocated fiscal spending to stimulate the economy, and after Tanaka became prime minister in April 1927, promoted expanded military spending and a forceful foreign policy toward China. The views of Takahashi himself, who served for six weeks in 1927 as Tanaka's finance minister, and those of Inukai Tsuyoshi, who served as Seiyūkai prime minister from December 1931 until his murder on May 15, 1932, were situated between the two parties. As Seiyūkai politicians, they favored liberal fiscal spending for economically productive purposes, but at the same time they opposed their party's advocacy of unproductive military spending and of a positive foreign policy toward China. Takahashi and Inukai feared that intervention on the Asian mainland would both needlessly antagonize the Chinese and lead to Japan's estrangement from its natural allies, the United States and Great Britain.[10]

Hamaguchi, a former finance ministry bureaucrat, finance minister, and strident critic of Takahashi's "reckless" fiscal spending, formed his Minseitō government in July 1929 with four major objectives: participation in international naval disarmament arrangements to promote peaceful solutions to conflict and to reduce military spending; balanced budgets and a resultant elimination of governmental borrowing; a return to the gold standard at the prewar exchange rate to facilitate international trade; and a tight money policy that would "rationalize" the financial and industrial world, that is, that would cause an economic contraction to force weak companies into bankruptcy and leave the healthy ones to flourish: a "wringing out," as he called it. Hamaguchi selected a non-party member, Inoue Junnosuke, as his finance minister to execute his monetary and fiscal policies even though Inoue, as governor of the Bank of Japan, had helped Takahashi in his efforts to save failing companies in the early 1920s and again in 1927, and had publicly stated only ten days prior to his invitation to join the government that "To go on the gold standard now is like forcing a man with pulmonary disease to run a marathon."[11]

Why did Inoue make this dramatic turnabout in less than a fortnight? Much has been written about Inoue's classical economic approach, and its contrast with Takahashi's "Keynesian" views, but the fact of the matter is that before Inoue became finance minister in July 1929, the public considered him a member of Takahashi's "loose money" team. Why would Hamaguchi, a balanced-budget zealot, ask Inoue to serve as his finance minister to return to the gold standard, and why could Inoue accept? The answer, it has been suggested, was that Hamaguchi, the head of a party government, needed a respected, non-party financial statesman with good connections on Wall Street and in the City of London, such as Inoue, to promote his deflationary policies to the public, and that Inoue's prime motivation was his ambitiousness. In Japan in the 1920s, a civil bureaucrat or even a retired general such as Tanaka could become prime minister only by joining a political party, and Inoue had ambitions to head the government. If Hamaguchi intended a return to the gold standard anyway, should not Inoue be the one to lead the way? If he succeeded in this difficult assignment, he would prove he was of prime ministerial timber.[12]

Hamaguchi and Inoue shared another motivation for returning to the gold standard, one held in common with most of their contemporaries: a visceral pride in Japan's position as one of the "powers." The world's leaders, meeting in Paris in 1918–19 at the end of World War I, had anointed Japan one of the major victorious powers, and thus one of the five permanent members of the League of Nations, in addition to the United States, Great Britain, France, and Italy, and to the exclusion of the pariah states, Germany and the Soviet Union. The Japanese, only recently out from under the yoke of the imperialist unequal treaties, and in the process of creating another sign of great power status, their own empire, reacted with a pride that was understandable, but that sometimes stood in the way of clearheaded decision-making. At the Genoa Conference in 1922, all advanced industrializing countries pledged to return to the gold standard and by 1929, all had done so except Japan. National pride, and the related desire to meet the wishes of great power financiers such as Inoue's friend, Thomas Lamont of J. P. Morgan in New York, impelled the finance minister to join Hamaguchi in acting. Takahashi, at least as nationalistic as Inoue, had a clearer understanding of Japan's place in the world: a country with a GNP one-seventh of the United States' and one-third of Great Britain's and France's should not blindly follow their lead out of a desire to prove that it deserved to be one of the powers. Takahashi's nationalism led him to believe that growing the Japanese economy came first, and proof of Japan's international status second; Inoue's priorities seemed to be the other way around.[13]

Inoue understood that a return to the gold standard would not be painless, but he believed that the long-term benefits of "rationalization" and a stable exchange rate outweighed what he viewed as a short-term cost, induced deflation. When the new government came to power, the yen-dollar exchange rate stood at 100 yen to 44.6 dollars. In order to return to the gold standard at the prewar parity, 100 yen to 49.875 dollars, Inoue needed to value the yen upwardly by more than 10 percent, which required monetary and budgetary austerity at home. In preparation for ending the embargo on gold exports, Inoue introduced stringent reforms: encouragement of household frugality to cut domestic consumption and especially imports, higher interest rates, and reduced government spending. Inoue not only attempted (unsuccessfully) to cut the salaries of civil servants, but he also curtailed a number of public works projects, such as construction of the new parliament and home ministry buildings and the police headquarters. Further, he also dispatched one of his lieutenants, Tsushima Juichi, to New York to win from Lamont and others financial backing to protect against the expected outflow of gold, essentially conceding that Inoue could not successfully carry out his policies without Wall Street support. From the point of view of returning to the gold standard, Inoue's policies succeeded splendidly: by the time Japan went back on gold in January 1930, the exchange rate had risen to its prewar parity. But in terms of the Japanese economy, Inoue's program was tragic. The value of Bank of Japan notes in circulation fell by 12.5 percent in 1930 and another 7.4 percent in 1931. Consumer prices fell by 8.3 percent in 1930, and 12 percent more in 1931. Accordingly, demand, production, and corporate investment in new facilities fell, companies laid off workers and reduced wages, and by the autumn of 1929, Japan descended into what the economic historian Nakamura Takafusa has dubbed the "Gold Standard Preparation Recession."[14]

Although most observers in 1929 approved of Japan's return to the gold standard, at least before the recession set in that autumn, the manner and timing of Inoue's policy did not go uncontested. The so-called New Par Gang of Four, the economic journalists Ishibashi Tanzan and Takahashi Kamekichi and their colleagues at the *Tōyō keizai shinpō*, a leading liberal economic journal and the donjon in Japan of what came to be called Keynesianism, opposed Inoue's patriotic decision to return to the gold standard at the prewar parity, and advocated returning at the current exchange rate, as Italy and France had done. This would grant Japan the benefits of a stable exchange rate system, yet avoid the deflation that would inevitably follow an upward revaluation of the yen. Ishibashi, who had translated *The Economic Consequences of Mr. Churchill*, Keynes's critique of Great Britain's return to the gold standard at the prewar parity in 1925, well understood the deflationary impact Inoue's policy would have on Japan's economy. Later, as Japan's leading inflationist in the 1930s, Ishibashi became a frequent supporter, and occasional critic, of Takahashi's monetary and fiscal policies.[15]

Another critic of Inoue was Takahashi. Like most of his contemporaries, Takahashi understood the benefits of adopting the gold standard, but he harbored grave misgivings over Inoue's timing as recession set in, and said so in a magazine article in November 1929 that must be one of the most engaging and cogent expositions of Keynesian economics ever published:

If a person has the ability to live on 5,000 yen per year, but saves and lives on 3,000, he saves 2,000 yen. He amasses savings year by year, and we heartily approve. But if we look at it from the point of view of the national economy, the 2,000 yen he saves through frugality lessens the demand for goods, and reduces national production by this amount. Thus, from the point of view of the nation, a person who can live on 5,000 yen per year should live profligately at that level.

To put it in plain language, if a person goes to a geisha house and calls a geisha, eats luxurious food, and spends 2,000 yen, we disapprove morally. But if we analyze how that money is used, we find that the part that paid for food helps support the chef's salary, and the part used to buy fish, meat, vegetables, and seasoning, and the part for transporting it is paid to the supplying merchants. That part then wets the pockets of farmers and fishermen.

The farmers, fishermen, and merchants who receive the money then buy clothes, food, and shelter. And the geisha uses the money to purchase food, clothes, cosmetics, and to pay taxes. If this hypothetical man does not go to a geisha house and saves his 2,000 yen, bank deposits will grow, but the efficacy of his money will be lessened.

But he does go to a geisha house, and the money is transferred to the hands of farmers, artisans, and fishermen. It goes in turn to various other producers and works twenty or thirty times over. From the individual's point of view, it would be good to save his 2,000 yen, but when seen from the vantage point of the national economy, because the money works twenty or thirty times over, spending is better. This is where an individual's budget and the national economy differ. This is an extreme example and I do not encourage people to go to geisha houses. People without the wherewithal should not borrow money to consume extravagantly. The point I want to make is that what is good for the individual and what is good for the nation are different.

Takahashi, having used his pithy geisha house analogy to encourage deficit financing, then went on to criticize the Hamaguchi government for its constrictive fiscal policies during the onset of a recession:

No matter how much we praise individual frugality, we do not applaud a national policy that reduces Japan's industrial power. Adopting a restrictive fiscal policy means constraining new governmental spending, and the finance minister has cancelled several projects already begun. If one passes through Nagata-chō these days, one sees the lonely structural steel framework of the new parliament building. The government stopped work on it midway through its construction, and the precincts look like a deserted old mountain temple. In Kasumigaseki, workers had put the foundations of the Home Ministry's new building in place, and across from the Sakuradamon gate to the imperial palace, the steel girders of police headquarters seemed completed. But when I drove by four or five days ago, I saw not a single construction worker on the job. Not even a cuckoo was singing.

When the government stopped work on these three projects, builders lost their contracts. They in turn laid off clerks, engineers, and construction workers, and ended contracts with suppliers of needed materials and merchants in general. All are the victims of government frugality. The people who lost their jobs lost disposable income. The workers' reduced buying power was passed on to their suppliers and to people not directly involved in this construction work. They too laid off workers and this led to further reductions in production. As a result, the government's policies invited general recession.

We have heard a great deal recently from the government about the need for contraction and frugality to prepare for ending the embargo on the export of gold. I think we must be cautious about the gold standard. Some people rhapsodize over our great chance to return to the gold standard while the yen rises against the dollar and while British and American interest rates are falling. But I think our celebration is premature. Of course we must think about foreign markets, interest rates, and exchange rates, but the best approach is to let the value of the yen adjust on its own without government intervention.

Takahashi concluded his little essay by returning to one of his lifelong mantras: the importance of Japanese economic development and his view that going back on the gold standard is not an end it itself, but a tool to aid in growing Japan's economy:

To prepare independently [to return to the gold standard], we must first build a firm basis for domestic industry, ocean-going transportation, etc., and not rely on foreign borrowing. When we have built a solid foundation for our own economy, we can then end the gold embargo. I think it is a delusion to think that we can, without this domestic foundation, depend on exchange rates, falling foreign interest rates, and the goodwill of the major powers to return to the gold standard. We must think primarily of the long-term benefits and the costs of the gold standard to Japan's economy.[16]

This is vintage Takahashi, indeed it is the capstone of his economic thinking up until this time. The Japanese government's primary concern should be Japan's economic development, not the promotion of an international system, no matter how orthodox. The finance minister thus should use the fiscal and monetary tools at his disposal to stimulate recovery from the depression and restart economic growth. In other words, it is his job to take the nation to the geisha house for dinner. Conversely, policies that contract demand and productive capital in Japan, and thus hinder economic growth, such as stopping work on the three buildings, are undesirable. While the finance minister has the obligation to use fiscal and monetary means to promote growth, the government should not play a direct role in the economy: Takahashi again states his belief in the efficacy of markets. Policies that place

Japan's economic health in the hands of the "major powers"—the Americans and the British—are to be avoided. In this short six-page essay, Takahashi, free from direct American or European influence, enunciated his ideas about Japan's recovery and growth. At a time when no financial leader in the world espoused such ideas, when the leaders of Britain's financial establishment did not yet know enough about Keynes's views to ridicule them as they would a few years later, and when Richard Kahn had not yet propounded his theory of the multiplier effect, Takahashi articulated, in his own uniquely entertaining way, Keynes's ideas about the use of a liberal monetary and fiscal policy to restart a stagnant economy.[17]

The World Depression Reaches Japan

Just as the "Gold Standard Preparation Recession" set in, the New York stock market crashed and a global economic tsunami swept across Japan's beaches. Like every other industrializing nation at the time, Japan had close financial and trade relations with the United States, Great Britain, Europe, and their empires. Japan relied heavily on the outside world for technology and natural resources and paid for them by exporting light industrial products, primarily, as the depression set in, textiles and raw silk. In 1929, they accounted for just under two-thirds of the value of Japan's exports: raw silk 36 percent, cotton textiles 19 percent, silk textiles 6 percent, and synthetic cloth a little over 1 percent. In 1929, 95 percent of America's raw silk came from Japan, whose industrial growth in the first third of the twentieth century depended on the "American women's habit of wearing silk stockings," and on South and Southeast Asian women's custom of dressing in cotton saris and sarongs.[18]

Foreign demand for Japanese textile goods fell precipitously after Wall Street's "Black Thursday," their export value decreasing by 53 percent, from 1,344,000,000 to 637,000,000 yen in two years, which superimposed the deadly effect of the world depression on Inoue's induced illness. Raw silk, the principal export product in 1929, provides a good example of how the crisis impinged on Japan. The price of raw silk per *kanme* (8.72 pounds) shrunk by 53 percent from October 1929 to November 1930, and accordingly its export value fell by a similar amount, 55 percent. American demand declined and undermined Japan's sericultural industry for three interrelated reasons: first, as the depression spread throughout America, women had less money to spend on luxury items like silk stockings.[19] Second, at the end of the 1920s, producers of rayon, a relatively inexpensive synthetic fiber, began to compete with silk in certain textile markets; rayon production in America grew by eight times from 1921 to 1929. Third, raw silk production and exports depended on borrowed capital, much of which dried up with the financial crises in New York, Tokyo, and Yokohama. New York financial houses lent money to Japanese raw silk exporters, who then lent money to regional producers to buy cocoons and to ship their finished goods to the ports for export. In 1929, borrowing from exporters and middle-sized banks in ports such as Yokohama reached 71 percent of the cost of buying cocoons and producing and transporting raw silk. The filature owners in turn lent money to farmers to raise silkworms and produce cocoons. Most of the loans were made without security, the borrower's only obligation being to sell his raw silk or cocoons to his creditor.

As the price of raw silk (along with securities and other commodities) collapsed in New York in 1929–30, American financiers had less money to lend, and Yokohama merchants and banks received both less credit and less money in payment for their exports. This reduced the capital they could lend to regional producers, who in turn had fewer funds to buy cocoons from farmers. Since farmers, expecting heavy demand for their cocoons, did not cut output, the only way they could sell their cocoons was to lower the price. In fact, farm households, rather than replanting their fields with other cash crops (which were also falling in value, but more slowly than mulberry, the food for silkworms), increased their cocoon production to compensate for lower prices, thus flooding the shrinking market and driving prices even lower. Most Japanese farm households relied on family labor to till their fields and raise silkworms: unlike urban white- and blue-collar workers, who received salaries and wages from their employers, farmers lived on the profits brought in from marketing their crops and cocoons. As their income from cocoons declined, farmers had to lower their own and their family members' "wages." Thus, they had less money to spend on other goods, including fertilizer, food, clothing, tobacco, liquor, etc., which reduced demand in other parts of the economy. It was this dramatic drop in the value of exports to America, Europe, and their colonies for products such as raw silk and cotton textiles, which had been central to Japan's economic development until 1930, and the attendant drying up of New York and Yokohama credit, that brought the world depression to Japan.[20]

Japan in Depression

Japan, buffeted by the double deflationary blows of Inoue's contraction and the world depression, could not escape falling national wealth, consumer prices, employment, wages, and farm household incomes— blows that, as one might expect, struck the urban and rural poor hardest. Gross national expenditure in current prices fell by 18.3 percent between 1929 and 1931, although when adjusted for deflation it rose slightly. Consumer prices plunged 19.3 percent and the price of agricultural products 39.3 percent by 1931. There are no reliable official statistics for unemployment during the depression, and scholarly estimates of unemployment in 1929–32 vary widely from the quantitative economic historians Satō Kazuo's and Odaka Kōnosuke's calculations of 1,200,000 at the low end of the scale, to Nakamura Masanori's of 2,500,000 and Sumiya Mikio's of 3,000,000 workers at the high. The lower estimates indicate an unemployment rate among non-agricultural workers of 8 percent; the higher ones of 20 percent. Miwa Ryōichi points out that 16 percent fewer employees worked in privately owned factories in 1931 than in 1929. Clearly, substantially more people were out of work in 1931 than in 1929. Nominal wages for industrial workers, the labor aristocracy, declined by 10.2 percent, although because consumer prices fell even more sharply, real wages rose by about 10 percent in the first two years of the depression.

But conditions were worse for the city and rural poor. Nominal wages for urban day laborers fell by 27.5 percent, and by 8.4 percent in real terms. Nominal wages for agricultural workers fell even more dramatically, by 37.5 percent, and by 21.4 percent in real terms. The nominal value of agricultural production per worker declined by 43.2 percent, and in real terms by 28.2 percent over these two years. And in Yamanashi Prefecture, one of the leading regions for cocoon and raw silk production in 1929, the value of production per farm household fell by 52 percent in nominal terms, and 40 percent in real terms.[21] Clearly the impact of falling raw silk and cotton exports hurt working-class Japan, but it devastated market-oriented agricultural regions such as Yamanashi, where farmers over time had transformed more and more of their dry fields into mulberry orchards. One could eat the grains and vegetables one cultivated if their prices fell too low; one could not eat mulberry leaves, silkworms, and cocoons.

After a long and painful period of preparation, Japan returned to the gold standard on January 11, 1930. Almost immediately, gold and specie began to flow out of Japan. The contractionary policies pursued by Hamaguchi, Wakatsuki Reijirō, and Inoue raised the value of the yen vis-à-vis foreign currencies, and consequently Japan's exports fell precipitously, by almost 50 percent from 2,150,000,000 in 1929 to 1,150,000,000 two years later. (Wakatsuki had succeeded Hamaguchi, who as prime minister in April 1931 ominously fell victim to a right-wing assassin's bullet.)

In September 1931, Japan and the world were stunned by two more major shocks. Overnight on the eighteenth and nineteenth, troops stationed in Manchuria to protect Japan's colonial leasehold blew up a section of their own railroad, blamed it on Chinese "bandits," and began the conquest of Northeast China. In the process, the staff officers of the Kwantung Army who planned and ordered the attacks ignored efforts of the Tokyo government to bring them under control. One may not necessarily follow the line of scholars who see this as the beginning of World War II; nevertheless, the "Manchurian Incident" irreparably enflamed Sino-Japanese relations and severely strained Japan's intercourse with the United States. Elite leaders such as Takahashi, who thought Anglo-American capital, markets, raw materials, and technology were essential to Japan's continued economic development (and national defense), were shocked by this event. As Arai Seiichirō, one of Takahashi's subordinates in the finance ministry during the 1930s, told an interviewer later, "Takahashi hated Manchuria. . . . The militarists wanted to take over Manchuria and China for Japan, but Takahashi absolutely opposed this. . . . Takahashi was raised on British and American values and was anti-militarist."[22]

Two days later, on the 21st, Great Britain, the pre–World War I linchpin of the world's financial system, re-embargoed gold and left the gold standard forever. The time seemed propitious for Japan, a minor player in the world of finance, to follow suit, but Inoue adamantly refused: he had staked his fledgling political career on this effort, and he saw no reason to give in now, when, in his evaluation, Japan had weathered the storm of his induced recession. But he had not planned for the next shock.

Major financial institutions, especially foreign ones, saw the potential for huge profits from these circumstances, and began to buy dollars. Assuming that Japan would be forced to leave the gold standard before the United States, National City, HSBC, Sumitomo, Mitsui, and Mitsubishi all converted yen into dollars. The bankers reasoned that when Japan did leave the gold standard, the value of the yen vis-à-vis the dollar would fall sharply. If they bought dollars at the current exchange rate, essentially $1 = ¥2, and it later fell to $1 = ¥2.5 or lower, they could buy back yen and make substantial amounts of money. From October through December of 1931, more than 300,000,000 yen were sold to buy dollars. Inoue's primary countermeasure was to raise interest rates to cool yen-dollar speculation by making foreign investments less attractive as compared with domestic ones. He succeeded in slowing the outflow of capital, but by raising the cost of borrowing, he also made it prohibitive for businessmen to borrow money for non-speculative, productive purposes. Investment in new facilities dried up completely by late 1931, unemployment rose further, wages and rural incomes fell even more, the stock market collapsed, and Japan fell more deeply into depression. On December 12, the cabinet was forced to resign.

Although the immediate catalyst that brought down the government was neither the Manchurian war nor the gold standard crisis, the machinations of the home minister, compounded by these two shocks, all on top of a deepening recession, fatally undermined the cabinet. The Seiyūkai formed a new cabinet the following evening that included two septuagenarians: Inukai Tsuyoshi as prime minister, and Takahashi as finance minister. Although both of these aging Seiyūkai leaders distrusted the military and had strong reservations about its actions in Manchuria, they agreed to shoulder the onerous task of running the government and leading a party in which many principal members had close ties to the army and supported its China policy.[23]

Takahashi Returns to the Finance Ministry

Takahashi accepted the finance ministry portfolio for the fifth time on December 13, 1931, immediately reversed Inoue's contractive monetary policies, and began to prepare for the introduction of an expansionary fiscal policy the following summer. At three in the afternoon of December 13, Fukai Eigo, Vice Governor of the Bank of Japan and Takahashi's close associate since their time together in London in 1904–5, visited the finance minister designate and recommended the following actions: Japan should leave the gold standard, and thus prohibit the export of gold as soon as possible, preferably that evening once the emperor officially appointed the new cabinet. Also, Takahashi should swiftly arrange to issue an emergency proclamation prohibiting the convertibility of currency to gold within Japan. If Japan re-embargoed the export of gold, inevitably the value of the yen would fall. Fukai feared that even if speculators could not sell gold and specie abroad, if they were still able to convert yen into gold within Japan, even for a few days, they would continue to do so in expectation of windfall profits after the yen devalued. Takahashi, before meeting with Fukai, had made up his mind to leave the gold standard, but vacillated on prohibiting convertibility. So strong was the commitment of Japan's financial leaders, including even Takahashi, to the gold standard, that he too was apprehensive about completely cutting the link between gold and the yen since, like most of his contemporaries, he expected a return to gold after recovery from the current financial crisis. Fukai met Takahashi a second time that day and once more urged a clean break from the gold standard. Takahashi, displaying his fear of allowing the yen to float without any anchor at all, again demurred. In the end, the two reached a compromise: conversion would be allowed with the finance ministry's permission, which clearly would be difficult to obtain. Since parliament was not in session in December 1931, Takahashi needed approval of the Privy Council to issue an emergency proclamation, a process that required three days. To deter speculators, Fukai decided to open only one window at the Bank of Japan to carry out gold-yen transactions, and to question each purchaser at length about their reasons for buying gold. As one can imagine, in the three days (one of which was a bank holiday) before Takahashi finally issued his emergency order on December 17, very little gold was bought.[24]

One fascinating dimension of these encounters, reported in Fukai's memoirs, is that the vice governor, a widely respected authority on monetary policy who as a career central banker was deeply committed to fighting inflation, urged Takahashi, the infamous "reckless spender," to abandon the gold standard completely and move to a managed currency, while the latter resisted. But both Takahashi and Fukai agreed that when Japan adopted a managed monetary and exchange-rate system, "it must carry out a monetary policy that balanced productivity and the money supply." Alas for Japan, Takahashi's successors in the finance portfolio increasingly ignored this dictum, which led Fukai in early 1937, during the tenure of Takahashi's successor as finance minister, Baba Eiichi, to resign his post as Governor of the Bank of Japan.[25]

The plans that Takahashi and Fukai devised were to devalue the yen in order to stimulate exports, and to create liquidity by issuing currency free from the constraints of the gold standard. These policies had the desired effect, although as we shall see, not everyone approved. The yen fell from a December 1931 high of just over ¥100=$49 to $28 a year later, then to $25 in 1933, before stabilizing at around $29–30 after the United States left the gold standard in 1933; in other words, the yen depreciated by around 40 percent, which made Japanese exports less expensive in foreign markets. Japan exported 2,150,000,000 yen worth of goods (excluding those to the rest of the empire) in 1929, the last pre-recession year, and by 1931, under Inoue's contractionary monetary policies, exports fell to 1,150,000,000 yen, a decline of almost half. But as soon as Takahashi removed Japan from the gold standard, exports began to rise: valued at 1,400,000,000 yen in 1932; 1,860,000,000 in 1933; 2,170,000,000 in 1934; 2,500,000,000 in 1935; and 2,700,000,000 in 1936. In 1935, Japan showed its first surplus of exports over imports since 1918, the last year of the World War I trade boom, even though imports from North America, Japan's major source of industrial technology and high-grade raw materials, had grown by almost two-thirds.[26]

In reaction to Takahashi's actions, informed public opinion at the time ranged from cautious optimism to adamant opposition. Editorials in newspapers such as the *Tōkyō nichinichi* and the Tokyo *Economist* viewed the decision to leave the gold standard as inevitable. The value of the yen, as described above, plummeted after Japan left the gold standard, and journalists predicted the resultant increase in exports. They expected a revival of wholesale and consumer prices, but wrote that the expansion must be carefully monitored to prevent inflation. Among journalists, only Ishibashi Tanzan and his colleagues at the *Tōyō keizai shinpō*, recognizing the deleterious effect of the sharp deflation since 1920 (33 percent) and 1929 (17 percent), argued that inflation would be salutary. The *Economist* wrote that academic economists universally opposed leaving the gold standard. It reported that, "academics, in their usual academic way," criticized Takahashi not because his policies would hurt the economy, but because they ran counter to orthodox economic theory. Although Keynes's 1924 book, *A Tract on Monetary Reform*, which called for a managed currency, had been widely read in Japan, only the Ishibashi group dared to advocate such a step. Everyone else—including even Takahashi to some extent—feared the consequences of severing the yen from some kind of systemic anchor. Oddly, given the deeply depressed economic conditions of December 1931, most analysts in Japan and elsewhere in the world for that matter were more anxious about inflation than deflation: widespread acceptance of Keynesianism was years away.[27]

The debate came to a head on January 21, 1932, when the two principals had an oratorical "gunfight at the O.K. Corral." On that day, Takahashi spoke to the House of Peers, Inoue replied, and then Takahashi responded to the reply. This exchange, which I shall paraphrase and quote at length, took place just as an election campaign was about to open: Inoue's Minseitō, elected in February 1930 while the euphoria over returning to the gold standard had not yet dissipated, held a 273–174 majority in the lower, but more important, House of Representatives at the time of the debate. When the votes had been counted a month later, Takahashi's Seiyūkai, benefiting from the widespread belief that Inoue's plans had failed, established a 303–146 lead. The shift in voter sentiment, already clear on January 21, provides a context for the Takahashi-Inoue debate: members of the House of Peers interrupted Takahashi 30 times with applause, shouted "No! No!" twice as the finance minister described alleged failures of his predecessor, and yelled, again in English, "Hear, Hear!" on another occasion. Inoue faced a cold, hostile audience and received no applause.

Takahashi got right to the polemical point by blaming Japan's depression on Hamaguchi's and Inoue's "extreme frugality budget." He added that the world depression, caused by similarly deflationary policies around the world, had an impact in Japan, but reiterated that Japan's economic woes should be attributed primarily to the Minseitō's policies.[28] People had warned Inoue of the risks when he began to prepare

in the summer of 1929 to return to the gold standard, but he had not listened. Contrary to Inoue's expectations, but not to those of his critics,
prices and investment declined, and capital dried up. "To sum up,"
Takahashi charged, "the previous government's policy of returning to
the gold standard and of a tight fiscal policy ran counter to the needs
of the times and threw the people's economy into extreme disarray.
[When the present cabinet came to power] Japan's future looked bleak."

As Finance Minister Inoue did not want Japan's exchange bank, the
Yokohama Specie Bank, to export gold and specie, it alone did not.
Therefore, foreign banks filled the vacuum, and in the first half of
1930 they controlled Japan's foreign exchange market completely. After
the twin crises of September 1931—the Manchurian Incident and the
United Kingdom's departure from the gold standard—Japan "hemor-
rhaged" specie to buy dollars. Japan should have left the gold standard
immediately to stop such speculation, but Inoue refused. In fact, the
government adopted the worst possible set of policies. It reversed its
policy and had the Yokohama Specie Bank buy gold and specie to slow
the outflow. When this failed, the government moved to a high interest
rate policy, and domestic capital dried up. But this did not stop the
buying of dollars either. Takahashi concluded by stating, "The government's policies oppressed the financial world, killed industrial production, and recklessly forced our economy into depression. . . . We have
left the gold standard to save the great bulk of the population from
dire straits, to promote industry, and to raise the people's standards of
living. We are reducing the exchange rate, inflating consumer prices,
and stimulating production."[29]

Inoue rose to reply. Takahashi was wrong. The depression hurt Japan
less than anywhere else in the world. This was not just Inoue's personal
opinion, but also that of the world's financiers. After the Hamaguchi
cabinet introduced its tight money policies, the trade surplus of imports
over exports declined, foreign borrowing was reduced, and the money
supply stopped growing.[30] According to Inoue, Takahashi exaggerated
the outflow of specie. "Where is his evidence that Japan cannot stay on
the gold standard?"

Inoue then presented the accusation, somewhat indirectly, but clear
to his listeners, that some of Takahashi's and the Seiyūkai's financial
supporters had said that they advocated leaving the gold standard to

restart the economy, but their true motivation was to garner their profits from dollars they had bought on speculation. Inoue conceded that there had been a large gold outflow after Great Britain left the gold standard. But he added that unlike Takahashi he did not blame foreign banks alone. Japanese capitalists had also bought dollars. "Isn't it interesting," Inoue asked provocatively, "that people who have sold a great deal of gold to buy dollars now preach leaving the gold standard?" Had Japan maintained its high interest rate policy and stayed on the gold standard, the speculators would have lost money, and the people's livelihoods would have been stabilized. Instead, gold flowed out of Japan to settle accounts after Takahashi's December decision; in other words, blame for the gold outflow rested with Takahashi, not Inoue. Because of Takahashi, the speculators—a small group of unpatriotic capitalists and bankers—won, while Japan lost.

Inoue next criticized Takahashi's plan to increase exports by lowering the exchange rate. He declared that devaluing the yen will not bring about Japan's economic recovery. First, raw silk exports to the United States will not benefit. Second, other countries will retaliate by devaluing their currencies or raising tariffs against Japanese imports. Third, increasing the money supply will lead to inflation and damage people's livelihoods. Finally, even if Takahashi's plans would help Japan, they breached international morality because they advanced Japan's interests at the expense of other countries. Inoue then concluded with an ominous warning: "In today's world, when political thinking has taken a turn for the worse, I am anxious. No announcement has been made yet about fiscal policy, but I fear we can expect a large increase in government spending before too long. Not just I, but the whole nation, worry about this." Perhaps the whole nation, but not members of the house. They began to drift out of the chamber as Inoue spoke. Takahashi hardly seemed to listen and carried on a whispered conversation with another Seiyūkai politician, Mori Kaku, as Inoue proceeded. The tide had turned against him and his speech had little effect on the audience.[31]

The finance minister then returned to the dais. Imamura Takeo describes the scene as follows: "Takahashi seemed, as usual, like a father telling a story. . . . The sails were already set. Takahashi had caught a good wind, and Inoue a reverse one." Takahashi stated that he could not answer all of Inoue's points in detail, so he would focus on one, the connection between gold and standards of living. Fundamentally, the gold standard, Takahashi agreed, has the potential to improve people's livelihoods, increase productivity, and give Japan the economic power to rival other countries. But in his opinion, Inoue's timing was wrong. Currently, Japan did not have the economic power to function successfully on the gold standard. The monetary and fiscal contraction that Inoue initiated to stay on the gold standard and stop speculation had hurt productive businesses and the people employed by them. Takahashi asserted, "To call speculators the enemy and to punish them by raising interest rates is unfortunate, I think. Farmers, fishermen, and foresters work from morning to night for a pittance. They are the backbone of our nation's production, the roots. They never think about exchange rates. Conversely, nobody thought of their needs" (when interest rates were raised to punish speculators). Japan must base its exchange rates on the foundation of the nation's real economic strength: in other words, its exchange rates should be determined by the market. When Japan borrows from abroad, it should borrow for productive purposes, not to support the exchange rate as Inoue had. Then Takahashi concluded, "All the nations of the world look inward and put their domestic problems first, and trade relations second. They guard against imports to develop their own industries. They establish national policies to expand production. Our country must follow suit." Takahashi took his seat to clamorous applause.[32]

Takahashi and Inoue laid out two sharply contrasting policy positions in their speeches to the House of Peers. Inoue advocated staying on the gold standard; borrowing abroad to protect Japan's specie reserves; instituting high interest rates to avoid speculation in foreign exchange and maintaining a tight capital market regardless of the short-term consequences; narrowing the trade imbalance even if it required a sharp curtailment of imports and exports; government frugality; and working within the existing international financial framework—in 1932, Inoue's views mirrored financial orthodoxy in New York, Washington, London, Paris, and Berlin. Possibly flattered by the attentions of metropole financiers such as Montagu Norman of the Bank of England and Lamont of Morgan, Inoue thought Japan was more of a financial power than it was. Takahashi, meanwhile, advocated leaving the gold standard, reducing interest rates to loosen capital and encourage private investment, borrowing abroad for productive purposes, stimulating exports, and putting Japan first and the crumbling international system second. He recognized that economically and financially, Japan was a minor player. Although Takahashi did not mention encouraging recovery through deficit governmental spending in his speeches, Inoue did: he feared a large increase in fiscal stimulation would come all too soon. A right-wing ideologue assassinated Inoue on February 9 as he went to make an electoral campaign speech, and he therefore did not live to see the beginning of Takahashi's deficit financing in late summer.

Takahashi had two more arrows in his monetary quiver before concentrating on fiscal stimuli. In the late spring of 1932, he took steps to allow for a substantial enlargement of the money supply, not only to increase liquidity and stimulate demand, but also to prepare for his intended spending policy. In June, Takahashi proposed and then saw passed a law raising the upper limit of paper money that the Bank of Japan could freely issue, unsupported by gold or specie, from 120,000,000 to 1,000,000,000 yen. Under the system in operation from 1900 to 1932, the Bank of Japan had to pay the government a penalty for all currency over 120,000,000 yen that it issued unconstrained by specie reserves; after July 1, 1932, the bank paid this fine only if it exceeded 1,000,000,000 in the issuance of unsupported currency. Some scholars have taken this as one more example of Takahashi's "recklessness" in financial matters. But in fact, during the Takahashi years, currency in circulation did not increase radically or unnaturally. In December 1931, when Inoue left office, 1,330,000,000 yen in Bank of Japan notes were in circulation, more than ten times the allowed limit. One year later, the amount had reached 1,430,000,000, an increase of 7.5 percent, and in December 1935, reached 1,767,000,000, 33 percent more than 1931. Throughout the same period, national income increased by 40 percent. In other words, in contrast to the Inoue years, when both money in circulation and nominal national wealth decreased by about one-fifth, during the Takahashi era, the money supply grew more or less according to Fukai Eigo's dictum that Japan's "currency should be managed so it grows in tandem with the growth of industrial production."[33]

Takahashi also encouraged lower interest rates, and his policies of devaluing the yen and increasing money in circulation had that effect.

The discount rate for Bank of Japan commercial notes fell from a peak of 5.84 percent when Takahashi came into office in December 1931 to 3.65 percent in 1933, a level at which it would remain through the rest of Takahashi's service as finance minister. Low interest rates had two benefits for Takahashi's broader policy. First, they allowed him to issue government bonds cheaply (in fact, one reason he delayed the issuance of government bonds until the late summer of 1932, more than six months after he re-assumed the finance portfolio, was because he wanted to wait until interest rates had come down). Second, they made it easier for businessmen to borrow money for industrial and commercial expansion. Takahashi understood that the government used monetary and fiscal policy only to prime the pump. As his stimuli took hold and the economy began to recover, people would spend more money, demand would increase, and businessmen would begin to look for capital to expand production to meet that demand; low interest rates were essential to this process.[34]

Government by Assassination: From Autarky to Autarchy

The depression had a traumatic impact on Japan, politically as well as economically. As the world's economies spiraled downward after 1929, nation after nation chose autarky, or economic self-reliance, as the answer to its economic woes. The United States Congress passed the Hawley-Smoot Tariff Act in 1930, which raised customs duties to their highest level in the country's history; Britain gave preferential treatment within its empire to various members; other nations retaliated by raising their tariffs against the United States and the United Kingdom.[35] In light of such actions, Takahashi saw no benefit for Japan alone to adhere to a collapsing world system. He abandoned the gold standard and devalued the yen in a domestic political atmosphere that had been radically changed by the economic crisis. Political party stalwarts such as Inoue, former Foreign Minister Shidehara Kijūrō, who was the architect of Japan's cooperative foreign policy in the 1920s, Prime Minister Inukai, and eventually Takahashi himself found themselves gradually discredited in wider and wider circles. Their opponents attacked them for relying on untrustworthy foreigners, and advocated diplomatic and military autonomy as well as an end to party governments.

The most powerful segment of the autarky group, or to use James Crowley's term, those who led "Japan's quest for autonomy," was the military. The army invaded northeast China in September 1931 to thundering public applause. The mass society that allowed the buds of democracy to sprout in the 1920s engendered something less attractive in the 1930s. Latent nationalism spread through the school system and organizations such as the Imperial Military Reserve Association (Teikoku zaigō gunjinkai), bitterness over America's tariffs and disgraceful treatment of Japanese immigrants, resentment toward what was seen as the powers' hypocritical unwillingness to allow Japan a "Monroe Doctrine" region in Manchuria, anger over nationalistic Chinese resistance to "righteous" Japanese actions in China, and the suffering of many Japanese during the depression converged to create a climate of enthusiastic support for the military, the men on horseback, the men with the easy answers, the men who advocated direct action and autarchy, not weak-kneed, democratic compromise.[36] Even prominent members of the governing Seiyūkai, men such as Kuhara Fusanosuke and Mori Kaku, joined the opposition to the very system that had brought their party to power.

From 1931 until 1936, various segments of the military instigated overseas aggression, coup d'état attempts at home, and assassinations that changed the nature of Japan's government and foreign policy. The military or sympathizing right-wing terrorists, the "double patriots," to borrow Richard Storry's apt phrase, killed or otherwise silenced the people who advocated cooperation. Assassins murdered three of five prime ministers and a fourth avoided death only when young army officers killed his brother-in-law by mistake. These terrorists killed two of three finance ministers, and the third probably escaped only by dying prematurely from ill health. And not only were temperate leaders eliminated; the threat of assassination also kept most remaining opponents quiet. No wonder the British-American journalist Hugh Byas, who worked in Japan from 1909 until April 1941, entitled his book on the 1930s in Japan *Government by Assassination*. The year 1932 was second only to 1936 in its bumper "red harvest" of Inoue in February, Dan Takuma, head of the Mitsui Corporation, in March, and Prime Minister Inukai in May. It was in this milieu that Takahashi became finance minister for the sixth time on May 26, 1932.[37]

Takahashi's Fiscal Policies

On Sunday, May 15, 1932, young naval officers burst into the prime minister's newly completed, pseudo–Frank Lloyd Wright–style official residence in the government district of Tokyo and brutally murdered Inukai. Although the premier, in the face of widespread public support for the army's actions in Manchuria, had not pressed the military as hard as his predecessor had over its aggression on the mainland, he nonetheless had two strikes against him: he had tried to limit the extent of the army's independent action in Northeast China, and he was a party politician. Although the military brass were apparently unaware of the assassination plans, they quickly viewed the prime minister's death as an opportunity to influence policy. Two days later, the jingoist Army Minister Araki Sadao informed Prince Saionji, the man responsible for selecting the next prime minister, that the army would not support another party government. Although technically in 1932 a prime minister could appoint a retired general as army minister, he would probably have been unwise, given the highly charged atmosphere, to attempt to do so. The prince faced another problem: he did not trust any member of the majority Seiyūkai party to succeed Inukai, with the possible exception of acting Prime Minister Takahashi, who was in ill health. Moreover, both Wakatsuki Reijirō, the last Minseitō premier, and Takahashi recommended to Saionji that he not appoint another Seiyūkai cabinet. Although the two men supported the principle of party government, they feared the majority party's ties to the military and its belligerent foreign policy views even more. Whether Takahashi was wrong in not pushing for another party government in May 1932 is a moot point. After all, it is difficult to say which was worse: a party government with close ties to the army or a less aggressive non-party government?

Ten days later, Saionji chose retired Admiral Saitō Makoto, by the standards of the times a moderate, to head a "transcendental," non-party government in which military, civil-bureaucratic, and party men would all serve. The Seiyūkai, although bitterly disappointed over the demise of their cabinet through what they perceived as no fault of their own—though the machinations of some of the more pro-army members had certainly played a part in the outcome—agreed to support the new government. They expected to return to power shortly and had no idea that the Inukai cabinet would be the last party government until after World War II. Saitō asked Takahashi to stay in office (in fact, the new prime minister needed Takahashi to provide moral ballast for his government) and Takahashi, despite his physical weakness, agreed to become finance minister for the sixth time.[38]

A week later, on June 3, and then again on August 25, Takahashi made two major speeches to parliament in which he presented his fiscal proposals. In these addresses, he proposed seven radical changes in policy, some of which were already underway. First, he would reverse the contractionary fiscal policy of his predecessor by dramatically increasing government spending. The new monies would be spent for productive public works projects such as riparian protection, improvement of harbor facilities, and building new roads. Most of this expenditure would be focused in depressed rural areas to increase employment and accordingly stimulate demand, as well as to improve local facilities for long-term economic growth. Takahashi proposed spending 600,000,000 yen in central government money over three years, but more than twice as much when local spending was added. The government would also provide funds to pay for the costs of the military's activities in Manchuria. Second, the government would sell treasury bonds to make up the difference between tax revenues, which had been reduced in the recession, and the government's expanded fiscal spending. Takahashi proposed selling half a billion yen worth of bonds in the current fiscal year. Third, the finance ministry would sell the bonds to the Bank of Japan, which would then wait for what it determined to be the most favorable time to sell them on the open market. Takahashi believed that more money needed to be pumped into the economy to ease capital; in other words, liquidity should be provided for "legitimate [non-speculative] business transactions."[39] Fourth, he proposed to increase the upper limit on guaranteed currency issuance from 120,000,000 yen to 1,000,000,000, as discussed above. Fifth, the government would work to lower interest rates to help industrialists, small businessmen, and farmers reduce the cost of borrowing for productive purposes. Sixth, Takahashi stated that he wanted to strengthen rural finance by providing regional banks with 700,000,000 yen for low-interest farm loans or to underwrite defaulted loans. Seventh, Takahashi proposed to raise tariffs on some goods, to be determined by the government.[40]

The Economic Efficacy of Takahashi's Policies

Having announced his plans for fiscal stimulation in the summer of 1932, Takahashi proceeded to implement a striking spending policy between then and 1936 (see Table 1). Governmental expenditures increased by one-third, from 1,500,000,000 in Inoue's last budget to 2,000,000,000 in Takahashi's revised 1932 budget (originally passed under Inoue in 1931, but revised upward by the new cabinet in the summer of 1932). Takahashi added another 15 percent in the 1933 budget, bringing the total of government expenditures in that fiscal year to 2,300,000,000, which the government held at this level until after Takahashi's death in 1936, when under his successor, Baba Eiichi, outlays quickly increased by another one-quarter, to 2,900,000,000 in 1937. Since Japan was in the depths of the depression when Takahashi instituted his spending policy in 1932, tax revenues had fallen sharply. To make up the difference, Takahashi issued 684,000,000 yen in government bonds. In 1933, the treasury sold even more bonds: 900,000,000 yen worth. The value of bond issuances as a percentage of government spending leaped from 2 percent in 1931 to over one-third in 1932, and would remain at this level through the Takahashi years. From November 1932, when the government first used the Bank of Japan *hikiuke* method, until the end of 1935, the finance ministry issued almost 2,800,000,000 yen worth of bonds, all sold directly to the central bank. By the end of 1935, the Bank of Japan had successfully sold more than 90 percent of these bonds, thus reabsorbing the increased liquidity after a suitable period of monetary expansion. The new system of selling bonds allowed Takahashi to wake up the lethargic economy while at the same time avoiding dangerous inflation. As Fukai Eigo stated in an oft-quoted remark, Takahashi, by selling treasury bonds to the Bank of Japan, "provided money to stimulate economic recovery, pay for the Manchurian Incident, and bring interest rates down—he hit three birds with one stone." And he did so with an increase in consumer prices of less than 3 percent per year.[41]

Takahashi's fiscal spending benefited three primary areas: the military, the civil bureaucracy to keep the government operational, and depression relief. Outlays to civilian ministries, excluding those for depression relief, rose by 16 percent from 1931 to 1933, and then declined slightly in 1934 and 1935. In 1931, the civil bureaucracy received almost three-quarters of the government's allocations; in 1935, only slightly more than half. The military was the primary beneficiary of this shift: its budget more than doubled from 1931 to 1933, and by 1935, exceeded 1,000,000,000 yen, or 46 percent of the total budget. The central government allocated 544,000,000 yen for depression relief in 1932–34, and then ended it altogether. Total central and local government investment in emergency relief reached 1.7 billion dollars in 1932–34, a substantial contribution, but still one third less than the army and navy received.[42]

As Table 2 illustrates, when viewed from a macroeconomic perspective, Takahashi's policies worked splendidly. National income increased by 60 percent between 1931 and 1936, but consumer prices by only 18 percent. In other words, after a 20 percent decline in nominal national income, and stagnation in real national income during the Inoue years of 1928–31, Japan experienced a sharp increase in both indicators under Takahashi between 1931 and 1936. Accordingly, more and more people went to work, and under- and unemployment declined—indeed, Japan returned to full employment by 1936. Non-agricultural workers increased in number by 2,000,000, and in percentage by 12.5, while workers in agriculture (the hiding place for those who had lost their jobs in the cities) declined by 354,000, or 2.5 percent. Workers in manufacturing, the most technologically advanced sector of the economy, increased by more than 800,000, 17.2 percent. Agricultural workers made up 47 percent of the work force in 1931, but only 44 percent in 1936.

Personal income also started to grow again after bottoming out in 1931–32, although it would not begin to outpace the increase in consumer prices until after 1936. Even the real wages of agricultural workers, the poorest segment in the poorest sector of the economy, began to rise in the mid-1930s, and surpassed their 1925–29 level in the period from 1935 to 1939. Real farm household incomes reached their prewar highs toward the end of the decade. By 1936, real disposable income in Japan had risen by 13 percent; in the United States over the same time period, it declined by 6 percent. In 1939, real disposable income in Japan was 37 percent higher than in 1929; in the United States, by contrast, it did not reach the 1929 level until 1940. All in all, Takahashi's use of monetary and fiscal policy to revive Japan's economy during the world depression of the 1930s succeeded. Japan recovered from the depression five years before the United States, and more dramatically over the whole decade than any of the powers except Germany.[43]

Table 1
Central Government Budgets, 1927–35

Year	Total Revenue	Treasury Bonds	Expenditures	For Military
1927	1,759	64	1,759	469
1928	1,721	64	1,721	488
1929	1,681	52	1,681	483
1930	1,611	00	1,611	474
1931	1,497	30	1,498	407
1932	2,018	684	2,018	699
1933	2,321	919	2,321	852
1934	2,224	881	2,224	943
1935	2,215	772	2,215	1,023

NOTE: Figures are given in millions of yen. (Nakamura 1983, 237) and (Bank of Japan 1966, 129) give slightly different data.
SOURCE: (Bank of Japan 1986, iv, 12).

Table 2
National Income and Consumer Price Index, 1931–36

Year	Ohkawa Estimate of National Income	Yamada Estimate of National Income	Consumer Prices
1931	10,583	10,678	100.0
1932	11,853	11,591 ·	101.3
1933	13,588	12,963	104.8
1934	14,161	13,670	109.8
1935	15,600	14,952	115.0
1936	17,229	16,645	118.3

NOTE: Figures are given in millions of yen.
SOURCES: (Bank of Japan 1966, 29, 32; Ohkawa and Shinohara 1979, 388).

To conclude this chapter, I would like to examine each of the questions posed at its beginning. First, was Takahashi guilty of social dumping or "beggar thy neighbor" policies? That is, did he think of Japan first and international cooperation second? The verdict on this count is guilty—except that at the time, social dumping was normal practice, not a crime. It is true that when he devalued the yen to reverse Inoue's overvaluation and its concomitant implosion of Japan's exports, Takahashi's primary goal was *Japan*'s economic recovery from the depression. But when one considers that the United States, Great Britain, and the other powers favored their own economies, workers, and empires over foreign ones, and what was called international economic cooperation at the time required financial leaders to follow the deflationary kinds of policies pursued by Inoue, Takahashi had no choice.[44] Why should he, the financial leader of a second-tier economic power, not beggar his richer neighbors when they were beggaring him? Takahashi's crime was that he was more successful than his foreign competitors were in growing his nation's exports in the 1930s. Masato Shizume argues that Takahashi carried out a one-time devaluation of the yen in 1931–32, and then restabilized the yen-dollar exchange rate at about 60 percent of its gold standard level—in other words, he was not abandoning the "Golden Fetters" of a fixed exchange rate, but simply revaluing the yen at a lower level, as the Italian and French governments had done when they returned to the gold standard in the 1920s. If Shizume is correct, Takahashi's "beggaring" was a one-shot devaluation of the yen from Inoue's artificially high price to its real 1932 value vis-à-vis the dollar.[45]

Was Takahashi guilty of a reckless fiscal policy when he increased government spending in 1932? The answer to this question depends on one's view of inflation. If one believes inflation is always and at any level unacceptable, even while deflation goes hand in hand with stagnation in national wealth, then Takahashi's policies in 1932–35 were lax. But if one believes that mild inflation is acceptable if it works in tandem with rapid growth, then one should encourage finance ministers to be reckless. Which would one prefer: a 20 percent decrease in prices and national income, and therefore a stagnant economy, or an 18 percent increase in prices and 60 percent growth of national wealth, and thus a rapidly growing economy? I leave it up to the reader to make his choice, but my view is that Takahashi was guilty of engineering a brilliant economic recovery between 1931 and 1936, or to invert John Kenneth Galbraith's pithy statement, he achieved a "triumph of thought over dogma."[46]

Was Takahashi responsible for the rapid inflation that occurred after his death, when the Japanese military invaded China in 1937, and then even more foolishly went to war with the United States and the British Empire in 1941? While consumer prices grew by about 3 percent per year during the Takahashi years of 1931 through 1936, they grew by more than 10 percent per year in the four years after his death, and then grew astronomically during and in the aftermath of World War II, between 1940 and 1948. At Takahashi's death, one could buy 3⅓ yen for every dollar; by the occupation period, the exchange rate had reached 360 yen to the dollar, a devaluation of the yen and resultant inflation of more than 100 times. This inflation was caused by incessant and grossly excessive borrowing from the Bank of Japan—actually, by printing money, since the central bank had no chance of reselling the bonds on the open market—in order to pay for the war. Those who blame Takahashi for the wartime inflation do so because it was he who instituted the system of selling treasury bonds to the Bank of Japan. These critics overlook that Takahashi regularly stated that his fiscal expansion and the increase in government spending were temporary expedients to be eliminated when Japan had recovered from the depression. As we shall see in the next chapter, Takahashi worked valiantly to cut back spending, particularly for the military, through 1935 and 1936, an effort that cost him his life in February 1936. I think it is safe to say that had Takahashi not instituted the Bank of Japan *hikiuke* system to create liquidity as he engineered Japan's recovery from the depression, the army and navy would have found other ways to obtain the money they needed to fight their war.

Did Takahashi's funding of depression relief in 1932–34 help the agricultural sector of the economy? The answer, I think, is no and yes. On the one hand, I agree with Nakamura Masanori and his seminar students, who investigated a village in Yamagata Prefecture and concluded that in the short run the spending brought minimal benefits to rural communities such as Miitsumi. But Takahashi's primary goal in his relief funding was a macroeconomic one, to pump money into the economy to stimulate demand and consumption and to bring about a nationwide recovery. Therefore, even if the expenditures did not help individual villages immediately, they did play a role in creating liquidity, demand, and eventual recovery. While rural Japan emerged from the depression more slowly than did urban areas, eventually even Yamagata farmers benefited from Japan's economic revival.[47]

Two questions remain to be answered, but are important enough to deserve chapters of their own: the connection between Takahashi's fiscal policies and the rise of militarism, that is, of the forces that took Japan into World War II, and a discussion of Takahashi's economic philosophy, and within it his views of government spending for rural relief.

THIRTEEN

Takahashi's Fiscal Policies and the Rise of Militarism, 1932–36

The decade and a half between the Manchurian Incident in September 1931 and Japan's surrender in August 1945 brought World War II to Asia, with its widespread death, destruction, and economic chaos. Over these years, military officers gradually replaced party politicians and civil bureaucrats in the critical positions of government, and led Japan toward an authoritarian political system and command economy at home, and aggression abroad. A combination of the world depression, with its rising unemployment and falling incomes; nationalistic feelings spread through the educational system; and resentment of external discrimination against Japanese goods and people discredited leaders who believed Japan benefited from participation in the Anglo-American world order, especially when dealing with China. The trend of the 1930s was away from international cooperation and toward diplomatic and military autonomy, economic autarky, and war. As this transition from "going along" to "going alone" occurred, Takahashi implemented fiscal policies to stimulate economic recovery. A large part of his government spending went to the military—its share grew from 27 percent in 1931 to 46 percent of a much greater total budget in 1936. This has led writers to raise the issue of a possible connection between Takahashi's fiscal policies and the rise of militarism. Did Takahashi, as some scholars assert, actively, knowingly, or at least unwittingly, encourage the rise of militarism by his fiscal policies?

Interpretations of the connection between Takahashi's policies and the rise of militarism fall into four broad categories. First, orthodox Marxist scholars, influenced by the view of Moscow and the Comintern, aver that Takahashi represented monopoly finance capitalism and as finance minister led Japan into the final stage of late capitalist development, "state monopoly capitalism," fascism, and war. Second, a number of historians emphasize Takahashi's participation in the Seiyūkai, a political party that, after Tanaka Giichi became its leader in 1925, advocated autarky, forceful intervention in China, an expanded military, and a positive spending policy. Takahashi also, they write, had a history of economic nationalism; thus, Takahashi must have actively supported increased military spending and aggression in China during the 1930s. His policies, according to this view, contrasted with those of Inoue and the Minseitō, a party that preferred peaceful diplomacy, disarmament, balanced budgets, and cooperation with the British and Americans on policy toward China and elsewhere. Third, still others believe that while Takahashi disapproved of excessive military spending and an aggressive foreign policy, because of Japan's political realities in 1932–34, he had no choice but to increase military outlays significantly when he designed a spending policy to bring about Japan's recovery from the depression. In the process, the army and navy enhanced their power to such an extent that Takahashi was unable to rein in military spending when he did try to eliminate Japan's budget deficits in 1934 and 1935. Thus, Takahashi's policies unintentionally unleashed the military and opened the potential for war. Fourth and finally, another group writes that Takahashi had no responsibility for the rise of militarism. He had a long-standing opposition to diplomatic and military adventurism in China and to excessive defense spending, and unlike most of his contemporaries in politics in the 1930s, he fought a desperate, courageous, and ultimately suicidal battle to keep the army under political control.[1]

To argue that Takahashi, because he represented "monopoly finance capital," helped lead Japan to militarism, fascism, and war is analytically meaningless since the proponents of this position contend that Japan's other bourgeois interwar leaders fell into the same category. Therefore, this paradigm cannot be used to distinguish between the actions of Takahashi and men such as Hamaguchi and Inoue who advocated orthodox classical financial policies. To take the second position, that

Takahashi was a long-standing supporter of militarism and aggressive imperialism, flies in the face of the evidence. One can make a stronger case for the third hypothesis, namely that Takahashi, by increasing military spending, unintentionally opened the way to militarism. But I shall argue that this was only partly true. Takahashi, even when he increased allocations to the army and navy, consistently offered them less than they demanded, and continually fought the military ministers and their minions both within government circles and publicly. Takahashi's angry confrontations with officers such as Generals Araki and Kawashima were widely reported in the Tokyo and regional press, and cost the finance minister his life in 1936. Thus, the fourth approach is the most accurate, but with some modification. Takahashi was neither an active nor a passive supporter of militarism and the army's aggression in Asia; however, his budgets did allow the military to fund the conquest of Manchuria and thus to take a preliminary step toward militarism and total war.

Takahashi's Opposition to Militarism

Takahashi's opposition to militarism, army and navy adventurism, and excessive military spending dates back to as early as 1885, when, as a young bureaucrat in charge of patent and trademark laws in the Ministry of Agriculture and Commerce, he sided with Maeda Masana's team in the debate over the latter's plan for Japan's economic development. Maeda's proposal to stimulate growth emphasized traditional endeavors such as agriculture, sericulture, and tea cultivation, and gave low priority to costly transplant industries such as steel, chemicals, and weaponry, all essential to the military. Maeda urged that government funds for building infrastructure be allocated for those projects that would encourage regional growth and raise standards of living rather than build central and military power. Takahashi took away several important lessons from Maeda's and his defeat at the hands of the two Meiji-period oligarchs, General Yamagata and Finance Minister Matsukata. Takahashi thought that enriching the country was more important than building a strong army, that the primary goal of the former was to raise the standard of living of all Japanese, not merely to make the state richer and more powerful, and that the prime movers in economic development were not Tokyo bureaucrats but regional entrepreneurs with their intimate knowledge of local markets and production techniques.[2]

From that time on, Takahashi's views continued to evolve, as he argued that an excessively strong and over-funded military not only hindered economic development, but also endangered Japan's security; that diplomats should lead and soldiers follow; that an aggressive, autonomous foreign policy toward China was dangerous, especially if it alienated China, the United States, and Great Britain; and that the army and navy should be under civilian control. In September 1905, just after Komura and Witte signed the Portsmouth peace treaty to end the Russo-Japanese War, Takahashi wrote from London to Bank of Japan Governor Matsuo, in what would become a recurrent theme throughout the last three decades of his life, "We must resolutely suppress efforts to replace and expand the army's and navy's armaments. It is crucial to avoid developing facilities beyond our nation's economic power. Each minister, and especially the army and navy ministers, must consider which facilities are most important to him, and whether or not the nation's wealth is adequate to support them."[3]

Takahashi, throughout his tenures as president of the Yokohama Specie Bank, as vice-governor and then governor of the Bank of Japan, as prime minister, four times finance minister, and agriculture and commerce minister between 1905 and 1927, consistently opposed an aggressive foreign policy, excessive military spending, and borrowing abroad if it threatened Japan's credit status. Takahashi rejected proposals to nationalize the railroad system in 1906 because he thought it would endanger Japan's newly won niches in the European and North American financial markets. The same year, Takahashi advocated a sinking fund in the annual budget to redeem the Russo-Japanese War loans. Takahashi, although head of the nation's central bank, sided with the political parties in opposition to the army's demand for two additional divisions in 1912, both because of the needs of Japan's financial probity but also because he anticipated that a stronger military would make foreign adventure—and thus war—more likely rather than less.[4]

As early as May 1911, Takahashi told a group of American businessmen that Japan should not act alone, but should follow the lead of the United States and Great Britain in their efforts to bring about the economic development of China. In 1915, Takahashi criticized Foreign Minister Katō Takaaki's handling of the Twenty-One Demands to China because it threatened Japan's relations with China, Great Britain, and the

United States. In December 1916, Takahashi criticized military demands for national defense spending that exceeded the economy's ability to pay for it. In the same article, he also called for practicing diplomacy first and the military action second, a peaceful foreign policy based on economic rather than military competition, and national defense planning that would not hinder the nation's economic growth. In 1918 Takahashi criticized the Nishihara loans as an illegitimate attempt to gain special rights for Japan in Manchuria, and in 1921, Takahashi called for an end to all efforts by the Japanese government to use loans to procure special rights in Shandong, Manchuria, and Mongolia. Takahashi opposed the army's adventurism in Siberia in 1917–22. In September 1920, Takahashi pressed for the abolition of the army's and navy's general staffs because they endangered Japan's relations with the United States and Great Britain. In 1921–22, as prime minister, Takahashi negotiated the treaty that terminated the Anglo-Japanese Alliance and enrolled Japan in the Washington Treaty System, the post–World War I Anglo-American world order. In 1922, Takahashi advocated the subordination of the two general staffs to the army and navy ministers, and called for the appointment of civilians to head the two military ministries. And in 1927, during his short, six-week service as finance minister in the Tanaka cabinet, Takahashi criticized his own prime minister for dispatching troops to interfere in China's domestic politics.

Takahashi, who began his education as a policy apprentice during the state-building decades of the 1870s and 1880s, was a nationalist who was deeply committed to Japan's economic development. Takahashi actively supported the first steps to create a Japanese empire in the late Meiji period. Indeed, he solidified his reputation as a financial statesman by raising in Europe and the United States almost half the monies needed to defeat Russia in 1904–5, and the Meiji emperor rewarded him for this service by honoring him as a hereditary peer. But the primary lesson he learned from this experience in London and New York was that Japan could not advance economically, diplomatically, or even militarily without the cooperation of the richer and stronger Western powers: Japan was able to annex Korea, for example, only because it had prior Anglo-American approval. Takahashi, like Shidehara, the architect of Japan's cooperative policy in the 1920s, believed that the capital, markets, technology, and raw materials provided by these two powers and the empires over which they ruled were essential to Japan's economic development. Takahashi spent years building a personal net-work of Japanese, British, and American bankers and later sent younger Finance Ministry and Bank of Japan officials such as Tsushima Juichi and Inoue Junnosuke abroad to nurture the network and at the same time to train them in the necessity of international financial cooperation. Takahashi believed Japan would commit military as well as financial suicide if it were to go to war with these two stronger states. Takahashi, who resented repeated Western slights toward Japan and the Japanese no less than anyone at the time, was not a slavish apologist for Anglo-American values, but rather was a hard-nosed realist who understood the power of Anglo-American capital and industrial capacity. As he said in his 1921 memorandum on China, "if China and Japan do not develop cooperatively their latent economic potential, the British and Americans will invade East Asia economically, and we will have no choice but to capitulate under that power."[5] Takahashi was clearly not an intentional supporter of militarism and the road to war when he returned to the finance portfolio in the 1930s.

Takahashi Fights the Military While Serving in the Saitō Cabinet

But what about the third interpretation of Takahashi's role in the rise of militarism, that by increasing the military budget, he unintentionally unleashed the army's and navy's power? As noted, the military budget more than doubled during the Takahashi years. Takahashi undertook his spending policies during the public euphoria over Japan's invasion of Manchuria, and although he opposed the attack and tried to limit its spread, he had no alternative but to give the army and navy their shares.[6] As a sitting finance minister, not an academic or journalist looking in from the outside, he had to deal with the realities of the military's power. He pragmatically acknowledged the political landscape in an interview with Ishibashi Tanzan, the Keynesian editor of the *Tōyō keizai shinpō*, who criticized Takahashi for his military spending even while praising him for his reflation of the economy. When asked by Ishibashi whether an increase in military allocations was the best kind of spending policy to stimulate economic recovery, Takahashi answered, "Of course military spending is not directly productive. . . . Warships do not produce other goods, but the money used to build warships is used productively. After the ships are launched, they need to be maintained. And the ships use coal, oil, and labor. These all create jobs and are expenditures that support people. . . . If in the political context of the times one has to spend money on the military anyway, it is better than nothing."[7] According to those who promote this third interpretation, Takahashi's defense spending allowed the two services to build up their strength and popularity, and in concert with the so-called new, revisionist civil bureaucrats, gradually to replace the political parties as the driving force of Japan's government, and eventually lead the nation to war. I concur that increases in military spending, which Takahashi had to allow despite his opposition to an aggressive foreign policy, played a supporting role in the early ascent of the military to power. But for the following reasons, I do not think Takahashi's contribution to the rise of militarism was a major one.

Military spending as a percentage of national wealth stayed steady at around 6.5 percent in all four Takahashi budgets from 1933 until 1936. The increases in military spending reflected the growth of the economy brought about by the success of Takahashi's monetary and fiscal stimuli, and were in line with his oft-repeated dictum that defense spending should not outrun national wealth. "We must prepare budgets in keeping with the people's income. Financial trust is an intangible matter. Maintaining that trust is our most important duty. If we focus too much on national defense, we will create runaway inflation and destroy that trust. Then our national defense will not be secure." Only after Takahashi's death did military spending as a percentage of national wealth grow dramatically, to 15 percent in 1937, 27 percent in 1941, and 76 percent in 1944.[8]

Takahashi stated repeatedly that he viewed the increases in budget allocations, including those to the military, as temporary measures. Once Japan had recovered from the depression and the Manchurian situation had been stabilized, Japan could return to balanced budgets. Fukai Eigo wrote in his memoirs that Takahashi understood from the beginning "that the policy of having the Bank of Japan undertake treasury bonds was a temporary expedient. He realized that it wasn't orthodox, and was something to do only when there was no liquidity in the money supply. . . . As industry recovered, government revenues would increase and budget deficits could be reduced. Thus, the sale of treasury bonds to the Bank of Japan could be cut back." Takahashi explained to the parliament on January 21, 1933, that the expenditures to pay for the Manchurian Incident, upgrading the army's and navy's weapons, and depression relief were temporary (*ichijiteki*) expenditures and would be reduced in a few years. With economic recovery, tax revenues would rise and Japan could return to a balanced budget. Takahashi repeated these views in a speech to the Bond Clearing House Association on April 21, and added, drawing on articles by Irving Fisher of Yale and a University of Chicago research group, that "One should not be concerned about balancing the budget in any one year, but over a number of years." In a speech to the parliament on December 23, 1934, Takahashi stated, "We must devise ways to reduce the issuance of treasury bonds. We must cut expenditures for national defense and other things."[9]

Takahashi courageously continued, almost single-handedly within the top levels of government, to fight army and navy policies, rhetoric, and demands for even larger outlays in an era when the cost of challenging the military could mean one's life. Takahashi publicly confronted the army and navy in the course of preparing all four budgets that he created between 1932 and 1936, and did so in an increasingly perilous milieu. Because he carried out a policy of liberal government spending during a popular war, he was constantly importuned to give the military its share or more. He operated in a political context in which off-stage negotiations and compromise, not public debate and principled argument, were normal behavior. He was also constrained by a system of budget-formation that required the unanimous consent of all cabinet ministers, including those from the army and navy. A look at the unfolding of the 1933 and 1934 budget negotiations illustrates the political difficulties Takahashi faced, the pressure on him to compromise in budgetary disputes, and his fighting spirit.[10]

Discussions on the 1933 budget opened later than usual, in the fall of 1932, because of a special summer session of parliament called to deal with supplemental spending for rural relief. Top army generals met and took a preemptive step on October 6, when they approved a broad budget plan and reported it directly to the emperor. Rather than follow the usual procedure of presenting his proposal through normal channels to the finance ministry, Army Minister Araki went around the entire cabinet to the monarch and only afterward publicly revealed the army's demands. The next day, Araki criticized Takahashi's plan to avoid raising taxes. In the army minister's view, the military needed more funds even if providing them slowed Japan's recovery from the depression and endangered its economic health. By the 8th, the finance ministry had received a total of 1,200,000,000 yen in proposals for new spending, an amount four times larger than those received in any previous year. More than half the amount demanded came from the army and navy.

On the 11th, Prime Minister Saitō announced a new process for deliberating on funding for the military. He would abandon the normal procedure of budget negotiations between sub-ministerial officials in the finance, army, and navy ministries, and henceforth Araki, Navy Minister Okada Keisuke, Takahashi, and he would determine the military budget before it went to the cabinet; in other words, two admirals, a general, and one civilian would be the principal negotiators. On the 25th, the cabinet (including Araki and Okada) agreed with Takahashi's view that it was too soon to raise taxes and therefore the finance ministry had to fund all new spending by selling treasury bonds to the Bank of Japan. On the 26th, Araki and Takahashi met, and the finance minister, under heavy pressure, recognized the urgency of the military budget, and Araki, as a quid pro quo, pledged budgetary self-control (without specifying what this meant). Takahashi went on to tell General Araki that as a member of the cabinet he should see himself as a politician responsible for national policy, not as a spokesman for his staff officers in the army ministry, and that a large increase in the army's budget endangered Japan's fiscal integrity as a nation.[11] The following day, Takahashi conferred with his subordinates, and the finance ministry agreed to restore 600,000,000 yen, or half the new demands, to the budget. Takahashi did not explain why he and his subordinates agreed to this concession. Possibly, in the face of right-wing terror in 1932 and because of his plan to stimulate the economy by government spending, Takahashi took the prudent way out and gave much of the new money to the military. Possibly he was under pressure from other ministers, particularly compromisers such as Prime Minister Admiral Saitō and Navy Minister Admiral Okada, who would become the next prime minister in 1934.

On November 1, Takahashi met with Araki and Okada, explained the government's financial problems, and asked them to accept a reduction in their demands. Okada, a member of the group that acquiesced to the naval limitations' treaties in 1922 and 1930, agreed, but Araki adamantly refused. By November 7, requests for new funds had risen by 200,000,000 yen to 1,400,000,000, but the finance ministry agreed to put only 610,000,000 yen, far short of what Araki wanted, back into the budget. At a cabinet meeting on the 7th, Araki told Takahashi that there was no reason the finance ministry could not issue 200,000,000 yen more in bonds. On the 8th, Takahashi met privately once more with Araki and Okada and at another cabinet meeting the next day, Takahashi agreed to give the army and navy 90,000,000 more, even though this required him to raise the issue of deficit bonds to over 900,000,000 yen, far more than the finance ministry thought healthy for the economy. He instructed the army and navy to work out between themselves how best to divide the extra 90,000,000, but they could not agree. Takahashi therefore made the decision for them; he provided 5,000,000 yen more, and the army received 50,000,000 and the navy 45,000,000. In the end, the 1933 military budget came to 852,000,000 yen, an increase of 22 percent over 1932 and more than twice that of 1931. But even if Takahashi gave the army and navy their largest appropriations up to that time, he also gave them far less than they had demanded; General Araki was not happy with the outcome of the 1933 budget.

The 78-year-old Takahashi, ill and unhappy with the process and results of the 1933 budget, considered resigning in April and May, but Prime Minister Saitō, who needed Takahashi's popularity and moral strength to govern, persuaded him to stay.[12] Once he decided to continue in the cabinet, Takahashi proposed a new approach to budget-making. Under the old system, each ministry presented its budget requests to the finance ministry. The accounting bureau of the finance ministry then determined what revenues were available, scrutinized each set of demands based on its detailed knowledge of the other departments' needs and costs, created a counter-budget for each ministry, and negotiated with them, almost invariably in an attempt to cut their requests. Only in the case of the military ministries did sub-ministerial negotiations not suffice; it was up to the finance minister himself to deal with his army and navy counterparts. After the finance ministry had successfully formed a budget acceptable to all ministries, the cabinet approved the budget and forwarded it to the lower house of the parliament for its rubber stamp. In Takahashi's view, probably an accurate one, each ministry argued from its own point of view, without considering national needs or fiscal limitations. In fact, the ministries tended to reintroduce programs that the accounting bureau had rejected in the past, or to make excessively large proposals as bargaining tools, as the army ministry had successfully done. The military ministries also tended to inflate the costs of the goods they proposed to purchase.

Takahashi wanted to proceed from the top down rather than the bottom up. The cabinet should set national priorities first, then consider income constraints, and finally ask each ministry for a broad outline of its needs. Takahashi wanted to use the leadership of the cabinet members to constrain excessive military spending; he wanted politicians, not finance ministry bureaucrats, to take the lead in budget-formation. Railroad Minister Mitsuchi Chūzō opposed Takahashi's plan because he feared that the various ministers would simply scratch each other's backs. No one would dare to oppose an increase for another ministry without expecting the same treatment in return. Mitsuchi believed that only finance ministry bureaucrats, who were not directly accountable to the public or to a ravenous ministry, had the expertise and the detachment to control spending. Needless to say, bureaucrats in the finance ministry, which Mitsuchi had headed in 1927–29, agreed. While the finance ministry officials argued in terms of the need for their expertise in the budget-making process, they opposed Takahashi's plan primarily because it would limit their power as members of the government's elite. Ultimately Takahashi's efforts failed, and the 1934 budget process went forward as usual.

In January 1933, the navy significantly intensified budgetary problems for Takahashi and the finance ministry by appointing Admiral Ōsumi Mineo to replace Okada as navy minister. Unlike Okada, a member of the so-called treaty faction of the navy that had supported the London naval disarmament negotiations in 1930, Ōsumi belonged to the "fleet faction" that had opposed them. Ōsumi proposed abrogating the treaty as a precondition to a large naval expansion. On July 10, the navy's general staff sent the navy ministry a plan for a naval buildup, and on July 21, Ōsumi met with General Araki and the two services agreed to cooperate "to complete the national defense." Meanwhile, some cabinet members proposed tax increases to pay for these expenditures, and even a group in the finance ministry made a study of the impact a tax increase would have on the economy. But Takahashi held his ground that it was too early in the recovery to raise taxes; he also announced that he wanted to reduce the level of bond issuance, which, of course, meant holding the line on government expenses.

Requests for new funds were delivered to the finance ministry by July 31, and not surprisingly, the military demands made up 64 percent of the total. The accounting bureau spent August and September hearing rationales from each ministry. But even while the accounting bureau did its research, many of the other actors were busy using private meetings and public opinion to sway Takahashi and Saitō. On September 9, Araki called on Takahashi and lectured him on the world situation. He told the finance minister that because of external crises, "Japan needed to build up its military to preserve peace." On the 12th, Ōsumi visited and discussed the dangers of the 1935 and 1936 crises—crises he, Araki, and other officers had conjured up to sway the government and public opinion—and called for a new plan of naval expansion. On September 28, the military distributed a press release announcing that the Soviet Union's current 5-year plan threatened Japan's "Manchurian ally." In reaction, the army proposed building stronger defenses there.

Saitō and Takahashi decided that a super-cabinet council of ministers was necessary to control the army and navy, and established the five ministers' council, made up of the prime, foreign, finance, army, and navy ministers, to coordinate defense planning and finance. The first meeting took place on October 3, 1933. Araki opened the meeting by explaining the dangerous international situation and the consequent need for a military build-up. Takahashi replied with his standard description of Japan's precarious fiscal position. The council met several times more. At these meetings, Takahashi and Foreign Minister Hirota Kōki argued that national defense should be subordinated to foreign policy, which should be set by the appropriate civilian authorities. Araki and Ōsumi countered that defense needs should come first, while foreign and financial policy should follow. Saitō, who wanted an outcome that would not threaten the stability of his government, straddled the fence and gave Takahashi only tepid support. On the one hand, the finance minister, in his words, seemed to get what he wanted: "Everybody agreed that foreign policy comes first, and that national defense policy backs it up as number two. And if the degree of national defense is not in accord with the people's financial power, it is like a painting of national defense. Thus, we must measure national defense by economic strength." The government announced on October 21 that all five ministers including Araki and Ōsumi had agreed to subordinate defense spending to fiscal strength, and to pursue a foreign policy based on peace and international cooperation, especially with China, the Soviet Union, and the United States. But the same day, Araki and the army put out a separate statement rejecting the conference results. Araki argued that because of the emperor's right of supreme command over the military, the army was not bound by the agreement he had agreed to. In spite of Takahashi's nominal victory, he reluctantly abandoned his plans for a cabinet-centered process.[13]

On October 22, most of the cabinet ministers left Tokyo to attend the army's annual maneuvers, and the government shut down. On the 23rd, the accounting bureau reported their funding decisions to Takahashi, who as usual had stayed behind in the capital. His subordinates called for substantial cuts in the military's, and especially in the navy's, proposals. They told the minister that the new demands could not be met without sharp increases in taxes or bond issues, neither of which he would support. Araki, on his return to Tokyo, immediately went to the prime minister to ask him to pressure Takahashi. Saitō visited the finance minister and told him that he wanted a harmonious, nonconfrontational outcome to the problem. He added that since the pressure for increased military spending came from within the army and navy, Takahashi must make concessions to the service ministers to help them control their subordinates, and that to satisfy the military, rural relief spending must be put off to the future.

Takahashi, who stood between his ministry and the prime minister, who in turn stood between Takahashi and the military, conferred with his subordinates, and on November 16, presented the finance ministry's budget proposal: a total of 2,017,000,000 yen, 3,000,000 more for the military than in 1933, and 700,000,000 in bond issues. The proposed budget recognized 620,000,000 in new funds, of which 400,000,000 was for the military. The budget cabinet met on the 17th, and the navy minister, whose branch had received only 39.5 percent of what it had requested, protested loudly and refused to accept the budget. General Araki, whose army had received 61.3 percent, acted the statesman and said he would negotiate privately with the finance minister. But the navy was particularly adamant, not only because of their cuts, but also because the accounting bureau claimed that the navy had overpriced the cost of the goods it wanted to purchase.

Over the next week, Prime Minister Saitō made the rounds of all of the relevant ministers in his effort to formulate an amicable conclusion to the budget debate. Takahashi made another, "final" proposal that raised the total budget by 89,000,000 yen and gave much of it to the navy. But Ōsumi still refused to sign off on it. Saitō called what he hoped was the final budget meeting for December 1, but it was postponed until December 2 after the emperor expressed his concern about the budget impasse. The emperor told his military attaché, General Honjō Shigeru, that if the cabinet fell over the finance ministry–navy conflict, it would have adverse effects abroad; Saitō used the opportunity to pressure Takahashi to give the navy 15,000,000 yen more. In the end, Saitō's seemingly endless round of private meetings with the various players (before the final meeting on December 2, the prime minister conferred with each cabinet member individually) brought a final budget of 2,224,000,000 yen with 943,000,000 for the military and 881,000,000 in government bonds.[14] Saitō's efforts to satisfy everyone ultimately satisfied no one. Takahashi fought hard in 1933–34 to limit military spending, and although he gave the army and navy more than he would have liked, he also gave them far less than they had demanded. The finance minister was not a free agent who could simply decree the budget his accounting department proposed. The interests and power of the various ministries (including the capacity of the army and navy to assassinate with impunity), a system that required unanimous cabinet approval of a budget, and the prime minister's desire for a harmonious outcome all intervened. To blame Takahashi for the increase in military spending in 1933–34 overlooks the constraints of the system in which he worked.

Takahashi did not oppose the military only at budget time. He consistently criticized the aggressive actions of the military, especially when they threatened Japan's relations with Great Britain, the United States, and China. According to one of his subordinates in the finance ministry, Saitō Toragorō, Takahashi asked Araki, "Are there really idiots in the army who think Japan can win a war against the United States?" Takahashi threatened in late December 1931 to resign from the government if the army carried out its proposed attack on Jinzhou, a city in China's Liaoning Province near the border with Manchuria. In Takahashi's view, this attack would bring the Japanese army too close to China proper, and thus place the possibility of a unified China under military threat. When the Japanese military dispatched troops to Shanghai in February 1932 during the seizure of Manchuria, Takahashi told Prince Saionji's secretary, Harada Kumao:

I have been absolutely opposed from the beginning to sending troops to Shanghai. At a recent cabinet meeting, I said [to Araki], "If the situation changes in Shanghai, can't you just bring the troops home?" The army minister replied, "If the army received an order [from the emperor] to do something, it would harm its dignity to withdraw." I answered, "The army's dignity is an internal matter, and when one faces a major international crisis of this sort, you can't say something as stupid as that (*sonna baka na koto o itte wa ikan*)." From the point of view of fiscal policy, if the incident turns into war, we don't have the funds to fight for more than half a year. Unlike the situation during the Russo-Japanese War, we do not have justice (*taigi meibun*) on our side and thus do not have the sympathy of the powers. Moreover, if we send out troops, the army will claim the so-called right of supreme command, and we won't know when they will bring the soldiers home.[15]

In December 1933, while Takahashi was preparing the 1934 budget, Foreign Minister Hirota asked at a cabinet meeting why the United States and Great Britain raised their tariffs against Japanese goods. Takahashi replied:

The foreigners have joined together to resist Japan not only because of trade friction. This trade resistance is the superficial symptom, but the real problem is the army and navy. The military clique goes all over Japan and talks about a 1935 or a 1936 crisis, and about beginning preemptive wars against the Soviet Union or the United States. Foreigners hear this kind of talk. It is unfortunate that Japan presents an attitude of favoring war when the Americans and Europeans want to avoid conflict. The military's attitudes provoke trade retaliation from foreign countries. The army should be careful in its language. There is no crisis of 1935 or 1936.

Araki turned pale with anger when he heard these words and said, "There will be a crisis. . . . We must prepare."[16]

In 1932–33, during a debate over which currency system should be adopted for Manchukuo, which the army leaders had just established as the capstone of their privately controlled empire (the army's "fireworks," in Takahashi's words), Takahashi objected to the military's plan to use Japanese yen on the grounds that Manchuria was not part of Japan, but was an independent, foreign country with a long history as part of China. He instead advocated the use of a silver-based currency, which would be linked with China's monetary system. His view prevailed until September 1935, only a few months before his death, when the government decided to tie the Manchurian currency to the yen at a rate of one-to-one. At that time he again expressed his apprehension that the army's planned export of capital to the colony would soak up specie needed for trade with other countries, and especially with technologically advanced countries. He thus proposed to the cabinet that the government limit investment in Manchuria.[17]

In July 1935, Takahashi alone among government leaders opposed a plan of the Kwantung Army to have the South Manchuria Railway Company establish a major company in North China, outside of the army's puppet state.[18] It is remarkable that a sitting finance minister would publicly take such a position in direct opposition to the views of the powerfully armed military services. Moreover, it is even more remarkable and ironic that Takahashi, ever the pragmatic rationalist, had a clearer view of the military's own reliance on the United States and Great Britain for technology and advanced raw materials such as aviation fuel than the army's leaders themselves. Takahashi recognized such dependence, in stark contrast to the perspective of generals such as Araki, who told Ishibashi Tanzan in a June 1, 1935 interview "if the people are determined to fight to the end, even three million bamboo spears will be adequate [to defend Japan]."[19] A war with the richer Anglo-Americans would not only require Japan to fight countries that were more advanced militarily, technologically, and industrially; it would also cut the Japanese army and navy off from sharing the benefits of those advances.

Takahashi Joins the Okada Cabinet

In the midst of Takahashi's struggle with the military, in July 1934, the Saitō Cabinet fell over suspicions that certain cabinet members would be arrested in connection with the Teijin incident, an alleged instance of official collusion and corruption, but which in fact was a case of "prosecutors' fascism." When the Suzuki Company (Suzuki Shōten) failed during the 1927 Financial Panic, the Taiwan Bank received 220,000 shares of the stock of Teijin, a rayon manufacturer owned by Suzuki. The bank was obliged to sell the shares over a ten-year period. A group of investors who bought some of this stock at an inexpensive price in mid-1933 made a windfall profit when its value rose sharply by year's end. Certain right-wing justice ministry officials, who wanted to replace the Saitō Cabinet with one headed by Hiranuma Kiichirō, a leading advocate of the mystical, emperor-cult approach to Japan's polity, used the Teijin affair as a way to take down the government. They arrested and interrogated under duress a number of officials and even ministers, including Railroad Minister Mitsuchi, a protégé of Takahashi, for conspiring to allow the investors to buy the stock at an artificially low price. Although in the end the charges turned out to be trumped-up and the arrestees found innocent of all charges, this was not until December 1937, far too late to save Saitō's cabinet, or for that matter, Takahashi's life.[20]

The prosecutors who pursued Mitsuchi and his fellow defendants in the Teijin case had a broader motivation than bringing down the Saitō government. Their real target was Takahashi and his "Takahashi line" (*Takahashi rosen*), an approach to Japan's depression-era problems that positioned Takahashi, not Saitō, as the cabinet's central figure.[21] One prosecutor tipped his hand when he asked leading questions to try to force an indicted finance ministry official named Kuroda Hideo to confess that profits from the alleged corruption were passed on to Takahashi. Hiranuma and his clique went after the finance minister because they opposed his "line": an arrangement to encourage economic growth through controlled inflation, to limit military spending, and to encourage a continued role for the parties in the political system. Takahashi had created a coalition that included large capitalists, small- and medium-scale businessmen, party politicians, mainstream bureaucrats, and the leaders of moderate, non-communist labor unions such as Sōdōmei, a federation that drew together almost three-quarters of all organized workers. Takahashi's idea was that economic growth through increased productivity should benefit everyone, not just big business. As profits rose, so too should wages: a bigger pie being cut into bigger slices for everyone. The Teijin prosecutors were not alone in their attack on the Takahashi line, a government-harmonized, antiwar "politics of productivity." They were joined by the military, the "new bureaucrats" who supported greater government involvement in the economy and collaboration with the military, chauvinistic civilian ideologues of various stripes, and some members of both parties who wanted to overthrow the Saitō and Okada governments for their own political gain.[22] This right-wing coalition rejected Takahashi's central coordination and supported movement toward an autarkic command economy, the abolition of political parties to form one top-down organization, an autonomous foreign policy, a powerful military, and aggressive expansion abroad, particularly in China.[23] It was in this atmosphere that Admiral Okada Keisuke, who had served as Saitō's first navy minister, was chosen to head the new government. As one can imagine, the Okada government was compromised from the beginning.

Before he formed his new cabinet on July 8, 1934, Okada asked Takahashi to stay on as finance minister, but Takahashi refused. On the one hand, the new prime minister needed him; no other politician had his knowledge of finance or his courage in standing up to the military. On the other, Takahashi felt burned by the Teijin scandal. Not only were his close associate Mitsuchi and several high-ranking finance ministry officials arrested, but his son Korekata was also implicated. Takahashi recommended as his successor Deputy Minister Fujii Sanenobu, a career finance ministry bureaucrat. Takahashi recognized in the summer of 1934 that the time had come to begin to rein in government spending; he thought that Fujii, an advocate of budgetary probity within the finance ministry, was the best man available to present to the cabinet the case for retrenchment. But Fujii, who had no political experience at the super-ministry level, was not up to the task; as one of his colleagues said, "Fujii was a ministry man replacing a legend." Physically unwell to begin with, he was caught in the midst of the sharp swords of the army and navy ministers and their allies, the anxiety of the compromisers such as Okada, and the rigor of his finance ministry colleagues, who criticized Fujii every time he made a concession to the military (an argument with Kaya Okinori, a ministry subordinate, over concessions to the military actually brought Fujii to tears).[24] The finance ministry drew up a 2,100,000,000 yen budget, presented it to the various ministries, and then brought it to the cabinet. But in November 1934, after only four months on the job, Fujii resigned and died soon after. Okada immediately visited Takahashi and persuaded him to return to the finance portfolio; in the car returning home, Okada surprised his secretary by telling him that since Takahashi had agreed to serve, "Everything is 'OK,'" using the English word. On November 27, amid the cabinet debate over the 1935 budget, the 80-year-old Takahashi, in ill health himself, returned to the ministry for his seventh and final time.[25]

The 1935 budget presented Takahashi with two problems: military pressure, which was predictable; and Fujii's plan to impose an excess business tax on companies, which was not to the finance minister's liking. Takahashi avoided a confrontation with the military by immediately giving them 100,000,000 yen more. Much as he disliked tax increases, Takahashi followed through on Fujii's proposal; it became the first tax increase during Takahashi's four years in office during the depression. The final budget reached 2,215,000,000 yen, slightly less than the 1934 budget, but included more than 1,000,000,000 for the military, or 46 percent of all government expenditures. In reaction to the growing economy, Takahashi reduced the issuance of treasury bonds from 881,000,000 in 1934 to 772,000,000 in 1935.[26]

Although Takahashi was now fully committed to limiting the sale of government bonds, he faced sharp criticism for the 1935 budget. Subordinates within the ministry opposed the additional 100,000,000 for the army and navy, and Minseitō politicians attacked him for breaking the "10,000,000,000 barrier" (with the additional sale of treasury bonds, the total value of outstanding bonds exceeded 10,000,000,000 yen).[27] For the first time since Takahashi had introduced his system of selling treasury bills to the Bank of Japan, the bank could not sell them all: as the economy expanded and companies began to invest in new facilities, the bonds had to compete with private borrowing for available capital. In January 1935, after the government had delivered the budget to the parliament for its rubber stamp, Minseitō politicians questioned Takahashi sharply for not returning to a "healthy" fiscal policy, meaning a balanced budget. Takahashi defended himself as follows:

Kawasaki-kun has said that we must emphasize fiscal policy, balance governmental income and expenditures, and avoid making up our deficits with treasury bonds. If we continue to do so our future is in doubt. As he said, military spending has exceeded a billion yen, and the cost of other ministries is over 500,000,000 yen. I am concerned because we have lost equilibrium. . . . But no one calls out, "reduce military spending!" This is because the people want defense spending. [At this point, someone in the chamber shouted, "No, no! It is because pistols are frightening!"] There is no other way to balance the budget than to reduce military spending. [Applause, and voices shouting, "Why doesn't the finance minister do it!"] You say, "Why doesn't the finance minister do it? Would you allow the finance minister to speak as the people's voice?" [Applause and laughter. Someone shouts, "The finance minister is the people's voice!"] In the final analysis, the bond issue is a serious problem. If we err on the bond issue now, we will cause Japan great harm. It troubles me greatly. But in the end, no matter how much we worry about bonds, if industry flourishes private capital will be necessary. At that time, people who now hold treasury bonds will go to the Bank of Japan to borrow money, and use the bonds as security. Thus, the danger of inflation because of a bloated money supply will be born. I believe this.[28]

Takahashi was caught on the horns of a dilemma from which neither he nor his successors in the finance ministry could escape. The military budget drove Japan toward economic disaster, and pistols were not only frightening, but also lethal.

The year 1935 brought other ominous events for the Okada government that would deepen Japan's gradual slide into autarchy, the most prominent of these being the "Emperor Organ Theory Affair" (Tennō kikansetsu jiken), or as opponents of the theory called it, the movement to "rectify the national polity." Minobe Tatsukichi, a legal scholar and professor of law at Tokyo Imperial University, had developed the "Emperor Organ Theory," an explanation of the Meiji Constitution of 1889 that allowed for the development of democratic institutions within a framework in which all sovereignty theoretically resided with the emperor. Minobe's advocacy of democratic government, unrestricted civil rights, disarmament, and his opposition to aggressive military expansionism had earned him the wrath of the army and the right wing. In the relatively liberal 1920s, Minobe and his theory held sway; in fact, as an eminent academic, Minobe was appointed to the House of Peers as a non-peer member in 1932. But, as we have seen, the atmosphere of 1935 differed dramatically from that of only three years earlier. In January, Minobe made a speech to the house in which he attacked the Justice Ministry's violation of human rights in its handling of the Teijin incident. Outraged, the right wing struck back. On February 28, Kikuchi Takeo, a retired army major general who served in the upper house, rose to counterattack—calling Minobe's theory a "negative, blasphemous, academic treason"—and the battle was on.

Over the next ten months, a coalition of new bureaucrats, retired and active military officers, Seiyūkai politicians such as Kuhara Fusanosuke who had close ties to the army, and right-wing activists enlisted mass organizations such as the Imperial Military Reserve Association to pressure Minobe and Okada. Hovering in the background was Hiranuma (in fact, the Minobe affair can be seen as a continuation of the Teijin incident), who strove to topple quasi-party cabinets such as those of Saitō and Okada and to replace them with pro-military, authoritarian governments. Okada, under pressure to save his cabinet, acquiesced to compromise after compromise. In the end, Minobe resigned from the House of Peers, and on February 21, 1936, a young student shot him in the leg in an attempted assassination. Takahashi, who admired Minobe for his support of civilian-directed diplomacy and his opposition to military expansionism, made no public statements in his defense.[29]

The Formation of the 1936 Budget

Given the atmosphere of late 1935, Takahashi's prospects for controlling military spending in the 1936 budget looked bleak. Nevertheless, he made one final effort to contain and even cut the army's and navy's budgets in the face of intense military opposition. The vituperative debate came to a head at an all-night cabinet meeting on November 29–30, 1935. The *Tōkyō asahi shinbun*'s reportage during the final weeks of budget-formation gives the reader a feeling of Takahashi's almost suicidal resolve to control military spending, the army's intense resistance, and Okada's equivocation. It runs as follows (paraphrased throughout, except where set off as quotations):

November 18. Now that the army's annual maneuvers have ended and the cabinet ministers are returning to Tokyo, the cabinet will open its budget discussions on the 22nd. Finance Minister Takahashi is committed to returning to a balanced budget and to gradually reducing deficit bonds. The military is his primary obstacle to achieving this goal. Army Minister Kawashima's stance in the debate depends on whether or not he can control the army internally. Does Prime Minister Okada, standing in the middle, have the skill to reconcile the two positions?

November 24. Headline: "The Government is Optimistic about the Budget!" The finance ministry's top officials met with Takahashi at his home in Omote-machi on the 23rd and have now finished their budget proposal. The army's top leaders met the same day to discuss their budgetary position; they have not agreed to the finance ministry's proposals and want more of the money they originally requested put back into the final budget. The top sub-ministerial officials from the finance, army, and navy ministries are conferring frequently to reach a compromise agreement before the cabinet meeting.

November 25. Takahashi proposed a "cooperative budget" process for 1936, so discussions had begun much earlier in the year; the army and navy agreed to this procedure at the time, but now are taking an unexpectedly strong stand and demanding tens of millions of additional funds. On the 24th, the finance ministry reached budget agreements with the interior, agriculture, and commerce ministries, so only the army and navy budgets remain unsettled. The prime minister still hopes that an "administrative" (sub-ministerial) agreement is possible, but if it cannot be reached, a "political" decision will have to be made at the cabinet level. Okada has postponed by one day the budget cabinet meeting, originally planned for the 25th, so that sub-ministerial negotiations between the finance and service ministries can continue.

November 26. Headline: "The Army Strongly Demands 60–70 Million More!" Although finance ministry officials worked hard on the 25th to reach a compromise agreement with the military and thus avoid an acrimonious confrontation at the cabinet meeting scheduled for the 26th, the army and navy refuse to back down. The army wants a total budget of 596,000,000 yen; the finance ministry offers 480,000,000 plus 10,000,000 more through the negotiating process. The navy wants a total budget of 580,000,000 yen; the finance ministry offers 530,000,000. The two services rejected the finance ministry's compromise proposal on the 25th, and want to make their case to the full cabinet on the 26th. After meeting at his home with his chief subordinates, Tsushima, Kaya, Ishiwatari, and Aoki, Takahashi made this statement: "We have no choice but to seek a political solution to the matter of national defense spending at a full cabinet meeting. We have reached administrative agreements with all ministries except the military ones. It is unfortunate that the army and navy do not have the same kind of cooperative spirit and we have had to break off negotiations. I shall strive to get the military officials to negotiate with sincerity."

November 27. The cabinet budget meeting scheduled for the morning of the 26th was postponed once more so that sub-ministerial negotiations could continue. Finally at 3:00 PM on the 26th, the budget meeting opened with the following statement by Takahashi (dubbed by the young officers who would lead the murderous 2/26 rebellion three months later the "Takahashi Proclamation"):

This year's budget was drawn up under principles agreed to by the whole cabinet. Each ministry agreed to cooperate and keep its demands for new funds to a bare minimum. We estimate that we shall have a natural increase in revenues of about 89,000,000 yen and that we can afford expenditures of 2,243,600,000 yen. We do not believe the economy has recovered to the point that we can increase taxes. Accordingly, we expect to reduce the issuance of bonds by about 80,000,000 yen. We asked each ministry to cooperate and put together a budget in keeping with our national and our citizens' incomes. If one compares Japanese per capita income with that of the Western powers, Japan has a per capita income of 165 yen, the United States 1,155 yen, England 863 yen, and France 465 yen. Japan has many wretchedly poor people, who are hit by natural disasters and are in pain. We have many social problems to solve. If the military pushes for larger budgets unreasonably, I think they will lose the trust of the people. We must gradually eliminate deficit bonds to stabilize the people's economy. Our primary purpose in reducing bonds is to reduce the people's fears. Thus, we have switched to our current policies.

To which Takahashi then added:

Our country is poor in natural resources and I doubt that we can compete in an autarkic economic environment. We must think about our position in the world and form a budget in keeping with our people's wealth. Financial trust is an intangible. Maintaining that trust is our most urgent duty. If we focus only on defense, we will cause bad inflation and that trust will collapse. Thus, our national defense will not be secure. The military should think about this. I have agreed to restore ten million yen to each service's budget. I can go no further than this.[30] [On page 4 of the evening edition a small article announced that the business world welcomed Takahashi's effort to reduce deficit bonds in 1936.]

November 28. The morning paper highlighted the army's "unofficial" reply to Takahashi:

There seems to be some misunderstanding concerning the coordination of defense and fiscal policy. It is deplorable for someone to leak out that the army has fabricated the current sense of crisis at a time when we have a real crisis that can only be met through national unity. Japan has the important and unprecedented duty to maintain peace in the Far East. The independence of Manchuria is the cornerstone to that effort. To strengthen Japanese-Manchurian ties, the country must strive as one. A policy that forgets our national destiny and doubts the fulfillment of this national duty hinders the advancement of our nation and race (*minzoku*). We absolutely oppose this kind of negative thinking. We feel compelled to state that our nation's central and urgent purpose is to prepare militarily to carry out Japan's righteous national duty. . . . The current budget demand is necessary to build an enduring foundation of military preparedness in order to secure our nation's defense. To say that the Japanese people resent the army's efforts because it has pushed too far in its budget demands in the past and present slanders the military to the extreme. The military believes that national defense must be based on real national unity. This will allow the populace to feel secure. We believe that the idea that the military's demands for more money are a burden on the people that impoverishes some of them must be corrected. Our nation's wealth grows year by year. We must have adequate funds to carry out our national policies based on the insoluble bonds between Japan and Manchuria.

The declaration then concluded, ominously in light of the murderous events of the following February: "In order to assist in the development of our national power and meet the demands of the populace, our leaders must be completely changed and renewed. We earnestly hope for the establishment of a fiscal policy that will increase our national strength."

The *Asahi* reported signs of compromise as the day ended. Army Minister Kawashima thanked the finance ministry for finding more money for the military budget, but argued it was still not enough. The finance ministry announced that it could not increase deficit bonds further, but that it might be able to find more money for the army and navy with the help of other ministries. But the young officers' movement, which concerned itself more with a "Shōwa Restoration," in which the emperor would be rescued from his misguided (and misguiding) advisors like Takahashi, than with budgetary matters, was not ready to compromise. As one of the leaders of the February 26, 1936 uprising would declare at his court martial, "Finance Minister Takahashi's statement to the army minister at a budget cabinet meeting in

October [sic] that the army's efforts to increase the military budget made it the focus of the people's resentment was something a finance minister must not be allowed to say. He did this to drive a wedge between the military and the people so he could defend the established order." Or as another stated, "Finance Minister Takahashi's fiscal policies were meant to prevent our restoration. . . . The fiscal policies of the restoration must increase government bonds and destroy the *zaibatsu.*" Suzaki Shin'ichi, in his book on the February 26 Incident, argues that the "Takahashi Proclamation" was an important cause of the incident, and the reason Takahashi became one of the assassins' primary targets.[31]

November 29. Prime Minister Okada met with the commerce, transportation, colonial, and railroad ministers to persuade them to transfer money voluntarily from their budgets to the military. Although the transportation and railroad ministers stated that such sacrifices would cause their ministries hardships, Okada was able to find 10,000,000 yen, which, the *Asahi* reported, was not enough to satisfy the army and navy. Takahashi restated his opposition to an increase in deficit bonds. The Seiyūkai publicly attacked the finance minister for trying to reduce deficit spending, and concluded its critique of its former president and prime minister by stating, "The Takahashi cabinet has lost its mandate."[32]

November 30. The cabinet budget meeting opened at 10:30 AM and immediately recessed, to reconvene at 3:00 PM. Army and finance ministry administrative officials met in the meantime in an attempt to find a compromise. After the reopening, Takahashi stated that the army must reduce its demands because of the difficulty of liquidating deficit bonds on the market. Kawashima countered that given the current world situation the army can compromise no further. At 5:30 PM, the cabinet adjourned for dinner and the physically fragile finance minister went home to rest. By the time Takahashi returned to the meeting at nine, his subordinates had agreed to increase the two services' budgets by 10,000,000 yen (8,000,000 for the army, 2,000,000 for the navy) and the two military ministers had accepted this compromise. Only one last step, obtaining agreement of the army general staff, remained before the cabinet could approve the budget.

Accordingly, Army Minister Kawashima stated that "The budget is generally resolved. I'll be back very soon for the final approval," and left for general staff headquarters at midnight to explain the compromise.

But when Kawashima returned at 1:40 AM, his attitude had changed completely. He reported that the general staff refused to accept the compromise and demanded 10,000,000 yen more. General Sugiyama, deputy chief of staff, even took the unprecedented step (infringing on the army ministry's authority) of visiting the prime minister's residence to explain the general staff's demands. Kawashima found himself in an untenable position; he had approved the army's budget, only to have another part of the army undermine his authority. The general staff nonetheless refused to compromise, even though its refusal meant that General Kawashima might be forced to resign as army minister.

At this point, the *Asahi* went to press and public knowledge of the end of the budget story had to be postponed until the next day's issue.

December 1. The headline of the *Asahi shinbun* that morning screamed:

> Twenty-one Hours in a Can/
> The Longest Cabinet Meeting in History/
> The 82-Year-Old Finance Minister's Tenacity/
> The Endurance King, Takahashi-san!

The *Asahi* reported that thirteen cabinet members had spent 20 hours and 50 minutes, from 10:30 AM on November 29 to 7:20 AM on November 30, at the prime minister's official residence. The person who persevered the most and defended his position to the end was the "miracle-working *daruma*," who was born in the first year of Ansei, that is, 1854. Because Takahashi had already decided to reduce the issue of deficit bonds beginning with the 1936 budget, he rejected any increase in military spending that could not be funded with transfers from other ministries. In the end, civil ministries provided 30,000,000 in funds for the army and navy in the last few days of the budget-making process. Thus, Takahashi did not have to bend on his bond-reducing plan. The general staff also backed down in the end and accepted Army Minister Kawashima's compromise.[33]

What clearly emerges from this description of the 1936 budget creation is that Takahashi did not have a free hand in the process. He and his ministry's firm opposition to increased military spending did not guarantee that the army and navy would not ultimately receive more money. The formal approval of a budget required the support of every member of the cabinet, including of course the army and navy ministers. A case in point was that only two years earlier, Transportation Minister

Mitsuchi, by stubbornly refusing to approve any kind of multi-year appropriation, had single-handedly blocked Takahashi's efforts to extend funding for rural relief beyond the 1934 budget. Furthermore, Prime Minister Okada was a retired admiral who himself, when serving as navy minister during the previous Saitō government, had pressured Takahashi to give the navy more money. As a result of his naval background and his desire as prime minister to emphasize the benefits of a harmonious outcome to the budget-making process over a gradual return to fiscal rectitude, Okada was more likely to compromise with the military than Takahashi was. One can appreciate why the military preferred that the final budgetary decisions be made at the cabinet rather than at the ministerial level, especially since the army could pressure recalcitrant ministers with its ultimate persuasive tool: pistols.

The End of the Takahashi Line

Takahashi continued to stand up to the army for the remaining months of his life. On January 5, 1936, the *Tōkyō asahi shinbun* carried a new year's interview with Takahashi in which he criticized Italy's invasion of Ethiopia by saying, "If a country increases its empire and pours money into it, how big a profit is it going to have? Until the profits come in, the home country has to carry [the colony.]" As Sugiyama Heisuke, the interviewer, explained, "This was an indirect way of speaking to the Japanese people about the dangers of empire." In a speech on January 15, Takahashi said, "Even if the disarmament conference does not reach an agreement [on naval armaments limitations], we cannot think of increasing defense spending. The basic premise of our foreign policy since leaving the League of Nations continues to be the support of world peace. Our current efforts at disarmament are based on a policy of not threatening other countries and of non-aggression, so even if the disarmament conference breaks up, there is no reason for additional military spending." On February 17, Takahashi told an overflow audience of more than 2,000—people began lining up five hours in advance to hear him speak—at Hibiya Public Hall that he was committed to the "smooth elimination of deficit bonds," which the army and navy understood to mean the smooth reduction of military spending.[34] A general election held on February 20 gave Takahashi a powerful vote of confidence. In spite of the efforts of the military and right wing to elect "patriotic" candidates, and of his former party, the Seiyūkai, to oppose cuts in military spending, the Minseitō, the party that campaigned in support of Takahashi's efforts to reduce budget deficits, won the most seats in the election. Takahashi's new party gained 59 seats over the 1932 election, while his old party lost 132. Ironically, it was Takahashi's expansion of the money supply and demand in 1932 that decided the election for the Seiyūkai; it was his efforts to reverse the trend in 1936 that won the election for the Minseitō.[35] It is hard to avoid reaching the conclusion that there was a connection between the election results and the murderous uprising only six days later.

Takahashi undoubtedly understood the risks of his opposition to increased military spending in the mid-1930s. After the octogenarian joined the Okada cabinet in November 1934, he told an acquaintance, "If I were younger and could serve the emperor in the future, I would worry about [the young officers], but at my age I have no future. I have to do my service now. I entered the government again thinking that this is my last chance to serve. I am prepared to die now." And in the autumn of 1935, when one of Takahashi's subordinates told him that a young army officer had shouted, "Bury Finance Minister Takahashi!" Takahashi had replied, somewhat flippantly for a man in such danger, "I don't know how many first and second lieutenants there are, but if each one shot me it would be too much."[36]

Takahashi's secretary Kubo Bunzō, Vice Minister Tsushima, and Takahashi's grandson Korenobu have all spoken or written of the procedures in place to protect the finance minister from attack in 1935–36. His staff members had a system in the minister's office to bolt the door from the inside, they had a concealed staircase exit, they practiced guarding his Omote-machi home against attack, and they had a secret hiding place for him under the roof of the Western-style part of the house. In the last week of Takahashi's life, Kubo told him to lower his head if gunmen attacked his car. Takahashi pointed out that when Minobe was attacked on February 21, the gunmen fired for the lower part of his body. "If Minobe-san had lowered his head, they would have killed him." Kubo concluded his recounting of these safety precautions by stating, "Takahashi knew at the time he would be a target of attack. Since I always rode next to him, I was prepared to die too."[37] It is hard not to admire Old Takahashi (Takahashi-ō), one of the few leading officials in the 1930s willing to risk his life in standing up to the "double patriots."

Takahashi, planning to take February 26th off from work, returned home early on the evening of the 25th to see his married daughter who had come for a visit. The whole family dined together, and Takahashi enjoined his daughter to follow the customs of her new family. Before dawn the next morning, more than 1,000 troops of the Third Imperial Guards Regiment, commanded by young, junior officers, seized central Tokyo and assassinated a number of leading government officials for the crime of misadvising the emperor, that is, of pursuing rational polices that prevented the monarch from ruling according to his true spiritual essence as Japan's man-god (*arahitogami*). Two of the officers led 100 of their men, armed with rifles and machine guns, through the snowy streets of Takahashi's lifetime nest (their base in Roppongi was within easy walking distance of the homes where Takahashi was born, brought up, and now lived) to his house in Aoyama. Just before 4:00 AM, Kubo received a telephone call from Takahashi's house: "Kubo-san. It's an emergency. The soldiers are here." Although they were still outside at that moment, there was nothing he could do. The soldiers smashed open Takahashi's front gate, pushed into the house with their boots on, and rushed to his bedroom. Takahashi looked at them severely and said, "What are you doing?" At that very instant, one of the officers shouted "traitor!" and fired bullet after bullet into Takahashi's chest and abdomen. The other screamed "heavenly punishment!" as he used his sword to hack the octogenarian repeatedly—the finance minister's right arm was almost severed from his body. Takahashi's pajamas were soaked red with his blood, and the tatami mats of his room covered with mud from the soldiers' boots. At 5:30, Vice Minister Tsushima received a call from Kubo to tell him that the finance minister was dead and that his house was surrounded by soldiers. Tsushima walked to Omote-machi, was allowed to enter the house, viewed Takahashi's mutilated body, and met with his family. Tsushima wrote tersely in his memoirs, "I was moved deeply." After completing their assassinations of the men they viewed as traitors, the rebels then called for a military government headed by their tacit supporter and Takahashi's former nemesis, General Araki. It took four days for the army to crush the rebellion.

Many generals, including Araki, supported the young officers' goals. Others, such as Army Minister Kawashima, wanted a compromise settlement that would not embarrass the army. Tsushima and others, most notably the emperor, called on the army to suppress the attempted coup d'état. Finally, on February 29, the army re-established discipline by ordering the young rebel officers to surrender. Ironically, the army's generals would take advantage of the suppression of a rebellion raised by their own subordinates to increase the military's power within the government and to elicit far larger budget allocations from the government: the 1937 military budget was triple the average of 1934–36; by 1939 it had doubled again, and by 1944, during the rapid wartime inflation, it reached a level 70 times larger than in Takahashi's final budget.[38] It is hard not to agree with the Marxist economist, Ōuchi Hyōe, who wrote in praise of Takahashi:

The February 26 Incident occurred shortly after a picture of Takahashi, reading Sidney and Beatrice Webb's book, *Soviet Communism: A New Civilization?*, appeared in the newspaper. I was impressed that Takahashi sat in his study and read about Russian communist politics and economics in the midst of the debate [over the military budget]. I was astonished by the aged politician's actions as I was by the achievement of the aging Webbs, and placed great hope in the efforts of this skilled financier to defend Japan's fiscal health. It goes without saying that the February 26 Incident robbed me of this hope.[39]

Tokyo was placed under martial law on February 26, and the army general in command, afraid of a popular uprising against the military, refused to allow the Takahashi family to hold a funeral for the dead finance minister. At last, however, the army relented, and Takahashi's funeral took place on March 26, one month after his murder. The military nevertheless refused to permit an official funeral in the finance minister's honor, no announcement was made ahead of time, and the military police (*kenpeitai*) directed the funeral procession over the three-mile course through central Tokyo from his home to his Buddhist temple, the Tsukiji Honganji. But in spite of the army's efforts, finance ministry members and their families turned out as the cortege passed the ministry, hundreds of people lined the streets, and buses and trams all stopped to express the people's feelings about Takahashi. Tsushima, who went to the minister's home to chant Buddhist sutras every evening between Takahashi's death and funeral, wrote, "Many ordinary people attended the funeral. It was a demonstration against one part [Araki's?] of the military." The empress and the royal family sent flowers. People abroad and at home recognized Japan's loss. The *New York Times* carried an obituary in appreciation of Takahashi's value to Japan, and in mourning of his nation's great loss. Takahashi's death removed Japan's "last resistance" to prewar militarism.[40]

CONCLUSION

Takahashi's Economic Philosophy
and Its Roots

Takahashi Korekiyo was an important financial statesman because as an economic and political thinker he was well ahead of his time. Before resuming the post of finance minister in December 1931 during the depression, Takahashi understood a baker's dozen of important principles, which in combination seem not to have been held by any other Japanese financial or political leader before the post–World War II Keynesian revolution—and perhaps not even then.

These principles were that the primary task of government is to encourage its nation's economic growth. The purpose of economic development is not only to make the state wealthy and powerful, but also to raise the standards of living of the nation's people. A nation best raises its wealth and its citizens' incomes by encouraging business enterprises to improve their workers' productivity and to share its benefits with them. The government should use a graduated income tax to narrow the gap between rich and poor, as a relatively equal distribution of wealth is necessary in all countries. Not only should the government adopt policies to enhance people's standards of living, but it should also encourage them to play a larger role in their own governance—thus Takahashi's advocacy of universal suffrage and the popular election of prefectural governors. By increasing spending over revenue and devaluing its currency, a government can use fiscal and monetary policy to stimulate growth, especially in times of recession. By balancing or running a surplus in its current accounts budget and upwardly valuing its currency, a government can use fiscal and monetary policy to contract demand and fight inflation when the economy overheats. Excessive military spending endangers not only the nation's economic health, but also its defense. In foreign policy, civilians should lead, the military follow. Japan's foreign and financial policies should be carried out cooperatively within an Anglo-American framework not only because war with the United States and Great Britain would be futile, but also because the two English-speaking nations and their empires provided Japan with its most important foreign markets, as well as sources of capital, raw materials, and technology. Japan's competition with other nations should be pursued through trade, not through empire-building and war. Japan should strive to build a strong, unified China, which would then become a partner, rather than a target, in world trade competition. And finally, market information, not centralized decision-making, is crucial for sustained economic growth. Takahashi, like Keynes himself, was both a "Keynesian" and a "Hayekian" at the same time.[1]

One of the primary goals of this book has been to investigate how Takahashi, an illegitimate child who as an infant was adopted into the lowest echelon of the samurai class, in his maturity came to hold this multifaceted set of ideas. Unlike higher-ranking samurai children in his or the previous generation in late-feudal Japan, most of whom studied Chinese literature (which meant the conservative neo-Confucianism of Zhu Xi) or Dutch learning (which meant Western military and medical sciences), as a youth Takahashi was poorly educated. He did not matriculate even at a *terakoya*, the typical kind of lower-level school for commoners and hereditary foot soldiers. From the letter the thirteen-year-old Takahashi wrote to his parents in 1867 while in San Francisco, we know that as a teenager he could read and write Japanese, but he apparently learned these skills from his grandmother and the priest at Jushōji, not in school. Takahashi, unlike the generation of educated men after him, did not have the opportunity to matriculate in the new Meiji-period universities such as Tokyo Imperial University, Fukuzawa Yukichi's Keiō Gijuku, or the Amherst graduate Niijima Jō's Christian college, Dōshisha, where students learned philosophy, economics, and law from bona fide Western or Western-trained teachers.

Through study, Takahashi developed only one utile skill in his youth, a command of English. His superiors in Sendai domain sent the ten-year-old Wakiji, probably because of his low status, to Yokohama in 1864 to learn English from American missionaries. Because Takahashi studied with native speakers and at an early age, he developed a fluency beyond that of either his samurai predecessors such as Fukuzawa, who studied English by reading and rote memorization, or his successors such as Inoue Junnosuke, who studied English in the formally structured classrooms of the elite Tokyo Imperial University. Takahashi, whose worldview was constrained neither by a late-feudal classical education nor by an orthodox modern one, had an insatiable desire to read, talk, and learn, and an ability from his youth to do that reading, talking, and learning in both Japanese and English. Because of his low status within the samurai class, his birth between generations, his unusual childhood and teenaged years, and his outgoing, unrestrained personality, Takahashi had the opportunity to develop an eclectic pragmatism and a detachment: an ability to look at his own society both from within and without at the same time. This was unusual among pre–World War II Japanese statesmen.

Takahashi's command of the most important foreign language during Japan's rapid modernization brought the insouciant fourteen-year-old his first government job, as a teacher at the Daigaku Nankō; in 1869, the ill-educated upstart began his career by teaching better-educated and higher ranking members of the samurai elite, for the most part older than he. His knowledge of English (including colloquial and vulgar English) brought him into contact with foreign employees of the Meiji government such as A. A. Shand, Guido Verbeck, William Elliot Griffis, and David Murray, all of whom served as his mentors during his teens and early 20s. Takahashi's knowledge of English led important government leaders such as Itō Hirobumi, Inoue Kaoru, Matsukata Masayoshi, and Yamagata Aritomo, although they often differed with him on policy issues, to entrust Takahashi with important assignments. His knowledge of English garnered Takahashi the assignment to write Japan's first and second sets of trademark and patent laws, and thus to meet Maeda Masana when they both served in the Ministry of Agriculture and Commerce in the 1880s. Because of his command of the primary language of international commerce, Takahashi became Vice

Governor of the Bank of Japan and was sent to London to sell Japanese war bonds in 1904, where he met Jacob Schiff. Takahashi was an autodidact who read and conversed voraciously, both in Japanese and English; but of the many men with whom he corresponded and talked, these two, an acerbic, French-educated Japanese industrial planner, and a German-Jewish-American financier, stand out as having had a particularly deep and lasting influence on him. Takahashi was attracted to them, I think, because they too were strong-willed men who had unusual backgrounds and careers, and thus, in spite of their service at the highest levels of their societies, they were men who had the ability to look at their own societies critically.

Maeda's effect on Takahashi's intellectual development as an economic and political strategist began from their first meeting in 1883. Although virtually all of Japan's leaders in the 1870s understood the importance of economic development to Japan's survival in the post–Industrial Revolution, imperialist world; although mentors such as David Murray had already spoken to the youthful Takahashi about the centrality of patent laws in protecting inventions and industrial processes as that development took place; and although Takahashi had already translated works by leading Western economists such as Alfred Marshall, it was Maeda who focused Takahashi's attention on a particular way of development that would become the central leitmotif of Takahashi's career. Maeda, who made his proposal for economic growth based on traditional, regional industry in the midst of a severe rural recession engineered by Finance Minister Matsukata to check inflation before it got out of hand, emphasized the importance of economic growth that benefited yeoman farmers and local, small-scale businessmen, not the central government and well-connected *zaibatsu*-in-the-making such as Mitsubishi and Mitsui. In the pages of his *Kōgyō iken*, Maeda harshly criticized Matsukata for sacrificing the countryside and traditional enterprises in the process of transplanting heavy industry from the West. While Takahashi, by the post–World War I era, had moved beyond Maeda's "regional growth first, heavy industry later" concept to a more comprehensive approach to development, he never gave up on the idea, first learned from Maeda, that raising people's standards of living was the primary purpose of economic development, which at the same time stimulated further development. Takahashi began to formulate an economic approach, which he later applied while serving as finance minister in the Hara, Takahashi, Inukai, and Saitō cabinets, that higher wages increased consumption and demand, which in turn stimulated more consumption and demand many times over: the multiplier effect. Maeda also planted in Takahashi's thinking the seeds of his belief that economic growth was more important than military power, and that an army and a navy that were too strong and rich endangered rather than strengthened national defense. While Field Marshal Yamagata and many generals after him advocated a policy of "national defense is fundamental and financial policy comes afterward," Takahashi, from the time of his service with Maeda on, reversed the formula.[2]

Takahashi also learned the efficacy of local decision-making and of reliance on market information from Maeda, who believed that regional entrepreneurs and officials had a better understanding than did central bureaucrats of local conditions and markets. Scholars have criticized Takahashi for carrying out rural relief efforts during the depression for only three years, 1932–34, while he was spending larger sums of money on the military. In his defense, however, Takahashi attempted to continue relief spending after 1934, only, as we have seen, to have his effort blocked by a cabinet colleague, Mitsuchi Chūzō. At the same time the finance minister also had serious doubts about the value of centrally directed relief efforts. Thus, although Takahashi believed Tokyo should provide local government with funds for basic rural assistance through public works and the provision of inexpensive capital, he returned to an advocacy of rural economic development through bottom-up, decentralized decision-making and attentiveness to grassroots market information as Japan began to recover from the worst of the economic slump. Takahashi stated at the time, "Because each farmer and the situation in each village differs, it would be wrong to impose a comprehensive relief program. . . . Each region has its unique disease. We must begin by investigating these sicknesses and applying the correct cures. If we scatter money uniformly from the center to the regions, we cannot eliminate the diseases."[3] It was Takahashi's view even during the 1932–34 period that decisions about how to use the government's relief funds should be made by local, not central, officials; he called even more strongly for grass-roots initiatives in the last two years of his life. This reflects Maeda's and Takahashi's 1885 plan for regional industrial banks, under which the central government's only role would have been to match funds raised locally yen for yen; if the centralizers had not blocked their proposal, Maeda and Takahashi would have established regionally controlled banks that made all lending decisions at the local level. It also reflects Takahashi's efforts as finance and prime minister between 1918 and 1922 to devolve control over the land tax and elementary education to local government. It was because of his commitment to decentralized decision-making, which he had first learned from Maeda, that Takahashi became a leading advocate of "rural revitalization," that is, of a movement to encourage local self-help, during the depression years.[4]

Schiff's influence was equally important. Takahashi learned from him in London and New York, and through their later correspondence, the importance of international cooperation, knowledge of world financial markets, the necessity of fiscal probity when borrowing abroad, the dangers of militarism, and perhaps surprisingly, considering Schiff's position as one of the world's richest financiers, the importance of sharing the rewards of economic growth with the working class. Takahashi also learned in London in 1904–5 of Japan's dependence on the Anglo-Americans for capital, modern technology, and advanced raw materials: largely the British during the Russo-Japanese War, but primarily the Americans after World War I. British, American, and later German and French financiers paid for 47 percent of the cost of Japan's victory over Russia. Schiff and his German in-laws, the Warburgs, alone underwrote more than one-quarter of the funds raised during the war. After Japan's victory, European financiers helped it restructure its bonds to lower the cost of its wartime borrowing. Fourteen of the seventeen battleships and protected cruisers that defeated the czar's navy were built in Glasgow, Liverpool, Barrow-in-Furness, and on the Thames; the range-finders that allowed the Japanese gunners to hit their targets in the Battle of Tsushima were developed by two professors at the University of Glasgow; the fuel that powered the ships was bought from Shell Oil; and the original technology for many of the army's small arms came from the United States.[5] A primary lesson that Takahashi learned from Schiff and others in 1904–5 was that the Anglo-Americans were Japan's most profitable allies. Another, expressed in the Takahashi-Schiff correspondence in 1915 over their opposition to Foreign Minister Katō's handling of the infamous Twenty-One Demands, was their belief that

Japan benefited from a "natural alliance" with a strong, unified China; picking China apart through diplomatic pressure, loans, and military intervention threatened Japan's relations with its three "natural" allies: China, Great Britain, and the United States. Yet another lesson was that Japan must practice financial responsibility in order to borrow money abroad; excessive spending threatened Japan's credit in international markets. By joining the Anglo-American team, especially over China, as Takahashi did when he was prime minister and participated in the Washington treaty negotiations in 1921–22, Japan gained access to capital, markets, technology, raw materials, and protection. Those who advocated an autonomous approach to foreign policy that increased the likelihood of war with the Anglo-American powers cut Japan off from these benefits—and courted the disaster of fighting a war with enemies that Japan could not defeat. Japan could use fiscal spending to stimulate economic growth, as Takahashi had in 1932–35, but over long periods of time, it must balance its budgets: it was essential to limit military spending to maintain credit abroad. In other words, bloated military spending not only threatened runaway inflation and war, it also endangered Japan's safe haven in the Anglo-American world.

There are two areas of Takahashi's mature economic thought for which it is difficult to pinpoint sources. We have seen that Takahashi had learned from Maeda, and to some extent Schiff, the importance of sharing the benefits of economic development with the workers who produced it. But Takahashi went a step further, and since his days as Hara's finance minister following World War I, advocated the creation of a system to create a fairly equal distribution of wealth between capitalists and workers. He decried the widening gap between rich and poor in interwar Japan. To Takahashi, a large, healthy middle class was essential to Japan's economic development and he therefore promoted a graduated income tax regime under which the rich would pay at substantially higher tax rates than the poor. Society, Takahashi thought, had a duty to help the poor, who fell into poverty for the most part through no fault of their own.[6]

Although Takahashi, under Maeda's influence, had already begun in the late nineteenth century to consider the importance of consumption to economic growth, it is unclear when and from where he developed the idea that the government could use deficit fiscal spending to stimulate demand, particularly during economic downturns. We have seen that Takahashi read the writings of Anglo-American economists in Japanese and English, had long-standing friendships with a number of British and American financiers and writers, and had periodic meetings with younger economic thinkers such as Fukai Eigo and Ishibashi Tanzan; however, we have no direct evidence that Takahashi was aware of Keynes's mature ideas. In fact, in 1929, when Takahashi published his geisha-house analogy, and in 1932, when he implemented his fiscal stimuli, Keynes and his young Cambridge colleagues such as Richard Kahn and Joan Robinson were still in the midst of formulating what later came to be called "Keynesianism." According to scholarly estimates, the earliest Keynes could have arrived at the "theory of effective demand," that is, "the theory of how aggregate supply adjusts to aggregate demand," is the summer of 1932, about the same time that Takahashi began his deficit spending to stimulate demand.[7]

Although we can probably rule out direct inspiration or contact, we should not assume out of hand that Takahashi was unlikely to have been influenced indirectly by Keynes or by any of the other many people whose works he read or with whom he spoke, even if we cannot "footnote" those influences. Educated Japanese, even self-taught ones, by the interwar years were not living in an exotic "backwater" far from a European and North American "center." Japan had moved into the mainstream of the West's, or more appropriately, the world's, intellectual life, and given the educational biography offered here, we can see that Takahashi was no exception. There is no reason that a cosmopolitan Japanese finance minister, especially one with highly trained and innovative advisors such as Fukai and Ishibashi, would be any less likely than one who was British, American, or Swedish to endorse graduated income taxes or a "Keynesian" solution to his nation's problems. Takahashi, a well-read and well-conversed autodidact with long experience in various parts of government, was a modern finance minister, and as such he chose modern solutions to the problems his country faced. Ironically, the pragmatic and non-dogmatic Takahashi often followed routes that most of his more formally educated Japanese and Western counterparts would or could not follow.

APPENDIX

Takahashi's Memoirs

Takahashi dictated his memoirs to his amanuensis, Uetsuka Tsukasa, in the late 1920s and early 1930s. The memoirs, which cover the first 51 years of Takahashi's life (1854–1905), were first published serially in the *Asahi shinbun*, then published posthumously in book form in 1936, and republished in the Chukō Bunko series in 1976. They remain in print today.

Memoirs are notoriously difficult sources on which to rely because in them their authors describe events that occurred years earlier; memory lapses, the advantage of hindsight, and changing ideas and agendas may lead the writers to describe these earlier events in ways that fit their current thinking or the current political and ideological environment. While Takahashi, like many writers of memoirs and autobiographies, may have exaggerated his role in certain of the events he describes, we can approach his reconstructions of meetings, events, and other occurrences in his life with a reasonable degree of confidence for several reasons (although I point out discrepancies from time to time). Imamura Takeo, Takahashi's first postwar biographer and one of his most critical evaluators, reported that when he visited Takahashi's room in his home in Omote-machi shortly after the finance minister's assassination, he found rows and rows of diaries and notebooks with letters and other documents that Takahashi had collected throughout his life. Takahashi wrote that before he dictated his memoirs to Uetsuka, they both read these materials to refresh Takahashi's memory about events that had occurred earlier in his life, and to prepare Uetsuka for Takahashi's dictation. Uetsuka then prepared a first draft of the memoirs, which the two men compared item by item with the relevant documents in order to look for inconsistencies, often revising passages four or five times. But most important, although the American firebomb raids of 1945 destroyed most of these documents, many still exist in the archives of the National Diet Library, Tokyo Metropolitan University, and the Institute for Monetary and Economic Studies of the Bank of Japan. These collections contain many of the documents Takahashi used in writing his memoirs. I have compared the two and found that he used them accurately and carefully.

Having said that, I should point out that most of the extant documents cover 1885–1905, the second half of the period described in his memoirs. Few remain from his youth. There is one notable exception, however; at the end of Chapter 1, I present the translation of a letter, available in the Tokyo Metropolitan University collection, that Takahashi wrote from San Francisco in 1867 to his parents and grandmother in Edo. He quotes sections of this letter verbatim in his memoirs, from which we may conclude that he had this letter in front of him as he dictated. I think we can surmise, given Imamura and Takahashi's statements on the process of reconstructing the set of memoirs, that he had other such letters as well.

Reference Matter

Notes

Introduction

1. (Ōtani 1986, 141; Shimizu Takayuki in *Tōkyō shinbun*, May 15, 2005; Imamura 1985, 329–41).
2. (Gotō 1977; Kindleberger 1986, 163; Skidelsky 1992, 488).
3. (Patrick in Morley 1971, 256).
4. See Appendix for a discussion of the provenance of these memoirs.

Chapter One

1. (Takahashi 1976, II: 301).
2. (Dore 1965, 84–85, 230).
3. (Takahashi 1976, I: 16).
4. The sections of Edo mentioned in this chapter, the places where Takahashi was born and grew up, are mostly in Minato Ward, the part of Tokyo where expatriate Europeans and Americans, that is, the representatives of major foreign companies and financial institutions, live today. Shiba, Mita, Atagoshita, Hamamatsu-chō, Zōjōji, and even Gotanda are within walking distance of the Minato Ward government offices.
5. (Takahashi 1976, II: 308).
6. (Takahashi 1976, II: 308–9).
7. (Takahashi 1976, II: 311–12).
8. (Takahashi 1976, I: 17).
9. (Takahashi 1976, I: 20–22).
10. (Takahashi 1976, I: 22–23).
11. Ōwara, who was a confidant from childhood of Sendai's lord, Date Yoshikuni, played a leading role in his domain's support of the shogun and

opposition to the establishment of the Meiji government in 1868, for which he was punished. Four years later, Ōwara entered the government he had resisted and before his death in 1900, served in the finance, education, and home ministries, and in the national police force.

12. (Smethurst 2001, 260–88).

13. (Takahashi 1976, I: 23–26; Tamaki 2001, 56, 69, 185, 197; Imamura 1985, 13–14).

14. (Takahashi 1976, I: 16–18).

15. (Griffis 1913, 116).

16. (Griffis 1913, 116–17). Satō was the grandson of the doctor Satō Taizen, founder of Juntendō Hospital. Like Takahashi, Momotarō eschewed medicine, but in his case to become an exporter of raw silk. Satō and Takahashi, both born in 1854, became close associates in San Francisco in 1868. Satō married an American woman in the 1880s and returned to Japan to live in Yokohama. (Reischauer 1986, 190–225).

17. (Checkland and Tamaki 1997, 66; Takahashi 1976, I: 31).

18. (Takahashi 1976, I: 32).

19. (Takahashi 1976, I: 35–38).

20. (Takahashi 1976, I: 38–39).

21. Tomita (1835–1916) had a long career as an official and entrepreneur. After studying economics in America, Tomita served as Japan's Vice Consul in New York, Consul General in Shanghai, and First Secretary in London. A protégé of Finance Minister Matsukata Masayoshi, in 1882 Tomita became the first Vice Governor, and in 1888 the second Governor of the Bank of Japan; he was dismissed from the latter job in 1890 because of a falling out with Matsukata over methods of financing foreign trade. He then entered the House of Peers and served as Governor of Tokyo in 1891–94, before retiring to private life. He subsequently founded a cotton textile company, an insurance company, and served as a director of a major railroad company.

22. (*Kengun seishin futkyūkai* 1941, 18–23). Itō commanded the Japanese fleet that defeated the Chinese in the Battle of the Yalu River on September 13, 1894. The Kanze school of *nō* drama wrote a play entitled *Yūkō* (an alternative reading of the characters Sukeyuki), in which the *shite* or main actor represents Itō as he reports to headquarters in Hiroshima about the battle.

23. (Takahashi 1976, I: 40–42). Ninety-one years later, in June 1958, the author, a young lieutenant in the army, sailed from Yokohama to San Francisco in a stateroom on a United States military transport. One of his tasks was to inspect the troops down below, who slept in large rooms in hammocks. Luckily, sanitary conditions seemed to have improved over the century between Takahashi's voyage and the author's.

24. (Takahashi monjo 1). Takahashi's letter is reproduced verbatim in (Takahashi 1976, I: 45). Nowhere in his memoirs does Takahashi tell us where he learned to read and write. He does not mention attending a domain school for samurai or a *terakoya* (temple school), where *ashigaru* and commoners' children often studied. But when I showed Takahashi's letter, written when he was thirteen, to Fujii Noriko, a specialist in reading Edo-period documents at the Bank of Japan's Institute for Monetary and Economic Studies, her immediate reply was that Takahashi had had a good late-Edo-period samurai education. I surmise that Takahashi learned *kanji* and *sōrōbun* from Jushōji-sama and his grandmother.

Chapter Two

1. (Takahashi 1976, I: 42–47).
2. (Takahashi 1976, I: 47).
3. (Takahashi 1976, I: 48).
4. (Takahashi 1976, I: 49–54).
5. (Takahashi 1976, I: 57).
6. (Takahashi 1976, I: 58).
7. (Takahashi 1976, I: 58–59). It is standard for biographers of Takahashi to use the phrase "sold into slavery" (*dorei ni ureru/urareta/sareta*) in describing this incident. A random survey of the bookshelves in my study came up with six examples: (Imamura 1958/1985, 16; Ōshima 1969, 15; Ōishi 1992, 14; Tsumoto 1998, 74; Kitawaki 1999, 14; Kimura 1999, 26). It is worth pointing out that although the continuation of the practice of indentured servitude in California in 1867—two years after the ratification of the Thirteenth Amendment of the Constitution made it illegal—demonstrates condescending American attitudes toward Asians, short-term bondage was far different from the kind suffered by slaves brought in chains from Africa. Yet Takahashi's biographers use the same word, *dorei*, for his indentured servitude as is generally used for hereditary slavery.
8. (Takahashi 1976, I: 59–60).
9. (Takahashi 1976, 60). The elder Browne was born in Dublin in 1821, had a long career in the United States government, wrote a book on whaling that apparently influenced Herman Melville in his writing of *Moby Dick*, and was appointed Minister to China by President Andrew Johnson in 1868. He was replaced in his diplomatic post in 1869, and died in Alameda, California in 1875.
10. (Takahashi 1976, I: 61–62).
11. (Takahashi 1976, I: 62–63).
12. Takagi (1841–1909) served as a diplomat in the United States from 1871 until 1880. He left the government to set up a company to export raw silk to

America. He played an important role in improving methods of producing, financing, packing, and shipping Japanese raw silk exports.

13. (Takahashi 1976, I: 64–65).

14. (Takahashi 1976, I: 65–68). The San Francisco couple's son Eugene in Yokohama, who, as we have seen, arranged for Takahashi and Suzuki to work for his parents, developed a somewhat unsavory reputation at this time. According to Takahashi, a San Francisco newspaper reported that he had arranged for 300 Japanese agricultural workers to go to Hawaii to work for a wage of four dollars per month. If they got sick and could not work, they lost their wages. One young woman, who was forced by these circumstances to give birth unattended by medical assistance, subsequently committed suicide. This report led Takahashi and Suzuki to realize how lucky they had been to escape their service contracts.

15. (Takahashi 1976, I: 70–71).

16. (Takahashi 1976, I: 74–75).

17. (Takahashi 1976, I: 77–78; Hall 1973, 146–47).

18. Takahashi was able to escape the assassins of 1869, but not those of February 26, 1936.

19. (Takahashi monjo 138; Takahashi 1976, I: 81–82). In the first poem, Takahashi misquotes an ode by Joseph Addison from 1712—"permanent" should be "firmament"; the second poem I cannot identify.

20. (Hara 2001, 345–46). One wonders why Takahashi, writing his memoirs while he was finance minister in the 1930s, gave so much space to childhood (and later, as we shall see) drinking and indiscretions. Was he giving us the unvarnished story of his life, or did he have some purpose in emphasizing his occasionally wayward early life? Did the nonconforming finance minister of the 1930s want to show that he had always been a "free spirit"?

Chapter Three

1. Takahashi tells us that one reason Mori was sent abroad was to protect him from possible assassination. After a Tosa domain warrior slashed two foreign teachers at Daigaku Nankō for consorting with Japanese women, Mori presented to the government a memorial to abolish the samurai right to carry swords. The government rejected his proposal—in fact, conversely, it required for a short time that all government officials carry swords—and nativist samurai, especially from Mori's own Satsuma domain, threatened his life (Takahashi 1976, I: 83–90; Takahashi 1936a, 91).

2. (Griffis 1900, 180–300).

3. (Imamura 1985, 31–32).

4. (Imamura 1985, 23–24. 30–32).

5. (Takahashi 1976, I: 92–97).

6. (Takahashi 1976, I: 97–102). Takahashi cherished this Bible all his life. After his death, there was an exhibit of political mementoes in Hibiya in Tokyo, and Takahashi's family sent Verbeck's Bible. On page one, Takahashi had inscribed that he read the book to correct his bad habits (Imamura 1985, 29–30).

7. (Takahashi 1976, I: 102–4). Before Takahashi left, he had one more issue to deal with—he and Okimi expected to marry each other. Although Takahashi's adoptive grandmother approved, perhaps because of her own youthful experience at love, Okimi still had her contract as a geisha, and in the end the marriage did not take place. Okimi later married, and managed a restaurant in Nihonbashi.

8. (Takahashi 1976, I: 103).

9. (Takahashi 1976, I: 103–21).

10. (Takahashi 1976, I: 121–25).

11. (Takahashi monjo: Takahashi letter to "Nobu," 15 December 1872).

12. (Takahashi 1976, I: 125–31).

13. (Takahashi 1976, I: 140–47).

14. (Takahashi monjo: Takahashi letter to "Naiki," 10 August 1974).

15. (Takahashi 1976, I: 147–50).

16. (Takahashi 1976, I: 157–58). The entire speech is reprinted in (Takahashi 1936b, 98–112).

17. (Takahashi 1976, I: 162).

18. (Takahashi 1976, I: 160–70; Imamura 1985, 35–38).

19. (Takahashi 1976, I: 170–72).

20. (Takahashi 1976, I: 172–81; Imamura 1985, 39). Takahashi wrote his memoirs while he was finance minister in the early 1930s, but in them he makes no apology for his unscrupulous behavior as a stockbroker in 1880–81.

21. (Takahashi 1976, I: 182–84).

22. (Takahashi 1976, I: 135–37; II: 76).

Chapter Four

1. The government promulgated patent regulations in 1871, but quickly withdrew them. Therefore I have called the 1885 law Japan's first.

2. (Imamura 1985, 39–40; Takahashi 1976, I: 184–86).

3. (Takahashi 1976, I: 187–89).

4. (Takahashi 1976, I: 190–91).

5. (Takahashi 1976, I: 191–92).

6. (Takahashi 1976, I: 207–9). Tomita was a member of the Meirokusha. The Takahashi papers include four English-language letters to Takahashi from

Kushida in Philadelphia, where he was studying at the University of Pennsylvania. Takahashi monjo: 26 October 1886; 2 November 1886; 12 February 1887; 3 April 1887. He tells Takahashi that he is studying with "Prof. Thompson of the University, [who] is the leading protectionist in the country," compares American and German universities, and adds that The Johns Hopkins University in Baltimore is unusual in America in that it is a German-type university.

7. (Takahashi 1976, I: 210).

8. (Takahashi 1976, I: 209–11).

9. (Takahashi 1976, I: 214–15). Takahashi tells us that Verbeck failed as a missionary when he returned to Japan because his fellow missionaries distrusted him. In their view, he spoke Japanese too well and had too many Japanese friends.

10. (Takahashi 1976, I: 215–17).

11. (Takahashi 1976, I: 217–20). It was not unusual in the late nineteenth century for military men to hold civil cabinet portfolios. Generals such as Tani, Yamagata Aritomo, and Saigō Tsugumichi, all key figures in the founding of Japan's army and navy, headed non-military ministries. However, leading civilian officials such as Itō Hirobumi and Matsukata Masayoshi were not appointed to head the Army or Navy ministries.

12. (Takahashi 1976, I: 219–22). The official history of the United States Patent Office includes a paragraph about Takahashi, and a picture of him from his 1886 visit (Dobyns 1994, 198). Takahashi, according to Dobyns, told Dr. P. B. Pierce, the chief examiner, that it was patents that made the United States a great country, and that "we (Japan) will have patents." Pierce took this as the most "unbiased testimony to the value and worth of the patent system as practiced in the United States . . . in all history." Dobyns adds that Takahashi went on to become prime minister, advocated economic, not military competition with the Western powers, and paid for this view with his life.

13. (Takahashi 1976, I: 221–25).

14. (Takahashi 1976, I: 225).

15. (Takahashi monjo, undated).

16. (Takahashi 1976, I: 225–27).

17. (Takahashi to Duryee, 20 December 1886; Duryee to Takahashi, 28 December 1886, Takahashi monjo).

18. (Takahashi 1976, I: 225–30). The Takahashi monjo include a letter dated 18 March 1886, from Welsh to Takahashi. Welsh thanked Takahashi for sending a photograph of himself, and included one of himself for Takahashi. Welsh also enclosed a letter of introduction to a Mr. White, Secretary of the American Legation in London.

19. (Takahashi to Takamine, 16 April 1886, Takahashi monjo).

20. (Takahashi 1976, I: 235–37).

21. (Takahashi 1976, I: 240–43). The Takahashi monjo includes a letter, date 25 June 1886, from J. Lowry Whittle of the Patent Office, introducing Takahashi to colleagues in Sheffield and Manchester.

22. (Takahashi 1976, I: 245–56).

23. (Takahashi, 1976, I: 258–59).

24. (Takahashi 1976, I: 257–62).

25. (Takahashi 1976, I: 279–82).

Chapter Five

1. For this view, see (Ōshima 1999, 39; Crawcour 1997, 69–104). For an excellent, succinct description of Maeda's proposal, see (Hashimoto and Ōsugi, 2000a, 55–57, 147–48).

2. (Takahashi 1976, I: 193; Ōshima 1999, 39).

3. (Soda 1973, 85–86).

4. (Takahashi 1976, I: 196–97; Ōshima 1974, 291; Takahashi 1936a, 274).

5. (Takahashi 1936a, 398).

6. (Soda 1973, 86, 96, 98, 106–9; Shinobu 1958, II: 601; Crawcour 1988, 418; Ōshima 1974, 291–93, 315–16; Smith 1955, 37–38).

7. (Ōshima 1974, 278–80).

8. (Ōshima 1974, 281–83).

9. Maeda apparently did not consider his sojourn in Shanghai as a trip abroad.

10. (Ōshima 1974, 283–85).

11. (Ōshima 1974, 285–87; Umemura 1983, 245–46).

12. (Ōshima 1974, 287; Umemura 1983, 246; Francks 1984, 55–63; Francks 1992, 120–28; Smethurst 1986, 150–52, 222–25; Smethurst 2000, 8–9). Marxist historians have criticized Maeda because his agricultural development plans aimed at helping owner farmers and small and medium-scale regional entrepreneurs and "did nothing for the victims of capitalist development" (Imamura 1985, 47). Actually, Maeda recognized, quite progressively for the mid-Meiji period, that rural middle-class farmers, not the larger landlords who dominated village life at the time, were the key to rural economic development. By encouraging middle-level farmers to improve their farming methods, adopt new technology, and increase productivity, that is, to modernize, Maeda's proposals actually undermined the existing rural order so that by the 1930s owner farmers and owner-tenant farmers had replaced landlords as the economic and political leaders of their villages (Masumi 1979, 342, 344–51).

13. (Ōshima 1974, 287–89).

14. (Umemura 1983, 246–47).

15. (Ōshima 1974, 290–91; Umemura 1983, 247).

16. (Ōshima 1974, 291; Soda 1973, 84; Tamaki 1995, 51).

17. (Takahashi 1976, I: 193; Takahashi 1936a, 269–70).

18. (Takahashi 1976, I: 194; Soda 1973, 88–89).

19. (Soda 1973, 91).

20. (Soda 1973, 91–93).

21. (*Keizaigaku kojiten*, quoted in Ariizumi 1969, 1–16).

22. (Ariizumi 1969, 4, Umemura 1983, 148–49, Soda 1973, 101–3; Fujita 1989a, 80).

23. (Takahashi 1976, I: 197–98; Ōshima 1974, 296–97).

24. (Soda 1973, 107–8).

25. Many historians emphasize *hanbatsu*, that is, the domain from which various government leaders hail, as the key to understanding Meiji politics. But in the *Kōgyō iken* debate, Matsukata of Satsuma, with the support of Yamagata, Inoue, and Itō of Chōshū, directly confronted Maeda and Kuroda of Satsuma. Policy differences also counted.

26. (Takahashi 1976, I: 200–1).

27. (Takahashi 1976, I: 202–3; Soda 1973, 114–18).

28. (Smethurst 2000, 14–15; Umemura 1983, 249–51; Ōshima 1974, 295, 299; Hashimoto and Ōsugi 2000a, 147–48).

29. I have no explanation for the seeming inconsistency between the support for Maeda's proposal at the meeting with Saigō and the views stated in the letters to the two ministers.

30. (Umemura 1983, 250–51; Mikuriya 1980, 117–18).

31. (Asō 1929, 379).

32. (Takahashi 1936a, 276; Fujita 1989a, 82).

33. (Shinagawa letter to Takahashi, 27 January [no year given, but probably 1886], Takahashi monjo).

Chapter Six

1. (Imamura 1985, 45–47).

2. (Takahashi 1976, I: 283–84).

3. (Takahashi 1976, I: 284–85).

4. (Ogura 1979, 14).

5. For Fujimura's career as a Maeda-type developmental governor of Yamanashi from 1874 to 1887, see (Smethurst 1986, 151–52, 222–23; Ariizumi 1979, 27–48).

6. (Takahashi 1976, I: 288).

7. (Takahashi 1976, I: 289).

8. (Takahashi 1976, I: 288–94).

9. Takahashi throughout his life tended in writing to repeat the same point two or three times in slightly different words. His memoirs, speeches, and other writings are replete with such redundancies.

10. (Takahashi 1976, I: 294–96).

11. (Takahashi 1976, I: 298–99).

12. (Takahashi 1976, I: 304).

13. (Takahashi 1976, I: 305–13).

14. (Takahashi 1976, I: 315–16).

15. (Takahashi 1976, I: 318–21).

16. (Takahashi 1976, I: 324–26).

17. (Takahashi 1976, I: 326–31).

18. (Takahashi 1976, I: 330–35; Guyer to Heeren and Takahashi, 13 May 1890, Castle Brothers to Lima, 27 May 1890, Takahashi monjo).

19. (Takahashi 1976, I: 335–36).

20. (Takahashi 1976, I: 336–37).

21. (Takahashi 1976, I: 337–41).

22. (Takahashi 1976, I: 341–52).

23. (Takahashi 1976, I: 352).

24. (Takahashi 1976, I: 352–54).

25. (Takahashi 1976, I: 354–58; Imamura 1985, 57).

26. (Takahashi 1976, I: 286–87). On the occasion of the 182nd anniversary of Peru's independence, Luis J. Macchiavello, Peru's Ambassador to Japan, wrote a short essay in the 2 September 2004 edition of the *Mainichi Daily News*, one of Japan's primary English-language newspapers, about Japanese-Peruvian friendship. He mentioned only one Japanese by name: Takahashi Korekiyo, leader of Japan's first investment project in Peru.

27. (Takahashi 1976, I: 364).

28. (Takahashi 1976, I: 364–65).

Chapter Seven

1. (Imamura 1985, 59–60; Tamaki 2001, 131–36). Kawada is listed among the "fifty leading entrepreneurs in the early Meiji era" (Hirschmeier 1964, 248–49). In addition to serving as Governor of the Bank of Japan, he was an associate of Iwasaki Yatarō in the formation of the Mitsubishi enterprises.

2. (Takahashi 1976, II: 11–14).

3. Tatsuno (1854–1919) studied in Tokyo with the British architect Josiah Conder and then in London. Eleven of his buildings still exist, including Tokyo Station, the Bank of Japan buildings in Tokyo, Osaka, and Otaru, the Nara Hotel, and the Bank of Korea building in Seoul.

4. (Takahashi 1976, II: 17).

5. (Takahashi 1976, II: 17–19).

6. (Takahashi 1976, II: 19–25). The architectural historian Botond Bognar describes the building slightly differently. According to him, the building had brick walls reinforced with iron rods and covered with stone on all three floors (Bognar 1995, 90).

7. (Takahashi 1976, II: 31–34; Ferber 2005).

8. (Ohnuki 2006, Table 2).

9. (Takahashi 1976, II: 35–36).

10. (Takahashi 1976, II: 37–46).

11. (Takahashi 1976, II: 46–55).

12. (Imamura 1985, 62).

13. (Berger 1982, 203).

14. (Takahashi 1976, II: 59–65).

15. (Takahashi monjo 13-1, 19 March 1895).

16. (Takahashi monjo 14, 31 March 1895).

17. (Takahashi 1976, II: 65).

18. (Tamaki 1995, 46–47, 51–53; Tamaki 2001, 108–11; Umemura 1983, 246–47).

19. (Takahashi 1976, II: 73–84, 88; Ishii Kanji, "Rivalry in Trading and Banking," in Hunter and Sugiyama 2002, 123–24).

20. (Takahashi 1976, II: 92–94). Asabuki ranks in Hirschmeier's list of the 50 leading entrepreneurs of the early Meiji era (Hirschmeier 1964, 248–49).

21. (Metzler 2006, 47–50; Tamaki 1995, 81–85; Hashimoto and Ōsugi 2000a, 104–6).

22. (Takahashi 1976, II: 102–12). Although Takahashi based this description of events in 1898 on a rereading of his diaries, one should bear in mind that he published his memoirs in the *Asahi shinbun*, a daily newspaper with a large circulation, in the early 1930s, just as the Japanese military began to take a different approach to empire. This kind of statement during the rise of militarism after the Manchurian Incident could not have endeared Takahashi to the radical young officers.

23. (Nakamura 1982, 10–11). Inoue's relationship to Takahashi was much like Takahashi's to Matsukata. In both cases, a younger man benefited from the patronage of an elder although they did not always see eye-to-eye on policy. Matsukata was nineteen years older than Takahashi, who in turn was fifteen years older than Inoue.

24. (Checkland and Tamaki 1997, 65–78; Tamaki 1995, 34–37, 95; Yoneyama 1927, 2–10; Takahashi 1976, II: 112–14). Parr's Bank later merged with the London County and Westminster Bank, which in turn merged with the National Provincial and District Banks to become NatWest, which in turn was bought

by the Royal Bank of Scotland. The Parr's Bank papers were found in the NatWest archive, which is now the RBSG Archives.

25. (Takahashi 1976, II: 112–14).

26. (Takahashi 1976, II: 114–16).

27. (Takahashi 1976, II: 116–20).

28. (Takahashi 1976, II: 121–25).

29. (Takahashi 1976, II: 125–32).

30. (Takahashi 1976, II: 132–55).

31. (Takahashi 1976, II: 155–58). One can visit the Japanese-style part of Takahashi's home, including the room in which he was assassinated, in the architectural park of the Edo Tokyo Museum.

32. (Satō 1985, 33). It is easy to oversimplify the party (democratic?) politics of prewar twentieth-century Japan. From 1913 on, both Yamamoto and Takahashi served in the Seiyūkai political party, known for its adherence to a "positive" fiscal and monetary policy. Machida joined the Kenseikai/Minseitō, known for a commitment to balanced budgets and high interest rates. Takahashi's economic views often differed from those attributed to his party.

Chapter Eight

1. (Bank of Japan 1966, 128).

2. (Takahashi 1976, II: 187).

3. (Takahashi 1976, II: 188–91; Fujimura 1992, I: 88–94) reprints these documents from the Finance Ministry archives. Both Hayashi and Takahashi studied English with Clara Hepburn in Yokohama in the mid–1860s (Griffis 1913).

4. (Takahashi 1976, II: 190–92; Takahashi 1936a, 498).

5. (Sherman 1983, 61).

6. (Takahashi 1976, II: 193, 199; Baring Letter Books, 200187, 4, 14, 19, 25, 26, 28, 30, Baring Archive at ING Baring, N. V.; Suzuki 1994, 31, 88, 92). The ambivalence toward Japan's prospects and the pressure for British neutrality at this time can be seen through the actions of Parr's, the bank with the strongest Japanese connection. On March 4 the board voted to contribute 100 pounds to the fund for the widows and orphans of Japanese soldiers. One week later, on March 10, the board voted to defer the contribution. On 30 June, after Japan's prospects had improved, the board voted to give 250 pounds in lieu of the deferred 100 (Parr's Bank records, RBSG Archives, 3 March, 10 March, 30 June 1904).

7. (Takahashi diary, 7 April 1904; Checkland and Tamaki 1997, 65–78; Tamaki 1995, 34–37, 95; Yoneyama 1927, 2–10).

8. The Japanese government had to repay a little over 800,000,000 yen for its foreign borrowing, but received only 690,000,000 yen, 86 percent of the

face value of the bonds. The difference was because the bonds sold for as much as 10 percent under their face value and the rest went for commissions. The financial burden of Japan's victory in 1905 was heavy (Ogawa 1923, 68–69).

9. (Takahashi 1976, II: 192).

10. (Fujimura 1992) has translated the diary into Japanese. In the process, he has made a spontaneous daily record, with its abbreviations, misspellings, and solecisms, into a more polished essay. The Takahashi monjo at the National Diet Library includes drafts as well as final versions of some of his English-language letters and other documents, which indicate that Takahashi took care in composing them; the diary, on the other hand, was written for his personal use only.

11. (Takahashi 1976, II: 201–2; Takahashi diary, 7–18 April).

12. (Takahashi 1976, II: 202).

13. (Imamura 1985, 67; Suzuki 1994, 95).

14. (Takahashi diary, 22 April, 16 December 1904). Takahashi refers to Sir Ernest Cassel as Earnest Cassel and Earnest or Ernest Cassell, Castle, or Casttle at different places in his diary.

15. (Takahashi diary, 22–29 April 1904). Samuel was descended from Dutch Jews who had immigrated to England in 1831. His companies were Samuel, Samuel Co. and the Shell Shipping Line, both with a major presence in Yokohama, and Shell Oil, a major supplier of oil to the Japanese navy during the war. In 1907, Shell merged with Royal Dutch Petroleum to form one of the world's largest oil companies. In World War I Samuel was decorated for service to the British navy, and later became a viscount (Fujimura 1992, I: 115). (The Japanese Loans, HSBC Group Archives, London, LOH I: 57) indicates that Samuel purchased 100,000 pounds (out of 12,000,000 total) of the November 1904 second issue of Japanese war bonds. P. G. Wodehouse, who worked for HSBC as a young man, writes of the Japanese loans of 1902 in *Psmith in the City*.

16. (Takahashi diary, 3 May 1904; Takahashi 1936a, 86).

17. (Cohen 1999, 1–144).

18. (Takahashi diary, 3–10 May 1904). Otto Hermann Kahn, like Schiff, was born in Germany of Jewish ancestry, but two decades later. He immigrated to New York in 1893, became an expert in railroad finance for Kuhn, Loeb, and later became an extraordinary patron of the arts; he served as chairman of the Metropolitan Opera from 1908 to 1931 (Jackson 1995, 630).

19. (Takahashi 1976, II: 203–4).

20. (Takahashi 1976, II: 203).

21. See for example, (Shillony 1991, 147–49, Reischauer 1986, 138–40). For a contrasting view, see (Guttwein 2005).

22. (Cohen 1999, 124).

23. (Cohen 1999, 134).

24. (Cohen 1999, 11–12; Allfrey 1991, 137–51, 215; Thane 1986, 80–99; Suzuki 1994, 97).

25. (Allfrey 1991, 215; Cohen 1999, 33–34).

26. (Baring Letter Books, 200187: 33, 34, 35, 38, 39, 45).

27. (Takahashi 1976, II: 222–24; Alfrey 1991, 215). Parr's Bank, however, recognized Shand's importance in attracting the Japanese business. On each of five separate occasions, 23 June 1904, 29 December 1904, 30 March 1905, 20 July 1905, and 7 December 1905, the directors voted him bonuses of 1,000 pounds (Parr's Bank records, RBSG Archives).

28. Letter from Takahashi to Inoue Kaoru, 11 July 1905, Matsuo Shigeyoshi Papers, Bank of Japan Archive. I have not seen Cassel's original letter. The excerpt above is my retranslation of Takahashi's translation of Cassel's letter, quoted in the 11 July communication to the elder statesman Inoue in Tokyo.

29. (Takahashi 1976, II: 206; Japanese Loans, HSBC Group Archives. London).

30. (Baring Letter Books, 200187: 39; Takahashi diary, 12 May 1904).

31. (Best 1972, 315).

32. (Imamura 1985, 71). Again I am retranslating a statement written originally in English.

33. A. J. Sherman, an investment banker himself, argues that Schiff, as a prudent investor, would not underwrite Japanese war bonds for purely political reasons. "Investors' money was not to be tossed away for political ends." This is undoubtedly true. But at the same time, Stillman, Morgan, and other gentile New York financiers had the same chance as Schiff to underwrite the Japanese bonds, and did not, because they found them too risky. I agree with Sherman that in this case Schiff was "daring," but not "imprudent." But I also think that Schiff's interest in Japanese war bonds would have been tepid at most if it were not for his anger over Russian anti-Semitism (Sherman 1983, 73).

34. (Suzuki 1994, 100).

35. (Takahashi 1976, II: 206). On 13 July 1911, Admiral Tōgō, the Japanese admiral who commanded the Japanese fleet at the Tsushima Straits, visited a shipyard in Glasgow and told the workers, "You won the battle of Tsushima for me" (Checkland 1998, 49).

36. (Baring Letter Books, 200189: 44).

37. For example, Takahashi, in his eulogy for former Finance Minister Inoue Junnosuke after the latter's assassination in 1932, wrote that in 1911 he had sent Inoue to New York and future Governor Hijikata to London so that they could study "foreign capital deeply" (Takahashi 1936a, 58).

38. (Takahashi diary, 13 May–27 June 1904).

39. (Takahashi diary, 30 June, 1 July 1904).
40. (Takahashi diary, 3, 12, 15 August 1904).
41. (Takahashi diary, 8, 13, 15 September 1904).
42. (Baring Letter Books, 200188: 2–6).
43. (Takahashi diary, 28 September, 1, 2, 4 October 1904).
44. (Takahashi diary, 6, 7, 11, 12, 13, 15, 17 October 1904; Baring Letter Books, 200188: 28).
45. (Takahashi diary, 17, 18 October 1904, Baring Letter Books, 200188: 30) Kuhn, Loeb and Speyer Brothers were the two most powerful Jewish financial houses in New York in 1904, but Schiff and James Speyer were "usually rivals" (Cohen 1999, 23).
46. (Takahashi diary, 19, 22 October 1904; Baring Letter Books, 200188: 46).
47. (Takahashi diary, 26 October, 1, 2, 3 November 1904; Baring Letter Books, 200188: 78; Ogawa 1923, 94; Japanese Loans, HSBC Group Archives, London).

Chapter Nine

1. (Takahashi diary, 11 November, 8, 10 December 1904).
2. (Takahashi diary, 13 December 1904).
3. (Takahashi 1976, II: 218).
4. (Takahashi 1976, II: 219–22; Baring Letter Books 200188: 216; 200189: 1–3). Revelstoke of Baring Brothers received the highest decoration although he represented the only financial house that did not underwrite Japanese bonds.
5. (Takahashi 1976, II: 223–24; Baring Letter Books 200189: 4).
6. (Takahashi 1976, II: 224–30). The Parr's Bank records in the RBSG Archives contain an English-language copy of the orders Takahashi received from Katsura, signed by Finance Minister Sone, which gave him the authority to go to London to carry out "a negotiation with capitalists."
7. (Takahashi 1976, II: 230–32).
8. (Takahashi 1976, II: 232–35; Japanese Loans, HSBC Group Archives, London; Baring Letter Books 200189: 19, 24, 26, 37, 70).
9. (Metzler 2006, xvi–xvii, 32, 209–12, 248–56).
10. (Takahashi 1976, II: 236).
11. (Takahashi 1976, II: 237–39).
12. (Takahashi letters to Prime Minister Katsura and Finance Minister Sone, 1 April 1905, 6 June 1905, Matsuo Shigeyoshi Papers IAX 23:1, IAX 23:2, Bank of Japan Archive).
13. (Takahashi 1976, II: 239–42).
14. (Takahashi 1976, II: 244–46).
15. (Takahashi 1976, II: 246–49).

16. (Takahashi letters to Inoue Kaoru, 3 July, 11 July 1905, Matsuo Shige-yoshi Papers IAX 23:2, Bank of Japan Archive).

17. (Takahashi 1976, II: 249–50).

18. (Takahashi 1976, II: 251).

19. (Kobayashi 1922, 79–80; Suzuki 1994, 116–17; Takahashi 1936a, 90; Japanese Loans, HSBC Group Archives, London; Lists of Japanese Loans, Parr's Bank records, 13 July 1905, RBSG Archives).

20. (Takahashi 1976, II: 258–59, 265–57; Takahashi cable to Governor Matsuo, 27 July 1905, Matsuo Shigeyoshi Papers, IAX 23:1, Bank of Japan Archive).

21. (Takahashi 1976, II: 261–62, 277–79; Takahashi cable to Governor Matsuo, 6 September 1905, Matsuo Shigeyoshi Papers IAX 23:1, Bank of Japan Archive).

22. (Takahashi 1976, II: 280; Takahashi cable to Governor Matsuo, 5 September 1905, Matsuo Shigeyoshi Papers IAX 23:1, Bank of Japan Archive).

23. (Takahashi 1976, II: 282–85).

24. (Takahashi 1976, II: 285–87).

25. (The Rothschild Archive, November 1905 Japanese Loan File).

26. (Takahashi 1976, II: 287–91). For Takahashi's dealings with the Rothschilds, see (Smethurst 2006).

27. Schiff was unhappy that Kuhn, Loeb received such a small allotment in this bond issuance. In a letter to Whalley of Parr's Bank, Schiff chastised the British bankers for relegating Kuhn, Loeb to a secondary role, and wrote, "We have accepted your proposition . . . only at Mr. Takahashi's urgent request and in order to be agreeable and helpful to him. . . . We have not received from the Associated Banks that consideration on which we feel in fairness to ourselves we should have insisted" (The Rothschild Archive, 1905 Japanese Loan File).

28. A preliminary and final version of the loan agreement can be found in (The Rothschild Archive, November 1905 Japanese Loan File).

29. (Parr's Bank records, RBSG Archives, 23, 30 November 1905; Baring Letter Books, 200189: 7).

30. The original of the picture is found in the Parr's Bank records in the RBSG Archives.

Chapter Ten

1. See (Dickinson 2005) for a discussion of the "deification" in the 1930s of Admiral Tōgō, Japan's victorious admiral in the 1905 Battle of Tsushima, and even of General Nogi, whose infantry tactics cost Japan thousands of lives at Port Arthur. The patriots who invoked the names of Tōgō and Nogi did not mention the British shipyards, Shell Oil, Schiff, the Rothschilds, or

Takahashi for their important roles in Japan's victory over Russia. By glorifying martial "spirit" over finance, technology, and raw materials, men such as Araki Sadao played "a pivotal role in stoking the fires for war against an enemy . . . they could not defeat" (543). The 1941 edition of *Japan: The Official Guide* (Board of Tourist Industry 1941), lists the homes of Tōgō and Nogi as places to visit, but makes no mention of Schiff or Takahashi. The 1975 revision does the same, and goes so far as to mention the Tama Cemetery as the site of Tōgō's grave. Takahashi, unmemorialized, is also buried there.

2. (Bank of Japan 1966, 130, 143).

3. (Shirayanagi 1930, 83).

4. (The Rothschild Archive, File XI/130A/19060306, 19060309).

5. (Inoue 1968, 162–65; Shirayanagi 1930, 83; Ericson 1996, 277–84).

6. Schiff wrote an account of his trip to Japan, *Our Journey to Japan* (Schiff 1907), privately published as a surprise to Schiff in January 1907. It is unpaginated and is available at the American Jewish Archives in Cincinnati. A Japanese translation (Tabata, 2005) was published in time for the centennial of the Russo-Japanese War (Adler 1929, vol. 1, 232).

7. (Hara 2001, 231–32).

8. (Checkland 1998, 49).

9. And for a different port. On the trip to New York, Wakiko missed the opportunity to visit San Francisco and Oakland, where her father had lived as a youth. While Schiff was in Japan, the Great San Francisco Earthquake occurred, and he and his party returned home through Vancouver.

10. For trust in Takahashi and Japan, see (The Rothschild Archive, XI/130A/0/19060125, XI/130/0/19060129, XI/130/0/19060212); for the "devoted head" letter, see (The Rothschild Archive, XI/130/0/19060507); see also (Ferguson 1999, 396–99).

11. (The Rothschild Archive, XI/130A/0/19060508, XI/130A/1/19070218, 19070225, 19070226, 19070227, 19070228, 19070301, 19070307, 19070308).

12. The agreement, Imperial Ordinance No. 23 approving the loan, and instructions from the Finance Minister in Tokyo to Takahashi and Ambassador Komura in London, can be found in (The Rothschild Archive, March 1907 Loan File; Suzuki 1994, 134–36).

13. (The Rothschild Archive, XI/130A/1/19070507).

14. (Adler 1929, I, 239–40).

15. (Metzler 2006, 80–85).

16. In this discussion of Takahashi's fiscal and monetary views between 1907 and 1914, I follow (Kamiyama 1989, 48–80).

17. (Ohkawa, 1965, 81; Bank of Japan 1966, 28, 130–31).

18. (Kamiyama 1989, 64).

19. See, for example, (Smethurst in Andrews and Chapman 1995, 71–89) for a discussion of this debate.

20. (Smethurst in Andrews and Chapman 1995, 72–81).

21. (Hackett 1971, 250–66; Imamura 1985, 75).

22. (Hackett 1971, 266; Imamura 1985, 75–76; Itō 2002, 51–56).

23. (Kyoto 1960, 768; Bank of Japan 1966, 28; Najita 1967, 191–94).

24. (Imamura 1985, 76; Kamiyama 1989, 68–70).

25. (Young in Kodansha 1983, 8: 120–21).

26. (Dickinson 1999, 86).

27. (Smith 1972, 343).

28. (Takahashi monjo, 22; Spence 1999, 362–63).

29. (Takahashi to Schiff, 20 April 1915, Takahashi monjo; Kimura 1999, 55; Ogawa 1973, 137–38).

30. David Starr Jordan (1851–1931) was chancellor of Stanford University and a director of the World Peace Congress. Charles William Eliot (1834–1926) was the former president of Harvard University and a trustee of the Carnegie Foundation for the Advancement of Teaching. They advocated resolving international conflicts through arbitration.

31. (Takahashi to Schiff, 24 January 1914, Schiff Papers, American Jewish Archives).

32. (Takahashi 1936b, 655–62).

33. (Bank of Japan 1966, 28, 32, 132, 158).

34. See (Metzler 2006), Chapter Five, "Divine Providence, 1914–1918" for a lucid discussion of Japan and its economy during World War I.

35. (Bank of Japan 1966, 169, 278; Ohkawa and Shinohara 1979, 392).

36. (Ohkawa and Shinohara 1979, 387, 390).

37. The classic work on the Rice Riots is (Inoue and Watanabe 1959–62). In English, see (Lewis 1990).

Chapter Eleven

1. (Bank of Japan 1966, 28–29; Ohkawa and Shinohara 1979, 387).

2. (Ōkurashō 1969 vol. 3, 134–35).

3. (Metzler 2006, 135).

4. (Metzler 2006) presents an excellent account of the financial recession, its origins and impact, in Chapter 6, "The Great Divide, 1918–1921." See "A History of Financial Instability in Japan after the End of the World War" (*Sekai sensō shūryōgo ni okeru honpō zaikai dōyōshi*) in (Bank of Japan 1958, 22: 385–735) for a detailed report of the recession and its impact.

5. (Imamura 1985, 90–92; Ōshima 1999, 72).

6. (Imamura 1985, 93–94; Schencking 2005, 214–17).

7. (Ogawa 1973, 140–41; Shinobu 1958, vol. 2, 601; Itō 2000, 261–63; Hackett 1971, 331).

8. (Ōshima 1999, 67).

9. I wrote these words on April 16, 2005, the same day that the *New York Times* reported mass anti-Japanese demonstrations in China. Takahashi, if he were alive today at 150, would be in a position to say, "I told you so."

10. (Ogawa 1973, 146–47; Kimura 1999, 54–57; Kobayashi 2001, 81–83, 116–17; Itō 1987, 69; see also Ōshima 1999, 75–76).

11. (Ogawa 1973, 148; Mitani 1974, 140; Banno 1985, 173–75; Itō 1987, 66–73; *Ōsaka asahi shinbun* 21 July 1928; Metzler 2006, 206–9).

12. (Imamura 1985, 106).

13. (Imamura 1989, 107–8).

14. (Imamura 1989, 109–10).

15. (Itō 1987, 74–75).

16. (Itō 1987, 60–62; Itō 1997, 173; Nakamura and Odaka 1989, 29–30).

17. (Itō 1997, 173).

18. (Takahashi 1936b, 21–23).

19. (Itō 1987, 175).

20. (Imamura 1989, 113–16).

21. (Itō 1987, 73; Matsuo 1974, 232–35; Itō 1997, 175; Takahashi 1936b, 645–46).

22. (Itō 1987, 51–52, 63, 85–86; Itō 1997, 174–75; Itō 2002, 130–31; Mayer-Oakes 1968, 274).

23. (Itō 1987, 81–83).

24. (Masumi 1979, 44–82).

25. (Imamura 1985, 116–23; Ōshima 1999, 88; Masumi 1988, 30).

26. (Eibun bunsho 1: 11, Bank of Japan Archive).

27. Hamaguchi presented a sharply reduced supplementary budget for 1924, and urged the public "to follow the beautiful custom of self-denial and frugality" (Naraoka 2002, 77).

28. (Imamura 1985, 124–33; Ōshima 1999, 90–92). Although the Katō government advanced the principle of popular rule, only four members of his cabinet served in the House of Representatives: Takahashi and Yokota of the Seiyūkai, Inukai Tsuyoshi of the Kakushin Kurabu, and Hamaguchi of the Kenseikai. Katō himself was a peer (Masumi 1988, 36).

29. (Eibun bunsho 1: 19, Bank of Japan Archive).

30. (Itō 1987, 201–3).

31. (Gotō 1977, 10–33; Imamura 1985, 134–40).

32. (Gotō 1977, 34–62; Morton 1980, 87; Itō 2005, 309).

Chapter Twelve

1. Most writers on the depression give Takahashi credit for Japan's recovery, but they often differ on whether monetary or fiscal policy played a greater role. See, for example, (Nanto and Takagi 1985; Cha 2003; and Iwata 2004, 249–76).

2. (Smethurst 1998; Cha 2003; Statistical References: Bank of Japan 1966 and 1982–86, vol. 7; Ohkawa and Shinohara 1979).

3. (Hugh Patrick in Morley 1971, 256). For positive interpretations of Takahashi's policies, see, for example, (Nakamura 1984, 125–30 and 1987, 63–94; Nakamura and Odaka 1989, 57–61, 308–12; Miwa 2003, 124–39; Gotō 1979, 180–87; Ōshima 1999 166–91; Kindleberger 1986, 162–64).

4. The economist Gary Saxonhouse made this point to the author at a presentation on Takahashi's policies at the University of Michigan on 6 November 2003. See (Patrick in Morley 1971, 258). Two other governments have been accused of carrying out "beggar thy neighbor" practices during the first half of the 1930s: the Social Democrats in Sweden and the Roosevelt administration in the United States (Kindleberger 1986, 181, 233).

5. (Shima 1983, 120–22; Bank of Japan 1986).

6. (Allen 1962, 137). At the Tokyo war crimes trials, the economic journalist Ishibashi Tanzan attempted to distinguish between Takahashi's financial policies and post-1936 wartime economic controls, but the prosecution rejected his distinction (Nolte 1987, 301).

7. (Nakamura et al. 1975, 2–48).

8. (Smethurst 2000).

9. (Satō in Nakamura 1981, 4).

10. (Smethurst in Andrews and Chapman 1995, 71–89; Smethurst 2001).

11. (Nakamura 1993, 114); Nakamura Takafusa has written a splendid book on Hamaguchi's and Inoue's "tragic" efforts to put Japan on the gold standard. In English, see (Metzler 2006).

12. (Nakamura 1993, 114).

13. (Nakamura 1982, 46).

14. (Nakamura 1993, 115; Bank of Japan 1966, 166–67).

15. (Nakamura 1982, 45–46; Jiang 1989, 22–49).

16. (Takahashi 1936a, 247–52).

17. Nakamura Takafusa calls the geisha house analogy "playful," and writes that Takahashi used it to make his arguments understandable to ordinary citizens (Nakamura 1994, 56).

18. (Mizunuma in Sumiya 1974, 116–17, 121, 189; Sugihara 1989, 152; Reischauer 1986, 256).

19. A leitmotif of Dashiell Hammett's detective novel, *The Red Harvest*, set during the depression, is that of the continental op's unnamed girlfriend continually darning holes in her silk stockings to make them last longer.

20. (Mizunuma in Sumiya 1974, 132–33, 155–56, 160, 182; Smethurst 1986, 157; Kindleberger 1986, 113).

21. (Ohkawa and Shinohara 1979, 251–58; Miwa 2003, 120; Nakamura 1982, 242–44; Nishikawa 1985, 267–68; Nakamura 1984, 100; Smethurst 1986, 164).

22. (Ōkurashō 1977, 287)

23. (Nakamura 1986, 160–78; in English, see Metzler 2006, 233–39; Imamura 1985, 177–78).

24. (Fukai 1941, 259–63).

25. (Nakamura and Odaka 1989, 306, 320 fn. 37).

26. (Bank of Japan 1966, 280–81, 320; Nakamura and Odaka 1989, 310).

27. (Bank of Japan 1986, vol. 4: 6–8). The liberal Ishibashi wrote that the global depression, both in Japan and elsewhere, occurred because of the deflation and contraction of demand caused by the decision of most nations to return to the gold standard at the pre–World War I exchange rate. He believed recession set in because of bad management of the money supply worldwide, not because of some sort of "crisis of capitalism" (Jiang 1989, 28).

28. Ishibashi called Inoue's encouragement of frugality, "the empire's shame" (Jiang 1989, 25–26).

29. (Bank of Japan 1961, vol. 21: 151–52).

30. Inoue's report about trade is technically correct: the surplus of imports over exports (excluding those to and from the empire) declined by 60 percent from 1928 to 1931. But this hardly gave him bragging rights. It occurred because trade declined sharply, exports by 42 percent and imports by 44 percent. That is, Inoue shrank the trade imbalance by shrinking trade (Bank of Japan 1966, 281).

31. (Bank of Japan 1961, vol. 21: 153–57; Imamura 1985, 171–72).

32. (Bank of Japan 1961, vol. 21: 157–59).

33. (Bank of Japan 1966, 29; Bank of Japan 1986, vol. 7: 329; Fukai 1941, 267). By December 1940, five years after Takahashi's death and three years into Japan's aggressive war in China, money in circulation exceeded 4,700,000,000, an increase of 270 percent over 1935, well ahead of industrial production and real national wealth. We shall return to the question of whether, as some argue, this was part of Takahashi's legacy.

34. (Nakamura 1984, 125).

35. (Hashimoto 2000b, 26).

36. As a graduate student, the author was amazed to find in a Tokyo used bookstore four or five shelves of books with the word *monrōshugi* (Monroe

doctrine) in the title. Why, he wondered, did so many Japanese writers have an interest in an arcane aspect of American diplomatic history? The answer, he found out through a bit of browsing, was that the books had been written in the 1930s in an effort to justify Japan's establishment of a puppet state in Manchuria.

37. (Byas 1942; Storry 1957; Crowley 1966).

38. (Byas 1942, 22–28; Storry 1957, 126–27; Berger 1977, 51; Imamura 1985, 180–84).

39. Fukai wrote that this idea was uniquely Takahashi's, but Jiang argues that Ishibashi had recommended having the Bank of Japan buy treasury bonds a year earlier (Jiang 1989, 32). We have no evidence that Takahashi knew of Ishibashi's idea.

40. (Ōkurashō 1955, vol. 1: 408–12). Fukai Eigo said in 1941 that he erred in allowing the Bank of Japan to buy bonds from the treasury (Yoshino and Tsuchiya 1957, 185). But in his study of monetary systems, first published in 1928, he wrote that in times of emergency such as war or economic crisis, a central bank could exceed the normal restraints in the money supply (Fukai 1938, 75–77).

41. (Bank of Japan, 1986 24–26, 44–45). Ishibashi praised Takahashi for his fiscal stimuli, but at the same time criticized him for worrying too much about inflation and not spending more (Jiang 1989, 34–35).

42. (Nakamura 1983, 237–38).

43. (Ohkawa and Shinohara 1979, 267–68, 387–94; Kindleberger 1986, 261; Napier in Najita and Koschmann 1982, 346; Skidelsky 1992, 603–4; Smethurst 1986, 97; United States Department of Agriculture 1949, 136–37, 140; Nakamura Takafusa in Dore and Sinha 1987, 63).

44. (Takahashi 1936c, 263–64; Kindleberger 1986, 123–27, 176–82; Ōuchi 1974, 260–62).

45. (Shizume 2009; Eichengreen 1995).

46. (Galbraith 1988, 186) calls the "rejection of all affirmative government economic policy" during the depression "a triumph of dogma over thought."

47. (Nakamura et al. 1975, 34–38).

Chapter Thirteen

1. (Bank of Japan 1961, vol. 27: 16–18; Chō 1973, 210–11; Chō in Sumiya 1974, 352–53; Tanin and Yohan 1934, 17–18, 169, 270; Shima 1983, 115–19; Imamura 1985, 188–91, 211, 240; Nakamura 1982, 307–8; Ōshima 1969, 166–84; Shima 1949, 115, 124; Tōyama, Imai, and Fujiwara 2000, 99–103; Bisson 1973, 214–16; 238–39; Maxon 1957, 93; Allen 1962, 137).

2. (Smethurst 2000, 1–24; Smethurst 2001, 282–84).

3. (Takahashi 1976, II: 279).

4. (Takahashi's letter to Jacob Schiff, 26 June 1915, Takahashi monjo 110–14).

5. (Ogawa 1973, 148). Japan's share of world manufacturing in 1925–29 was 2.5 percent; the United States' 42.5 percent. Takahashi, if he had lived through World War II, would not have been surprised to learn that the United States produced 4.5 times more, and even the Soviet Union twice as many airplanes as Japan in 1941–44 (Francillon 1970, 10).

6. (Nish 1993, 12, 95).

7. (Takahashi 1936a, 247–49). As early as 1915, Takahashi made a distinction between "war loans and productive loans" (Takahashi to Schiff, 26 June 1915, Takahashi monjo, 110–14).

8. (Bank of Japan 1982–86, vol. 4, 169; *Tōkyō asahi shinbun*, 27 November 1935; Chō 1973, 222; Hara in Harrison 1998, 257).

9. (Ōkurashō 1955, I: 414–25; Gotō 1977, 134–37; Fukai 1941, 270–72).

10. The following discussion of the making of the 1933 and 1934 budgets is taken from (Ōmae 2000, 29–46).

11. (Shillony 1973, 30; *Tōkyō asahi shinbun*, 27 October 1932).

12. (Aritake 1986, 177–84; Nakamura 1993, 166).

13. (Fujita 1989, 17–19).

14. (Aritake 1986, 199–204). General Honjō Shigeru, the emperor's chief military aide-de-camp, described in his diary the 1934 budget conflict between Ōsumi and Takahashi. He wrote that the navy attempted to use the "right of supreme command" ploy to outmaneuver Takahashi. The navy claimed that since its chief of staff had already reported on the spending plans to the emperor, the finance minister did not have the authority to deny the navy's requests. In the end, Admiral Saitō, to save his government, was able to persuade both Ōsumi and Takahashi to compromise (Hane 1982, 86–90).

15. (Harada 1950–56, vol. 2: 204–5; Ōkurashō 1977, 328; Itō 2005, 351). Takahashi's remark here was a repetition of what he had written in 1920 during the army's Siberian adventure.

16. (Harada 1950–56, vol. 3: 198–99).

17. (Takahashi 1936c, 323–25; Takahashi 1936b, 652–63; Ōkurashō 1977, 134).

18. (Hane 1982, 150).

19. (*Tōyō keizai shinpō* 1935, 30–31).

20. (Aritake 1967, 495–642, especially 524–34, 603–13; Aritake 1986, 222–29, 249; Imamura 1985, 202).

21. Prince Saionji recognized Takahashi's centrality to the government. He told his secretary Harada Kumao in February 1934, "People like Itō (Miyoji) and Hiranuma cause the government a great deal of trouble by their maneuverings and should be avoided. On the other hand, while Saitō should listen to Taka-

hashi on fiscal policy and economics, the prime minister does not need to do everything the finance minister says about politics" (Harada 1950–56, IV: 152).

22. Kuhara Fusanosuke, an entrepreneur and Seiyūkai politician with investments in Manchuria, was a particularly harsh critic of the Takahashi line (Shillony 1973, 88).

23. (Matsuura 2000, 63–67; Spaulding in Wilson 1970, 51–70; Aritake 1967, 610).

24. (Okada 1950, 39; Ōkurashō 1977, 77). Ironically, the 1938 budget, formed by Kaya when he served as finance minister in the first Konoe cabinet, increased the military budget over 1937 by 80 percent. The army and navy in 1938 received 6,770,000,000 yen, more than six times the amount they received in the Fujii/Takahashi 1935 budget (Hara 1998, 257).

25. (Okada 1950, 100).

26. (Imamura 1985, 206–8; Ōkurashō 1977, 79).

27. Kaya criticized Takahashi, as he had Fujii, for giving in to the military. "Takahashi is senile. He threw them a hundred million [yen] just like that" (Ōkurashō 1977, 79).

28. (Imamura 1985, 208–10).

29. (Okada 1950, 127; Imamura 1985, 214–16; Miller 1965, 183; Smethurst in Wilson 1970, 1–23).

30. This report is supplemented by one from the *Yomiuri shinbun* of November 27.

31. (Suzaki 2003, 113–15).

32. A number of observers at the time viewed Takahashi as the government's central figure and called him "Prime Minister Takahashi," or called the Okada cabinet the "Takahashi cabinet." See (Okada 1950, 101, and Matsuura 2000, 65–66).

33. See also (Tsushima 1962, 258–94; Imamura 1985, 218–24).

34. (*Tōkyō asahi shinbun*, 5, 16 January, 18 February 1936).

35. Nakamura and Odaka make this point, that Takahashi's policies in 1934–36 were like those of the Kenseikai (Minseitō predecessor) in the mid-1920s. The authors add that the shift between negative and positive fiscal policies should not be interpreted as merely a result of "the political cycle." That is to say, leaders such as Takahashi could rise above party platforms (Nakamura and Odaka 1989, 75, fn. 37).

36. (Imamura 1985, 235).

37. (Ōkurashō 1977, 130–37).

38. (Shillony 1973, 135–36; Ōkurashō 1977, 136–37; Tsushima 1962, 303–14; Imamura 1985, 230–32).

39. (Chō 1973, 222).

40. (Tsushima 1962, 314; *New York Times,* 27 February 1936: Otani 1986. 141; Shimizu Takayuki in the *Tōkyō asahi shinbun,* 15 May 2005).

Conclusion

1. See (Skidelsky 2000, 284–86), for a discussion of Keynes's agreements (and differences) with the view expressed in Hayek's *Road to Serfdom* that markets were the only efficient transmitters of economic information. Takahashi, like Keynes, was an advocate of a "middle way" between a free market and a government-influenced economy. Hayek's classic book was published in 1944, eight years after Takahashi's death.

2. (Takakura 1957–60, vol. 1, 497).

3. (Fujita 1989a, 93; Takahashi 1936a, 422).

4. (Takahashi 1936c, 285–87; Smith 2001, 155–66).

5. (Checkland 1998, 46–49).

6. (Takahashi 1936b, 645–66).

7. (Skidelsky 1992, 443).

Works Cited

Newspapers

Kyōto hinode shinbun
Mainichi Daily News
New York Times
Ōsaka asahi shinbun
Tōkyō asahi shinbun
Tōyō keizai shinpō
Yomiuri shinbun

Primary Sources

Baring Archive at ING Bank, N. V., London
Eibun bunsho, Bank of Japan Archive, Tokyo
Hongkong and Shanghai Bank Corporation (HSBC) Group Archives, London
Matsuo Shigeyoshi Papers, Bank of Japan Archive, Tokyo
The Rothschild Archive, London
Royal Bank of Scotland Group Archives (RSBG Archives), London
Schiff Papers, American Jewish Archives, Cincinnati
Takahashi diary (techō) 4 March–18 December 1904. In English and Japanese.
   Takahashi Korekiyo monjo, National Diet Library, Tokyo
Takahashi Korekiyo monjo, National Diet Library, Tokyo

Other Sources

Adler, Cyrus. 1929. *Jacob Schiff: His Life and Letters*. London: William Heine-
mann, Ltd.

Allen, G. C. 1962. *A Short Economic History of Modern Japan, 1867–1937.* London: George Allen & Unwin.

Allfrey, Anthony. 1991. *Edward VII and His Jewish Court.* London: Weidenfeld and Nicolson.

Andrews, George Reid, and Herrick Chapman. 1995. *The Social Construction of Democracy, 1870–1990.* New York: New York University Press.

Ariizumi Sadao. 1969. Kōgyō iken no seiritsu. *Shigaku zasshi* 78 (10): 1–30.

———. 1979. *Yamanashi: Meiji no hatten.* Kui shinsho, no. 3. Kōfu: Yamanashi kyōdo kenkyūkai.

Aritake Shūji. 1967. *Shōwa ōkurashō gaishi.* Vol. 1. Tokyo: Shōwa ōkurashō gaishi kankōkai.

———. 1986. *Saitō Makoto.* Vol. 14 of *Nihon saishō retsuden.* Tokyo: Jiji tsūshinsha.

Asō Daisaku. 1929. *Takahashi Korekiyo den.* Tokyo: Takahashi Korekiyo den kankōkai.

Bank of Japan. 1958. *Nippon kinyūshi shiryō: Meiji Taishōhen.* 25 vols. Tokyo.

———. 1961. *Nippon kinyūshi shiryō: Shōwahen.* 31 vols. Tokyo.

———. 1966. *Honpō shuyō keizai tōkei.* Tokyo.

———. 1982–86. *Nippon ginkō hyakunenshi.* 7 vols. Tokyo.

Banno Junji. 1985. *Kindai Nihon no gaikō to seiji.* Tokyo: Kenbun shuppan.

Berger, Gordon Mark. 1977. *Parties out of Power in Japan, 1931–1941.* Princeton, NJ: Princeton University Press.

———, trans. and ed. 1982. *Mutsu Munemitsu Kenkenroku: A Diplomatic Record of the Sino–Japanese War, 1984–1895.* Princeton, NJ: Princeton University Press.

Best, Gary Dean. 1972. Financing a Foreign War: Jacob H. Schiff and Japan, 1904–5. *American Jewish Historical Quarterly* 61: 313–24.

Bisson, T. A. 1973. *Japan in China.* New York: Octagon Books.

Board of Tourist Industry. 1941. *Japan: The Official Guide.* Tokyo: Japan Government Railways.

Bognar, Botond. 1995. *The Japan Guide.* New York: Princeton Architectural Press.

Byas, Hugh. 1942. *Government by Assassination.* New York: Alfred A. Knopf.

Cha, Myung Soo. 2003. Did Takahashi Korekiyo Rescue Japan from the Great Depression? *Journal of Economic History* 63 (1): 127–44.

Checkland, Olive. 1998. The Iwakura Mission, Industries and Exports. In *The Iwakura Mission in Britain, 1872,* ed. Andrew Cobbing et al., 37–51. London: The Suntory Centre, London School of Economics and Political Science.

——— and Norio Tamaki. 1997. Alexander Allan Shand, 1844–1930—A Banker the Japanese Could Trust. In *Britain and Japan: Biographical Portraits,* ed. Ian Nish, 65–78. Richmond, Surrey: Japan Library.

Chernow, Ron. 1993. *The Warburgs: The Twentieth Century Odyssey of a Remarkable Jewish Family.* New York: Random House.

Chō Yukio. 1973. *Shōwa kyōkō*. Tokyo: Iwanami shinsho.

Cohen, Naomi W. 1999. *Jacob H. Schiff: A Study in American Jewish Leadership*. Hanover, NH: Brandeis University Press.

Crawcour, Sydney. 1988. Industrialization and Technological Change, 1885–1920. In *The Twentieth Century*. Vol. 6 of *The Cambridge History of Japan*, ed. Peter Duus, 385–450. Cambridge, UK: Cambridge University Press.

———. 1997. "Kōgyō Iken": Maeda Masana and His View of Meiji Economic Development. *Journal of Japanese Studies* 23 (1): 69–104.

Crowley, James B. 1966. *Japan's Quest for Autonomy: National Security and Foreign Policy, 1930–1938*. Princeton, NJ: Princeton University Press.

Dickinson, Frederick R. 1999. *War and National Reinvention: Japan and the Great War, 1914–1919*. Cambridge, MA: Harvard University Asia Center.

———. 2005. Commemorating the War in Post-Versailles Japan. In *The Russo-Japanese War in Global Perspective: World War Zero*, ed. John W. Steinberg, et al., 523–44. Boston: Brill.

Dobyns, Kenneth W. 1994. *History of the United States Patent Office*. Washington, DC: US Patent Office.

Dore, Ronald. 1965. *Education in Tokugawa Japan*. London: Routledge and Kegan Paul.

——— and Radha Sinha. 1987. *Japan and the Depression: Then and Now*. New York: St. Martin's Press.

Eguchi Keiichi. 1994. *Jūgonen sensō no kaimaku*. Vol. 4 of *Shōwa no rekishi*. Tokyo: Shōgakukan.

Eichengreen, Barry. 1995. *Golden Fetters*. Oxford: Oxford University Press.

Ericson, Steven J. 1996. *The Sound of the Whistle: Railroads and the State in Meiji Japan*. Cambridge, MA: Harvard University Asia Center.

Ferber, Katalin. 2005. Professionalism as Power: Tajiri Inajirō and the Modernization of Meiji Finance. In *Institutional and Technological Change in Japan's Economy: Past and Present*, ed. Janet Hunter and Cornelia Sturz, 100–25. London: Routledge.

Ferguson, Niall. 1999. *The House of Rothschild: The World's Banker, 1849–1999*. New York: Viking.

Francillon, René J. 1970. *Japanese Aircraft of the Pacific War*. Annapolis, MD: Naval Institute Press.

Francks, Penelope. 1984. *Technology and Agricultural Development in Pre-War Japan*. New Haven, CT: Yale University Press.

———. 1992. *Japanese Economic Development: Theory and Practice*. New York: Routledge.

Fujita Yasukazu. 1989a. Takahashi zaisei keizai shisō kenkyū josetsu. *Keizai ronsō* 144 (2): 74–93.

———. 1989b. Takahashi Korekiyo to goshō kaigi. *Seiji keizai shigaku* 274: 1–21.

———. 1989c. Takahashi Korekiyo to naisei kaigi. *Seiji keizai shigaku* 275: 20–36.

Fujimura Kin'ichirō. 1992. *Takahashi Korekiyo to kokusai kin'yū*, 2 vols. Tokyo: Fukutake shoten.

Fukai Eigo. 1938. *Tsūka chōsetsuron.* Tokyo: Nihon hyōronsha.

———. 1941. *Kaiko nanajūnen.* Tokyo: Iwanami shoten.

Galbraith, John Kenneth. 1988. *The Great Crash: 1929.* Boston, MA: Houghton Mifflin Company.

Gotō Shin'ichi. 1977. *Takahashi Korekiyo: Nihon no Keinzu.* Tokyo: Nihon keizai shinbunsha.

Griffis, William Elliot. 1900. *Verbeck of Japan: Citizen of No Country.* New York: Fleming H. Revell.

———. 1913. *Hepburn of Japan and His Wife and Helpmates: A Life Story of Toil for Christ.* Philadelphia, PA: The Winchester Press.

Gutwein, Daniel. 2006. The Background of Jacob H. Schiff's Financial Support for Japan during the War. In *Rethinking the Russo-Japanese War: Centennial Perspectives*, ed. Rotem Kowner. London: Global Oriental.

Hackett, Roger F. 1971. *Yamagata Aritomo in the Rise of Modern Japan, 1838–1922.* Cambridge, MA: Harvard University Press.

Hall, Ivan. 1973. *Mori Arinori.* Cambridge, MA: Harvard University Press.

Hane, Mikiso, trans. 1982. *Emperor Hirohito and His Chief Aide-de-Camp: The Honjō Diary, 1933–36.* Tokyo: Tokyo University Press.

Hara, Akira. 1998. Japan: Guns before Rice. In *The Economics of World War II*, ed. Mark Harrison, 224–67. New York: Cambridge University Press.

Hara, Fujiko, ed. and trans. 2001. *The Autobiography of Ozaki Yukio.* Princeton, NJ: Princeton University Press.

Harada Kumao. 1950–56. *Saionji-kō to seikyoku.* 9 vols. Tokyo: Iwanami shoten.

Hashimoto Jurō and Ōsugi Yuka. 2000a. *Kindai Nihon keizaishi.* Iwanami tekisutobukkusu. Tokyo: Iwanami shoten.

Hashimoto Jurō. 2000b. *Gendai Nihon keizaishi.* Iwanami tekisutobukkusu. Tokyo: Iwanami shoten.

Hein, Laura. 2004. *Reasonable Men, Powerful Words.* Berkeley, CA: University of California Press.

Hirschmeier, Johannes. 1964. *The Origins of Entrepreneurship in Meiji Japan.* Cambridge, MA: Harvard University Press.

——— and T. Yui. 1975. *The Development of Japanese Business, 1600–1980.* London: George Allen & Unwin.

Hunter, Janet, and S. Sugiyama. 2002. *Economic and Business Relations.* Vol. 4 of *The History of Anglo-Japanese Relations, 1600–2000.* New York: Palgrave Macmillan.

Imamura Takeo. 1985. *Takahashi Korekiyo*. Vol. 8 of *Nihon saishō retsuden*. Tokyo: Jiji tsūshinsha. (Orig. pub. 1958.)

Inoue Kaoru-kō denki hensankai, ed. 1968. *Segai Inoue-kō den*. 5 vols. Tokyo: Hara shobō.

Inoue Kiyoshi and Watanabe Tōru. 1959–62. *Kome sōdō no kenkyū*. 5 vols. Tokyo: Yūhikaku.

Itō Takao. 2000. *Taishō demokurashiiki no hō to shakai*. Kyoto: Kyōto daigaku gakujutsu shuppankai.

Itō Yukio. 1987. *Taishō demokurashii to seitō seiji*. Tokyo: Yamakawa shuppansha.

―――. 1997. Daiichiji taisen to sengo Nihon no keisei. *Hōgaku ronsō* 140 (4): 155–211.

―――. 2002. *Seitō seiji to tennō*. Vol. 22 of *Nihon no rekishi*. Tokyo: Kōdansha.

―――. 2005. *Shōwa tennō to rikken kunshusei no hōkai*. Nagoya: Nagoya daigaku shuppankai.

Iwata Kikuo, ed. 2004. *Shōwa kyōkō no kenkyū*. Tokyo: Tōyō keizai shinpōsha.

Jackson, Kenneth T., ed. 1995. *The Encyclopedia of New York City*. New Haven, CT: Yale University Press.

Japan National Tourist Organization. 1975. *Japan: The Official New Guide*. Tokyo: Japan Travel Bureau.

Jiang Keshi. 1989. Ishibashi Tanzan no sekkyoku zaiseiron: Takahashi zaisei to no kakawari. *Nihonshi kenkyū* 328: 22–49.

Kamiyama Tsuneo. 1989. Nichiro sengo no seika seisaku to zaisei. *Shigaku zasshi* 98 (1): 48–90.

Kengun seishin fukyūkai. 1941. *Kaigunhen*. Vol. 2 of *Taishōden*. Tokyo: Kengun seishin fukyūkai.

Kimura Masato. 1999. *Takahashi Korekiyo to Shōwa kyōkō*. Tokyo: Bungei shunjū.

Kindleberger, Charles P. 1986. *The World in Depression, 1929–1939*. Berkeley, CA: University of California Press.

Kitawaki Yōko. 1999. *Hitsugi o ōite koto sadamaru: Takahashi Korekiyo to sono jidai*. Tokyo: Tōyō keizai shinpōsha.

Kobayashi Michihiko. 2001. Takahashi Korekiyo "Tōa keizairyoku jūritsu ni kansuru iken" to Inoue Junnosuke. *Kitakyūshū shiritsu daigaku hōsei ronshū*. 29 (1–2): 81–132.

Kobayashi Uchisaburo. 1922. *War and Armament Loans of Japan*. London: Oxford University Press.

Kodansha. 1983. *Encyclopedia of Japan*. 9 vols. Tokyo: Kodansha, Ltd.

Kyōto daigaku bungakubu kokushi kenkyūshitsu. 1958. *Nihon kindaishi jiten*. Tokyo: Tōyō keizai shinpōsha.

Lewis, Michael. 1990. *Rioters and Citizens: Mass Protest in Imperial Japan*. Berkeley, CA: University of California Press.

Masumi Junnosuke. 1979. *Nihon seitōshi ron.* Vol. 5. Nihon seiji kenkyū sōsho, no. 1. Tokyo: Tōkyō daigaku shuppankai.

———. 1988. *Nihon seitōshi ron.* Vol. 3. Nihon seiji kenkyū sōsho, no. 1. Tokyo: Tōkyō daigaku shuppankai.

Matsuo Takayoshi. 1974. *Taishō demokurashii.* Tokyo: Iwanami shoten.

Matsuura Masataka. 2000. Takahashi Korekiyo to "kyōkoku itchi" naikaku. In *Sensō-fukkō-hatten: Shōwa seijishi ni okeru kenryoku to kōsō.* ed. Kitaoka Shin'ichi and Mikuriya Takashi, 63–85. Tokyo: Tōkyō daigaku shuppankai.

Mayer-Oakes, Thomas Francis. 1968. *Fragile Victory: Prince Saionji and the 1930 London Treaty Issue.* Detroit, MI: Wayne State University Press.

Maxon, Yale. 1957. *Control of Japanese Foreign Policy: A Study of Civil–Military Rivalry, 1936–45.* Westport, CT: Greenwood Press.

Metzler, Mark. 2006. *Lever of Empire: The International Gold Standard and the Crisis of Liberalism in Prewar Japan.* Berkeley, CA: University of California Press.

Mikuriya Takashi. 1980. *Meiji kokka keisei to chihō keiei, 1881–1890.* Tokyo: Tōkyō daigaku shuppankai.

Miller, Frank O. 1965. *Minobe Tatsukichi: Interpreter of Constitutionalism in Japan.* Berkeley, CA: University of California Press.

Mitani Taichirō. 1974. Nihon no kokusai kin'yūka to kokusai seiji. In *Kindai Nihon no taigai taido,* ed. Satō Seizaburō and Roger Dingman, 123–54. Tokyo: Tōkyō daigaku shuppankai.

Miwa Ryōichi. 2003. *Gaisetsu Nihon keizaishi: kingendai.* Tokyo: Tōkyō daigaku shuppankai.

Morioka Kiyomi. 2004. Meiji zenki ni okeru shizoku to kirisutokyō. *Shutoku daigaku shakai gakubu kenkyū kiyō* 38: 125–69.

Morley, James W. 1971. *Dilemmas of Growth in Prewar Japan.* Princeton, NJ: Princeton University Press.

Morton, William Fitch. 1980. *Tanaka Giichi and Japan's China Policy.* New York: St. Martin's Press.

Najita, Tetsuo. 1967. *Hara Kei in the Politics of Compromise, 1905–1915.* Cambridge, MA: Harvard University Press.

——— and J. Victor Koschmann. 1982. *Conflict in Modern Japanese History.* Princeton, NJ: Princeton University Press.

Nakamura, James. 1966. *Agricultural Production and the Economic Development of Japan, 1873–1922.* Princeton, NJ: Princeton University Press.

Nakamura Masanori, et al. 1975. Shōwa kyōkōka no Tōhoku nōson. *Hermes* 26.

Nakamura Masanori. 1982. *Shōwa no kyōkō.* Tokyo: Shōgakukan.

Nakamura Takafusa, ed. 1981. *Senkanki no Nihon keizai bunseki.* Tokyo: Tōkyō daigaku shuppankai.

Nakamura Takafusa. 1982. *Shōwa kyōkō to keizai seisaku: aru ōkura daijin no higeki.* Nikkei shinsho 288. Tokyo: Nihon keizai shinbunsha.

————. 1983. *Economic Growth in Prewar Japan.* New Haven, CT: Yale University Press.

————. 1984. *Nihon keizai: sono seichō to kōzō.* Tokyo: Tōkyō daigaku shuppankai.

————. 1986. *Shōwa keizaishi.* Iwanami Seminar Books 17. Tokyo: Iwanami shoten.

————. 1993. *Shōwashi.* Vol. 1. Tokyo: Tōyō keizai shinpōsha.

————. 1994. *Lectures on Modern Japanese Economic History, 1926–1994.* Tokyo: LTCB International Library Foundation.

———— and Odaka Kōnosuke, eds. 1989. *Nijū kōzō.* Vol. 6 of *Nihon keizaishi.* Tokyo: Iwanami shoten.

Nanto, Dick K., and Shinji Takagi. 1985. Korekiyo Takahashi and Japan's Recovery from the Great Depression. *American Economic Review* 75 (2): 369–74.

Naraoka Sōchi. 2002. Katō Takaaki naikaku no seiji katei (1), *Hōgaku ronsō* 152 (3): 65–87.

Nish, Ian. 1993. *Japan's Struggle with Internationalism: Japan, China, and the League of Nations, 1931–3.* New York: Kegan Paul International.

Nishikawa Shunsaku. 1985. *Nihon keizai no seichōshi.* Tokyo: Tōyō keizai shinpōsha.

Nolte, Sharon H. 1987. *Liberalism in Modern Japan: Ishibashi Tanzan and His Teachers, 1905–1960.* Berkeley, CA: University of California Press.

Ogawa, Gotaro. 1923. *Expenditures of the Russo-Japanese War.* New York: Oxford University Press.

Ogawa Heikichi. 1973. *Ogawa Heikichi kankei monjo.* Vol. 2, ed. Ogawa Heikichi monjo kenkyūkai. Tokyo: Misuzu shobō.

Ogura, Takekazu. 1979. *Can Japanese Agriculture Survive? A Historical and Comparative Approach.* Tokyo: Agricultural Policy Research Center.

Ohkawa, Kazushi, and Miyohei Shinohara. 1979. *Patterns of Japanese Economic Development: A Quantitative Appraisal.* New Haven, CT: Yale University Press.

Ohkawa, Masazo. 1965. The Armaments Expansion Budgets and the Japanese Economy after the Russo-Japanese War. *Hitotsubashi Journal of Economics* 5 (2): 68–83.

Ohnuki Mari. 2006. Nippon Ginkō no nettowāku to kin'yū shijō no tōgō—Nippon Ginkō setsuritsu zengo kara nijusseiki shotō ni kakete. *Kin'yū kenkyū* 25 (1): 183–214.

Ōishi Tōru. 1992. *Ōkura daijin Takahashi Korekiyo: fukyō norikiri no tatsujin.* Tokyo: Manejimentosha.

Okada Keisuke. 1950. *Okada Keisuke kaikoroku.* Tokyo: Mainichi shinbun.

Ōkurashō. 1954–65. 18 vols. *Shōwa zaiseishi.* Tokyo: Tōyō keizai shinpōsha.

Ōkura daijin kanbō chōsa kikaku ka. 1977. *Ōkura daijin no omoide.* Shōwa zaisei-shi shidankai kiroku, no. 1. Tokyo.

Ōkurashō hyakunenshi henshūshitsu, ed. 1969. *Ōkurashō hyakunenshi.* 3 vols. Tokyo: Ōkura zaimu kyōkai.

Ōmae Nobuya. 1999. Saitō nakikakuki no yosan hensei to ōkurashō (1). *Hōgaku ronsō* 145 (3): 28–50.

———. 2000. Saitō naikaku no yosan hensei to ōkurashō (2). *Hōgaku ronsō* 147 (3): 29–50.

Ōshima Kiyoshi. 1999. *Takahashi Korekiyo: zaiseika no sūkina shōgai.* Chūkō shinsho. Tokyo: Chūō kōronsha. (Orig. pub. 1969.)

———, Katō Toshihiko, and Ōuchi Tsutomu. 1974. *Shokusan kōgyō.* Vol. 2 of *Jinbutsu: Nihon shihonshugi.* Tokyo: Tōkyō daigaku shuppankai.

Ōtani Ken. 1986. *Ōkura daijin no Shōwashi.* Vol. 7 of *Kenryokusha no jinbutsu Shōwashi.* Tokyo: Bijinesusha.

Ōuchi Tsutomu. 1974. *Fuashizumu e no michi.* Vol. 24 of *Nihon no rekishi.* Chūkō bunko. Tokyo: Chūō kōronsha.

Reischauer, Haru Matsukata. 1986. *Samurai and Silk: A Japanese and American Heritage.* Cambridge, MA: Harvard University Press, The Belknap Press.

Satō Masanori. 1985. Meiji sanjūyonen zengo ni okeru Takahashi Korekiyo no Nichigin kinyū seisaku. *Shakai keizai shigaku* 50 (5): 30–52.

Schencking, Charles, 2005. *Making Waves: Politics, Propaganda, and the Emergence of the Imperial Japanese Navy, 1868–1922.* Stanford, CA: Stanford University Press.

Schiff, Jacob. 1907. *Our Journey to Japan.* New York: privately published.

Sherman, A. J. 1983. German-Jewish Bankers in World Politics: The Financing of the Russo-Japanese War. *Year Book XXVIII.* New York: Leo Baeck Institute.

Shillony, Ben-Ami. 1973. *Revolt in Japan: The Young Officers and the February 26, 1936 Incident.* Princeton, NJ: Princeton University Press.

———. 1991. *The Jews and the Japanese: The Successful Outsiders.* Rutland, VT: Charles E. Tuttle Company.

Shima Kinzō. 1983. Iwayuru 'Takahashi zaisei ni tsuite.' *Kinyū kenkyū* 2 (2): 83–124.

Shima Yasuhiko. 1949. *Ōkura daijin.* Tokyo: Iwanami shinsho.

Shinobu Seizaburō. 1958. *Taishō demokurashiishi.* 2 vols. Tokyo: Nihon hyōronsha.

Shirayanagi Shūko. 1930. *Zoku zaikai taiheiki.* Tokyo: Nippon hyōronsha.

Shizume Masato. 2009. *Kyōkō to keizai seisaku: kaihō shōkoku Nihon no 1930 nendai no keiken.* Tokyo: Nihon keizai shinbun shuppansha.

Skidelsky, Robert. 1992. *John Maynard Keynes: The Economist as Savior, 1920–1937.* New York: Penguin Books.

———. 2001. *John Maynard Keynes: Fighting for Freedom, 1937–1946.* New York: Viking Penguin.

Smethurst, Richard J. 1986. *Agricultural Development and Tenancy Disputes in Japan 1870–1940.* Princeton, NJ: Princeton University Press.

———. 1998. The Self-Taught Bureaucrat: Takahashi Korekiyo and Economic Policy during the Great Depression. In *Learning in Likely Places: Varieties of Apprenticeship in Japan*, ed. John Singleton, 226–38. Cambridge, New York, and Melbourne: Cambridge University Press.

———. 2000. Takahashi Korekiyo's Economic Policies in the Great Depression and their Meiji Roots. In *Politics and the Economy in Prewar Japan*, 1–24. London: The Suntory Centre, London School of Economics and Political Science.

———. 2001. Takahashi Korekiyo's Fiscal Policy and the Rise of Militarism in Japan during the Great Depression. *Kindai Nihon kenkyū* 18.

———. 2006. Takahashi Korekiyo, the Rothschilds, and the Russo-Japanese War, 1904–1907. *The Rothschild Archive Review of the Year, April 2005 to March 2006*, 20–25. London: The Rothschild Archive.

Smith, Daniel M. 1972. *The American Diplomatic Experience.* Boston: Houghton Mifflin.

Smith, Kerry. 2001. *A Time of Crisis: Japan, the Great Depression, and Rural Revitalization.* Cambridge, MA: Harvard University Asia Center.

Smith, Thomas C. 1955. *Political Change and Industrial Development in Japan: Government Enterprise, 1868–1880.* Stanford, CA: Stanford University Press.

Soda Osamu. 1973. *Maeda Masana.* Tokyo: Yoshikawa kōbunkan.

Spence, Jonathan D. 1999. *The Search for Modern China.* New York: W.W. Norton.

Stegewerns, Dick. 2002. The End of World War II as a Turning Point in Modern Japanese History. In *Turning Points in Japanese History*, ed. Bert Edström, 138–62. London: Japan Library.

Storry, Richard. 1957. *The Double Patriots: A Study of Japanese Nationalism.* Boston: Houghton Mifflin Company.

Sugihara, Kaoru. 1989. Japan's Industrial Recovery, 1931–36. In *Economics of Africa and Asia during the Inter-War Depression*, ed. Ian Brown, 152–69. London: Routledge.

Sumiya Mikio, ed. 1974. *Shōwa kyōkō.* Tokyo: Yūikaku sensho.

Suzaki Shin'ichi. 2003. *Niniroku jiken: seinen shōkō no ishiki to shinri.* Tokyo: Yoshikawa kōbunkan.

Suzuki, Toshio. 1994. *Japanese Government Loan Issues on the London Capital Market, 1870–1913.* London: Athlone Press.

Tabata Norishige. 2005. *Nichiro sensō ni tōshishita otoko: Yudayajin ginkōka no nikki.* Shinchō shinsho, no. 143. Tokyo: Shinchōsha.

Takahashi Korekiyo. 1936a. *Zuisōroku.* Tokyo: Chikura shobō.

———. 1936b. *Takahashi Korekiyo keizairon,* ed. Uetsuka Tsukasa. Tokyo: Chikura shobō.

———. 1936c. *Kokusaku un'yo no shō.* Tokyo: Tōnan shoin.

———. 1976. *Takahashi Korekiyo jiden,* ed. Uetsuka Tsukasa. 2 vols. Chūkō bunko. Tokyo: Chūō kōronsha. (Orig. pub. 1936.)

———. 1997. *Takahashi Korekiyo den* (abridged). Transcribed by Uetsuka Tsukasa and translated into modern Japanese by Yajima Yukihiko. Chikyūjin Library, no. 3. Tokyo: Shōgakukan.

Takakura Tetsuichi. 1957–60. *Tanaka Giichi denki.* 3 vols. Tokyo: Tanaka Giichi denki kankōkai.

Tamaki, Norio. 1995. *Japanese Banking: A History, 1859–1959.* New York: Cambridge University Press.

———. 2001. *Yukichi Fukuzawa, 1835–1901: The Spirit of Enterprise in Modern Japan.* New York: Palgrave Macmillan.

Tanin, O. and E. Yohan. 1934. *Militarism and Fascism in Japan.* London: Martin Lawrence, Ltd.

Thane, Pat. 1986. Financiers and the British State: The Case of Sir Ernest Cassel. *Business History* 38 (1): 80–99.

Tōyama Shigeki, Imai Seiichi, and Fujiwara Akira. 2000. *Shōwashi.* Tokyo: Iwanami shinsho. (Orig. pub. 1959.)

Tsumoto Yō. 1998. *Sei o funde osorezu: Takahashi Korekiyo no shōgai.* Tokyo: Gentōsha.

Tsushima Juichi. 1962. *Takahashi Korekiyo-ō no koto.* Vol. 9 of *Hōtō zuisō.* Tokyo: Hōtō kankōkai.

Umemura Mataji and Nakamura Takafusa, eds. 1983. *Matsukata zaisei to shokusan kōgyō seisaku.* Kokuren daigaku purojekuto "Nihon no keiken" shiriizu. Tokyo: Kokusai rengō daigaku.

United States Department of Agriculture. 1949. *Consumption of Food in the United States. 1909–1948.* Washington, DC:

Wilson, George M., ed. 1970. *Crisis Politics in Prewar Japan.* Tokyo: Sophia University.

Yoneyama, Umekichi. 1927. *Alexander A. Shand: A Friend of Nippon: Interesting Chapters from a Banker's Reminiscences.* Tokyo: Japan Times.

Yoshino Toshihiko and Tsuchiya Takeo. 1957. *Rekidai Nihon ginkō sōsairon: Nihon kin'yū seisakushi no kenkyū.* Tokyo: Daiyamondosha.

Index

budget of 1933, 275, 277; Saitō
government and, 281
budget of 1934, 294; Saitō government and, 278, 280–82
budget of 1935, 279; Okada government and, 286
budget of 1936, 279; military
spending and, 288–92; Takahashi line and, 295
budgets, 3–4, 171–72; 1934 conflict
over, 332*n*14; cooperative process and, 289, 291; economic
philosophy and, 305; frugality
and, 245; gold standard and,
241–42; industrial development
and, 174; Okada government
and, 286–87; opposition to
militarism and, 273–77; parliament and, 202; positivists *vs.*
negativists on, 200; postwar
hard landing and, 217–18; rise
of militarism and, 269–71; Saitō
government and, 278, 281;
Takahashi line and, 294–98,
297; Takahashi's proposed
(1914), 205–6
Burchard, Ludwig, 162
bureaucracy, 2, 204–5; economic
philosophy and, 303; opposition to militarism and, 274; patent law travels and, 66; rise of
militarism and, 268; Takahashi
government and, 227
Byas, Hugh, 260

Cameron, Ewen, 146, 159; first
Russo-Japanese War bonds and,
148–50, 154; second Russo-
Japanese War bonds and, 160,
162

capital, 183, 227–29, 262; Agricultural College and, 97; economic
growth and, 116; gold standard
and access to, 127; industrial
development and, 175–76; industrial policy and, 81; interest
rates and, 201; Japan's reliance
on foreign, 188, 195; opposition
to militarism and, 272–73; silver
mining and, 100, 102, 110–13,
113; Sino-Japanese War and, 123;
Takahashi's views on, 138–39,
222–23; Yokohama Specie
Bank as provider of, 128, 135–36
Cassel, Ernest, 7, 141; Brazilian
loan and, 159; decorations
granted to, 155; English royalty
and, 153, 180–81; fifth Russo-
Japanese War bonds and, 184;
first Russo-Japanese War
bonds and, 148, 150, 152–55;
Inoue and, 323*n*28; Japan's recognition of, 195; second Russo-
Japanese War bonds and, 163;
Takahashi meets, 167
Castle Brothers: silver mining and,
107
central government: economic
philosophy and, 229–30, 304,
Chartered Mercantile Bank of India, London, and China (Iron
Pillar Bank), English language
and, 20; youthful carousing at,
20, 22, 25
China: anti-Japanese sentiment
in, 125–26; autarchy and, 260;
Battle of the Yalu River and,
312*n*22; Browne as Minister to,
29; Brownes and, 30; decorates
Takahashi, 199; economic phi-

Harvard East Asian Monographs
(*out-of-print)

Harvard East Asian Monographs

Harvard East Asian Monographs

Harvard East Asian Monographs

Harvard East Asian Monographs

Harvard East Asian Monographs

Harvard East Asian Monographs

Harvard East Asian Monographs